THE FENCES BETWEEN

by
NORMA MARCERE

DARING PUBLISHING GROUP, INC.
DARING BOOKS • LIFE ENRICHMENT PUBLISHERS
CANTON • OHIO

Copyright © 1989 by Norma Marcere
All rights reserved.

Published by Daring Books
P.O. Box 20050, Canton, Ohio 44701

Printed in the United States of America.

Library of Congress Cataloging-in-Publication Data

Marcere, Norma, 1908-
   The fences between / Norma Marcere.
     p.   cm.
   ISBN 0-938936-87-5
   1. Marcere, Norma, 1908-   2. Afro-Americans--Ohio--Biography. 3. Ohio--Biography.
4. Ohio--Race relations. I. Title.
E185.97.M27A3   1989
977.1'00496073--dc19
  [B]   89-1362
                                          CIP

Dedicated to My Husband
of 42 years
1930 - 1972
Percy Alluren Marcere

At various stages of our togetherness, he fulfilled my need for
A big brother protector
A father advisor
A tender lover
A devoted husband

He was
A father and role model to our children
He was
A man who knew himself—and
He was
Always my best friend

Table of Contents

Foreword 7
1 New Beginnings 9
2 Culture Shock 25
3 College Life 35
4 How And Where Shall I
   Worship My God? 51
5 I'll Never Hire 63
6 A Friend's Proposal 75
7 The Most Educated Cook In Town ... 99
8 An Unexpected Happening 109
9 Philadelphia 125
10 Fenced In—By Our Own Four Walls . 137
11 Shuggie 151
12 Like Father—Like Daughter? 161
13 A 1935 Working Wife And Mother . 193
14 My Hand To The Plough 215
15 My Expanding World Of Many Circles . 227
16 My Work, Place, The Slums 253
17 Seeking Employment—
   After Pearl Harbor 267
18 Around My Dining Room Table 277
19 Racism, Pure And Lethal 293
20 Confusion, Conflict, Confession,
   Compliance 321
21 Teaching 341
22 Venturing Away From Home 365
23 The Touch Of Our Hands 379
24 Counseling 389
25 The Shocking Truth! 415
26 Stormy Weather 425
Author's Notes 445
INDEX 447

Photo Contents

Evans Album	87 - 93
Working	94 - 98
Snipes Album	184 - 192
Marcere Album	311 - 320

1

New Beginnings

In the summer of 1926, after high school graduation, I worked for a time for my Aunt Clella in her dry cleaning and alterations shop. Aunt Clella quit her job as cook for Attorney and Mrs. Harry Frease as soon as Grandma's house was paid for. My job was to mend and patch garments of all kinds. Buttons and snaps were added and removed, seams were let out to make a tight garment roomier and adult garments were made small enough for a child. This interesting, creative job, for which my aunt paid me six dollars a week, put to use my self-taught sewing skills built upon the basics I had learned in the seventh grade. I took no sewing or home economics classes in high school. Mom reasoned that she and Grandma, with their six and twelve children respectively, had more sewing and cooking expertise than any unmarried school teacher.

"You go to school to be taught the things we mothers never had a chance to learn," Mom emphasized.

My aunt's shop on Cherry Avenue between Eighth and Ninth Streets gave me the opportunity to become familiar with businesses I had never seen before. Everything a family needed could be supplied within a two or three block area. Daily I passed a dry cleaning shop, two restaurants, a plumbing and heating store, coal yard, two billiard parlors, a barber shop, a hand laundry, a grocery and meat market, a wholesale produce company, two poultry stores, and a drugstore. Each establishment gave that small compressed area a distinctiveness not found in any other section of town. The businesses were operated by Germans, Italians, Irish, Greeks, Jews, Negroes, Chinese, and people who tried hard to minimize their ethnicity and were just Americans.

Next door to Aunt Clella's shop, a Mr. and Mrs. John Premmer operated a family restaurant. They asked if I would wait tables for them during the busy dinner hour from 5:00 p.m. to 8:00 p.m. Before I could accept this job that would give me an additional income of five dollars a week, my mom and aunt had to be assured that a responsible person would walk me out of the Ninth Street and Cherry Avenue Southeast area to the Fifth Street and McKinley Avenue Southwest neighborhood, a distance of ten blocks. Safety, they believed, was assured once a pedestrian had passed through the business and red-light district, which covered a nine-by-four block area from East Tuscarawas to Ninth and Cherry Southeast. It also spread east and west into Walnut, Rex, Piedmont and Savannah Avenues.

Cherry Avenue, the main thoroughfare in the congested slum district, had a reputation as "little Chicago." It was rumored that murdered bodies were found almost every weekend on the streets, in freight yards, along the Pennsylvania Railroad tracks, in dark alleys and abandoned dwellings— victims of the Black Hand Gang! Whatever the rumors, and however true or exaggerated the facts or fantasies, we were warned as children to "Stay off Cherry Street!"

Most of the first generation Europeans and the largest portion of Negroes lived in the areas immediately adjoining Cherry Avenue. We, with perhaps twenty other Negro families, were widely dispersed in the southwest area of

Canton, a "full mile" away from Cherry Avenue.

True to her promise that she knew someone who would escort me to the southwest-section of town, Mrs. Premmer introduced to Aunt Clella and me one of her regular dinner customers, saying, "I want you to meet a first class gentleman. Percy Marcere, meet Norma Snipes and her aunt, Miss Evans."

Mrs. Premmer, a pleasingly plump, brown-skinned woman in her mid-30s, stood there with arms crossed over her bespattered cook's apron. The smile on her face gave the impression she had masterminded the impossible.

"Pleased to meet you both," Percy smiled pleasantly. "This marvelous cook here has served you, Miss Snipes, on a platter at all of my meals for the past three days. She's been telling me she needs you so badly as a waitress, that unless I promise to escort you home, she won't let me eat here anymore. So, I must eat, and you must get home. Agreed? Then, so be it. It's my pleasure."

"Can she start this evening?" Mrs. Premmer directed the question to my aunt.

"I think so. I'll tell Norma's mother not to look for her until . . . what time shall I say?" Aunt Clella asked.

"I try to close the restaurant between 8:30 and 9:00 p.m." Mrs. Premmer offered.

"Then I'll tell her mother to expect her between 9:00 and 9:15," Aunt Clella agreed.

"I promise you that Norma will always be home no later than 9:15," Percy said assuring my aunt.

Back in the shop, Aunt Clella commented, "Percy! Is that his name? Seems like an honest, sincere young man. I'll tell your mom not to worry, that you will get home safely."

My first thought, as I was introduced to this very tall, very slender, and very dark man was, "I will never let you walk me all the way home. You might be nice, but you are too dark.

Maybe not Aunt Clella, but I bet Mom might object to your darkness, if she were to see you."

As we left the restaurant that first evening, headed toward southwest Fifth Street and McKinley Park, I was terribly self-conscious. It was the first time I had ever walked the streets with a young man.

I felt as if Percy and I were standing in a revolving display window, and that the people passing by were looking, thinking, and commenting. Only the warm, star-studded July night, instead of a bright, sunlit day, made that first walk together bearable.

When we reached McKinley Park, I turned facing Percy and volunteered, "I can get home from here. I live just a few blocks down the street."

"I understood I was to walk you all the way home, right to your door," Percy tried to explain.

"Oh, no," I said, "Just past those busy streets back there. I am not afraid now. I know all the people from here to home and the lights are on in all of the houses. I could run up on anyone's porch if I thought I was being followed.

"Over there," I continued nervously, pointing to a large home on the corner of Fifth and Wells, "is the home of my Dueber School principal, Miss Lena Ritterspaugh. In the next block across the street live the Ballards, the people from whom we bought our house. Further down, there is Miss McGeehon's home. She was the fifth-grade teacher to all of my sisters and brothers. Just before I reach the B & O tracks, I pass Reverend and Mrs. Pemberton's house. Once across the tracks I am home safe. So do not worry about me, I shall be all right. I am a very fast runner besides."

"There's nothing more for me to say then, except 'Goodnight,' " Percy remarked, and we parted.

This young man, Percy Alluren Marcere, really impressed me with his gentlemanly behavior. He appeared to be a quiet, reflective individual; but as we became better acquainted, I discovered he was a great conversationalist. By the time my vacation jobs between my Aunt Clella's shop and Premmer's restaurant came to an end, I had several reasons to feel good about that summer.

On the evenings the restaurant closed early, I rather surreptitiously encouraged Percy to walk a route that covered every inch of Cherry Avenue, from Ninth Street South to Thirteenth Street and from Ninth Street North to East Tuscarawas Street and the public square. I was eager to satisfy my curiosity about this forbidden section of town. Fearing no danger, I was beginning to thoroughly enjoy those extended jaunts, properly escorted down mysteriously evil streets. My walking companion was a gentleman of the highest order and so entertaining. He was as different from my father as day is from night. My pop's reticence had prevented him from speaking a single word on our one mile walk to my high school and to his hotel job. Percy and I communicated nicely.

All about us were the noisy, discordant sounds of many languages, but my interest in language and ethnic differences began long before I heard the multiple babblings on Cherry Avenue. There were German-speaking Slovaks who attended St. Mary's School, and my grandfather spoke German fluently. We had Romanian, Italian, and Jewish neighbors living next door to us. From whispered conversations at home I gathered that quite a few Negroes had ambivalent feelings about foreigners. They often felt threatened, displaced, and excluded in the land that had been their forefathers' home for three hundred years. Negroes had no foreign allegiance. They had no second or third language. They were just English-speaking, brown-skinned Americans.

My maternal grandparents, James Robert Evans and Clella Dorsey Evans, were born free in 1841 and 1851 respectively. They claimed Pennsylvania and Bellevue, Ohio, as home. My mother, Ida Evans, was married to Norman Sherwood Snipes, from Raleigh, North Carolina, in 1906. They witnessed the heavy tide of immigrants who came to Canton in 1909. They often found themselves in the midst of strange-speaking peoples.

The Jews had a synagogue in Canton as early as 1869. The Italians arrived in 1884 only to learn the Swiss were here in 1883. With the 1900-wave of immigrants, Canton, like many industrial, midwestern cities, had all the ingredients for an international melting pot.

There was a carnival atmosphere about the sights, sounds and smells of Cherry Avenue that vanished in the '60s with the clearing out of the slums, the construction of a super highway, and the building of an industrial complex. The new skyline erased forever a whole area that surrounded the heart of the city like an alien squatters' village.

I was curiously fascinated by the business places we passed, partly because my father had owned a billiard parlor on the corner of Third and Walnut Avenue Southeast, and my grandfather had had his own barber shop in Bellevue, Ohio. It was exciting to observe the array of multi-ethnic entrepreneurs, excitedly serving the needs of their culturally different constituents.

Many of the businesses evidenced their owners' ethnicity by their wares and their services. Their collection of talents and skills undoubtedly contributed to Canton's reputation as the "City of Diversified Industry". Throughout the business day these proprietors served their patrons gratefully, displaying the highest art of salesmanship and persuasion.

Mobility and prosperity made it possible for these proprietors to move westward and northeastward, away from their humble beginnings. Their second businesses sought the patronage of a white-collar, upper-class clientele instead of their former blue-collar supporters. They established lodges, golf courses, churches, hotels, and restaurants, from which others, unlike themselves, were excluded. Negroes, in particular, were denied membership and entry.

Such discriminatory practices were defended on the grounds that certain gatherings, private if you please, were for the furtherance of their own ethnic traditions. They needed to sustain their "old world" values, while becoming Americanized.

Negroes had no such link with their ancient traditions. After three hundred years of agricultural servitude, after a complete divestiture of their African culture—family, language, tribal customs, and religion—Negroes were less than sixty-five years into the process of restructuring a Negro-American culture.

Percy and I engaged in deep philosophical prognostications about our people and the world in which we lived. We felt a sense of pride that in 1929 we had many community-service businesses up and down Cherry Avenue. There were three restaurants, a pharmacy, three physicians, two dentists, two barber shops, a beauty parlor, three pool halls, a gasoline station, two garage repair shops, an undertaking establishment, a grocery store, a bakery, a dance hall and lodge, and my aunt's dry cleaning and pressing shop. Outside the multi-ethnic thoroughfare, there was the Gillespie radio repair shop on Sixth and Cleveland Northwest and Jackson's fruit and vegetable produce stand in the Auditorium Market. It was whispered that a popular downtown business was run by a Negro who was passing as white. We expressed confidence, much as my father had in 1904, that in America the opportunity to do, and to become, was beckoning with open arms.

Percy and I talked a lot about ourselves. We spoke of our likes and dislikes, our sisters and brothers, our hometown, and of our hopes for the future. Each of us was the oldest of a family of six children. He had four sisters and a brother, which paralleled my family of four girls and two boys. He was six years my senior, and we both had October birthdays. He was born in Meridian, Mississippi. His father was a Baptist preacher. Percy, on his way to New York, stopped to visit a childhood friend of his, Dr. Simon Cole, a dentist. Dr. Cole advised him to remain in Canton, saying it was a good place to earn money and to save it.

Percy was supporting his sister, Alberdeen, at Columbia University. She was in nurse training. He had dated no one since his arrival in Canton in 1924 and declared he never planned to marry. Neither did I.

Occasionally during my senior year, as I passed the square on my way to high school, I had heard a man whistling a block away on East Tuscarawas and Piedmont. With a resonance of unique quality, the tunes of My Blue Heaven, Let Me Call You Sweetheart, Ain't Misbehavin', and other popular ballads of the day, caught the attention of scores of people headed for work. Often I wondered who was the person of such happiness, joyfully rendering such beautiful music. Now I knew! Percy was the whistling porter-custodian at the Richman Brothers Men's Clothing Store. At 7:30 a.m. he could be seen washing the display windows and mopping the foyer. When the opportunity arose, I would stop outside Richman's for a chat while he went about his work.

Kent State University had just opened a one-year Normal School Extension Unit at the Canton City School Administration Building. Simultaneously, Mrs. John Leonard offered me a job as a live-in maid and cook with time off to go to school. My pay was ten dollars a week. With the fifty dollar Menelick Culture Club Scholarship and nearly half the salary I had saved from my two summer jobs, I was able to enroll in college. I was also able to give Mom half of my salary, twenty dollars a month.

As soon as that school year was over, I became a full-time cook with the Arthur Reeves family at Congress Lake, from June to December. I would enroll at Kent in January.

Just before I was to leave for the main campus, I received a telephone call from the office secretary at Richman's. She asked me to stop by the store to pick up a going-away gift. With half the store clerks looking on, Percy gave me a small mirrored cedar chest, with a neat assortment of needles, thread, scissors, manicuring set, and six pairs of silk hose. A pair of silk hose cost a dollar and a quarter. Cotton stockings cost thirty-five cents. A respectable young lady did not accept personal items from a gentleman. I floundered for words to conceal my confusion, while expressing a cautious gratitude.

He explained, "My sister Alberdeen is always writing to ask for at least two pair of silk hose. I guess wearing silk stockings is very important when you're in college." Between December 1928 and August 1929, I saw Percy twice.

My determination to pursue this second year of college precipitated an explosive confrontation between me and Mom. It was traumatic. Thoroughly convinced I was right, I pushed aside the irritating anger and the guilt that tried to invade my conscience. I was eighteen and on the threshold of new beginnings.

I had always planned to teach and, having performed well that first year in the Kent Extension College in Canton, I was even more determined to continue my training on the main campus in Kent, Ohio. Neither mom's need for me to help her support the five younger children at home (now that pop had vanished, wherever a deserting parent hides) nor my nearly nonexistent college funds could quench my determination to pursue the training that would make teaching possible.

Mom and Grandma both lamented their unfulfilled dream

of becoming teachers. My great expectation was to fulfill three dreams in one, mine and theirs.

A recurring dream, which I had not fully shared with Mom or anybody, pretty well outlined my career and my future. I would live at home and pay room and board to help support the family. Teachers were not allowed to marry, and this appealed to me. There was nothing particularly attractive about my parents' marriage and subsequent separation. Knowing that marriage and babies went together made an unmarried teaching career even more attractive. I did not want babies, so a husband was expendable.

As a teacher, I could build a third bedroom over the kitchen replacing a pitch black, low-ceilinged storage room, cluttered with broken furniture and discarded toys. The new addition would be a large airy room with twin beds for my sister, Ethel, and me.

A teaching position would permit me to return to college for a part of each summer and then travel. The first place on my itinerary would be Raleigh, North Carolina. I could see what the South was like with its segregation and Jim Crow laws and look up my pop's relatives. Maybe I could locate my pop. I wondered if he was in school somewhere getting his law degree, now that he had divested himself of family obligations.

I tucked my dreams away and gathered together my belongings. My neatly packed leather-simulated cardboard suitcase reflected my meager finances as well as my feelings about the importance of clothing. I thought in threes: one garment being worn, one in the closet or dresser drawer ready for wear and one being laundered, dry cleaned or mended.

My college wardrobe consisted of two dresses, a two-piece suit with a blouse and sweater and an "after-school" dress. The lingerie and toiletries were kept to a minimum. There were three pairs of panties, three brassieres, two slips, one nightgown, three pairs of lyle cotton stockings, six neatly quilted three-by-twelve-inch flannel feminine pads, safety pins, needle and thread, a bar of P & G laundry soap, a bar of Ivory toilet soap, Mavis talcum powder, Mum, Vaseline, a toothbrush, comb and brush, two washcloths and a small-sized bath towel. Two pair of oxfords—one brown, one black, with matching shoe polish kits, a pair of patent leather pumps (my graduation shoes) for dress, a winter coat with hood and scarf, a pair of woolen gloves and a pair of rubber galoshes completed my wearing apparel. My wardrobe was not as collegiate as the well-dressed college miss, but I was fortified with a naive abundance of self-confidence and optimism.

My employer, Mrs. Arthur Reeves, a strikingly beautiful woman, congratulated me for my educational goals. "Stay with it, Norma. You know what your mother has suffered and what it means to be deserted. Look at me, I am surrounded by wealth and you can see for yourself what my life is like. As a teacher, you will have security and independence. I wish I had had the opportunity to go to college."

I was on my way, aware that my savings and a contribution from St. John's A.M.E. Zion Church would not cover all of the winter and spring quarter expenses.

The Kent Normal School campus did not present a particularly inspiring view that cold January morning. The taxi driver drove slowly and pointed out the Administration Building dominating the snow-covered campus. It was surrounded by Kent Hall, the University School and the dormitory. Alighting from the taxi with suitcase in hand, I was eager to get about the business of completing my registration.

After a morning of directions to "stay here" and "go over there," the long registration lines in the Kent Hall gymnasium were behind me. With my tuition receipt tucked inside one of the six text books cradled in my left arm and dragging my suitcase by a very tired right arm, I approached the dormitory registration desk. How nice it would be to get my room assignment, take a hot shower, stretch out on a comfortable bed and shout, "I made it! I am really here, Kent!"

I was totally unprepared for the face-to-face pronouncements of the dean of girls.

"I am sorry," an unfeeling feminine voice began as I placed my registration forms on the office counter. "We have no accommodations for your stay on campus. Your dormitory deposit will be returned to you. We just couldn't! It is our policy to recommend a couple of good colored homes where you may stay. The room rent is two dollars a week. You may board with your landlady or do your own cooking. We set the room rent, she sets the board rate, and we inspect the houses. You should be as happy as the other colored students—we haven't had too many—who have stayed off campus while attending Kent."

She moved away from the counter and returned with a sheet of paper. "Here are some addresses. Oh, how to get to these homes? Go to the main street just outside this administration building, turn left and walk to the center of town. A drugstore is on the corner. Turn left again and walk about five blocks. You will be in the colored section. Anyone can tell you where the Joneses, the Browns, the Fletchers or Howards live, if you ask. A couple of these families are related. It might be better if you chose this family here at this address." She circled a name, placed the sheet in front of me, and continued, "Two of these families, I am told, have teen-age boys living at home. We may have to reconsider and not allow our students to live where dating could be a temptation. Shall I call a cab or phone one of the families to drive up here for you? They all have automobiles. Just wait a few minutes in the outer office. I shall get your deposit."

Dean Verder never gave me a chance to open my mouth for any utterance, not a single word. It is difficult for me to recall exactly how I felt during her garrulous dissertation. I stood before her, looking at her, and yet not seeing her. With each spoken word, the vision of her diminished. Was I dreaming? Was I experiencing shock, fear, intimidation or anger? Disbelief overwhelmed me. What was I supposed to do? Was I to say "Thank you" . . . "Oh, that is all right" . . . "Yes, ma'am, I understand"?

I stood there. I was like someone standing outside a huge iron gate, locked out. Does the person wishing to pass through yell and call out, pound real hard with both fists or walk away? A brief thought crossed my mind to protest, to scream, to say that I had never spent a night in the home of strangers and to ask why it was so necessary for me to live outside the college campus in a colored home. Would it help to tell this person I was not seeing that I had looked forward to living in the same dormitory with some of my classmates of last year?

Then another thought followed that caused me to neither protest, beg, nor question, but to walk resolutely away. I had barely enough money to see me beyond that first month of the winter quarter. If Dean Verder knew this, she would probably see that I was sent home pronto, to "wait until you have adequate funds." It might be better for me to live off campus and do my own searching for work than to live on campus, looking for the approved jobs that the college catalog explained came through the Dean's Office.

I had planned to use my cooking experience to request work in the cafeteria dining room for my board. This college administrator would never help a student as unwelcome to the college as she indicated I was. Maybe a colored family would assist me in finding part-time work to earn at least three dollars a week. If the Kent colored residents would be anything like some of the choir members at St. John's A.M.E. Zion Church or some of Mom's Watkins Products customers, they would understand. They would be proud of me and encourage me. I backed away from the counter, picked up my belongings and walked outdoors to a waiting cab.

The taxi driver tossed my suitcase in the back seat of his conveyance. I held on to my purse with the dormitory deposit after extracting fifty cents for taxi fare. The textbooks that tumbled beside me on the seat were the only assurance that I was a bona fide college student. Later that week I would look at my *Hygiene of the Child, Elementary School Music, History of Lower and Middle Grades, Industrial Arts* and *English Grammar* books and wonder if I should not take them back, receive the full purchase price and return home.

The mile or so ride down narrow, snow-covered streets exacted no inquiring remarks from either the driver or me. The four- and five-room, two-storied wood frame houses in each block were typical of small-town neighborhoods. I was reminded of Norwalk, Ohio, where I had lived as a small child; but the moments in Dean Verder's office pushed aside any nostalgic memories of peace and beauty.

What I had been introduced to in the dean's office was a form of slavery: no voice, no choice, no access. Like an annoying traffic signal that catches the pedestrian halfway between the curb and the center lane, I was stopped dead in my tracks. With the signal lights flashing, "You can't! We won't let you!", the pedestrian has to decide whether to go back to the curb, stand in the center safety lane or chance rushing to the other side.

Slowly, a tingling, irritating sensation enveloped me as one by one all of the hushed conversations at home of racial injustice came to mind. Was I entering a hostile, separatist world whose racial tenets had birthed the N.A.A.C.P.? This organization's main function was to seek, by education, persuasion and legal decisions, justice and equality under the law.

Topping the list of "you can'ts," most of which I had only

heard about, would be today's experience.

You can't stay at the Kent State College dormitory!

How soon would I personally come face to face with other "can'ts" that my parents, my Uncle Eugene, the Methodist preacher, and the young Negro doctor had talked about from first-hand experience? A list of "you can'ts" flooded my brain. There were can'ts that shouted exclusion from theaters, hotels, restaurants, YWCAs, country clubs, neighborhoods, amusement parks, Pullman trains, hospitals and churches.

The "you can't" was like telling an individual he was less than a first class human being, incapable and unworthy of going places and doing things because of a personal inadequacy.

The "we won't let you" attitude suggested a near forcible restraint. Minus the seemingly polite rationalization of a Dean Verder, the law or any authority figure could prevent the victim's entry.

We won't let you in this restaurant, swimming pool or dance hall. We won't let Negro children enroll in the dancing classes, or participate in dramatics! We won't cut your hair in our barber shops, loan you money from the bank or hire you for skilled or professional jobs!

"Here you are, lady," the cab driver announced, breaking into my litany of can'ts and won'ts, "I'll knock on the door and see if anyone is at home. From the snow on the walk, it doesn't look like anyone's been in or out of the house today." He knocked loudly, "Yes, there's someone here. I'll bring your suitcase. This is going to be a long walk to the college, young lady."

"Thanks," I said politely. He pocketed his fare and drove off.

The couple who greeted me at the door would have made a perfect picture for Norman Rockwell's *Saturday Evening Post* magazine cover. This young artist on his way to acclaim might have caught the physical characteristics and the initial southern congeniality of Mr. and Mrs. Jones, but no artist or psychologist could have portrayed or analyzed the perplexity and the feelings I had, of being suddenly propelled into an alien, nonacademic, culturally different, colored world.

II

Culture Shock

Living in my college-approved, off-campus rooming facility dissipated thoroughly the mystery-shrouded curiosity I had about colored-family living. When Mom and I had canvassed for and delivered McBrady goods in the heavily populated colored sections of Canton, Massillon, and rural Aultman to prevent the foreclosure of our home, I wondered about many things. I was just thirteen. Mostly I was curious about the food and dietary patterns of these unfamiliar people.

My olfactory nerves frequently twinged at the odors that came from boiling kettles and frying skillets. From half-hidden strange kitchens, on waves of smoke and steam, smells poured forth saturating the already laden atmosphere, causing the excess redolence to cling to one's skin and clothing. None of Mom's beans, vegetable soup, fried potatoes and onions, applesauce, bread pudding or my homemade bread ever smelled singly or collectively like the strange odors some homes emitted.

That winter of 1928 I was introduced to a new dimension of peculiar experiences in the Jones' home. Mr. and Mrs. Jones were kind enough in a strange, restrained manner. They expressed to me a polite welcome the day I arrived.

"Youse be mos' we'come to oauh 'umble 'ome. We wusn't

'spectun no one cose we neber know if de be gwine to hab any us folks in de college."

I could hardly interpret their words, and as wafts of those unpleasant smells assailed me, I stood there thinking I should not stay. I ought to run after the taxi and return to school to request another rooming place. However, this couple rather interested me and I must not forget my good manners.

Mrs. Jones, a small woman whose real calico-dressed figure was hidden by layers of cotton petticoats and long winter underwear, had a joyless smile. Mr. Jones was a tall, friendly gentleman of few words. He was wearing heavy navy blue corduroy trousers and a heavyweight plaid shirt. Flannel underwear peaked through the shirt cuffs and lay in folds on his ankles, half-hidden by fleece-lined bedroom slippers.

Mrs. Jones explained they were upright church-going Christians. They had a son and daughter whom I would meet later. She announced in a decisively expectant tone that I was most welcome to attend Sunday morning church services with them. They would return for the evening services at their Baptist church, but it would be up to me whether to attend that second service or not. She invited me to eat Sunday dinner with them without charge. Mr. Jones nodded his head in agreement.

"Sho is good to mek you we'come to ouah home. Jes mek youhsef commptibal," Mrs. Jones remarked as she showed me the little windowless alcove bedroom on the first floor just off the chilly, plainly furnished front room. It contained a double bed and a mirrored dresser. A large nail on the wall supported four or five coat hangers. After emptying my suitcase and storing it under the bed, it was plain that only two of the dresser drawers were needed for all of my belongings. I placed my textbooks on top of the dresser with my toiletries. I explained to Mrs. Jones that I would need much less kitchen cupboard space, even after purchasing a supply of food in a day or two. I was shown the iceless icebox on the rear porch where I could keep perishables such as milk, oleomargarine and eggs.

As I undressed that night, after pulling shut the cretonne-curtained draperies separating the bedroom alcove from the adjoining room, I discovered I was to share my bed with the landlady's fifteen-year-old daughter, Susie. Susie had entered the dining room sometime during my orientation and had seated herself quietly, sullenly and disinterestedly in front of the small gas heater. She did not appear pleased with my formal invasion of her home. Susie was a plump but shapeless, old-looking teenager who appeared to be terribly ashamed of something—perhaps her femininity. She had nothing to say all evening. I was glad to retire after a disappointingly queer day.

I was sitting on the bed when Susie parted the draperies and said, "I hope you don't mind if I sleep next to the wall."

An angry feeling began to envelope me, and I wondered how to react to this sudden intrusion of an unexpected bedmate. I had become so used to the single bed in the private homes where I cooked that, even when I slept at home, I no longer shared a bed with my sister Ethel. I slept on the hide-a-bed davenport in our front room.

"Your mother did not tell me that we were to share the same bed," I said to Susie. "I have been sleeping alone since my freshman year in high school. I don't like for anyone to touch me, so I shall sleep as close to the edge as I can without falling out of bed." These defined bed perimeters indicated Susie and I would distance ourselves from each other as far as possible.

The voluminous straw-filled mattress and a deep depression in the middle of the time-weakened bedsprings caused each of us to roll toward the center of the bed. I awakened and recoiled every time Susie touched me or I touched her. I wanted to kick her and pinch her and fight a real bed fight, as Ethel and I had done a few times as young children. My restraint was not an act of kindness, but a loathing to touch her skin as though it were poison. My futile attempts to control the centrifugal force of colliding bodies ended with my sitting upright in a lumpy upholstered front room chair. With my pillow around my shoulders and my winter coat covering my lap, knees and feet, I awaited the dawn of my second day in Kent, Ohio.

The next night, Susie slept upstairs; but even sleeping alone, I never got used to that floppy traveling mattress, seesawing on a sagging bedspring. I never got used to most things in the Jones' home. I was bombarded with revolting sensations involving every sensory perception of sight, sound, smell, taste, and touch. The little annoyances became bigger day after day, even when I was invited to sit at the table and Mr. and Mrs. Jones welcomed me to share their blessings.

The fried salt pork (instead of bacon), the thick rough grits and the crisp, fried "caught-today-creek-fish"—foods I had never eaten before—initiated unpleasant smelling, tasting and feeling sensations.

The incredible scene that set me in orbit was Mrs. Jones' weekend chitterling cleaning ritual. Mr. Jones and some neighbors went to the slaughterhouse on Friday evening or early Saturday morning and returned home with two large galvanized laundry tubs filled with hog bowels bulging with the feces of recently slaughtered swine. The sight of Mrs. Jones, Susie and a neighbor or two extracting the bowel contents from long, curling, convoluted, grey intestines was revolting.

By noon the vaporous stench of the boiling excrement-scented chitterlings forced me wretching into the cold outdoors with no place to go except the college library or the streetcar and interurban train station downtown.

That first Sunday in Kent I accompanied my landlady, her

husband, and their daughter Susie to church. Mrs. Jones, dressed in finery that surprised me, seemed eager to introduce me to the congregation and to her friends. She proudly sat in the Amen corner to the right of the church and close to the pulpit. The choir was behind the pulpit and Susie, not nearly as well-attired as her mother, was surprisingly at ease there. Mr. Jones sat in the front row with a group of other well-suited, impressive-looking gentlemen. They looked so important, but I never knew if they had a specific church function. I sat halfway between the front and the back of the storefront church, which seated perhaps fifty worshipers when filled to capacity.

The Sunday morning service, although scheduled for 11:00 a.m., did not start until well after 11:30. The benediction at 2:00 p.m. signaled that a spiritual pinnacle had been reached and everyone could go home happy. It was an emotional service, far different from the Catholic and Methodist congregations I knew. Moment by moment, emotions gained momentum of uninhibited proportions. Susie—quiet, demure, awkward Susie—came to life in the choir. She swayed, clapped her hands and sang lustily. She was a kindred Christian spirit with the other choir members.

Repeated "Amens" and "Yes, Lords" expressed the congregation's agreement to the preacher's message. "It's a haud, sinful worl out there," the preacher shouted, "but God will take care of His own!"

A woman jumped up and shouted, "Yes, He will! Yes, He will!" The choir picked up the mood and started singing "God Will Take Care of You." Soon half the church was singing, and shouting and clapping hands. Mrs. Jones, and the ladies in the Amen corner, rocked back and forth, dabbed a tear from their eyes and uttered meditatively, "Yes, Lord! Yes, Lord!"

The minister concluded his message and welcomed sinners

and new members into the fold. The choir sang another song as the collection was taken. A deacon announced the weekly meetings and welcomed attendance at the Sunday School teachers' classes, choir practice, missionary society and prayer meeting. Then the visitors were asked to stand and introduce themselves. When I announced that I was a student at Kent Normal College and was staying at the Jones' home, Mrs. Jones stood and took a bow. The minister congratulated me with "It's good to see educated young people who hasn't forgotten God. College students sometimes gits so interested in big woids and science and a lot of 'ologies' and foolishness . . ."

"Amen. Amen," the congregation chanted.

". . . that dey think dey doan need God. You'se mose welcome to worship wid us, Sistah."

As we walked the Sunday silent street to the Jones' home, I was bothered by the high degree of church emotion and the pastor's remarks about education. People who can reach such heights of emotion can forget about meaningful life goals. People who reject knowledge cut themselves off from the mainstream of competitive pursuits. Where were these people going? What did they want from life, I wondered.

My mom had taught us that wisdom, knowledge and God were partners. "Every time you study, you are praising God. You are strengthening the mind and the intelligence He has given you," Mom repeated over and over.

Mom also taught us about emotional control in the areas of happiness, sorrow, fear, and anger by referring to a scale from one to ten. The higher the reaction, seven to ten, the more intense, more noisy, more violent the display. The lowest ratings of one to three meant one's emotions were so moderate as to make others wonder if they existed at all. Emotions at the range of four to six were average. They existed, but no one was greatly disturbed, hurt or inconvenienced by the individual's feelings and behavior.

We were taught, we observed, and we learned we could be deliriously happy; and yet our laughter, our joy, could not be heard beyond the four walls of our home or more than twenty feet beyond the front and back porch where we gathered for fun and games. We could become angry and not resort to name-calling or fighting or plan revenge. We could be afraid but we were taught to stop and think through our fears, rather than scream, panic, and fall apart. To wail and cry with sadness and sorrow was explained as shaking our fist in the face of God and being rebellious.

"Go into your closet and ask God for His comfort," Mom advised. "The world does not really care whether you are happy, sad, fearful or angry; so why be bothersome?"

That church service was somewhat bothersome to me and so was the Sunday dinner. At the table, as my plate was filled with potato salad, cole slaw, cornbread and chitterlings (often pronounced chiddlins), I was overcome with nausea and rushed first to the bathroom, then to my bedroom. I experienced a deep, deep longing to be back home.

I was not at all sure Mom would welcome me after my determined departure. If I went back so soon, it would be on her terms. "Get a job and help me support this family!" I could not go back to Mrs. Reeves because she needed me as a cook only six months of the year. I had to stay in school until June, but did it have to be with the Joneses? Their house, their daughter, Susan, my bedroom, their cooking smells, their church service, all annoyed me. It was not until I had a course in sociology at Temple University two years later that I understood the meaning of culture shock. I had maximum shock on the level of eight to ten. It was no average four to six or minimum one to three!

I began to make resolutions. I would begin to write letters home to Mom and the kids to let them know I would come home some weekends, especially when the Joneses had Sunday chitterling dinners. Even if I attempted to describe this food, no one at home would know what I was talking about. In the meantime, I absented myself from the Jones' home as much as possible. I would awaken at 6:30 a.m. and head for school by 7:00 with a small packed lunch of a peanut butter sandwich and two or three cookies.

I remained at the college later than most non-dormitory students, studying in the library or an empty classroom in Kent Hall. When I figured the Jones' supper hour was over, I returned home to prepare my evening meal, which usually consisted of a can of beans or vegetable soup and a boiled potato. The right amount of water to a can of soup could be very filling. I learned to drink cups and cups of coffee to keep awake while I studied.

It was difficult to concentrate in the gas heated dining room area with three people conversing about local gossip. The Jones' twenty-year-old son, Alvin, came in from work, ate a hurried supper and went out on the street. He gave the impression of not really living at home.

My college assignments were not like the high school homework or even that of the Canton College Center. I had to exert a new kind of discipline and concentration. Many evenings I started studying after the Joneses had retired and continued studying until midnight. Mrs. Jones warned me she would raise my rent if I continued to study after 10:00 p.m. "De college hab a lights out time, too," she reminded me.

Just when my money was running very low, I saw an ad in the daily paper for an evening cleaning woman at one of Kent's largest beauty shops. I applied for it and was hired. The pay would be seventy-five cents an hour and it was possible that I could earn three dollars a week. This would pay my room rent of two dollars and allow one dollar for food. This beauty shop job was not on the dean's list of "approved" places of employment, but it paid twenty-five cents an hour more than the college recommendation of fifty cents an hour.

I got behind in my room rent. The overwhelming urge to escape a nauseating and often morose Saturday and Sunday weekend was more compelling than paying my room rent, which was the exact train fair home to Canton. By the end of the winter quarter, Mrs. Jones threatened to report this fact to the dean of girls, along with my unauthorized evening employment. I was in a strange, strange world, a disconcerting real-life situation. An earlier curiosity about a different environmental lifestyle had been satiated.

III

College Life

What do I remember most about my matriculation at Kent Normal College? Fun and excitement? Friends? Parties? None of these. There was always the shortage of money. A nagging fear activated a concern that if I did not remain at Kent and did not return the next quarter, my goal to graduate and become a teacher would be more than temporarily postponed; it would be decisively aborted. That concern kept me going. Dean Verder set the stage for the unpleasant environmental complications by placing me outside the realm of intimate dormitory experiences. Nevertheless, except for the physical education classes, school was quite rewarding.

Learning has always created a sense of excitement within me. To read a book, to listen to a lecture, to absorb new facts, to exchange ideas, to experiment with materials, to be challenged by a new viewpoint, was like an adventurous journey. Not all of my classes, not all of my teachers, were super. One good, exceptional teacher, however, could make it worth my while to be in school every day and to absorb something even from a mediocre teacher. Of the nearly seventy or more different teachers I had from grade school through the second year of college, only a dozen or so stood out as exceptional. They were the teachers whose professional enthusiasm, whose encouragement and high expectations carried over to the next class, the next year, and the next challenge.

I began college with four high school years of perfect attendance. I set a goal of perfect college attendance, too. I nearly missed that perfect record when as a junior in high school, Mom insisted that I, not Ethel, stay home to care for my younger sisters, six-year-old Ruth and four-year-old Virginia. Ruth was recovering from a recurring chest carbuncle which caused her to fret and demand attention. Virginia was never ill.

"It is not my wish to keep you out of school, but I need the work and the girls must be looked after. You can study your lessons at home. You will not get behind. I shall write a note to your teachers and tell them of this emergency," Mom explained apologetically.

Mom left the house to board the 7:30 Sixth Street trolley to the square. She would arrive at her job by 8:00 a.m. Ethel, Eugene and Carl would leave for school a few minutes after Mom's departure. I had to think fast. I was determined not to be counted absent from school. Since I, like my father, could walk a mile in ten minutes, I could leave the house at 8:00 or 8:05 and be at my school no later that 8:15. Being present for homeroom exercises, I could then go down to the office with a note requesting permission to leave school because of a family emergency. Mom had taught me how to sign her name on Pop's money order support checks, so the note I would write would look authentic.

After surrounding Ruth and Virginia with an assortment of small playthings, I told them I had to go to Roberts Grocery, four blocks away, to get some food for lunch. "Be real good and Mr. Roberts is sure to give me some candy for each of you. If I am a little late, do not worry. You know how Mr. Roberts likes to talk."

With that, I hurried from the house and headed for

McKinley High. After making my presence known to my homeroom teacher, I was given permission to speak to several of my teachers and explain the emergency which required my going home. The forged excuse was on file in the attendance office. By 9:00 I was back home, and not a moment too soon because Mom phoned to ask, "Is everything all right?" My younger sisters never missed me. They never questioned why Mr. Roberts did not send them a penny treat. My perfect school attendance continued.

The health and physical education curriculum at Kent State revived all of the incidents and feelings that caused me to faint when gymnastics was a requirement in high school. I seldom had a gym partner and never a swimming partner. The girls would chatter and giggle with a friendly intimacy in the locker rooms, then run jubilantly to the gym floor, grab a friend and line up for games and exercises. I was always the girl without a partner, unless there happened to be a least preferable white girl left to be my reluctant teammate. On those occasions, we would stand there, each of us in our own thoughts, afraid to smile, forced to accept the fact we were undesirables trapped to perform together for that class period.

In high school I pretended a faint and sudden illness to cover my anger and humiliation. If I tried that at Kent, I feared I would be taken to the infirmary and my pretense would be exposed. How I wished the gym instructor would assign us partners by some method which would de-emphasize our physical appearance or our personal preferences.

After gym class one morning, the instructor called me aside and explained there was another colored girl at the college. "Would you mind, Norma, if I had your schedules changed so that you and Velma could be in the same class? She appears so lonesome, and that way you both . . ."

I did not hear the rest. My mind flashed back to other situations when teachers found unpaired Negro students a dilemma.

One and two scattered Negro students in college presented the same problem as the ten to fifteen Negro students at McKinley High School. Why?

One teacher came up to me in my sophomore year and asked if I would like to transfer to another biology lab period. "We have the nicest colored girl there, and she really needs a partner. We try to do our lab experiments in twos."

"I have a very good partner," I explained. "Ben Eppy and I work well together, and we take turns with other partners in our class," I explained.

She looked at me and that kind, patronizing smile disappeared as she walked away. But now that my college physical education teacher was asking favors, I would ask one, too.

"While you are changing the schedules to put us in the same class, could it be the last period of the day, on Friday?"

"I think so," she replied. "Come by my office tomorrow for your new schedule."

That way, I reasoned, I could hurry home after class, finish shampooing my hair, dry it, and press it properly. I dreaded revealing the fluffiness of my hair after water had seeped under the swimming cap and returned my hair to its natural expansive state.

Velma and I became good gym partners, but we did poorly as swim teachers for each other. In the swimming class, the instructor never touched Velma or me. She never took hold of our hands, never held our bodies to show us how to float or how to perfect a particular technique as she did dozens of other girls. She showed no concern for our progress. Yet I understood we were expected to swim across the pool, master certain strokes or fail the course. I made a "D" in swimming, the first near failing grade of fourteen years of schooling.

Oh how I disliked being treated so differently by some faculty and many of my fellow students! The students at Kent were being trained to go into their respective communities and teach young children. Their professors should have been the epitome of culture, wisdom, knowledge, democracy, fair play and justice. How could students learn what their teachers did not practice? A strong, fair teacher sets a positive atmosphere for the class. I learned in grade school that a student's personal biases were quickly put aside in the presence of a "fair play" teacher.

I became very perceptive of the weak, uncertain teacher or the deeply prejudiced one who kept alive in her charges the belief that I was different from those all around me!

How very lonesome it was not to have a friend to study with, not to have a classmate to share ideas with. I never reviewed examination questions with another student. In the midst of several hundred college students, no one knew me, no one spoke to me, no one became my friend.

One of my favorite courses at Kent was the two-unit industrial arts class. One unit was lecture, emphasizing purpose and objectives. The other was a practicum, actually working with materials and machinery to create furniture, toys and art objects from blueprinted designs. The finishing procedures with sandpaper, paints and lacquers made every object a superb work of art.

Miss Swan, the diminutive, effervescent instructor, was a versatile, entertaining person. She wove accounts of her European travels in between her demonstrations for the maximum utilization of electrical machinery and hand tools. From her, as from Miss Leichenstein, my eighth grade English teacher, I caught a glimpse of an exciting world of history, art, literature and music outside the United States. She was an enthusiastic world traveler. Like Mr. Gilmore, my art teacher at McKinley High and Sister Mildred, my first grade teacher at St. Mary's, I was inspired to perform beyond what I thought were my capabilities. Miss Swan extolled excellence. Her awareness of me made going to Kent worth the annoyances, the discomforts, the loneliness and everything.

Many, many hours I worked overtime in Miss Swan's workshop. In fact, her classroom, or any empty room in Kent Hall, became my study area long after most classes had ceased for the day. I saw very little of the college facilities beyond the classrooms to which I was assigned. Why I avoided the library I am not sure unless it was the distance that had to be walked across campus. The closed, isolated stillness, being boxed in by stacks and stacks of crowded bookshelves, were not conducive to study. If there had been a lounge where students gathered in comfortable surroundings to relax, to read the newspapers and to hear the excited conversations of other young people, I might not have stayed away. I know why I stayed away from the cafeteria. I had no money for the purchase of food or soft drinks.

Even my return to my off campus room after 7:00 p.m. was to avoid witnessing the Jones family enjoy their strange odorous foods. One dessert with a fragrance that pleasantly excited me, however, was Mrs. Jones' nutmeg spiced, orange-brown sweet potato pie. One weekend I asked to buy a pie to take home to my family. Like the fragrant piece of baked ham I impolitely filched from my Aunt Clem's kitchen table as a child of seven, I could not withstand the tantalizing aroma of this pie. I discreetly nibbled and consumed more than half the pie on the train ride home. It was the most delicious dessert I had ever tasted. It is still my favorite pie.

One Wednesday, I faced a situation which had all the ingredients for a happening that could have made the difference between where I am and what might have destroyed me. I was experiencing a most difficult crises. I was hungry. I was behind in my room rent, and I had no money to buy food. I had not eaten since Monday. That Monday morning my "Mother Hubbard cupboard," with its nearly empty box of buckwheat pancake mix, yielded two small pancakes. In the cupboard there was no syrup, no sugar, and no jelly to embellish the bare pancakes. On Mrs. Jones' kitchen table in the midst of the usual condiments and unstored tableware, I saw a jar of crystal clear, amber-colored syrup. I decided to borrow some and poured a generous amount on my two pancakes.

My taste buds were attuned for a gentle maple syrup flavor. My eyes had never seen such sparkling beauty. The Algae Syrup label on that well-filled bottle did not prepare me for its content of a bitter, strong taste of cooking molasses. I had to spit it out. That first mouthful shocked my taste buds and destroyed my appetite. The rest of the syrup-saturated pancakes, as hungry as I thought I was, were stuffed in the empty pancake box and tossed in the waste basket. Now it was Wednesday, and although I had drunk many cups of coffee, my food fast had been complete.

Thursday and Friday I would work at the beauty shop. If I could manage without eating until payday on Friday, I wondered how to spend my three dollars. Should I give Mrs. Jones two dollars for room rent, spend a dollar for food and be uncomfortably nauseated from the smell of chitterlings all weekend? Should I spend two dollars for train fare to and from Canton, give Mrs. Jones one dollar toward the ever-mounting back rent and hope? Hope for what? Food from heaven?

That Wednesday afternoon I asked Miss Swan's permission to spend an extra period or two in the workshop to start another project. "Of course, Norma, anytime," she agreed.

Within moments Miss Swan announced, "I must go to the office for a little while. Take care of things. If you leave before I return, just turn the lock on the door and turn out the lights." She disappeared.

I was busily engaged on my project when, reaching for a special tool, I spied Miss Swan's purse on her desk. It was a well-tooled, brown leather purse that might have been purchased in Italy, Spain, or some expensive shop on New York's Fifth Avenue. The owner had to have money to own such a purse. How penniless I was, and how hungry! I could slip up to the desk, open the purse and quickly reach in and get a dollar. With one dollar, I could buy enough food to last three or four days. A can of Campbell's pork and beans, a box of oatmeal, a can of evaporated milk, some mustard sardines and three or four potatoes was all I needed.

Three times I approached Miss Swan's desk, and three times I returned to my project. My brain was in a whirl of conflicting messages and my body was weak and trembling. A voice seemed to say to me: "Go ahead, do it. Take some money from that purse."

"How dare you even think of stealing! Shame on you!" I thought.

"What is wrong with that? You are hungry, aren't you?"

"Yes, but I would be crazy to . . ."

"Hungry people do crazy things. Society understands."

"No, no. When Miss Swan gets back, I may tell her how long it has been since I have eaten and ask her to loan me some money, but stealing? . . ."

"That would be borrowing. People in your family are not in the habit of borrowing either. Are they?"

"No, no one ever borrows a dime or a dollar from another person at our house."

"Stop thinking! You have wasted five minutes already. Hurry up and go take what you need."

"I can't! I have never stolen a penny in my life. Even when I went to the store for Mom as a little girl and wanted to buy a sucker, I would take that penny home and put it in the family coin jar for a real family treat later on."

"Which proves how dumb you are! Remember how the friends you visited in Cleveland called you dumb because you went all over Woolworth's store on Euclid Avenue and never thought to shoplift? Well, this is your chance to prove you have class. You take from the best."

"I cannot! I will not! Ever! The Bible says, 'Thou shalt not steal! Thou shalt not covet!' I have no right!"

"No one will ever know."

"My guardian angel knows. She is watching me now. And I would know."

"You are thinking strange, real crazy-like."

"Maybe, but what if I am caught with my hand in a purse that does not belong to me? What if I am suspended from school? The headlines would read: 'Nigger Student at State College Steals From College Professor!' I would be branded for life! I could never become somebody."

"Well, if you don't care about being hungry . . ."

"I don't care! I don't care!"

I wanted to run from the room to flee the temptation and the physical weakness sweeping over me. Something within urged me to stay. I returned to my project.

For a brief moment I thought to share with Miss Swan upon her return my knowledge that her purse had been carelessly left behind and that I stayed as long as I had to keep an eye on it. Mom used to relate how various housewives who employed her would leave coins on a windowsill or a dollar bill under a dresser scarf. She wondered if it was intentional bait to test her honesty or the thoroughness of her dusting. I did not want to believe Miss Swan had left her purse behind to deliberately test my honesty.

"Will you please inspect this, Miss Swan? I had not planned to work so late, but I got involved and could not stop. What do you think of this design?" I volunteered questioningly.

"Nice work, Norma. Lovely. Do you plan these Easter carts as gifts?"

"Yes. I hope to fill them with little trinkets for my two

younger sisters. They are seven and nine years old."

I did not elaborate by telling her they would be so much prettier than the cereal bowl Easter baskets my aunt had arranged for all of us a few years ago. Miss Swan and I left Kent Hall together. She never knew of my temptation, and I rejected the thought she had any intentions to test my honesty.

On the way home that cold wintry, late afternoon, I added several streets to my route and headed for St. Patrick's Catholic Church. I knew the doors would still be open. Catholic churches never locked their doors before the six o'clock Angelus. The church was empty, save for two stoop-shouldered old ladies with their heads draped in bandannas. Coming upon them from the rear I became aware they were fingering their rosaries in repetitious homage and beseechings to Mary, the Mother of Jesus. A barely audible utterance escaped their lips, but it was easy to know by a slightly elevated murmur and the shifting of gnarled fingers when the prayer began with the salutation, "Hail Mary, full of grace" and ended with the petition, "Pray for us sinners now and at the hour of our death."

I came to the church to pray for now, and to speak directly to the Almighty. I approached the communion rail and knelt before the Blessed Sacrament and began to pray silently.

"Dear Lord Jesus, I am hungry. I need help. This is the first time I have ever been tempted to steal. I want to stay at Kent, but not at the risk of becoming a thief. I was in great danger this afternoon. Remind my guardian angel to never leave my side and lead me not into temptation. You fasted forty days in the desert. How did you do it? For three days I have been hungry, and it is wintertime and so cold here. It will be five days by Friday before I get paid for my work at the beauty shop and can buy food. I don't think I can make it. Please give me my daily bread so this pain in my stomach will go away. Amen." I left the altar, smiled at the two women and hurried home.

With an "youse a bit late tanite," Mrs. Jones handed me the first letter to come from my family since my arrival at Kent. Aunt Clella, recently married and living in Sharon, Pennsylvania, wrote me a long newsy letter about her new home, new friends and activities. She hoped to have Grandma and Grandpa visit her in the spring. She sounded so happy. She wished me success and enclosed two dollars for "something nice." The one dollar I gave Mrs. Jones toward my back rent, and I hurried out into the darkness to buy some food. The little neighborhood store close by could not, at a reasonable cost, supply all I had envisioned purchasing earlier that day, but the sardines and crackers I bought tasted great. My fast was over.

The next morning, a secretary from the main office called me aside from my 8:00 a.m. class to announce: "A Mrs. Reeves of Congress Lake wants you to phone her as soon as you can. It is to be a collect call. There is no phone where you live, or we would have contacted you last evening. Would you like to use the phone in the registrar's office?"

That Friday evening at the close of my work at the beauty shop, Mrs. Reeves had a car driven by an Amish farmer waiting to drive me to Congress Lake. Mrs. Reeves was lonely and rather depressed. Her husband was on an extended business trip. Her children were all away at college and finishing schools. She needed someone to talk to who would give her understanding, companionship, and encouragement as she pondered some personal midlife concerns.

It was a revitalizing weekend for both of us. I, an eighteen-year-old Negro girl, and Mrs. Reeves, a wealthy mid-forty-year-old Caucasian woman, benefited from a sort of therapeutic rejuvenation. We both needed encouragement and understanding. I reached into her world of plenty and sophistication **and** learned that wealth and white skin does not necessarily guarantee happiness. She was uplifted by my naive enthusiasm for overcoming odds and gave me renewed hope to hold on.

Strange how this weekend also made it possible to solve an annoying problem with my music appreciation course. My piano background of music at home and Mom's singing of hymns and popular ballads was an inadequate frame of reference for the orchestrated operatic compositions we analyzed in class. I recalled the times when the Reeves family, dressed in formal attire, were patrons attending the opera performances in Cleveland. They also had a large collection of opera albums. Could I listen to them, and would Mrs. Reeves tell me about the operas she had seen?

She did just that. She and I, comfortably robed and fully relaxed, listened for hours to the music from her extensive phonograph collection. Even as the dining room draperies of my childhood years provided a backdrop for Mom's poetry, so, too, the view from the sun porch of the Reeves home gave substance to the sounds of music. Overlooking the expanse of lawn sloping to the lakefront, the winter scene became an uncaptured canvas. Bare maples and elms with stiff-frozen, corpselike appendages stood like motionless royal guards protecting and threatening nothing in particular. Oaks holding on to their dry leaves gave off mumbling, whimpering sounds in conversational argument with the luxuriantly green and singing pines. A subdued winter sun half-heartedly played peek-a-boo on the bare lawns and the ice-frosted banks of Congress Lake.

As the operatic melodies filled the house, the compositions of German, Italian, French and Russian artists were played and replayed. A few of my favorites were "LaBoheme" by Puccini, "Carman" by Bizet, "Lohengrin" by Wagner and "Don Giovanni" by Mozart. I would go back to class on Monday with a better knowledge of the historical origins, the plots, costumes and well-known operatic performers. I was likely to earn a decent music grade after all.

The Sunday dinner we prepared was a delicious, mouth-watering roast beef extravaganza. I wanted to tell Mrs. Reeves about the chitterling episodes at Kent, but she would have had no frame of reference to appreciate the irritating situation. I shared some of my pressing concerns, yet not everything. One in particular was about my work at the beauty shop to keep ahead of my room rent and incidentals. That was perhaps a concern I should not have mentioned since Mrs. Reeves had no access to money. That was one of her embarrassing annoyances.

She, a poor girl from the wrong side of the tracks, shared with me how she married a man of wealth. He had his methods of reminding his beautiful wife of her transplant from nothingness to plenty. She had to ask for and account for every cent she spent.

She evidenced her uneasiness about my health when, upon my departure that Sunday, she gave me a good-sized box of the small eight-ounce cans of fruit, vegetables, soups and juices from an abundance of canned foods stored in her attic. As the Amish farmer prepared to drive me back to Kent, Mrs. Reeves cautioned me never to go a day without eating some fruit. "You are much too thin. Take care of your health, Norma."

At Eastertime I wanted to go home to give my sisters the gaily decorated bunny wagons. It was also imperative I obtain some house-cleaning and catering jobs to take care of the next quarter fees, books and room rent. As I boarded the interurban train in Kent, laden with a suitcase of most of my belongings, I was well aware I only had seventy-five cents of the one dollar, one-way fair to Canton. The familiar conductor acknowledged the seventy-five cents and waited a moment for more change before asking, "Where to?"

"Canton, Ohio," I answered.

"That fare is one dollar, Miss. Remember?"

"I have only seventy-five cents."

"Well, that won't take you to Canton."

"I have to be home for Easter."

"Seventy-five cents will take you as far as North Canton. You will have to get off there and walk a distance of eight miles to Canton," he warned.

"That will be OK, sir. I am sure I can walk that," I answered gratefully. Settling down, I was content. I was on my way home.

As I got up, suitcase in hand, to leave the train at North Canton, the conductor stopped my departure with, "If you promise to bring the other twenty-five cents by the interurban office on the Canton Public Square Monday morning, I'll let you ride to Canton."

"Oh, thank you, sir," I said, startled and overjoyed at his unexpected consideration. "The first thing Monday morning I shall be there as soon as the office opens," I promised.

It was only as I walked the one mile home from the square, stopping at every block to change my heavy suitcase from one arm to the other, that I realized how impossible it would have been to have walked from North Canton to home. It was one of those pre-Easter days with the promise of spring in sight, but the temperature was freezing.

At home no one had any cash. There was not a red cent anywhere. Even the cookie jar was empty. The loss of my twenty-five dollar a month contribution was almost catastrophic. The boys had not caddied during the winter months. Many of Mom's four-dollar-a-day customers had cut back to an every other week schedule.

Four days later I walked into the interurban office to say, "Last Saturday I promised the conductor on the 8:00 train from Kent I would repay him this twenty-five cents on

Monday. Will you see that he gets it with my apologies for being so late? Thank you."

I spent my vacation phoning former employers to let them know I was in town and available for work. I gave them my school address and let it be known I was available for weekend catering at only six dollars plus transportation. The Urban League urged me to apply for a summer playground job.

From two days' earnings as a housecleaner, I gave Mom two dollars. I returned to school with two weeks' rent for my landlady and two dollars in cash. Grandma had given me several glasses of gooseberry and currant jelly. My diet that quarter would include a lot of peanut butter and jelly sandwiches and coffee; but I was not ready to apologize to my mom or to my siblings for the hardships in evidence at home. My determination to continue in college had not abated.

IV

How And Where Shall I Worship My God?

Shortly after I had prayed at St. Patrick's, "lead me not into temptation," I knocked on the rectory door and announced to an obliging young priest my desire to take instructions in the Catholic faith. This was not a totally unforeseen probability. My four-year attendance at St. Mary's Catholic School, upon the impetuous, naive invitation of Sister Mildred, had pretty well determined the mold of my Christian convictions.

All of Grandmother Evans' children had been baptized and enrolled in the high Episcopal church in Bellevue, Ohio. Mom, until the age of fourteen, when she moved to Canton, was a devout member of the Episcopal Church. She had begun to sing in the adult choir at the age of twelve. My father was the son of a Baptist preacher. He and Mom married in the African Methodist Episcopal (AME) church. We six children were baptized at the same Methodist altar where our parents exchanged their vows.

Grandfather Evans claimed to favor the Quaker concept of religious fervor. He liked to reminisce about the Quakers' involvement in the Underground Railroad and the Quaker assemblies his German foster parents introduced him to as a child. Even though any one of us might have been heard to say, "I do not like such-and-such a church as well as another," we nevertheless, as a family, had an ecumenical mentality long before we ever heard this terminology.

Our family's religious beliefs were not complicated. Our faith centered around a creator, Father-God, whose son Jesus came to earth to teach us how to live. In so doing, He died upon the cross for our salvation. We were taught that we truly loved God when we treated our fellow man with the same respect we preferred for ourselves. We were taught that low or high intelligence, even poverty or wealth, could determine an individual's religious inclinations. With an emphasis upon the search for knowledge and wisdom, we were reminded "to whom much is given, much is expected." We believed, too, that every individual had the right, and the obligation, to worship God in the manner he chooses, according to the grace and talents which God bestowed upon him or her.

My formal education began at St. Mary's multi-ethnic Catholic school, where I spent four joyous years. At the daily weekday masses and on Sundays, we knelt reverently and spoke devoutly to God. I sensed His presence every time I entered church. I knew that my Heavenly Father was my protector when I prayed, "lead us not into temptation." He supplied my needs when I prayed, "give us this day our daily bread." I was encouraged and challenged by the catechism classes, the Bible stories, and Mom's exhortation to seek wisdom and knowledge for the glory of God. I, with my brown skin in that Catholic sea of white faces, clung tenaciously and hopefully to the promise that I would inherit the earth if I obeyed God's commandments.

When we moved across town in 1918 to a more affluent, less ethnic-oriented Catholic parish, the pastor refused to enroll me in the fifth grade, my sister in the third grade, and my brother who was about to enter the first grade, in his school. His school, he said, was open only to born Catholics. Mom, knowing the priest was referring to her children's "born color" and not "born faith," expressed her indignation by forbidding me, in particular, to ever go near a Catholic church again. I sadly but obediently acquiesced until my senior year in high school.

With this rejection from St. Joseph's, I feared Mom would re-emphasize our identity with St. Paul's AME Sunday School. My intermittent attendance there between the ages of seven and ten was filled with hurt and rejection. There was much adulation and acceptance of light-skinned children, but there was almost a contemptuous rejection of the brown and dark-skinned boys and girls. There was no love or acceptance there. In addition to the color distinctions, the Sunday School gatherings were predominantly social events. To display one's expensive clothing, to detail a Sunday dinner menu, provided an intimate dialogue for a favored few. There was little time devoted to prayer, the memorization of a Bible verse or the discussion of a catechism lesson.

We always claimed it was by accident that we discovered St. John's, but one Sunday morning my sister and I went out of our way to find this little storefront church where people were so friendly and the minister preached intellectual sermons. There was no shouting or emotional hysterics, and no standards of physical beauty.

The dilapidated one-story frame building which housed the St. John's A.M.E. Zion congregation hugged the sidewalks on the corner of Eighth and Layfayette streets. Amateurishly constructed wooden benches rested unevenly on the pine floors. A one-step raised platform was the preacher's pulpit and the choir loft. The four or five oversized windows facing east and north had been papered with a gaudy transparent cellophane window covering through which no one could peer in or out. Someone must have thought this decorative necessity came close to the stained glass windows of the beautiful churches "up town."

We were comfortable there and I felt useful. I taught a Sunday school class of elementary boys and girls. I played the piano for the choir. I loved the singing, but a part of me would never acclaim this place as church.

Church to me was an architecturally magnificent place where people went to kneel before God in His holy of holies. Church was a house of prayer. There was very little prayer in this assembly. There was teaching, discussion, some differences of opinion, but no communion with the God of the universe. My soul was filled with yearning. I wanted to worship God in a temple or His great outdoors, not in a stable, not in an abandoned storeroom.

In the early 1920s, I was introduced to a spectacular type of religious service when Aimee Semple McPherson, a nationally renowned Evangelist, conducted a revival at the Canton City Auditorium. I was about fifteen years old. For several nights my mother permitted me to accompany my Aunt Clella to this unusual service. We joined the hundreds of spectators and worshipers, standing in a long line on Cleveland Avenue, eager to get the best seats in the auditorium to better gaze at this fantastic woman. As beautiful as she was in her flowing white robe, she reminded me more of a Theda Bara or Norma Talmadge movie star than one of God's saints. She did not fit the image I had of one proclaiming Jesus. She was not the counterpart of the biblical women or saints I had read about. Ruth, Vashti, Judith, St. Theresa, St. Cecilia, St. Anne, St. Monica, St. Agatha and even Mary the mother of Jesus were far different, God-loving, Jesus-adoring women. To my fifteen-year-old observation, each service reminded me of a theatrical performance with all the adulation heaped upon the star performer.

And then I entered college. My attendance at the Baptist church in Kent, sporadic as it was, alerted me to the realization that I was beginning to build up some negative attitudes about various religious gatherings. I found myself scrutinizing every action and analyzing every sermonized word.

Too often the prayers and exhortations were shouted and bellowed as though God was on the highest mountain top or blocks away somewhere. Exciting his congregation with moanings and groanings about the evils of this world, the preacher focused upon the heaven to which his congregation was bound. In equally intense oratory, he condemned dancing, drinking, playing cards and movies. Nothing was said about how to live a good life, how to use one's talents to serve mankind, or how to live in the world and not become a part of the world.

We did many things in our home which would have automatically disqualified us for membership in a Protestant church. We engaged in a variety of card games, and we went to the movies at least once a week. It was difficult for me to label any of the preacher's forbidden behaviors as sinful. The Ten Commandments did not mention them.

When Grandma taught me how to make elderberry wine and dandelion blossom wine, she reminded me of the first miracle Jesus performed, changing water into wine at the marriage feast. "The misuse of anything can be sinful. A thinking human being should never let an object or situation master him. He always remains in control. If he cannot, he should remove himself from the danger." We were permitted to taste our homemade wine at Thanksgiving or Christmas. A little glass of hot wine with lemon could be taken if we had a bad cold. Grandpa had his whiskey toddy every evening before bedtime. No one in our family was ever known to have been drunk or intoxicated.

Dancing, to me, (even though I could not dance a step) was a beautiful art form, like painting a picture, running a race, swimming, or playing a game of tennis. Every nation on earth had its distinctive dance. I was learning, through my music appreciation course, that there was a beauty of movement and a message in the waltz, the polka, hula, Virginia reel, tango, tap dance, ballet and other dance forms. Recognition was being given to the spiritual and jazz music as a distinctive Negro American contribution, but the African dance was still considered a barbaric ritual. So little of a positive nature was taught about our African heritage in the 1920s.

At age nineteen, I hoped to rekindle some of the sacred moments of my early childhood and to enjoy again the beauty and the ritual of the Catholic church. I needed to feel close to a source of strength and to recapture the sense of belonging to the whole human race, not just an isolated segment of humanity. I was hungry for in-depth religious instruction.

World history from the time of creation to the Caesars of Christ's time could be read in any ancient history book. The leadership of America could be traced from President Washington to each of his successors. I wanted to know who followed the twelve apostles. If Peter was the rock upon which the church was built, who succeeded him and who was the head of the church in the twentieth century? I wanted to know the history of Christianity, year by year, and generation by generation, since Christ walked the earth as man.

I satisfied my need to communicate with Jesus by entering the Catholic church nearly every time I passed its cross-adorned steeple. Always I entered the ediface alone, but once inside I believed I was surrounded by a host of saints who understood and strengthened me. I left the church refreshed and filled with a sense of peace, while at the same time, thirsting for something more.

Most of the above I shared with the young priest at St. Patrick's. He listened attentively with an occasional nod of his head. "I understand," he said. "Would you like to complete the series of instructions before your graduation? Just tell me when you want to begin."

August graduation was some weeks away and there were

many hurdles ahead. With budget adjustments here and there, money matters were a trifle better. It became necessary to discontinue my weekend trips home. The two-dollar train fare was applied to my ever-mounting delinquent room rent. I learned to escape some of the abhorrence to the weekly chitterling ritual by absenting myself from the Jones home as often as possible.

I began to study at the beauty shop and in the rear of St. Patrick's church. I now had two homes that welcomed me for a friendly visit and a meal at their table. Mrs. Brown, a younger married sister of Mrs. Jones, welcomed me to her home. I did not study there, but with her husband and two young children I enjoyed an evening of relaxation.

Velma, the girl who became my permanent gymnasium and swim partner, lived with relatives in Ravenna, Ohio, a town four miles east of Kent. Her parents drove from Cleveland frequently to take Velma home for the weekend. I became a regular guest. Not only did I enjoy this no-cost trip to Cleveland, but Velma's mother was a wonderful cook who spread a sumptuous table. Her father was a humorous gentleman who talked more than any man I had ever met. The whole family campaigned to put weight on my skinny frame by serving me extra generous portions of their food. I imagined my shrunken stomach expanding beyond my ability to satisfy it, and I winced when I thought of ballooning to one hundred and eighty pounds, which was about Velma's weight. She and her parents were wonderful to me.

Two events of considerable magnitude consumed my thoughts: my forthcoming graduation and my baptism. I wrote a two-part letter home to inform Mom of the dates of both. There was some uncertainty about my graduation, I explained, because I was short of money and behind in my room rent. If my landlady notified the college as she threatened to do, my diploma would be withheld and I would not graduate. I was hoping Mom could spare five or ten dollars to help. She had, till then, not given me a single dollar as help or encouragement. I had received nothing except meals on my weekends at home.

The second part of my letter announced with certainty that I was to be baptized and received into the Catholic church the week before graduation. I would become that which Sister Mildred had always predicted: a real, honest-to-goodness, full-fledged Catholic.

By return mail two or three days later, I opened my first letter from home. The only words on that sheet of tablet paper glared at me. I read, "It is bad enough to be a nigger, much less a Catholic. Don't be a fool!"

I was stunned! Stunned enough to stop dead in my tracks and not go through with my baptism. What did Mom mean by her comment? What did she know about the white world that I did not know? I knew the Ku Klux Klan hated Negroes, Jews and Catholics. Would I be in double jeopardy as a Negro and a Catholic?

A strong unifying force for the ethnic Catholic was that they were all Caucasian and all shared a common religious worship as members of the universal Latin rite Catholic church. That in itself excluded the Negro. His skin color and his unstructured Protestant worship was a distracting observation, separating him from the Caucasian majority.

The most recent immigrant to set foot on Ellis Island quickly discerned the American racist discrimination pattern. With prosperity, they moved across town where they were often the first to refuse service to Blacks. They supported restrictive covenants. Their churches made donations to support a "colored" Protestant church rather than run the risk of a Negro member worshiping beside them. There was no thought to include the Afro-American within the dominant white

Christian establishment. Maybe I needed time to look around before joining a white, ethnic-diversified Roman Catholic church, I reasoned.

If the feelings engendered by Mom's note stunned me to religious inaction, the threat of leaving school without a diploma spurred a renewed effort to get the money I needed for my graduation. The registrar's office had warned that unpaid bills and fees meant no cap and gown and no place in the graduation procession. I needed twenty-five dollars within days.

Mrs. John B. Leonard, my first employer after high school graduation, was a staid, class-conscious, aristocratic woman. She was graciously severe in the application of those skills needed to supervise a staff of qualified servants operating her spacious, beautifully furnished home. I sensed she felt that races and lower, poorer classes of people had their "place." I felt I had gained her respect for my cooking skills, if not her understanding of my educational pursuits. Our year-long communication level was strictly an employer-employee exchange that recognized only one common denominator: efficient service for the dollar received. A good worker was entitled to fair treatment and his paycheck. I would phone Mrs. Leonard and request a loan of twenty-five dollars. I could offer her three or four cooking or catering services or repay her in cash when I was hired as a teacher.

Mrs. Leonard hesitated long over the telephone call requesting money for me to graduate.

"How did you get into this situation, Norma? Why have you waited until the last minute . . . ? I don't know, Norma ... You need it tomorrow? . . . You had better call for it at the Western Union telegraph office . . . . First thing in the morning. Twenty-five dollars, you say?"

"Yes, please; and thank you, Mrs. Leonard."

"All right, Norma, and get in touch with me when you

return to Canton."

"I shall, I shall," I promised.

At nine o'clock the next morning, I informed the registrar I was going to town to pick up the money for my graduation fees. I would be right back. After pacing up and down in the telegraph office for nearly an hour, satisfying a clerk I was who I said I was, I collected the twenty-five dollars and ran the half mile back to college. My fees were paid. I was robed and capped and marched down the aisle at 12:00 noon.

I was the only Negro girl in the August 1929 Normal School graduation class at Kent. Not a member of my family was present. I was delighted to see Mrs. Brown, my new landlady, seated inconspicuously at the rear of the auditorium. Her face was aglow with a warm, sincere smile.

She had befriended me when her sister refused to allow me to stay the last three weeks in her home without paying my rent in advance. Mrs. Brown loaned me six dollars to pay her sister in full. She knew I had no money.

As I left Kent early the next day, she whispered, "Keep half of the twelve dollars you owe me as your graduation gift. You worked hard for this achievement. Congratulations and God bless you."

I returned to Canton, penniless, clutching my diploma, a priceless possession. No one had taken a graduation picture of me in my cap and gown. I had no class ring on my finger, proof positive of all my sweat and tears, but I had made it! I had completed two years of normal training, the maximum requirement for teaching in Ohio schools. I was prepared to teach! I would apply at the Canton School Board for an elementary school position in a day or two. I could see myself now as a teacher at the Liberty Avenue or South Market School where I had done two-thirds of my practice teaching.

With my first paycheck I would repay Mrs. Leonard her twenty-five dollars, since there was no response to my catering offer, and send six dollars to Mrs. Brown. I would buy myself two "teacher" dresses with the prettiest collar and cuff sets. Then I would begin to help Mom support my brothers and sisters. Maybe Mom and I could be pals again. We had really grown apart in the months I had been a student at Kent.

I pushed aside for the time being that unfulfilled yearning for a religious affiliation. I could adopt for awhile what my philosophy instructor repeated many times: "A religious church affiliation is not really necessary. No priest, rabbi or minister can make you good. It is good to be good for goodness sake."

V

I'll Never Hire

The Canton school superintendent's office and the Board of Education offices were housed in the same Administration Building where I attended my first year of college. The two-story complex was an attractive, cozy and inviting structure. It was ideal for the thirty aspiring young teachers who had insufficient funds to attend a distant state university and needed the encouragement from local educators.

To the administrative staff, department heads and secretaries, I was no stranger. Even Superintendent Wilson Hawkins, a veteran of seventeen years, knew me well enough to address me by name. I was on home territory when in August of 1929 I walked into that same building to be interviewed for a teaching position. Confidence enlivened every bone in my body. I was composed, alert and optimistic. The knowledge that Jesse H. Mason, the new superintendent appointed as of December 1, 1928, had never seen me, created no sense of fear or apprehension.

Superintendent Jesse H. Mason rose from his chair as his receptionist ushered me in saying, "Miss Norma Snipes to see you, sir."

He politely said, "Come in." He never asked me to be seated, as he stood towering above his impressive, highly polished executive desk. In his hand he held my application and my transcript revealing my academic performance at Kent Normal College. He also had a twelve-year record of my school work shared between St. Mary's, Dueber Avenue and McKinley High schools. Reviewing my records, he must have sensed my pride for a commendable fourteen-year school performance, with six years of perfect attendance and high grades.

With deliberation he walked to the rear of his office, stood there a moment and came back to the front of the room. The papers in his hand, he flung upon the desk as one tosses away an annoying bundle of useless junk mail. Pounding his now empty fist upon his desk, he literally shouted at me. "I shall never hire a colored teacher to teach here as long as I am the superintendent of these schools! Go South!"

He glared at me smirkingly, as though I was a foolish, silly girl. I had gone beyond my turf. I had no business being there in his office on his terrain, making such a ridiculous request— to teach!

The papers that he tossed away so carelessly on his desk did not annoy him. It was me. He was acting out that which he would have liked to be doing to my person. I felt he would have tossed me out of his office except for a degree of "civilized" northern restraint. Northerners did not harm Negroes as Southerners did.

How could I have so unnerved Jesse Mason, so threatened him by my presence? I carried no gun, no switchblade. I was a five-foot-four-inch, one-hundred-five-pound nineteen-year-old young lady. He was inches taller, much, much heavier and a mature adult. He could step on me like stepping on an earthworm. I felt as though he had thoroughly squashed me into a nonentity. Nineteen years of my life, recorded on those papers randomly scattered on his desk, were to him as useless as nothingness.

In 1926 I had seen a picture of a lynched Negro man. His

dangling, scorched, bulllet-ridden, blood-stained, castrated, death-stiffened body was hanging from a tree. There were twenty-three Negro lynchings the year I graduated from high school. I wondered how it could happen. I could not understand how one person or a mob, out of fear or anger, could express such contempt, such hate, such repugnance toward another.

That morning in Superintendent Mason's office, I became personally aware of the lynching mentality. I was witnessing a cowardly attempt to detach oneself from the reality of justice and honest leadership. What was even more shocking was that I had an embarrassingly guilty feeling of being to blame, of having said or done something wrong. I began to doubt myself. I felt unworthy. I was ashamed. I was humiliated. I wanted the floor to open up and swallow me into nothingness so I could die. And then I wanted to fight back!, to argue!, to demand! Was I really that un-deserving? What was wrong with me?

I stood there, fenced out once again, as I had been in Dean Verder's office eight months earlier. What could I say? What more would he say? This interview was to have been an inquiry about my interest in my chosen field of teaching and my practice teaching reactions. He was to have inquired about my educational philosophy, my moral values and my goals for contributing to the betterment of youth and the community. He had no intention to dignify me with the respect accorded an aspiring professional. To him, none of those measures pertained to me.

As Dean Verder spoke her edict of dormitory exclusion at Kent State, her countenance to me became an opaque, faceless blur. Her unseen image told me to remove my presence with the directive, "Have a seat in the outer office," and it walked away.

Jesse Mason had spoken his piece. He buttoned his suit

coat and turned his back on me. His dark blue-suited shoulder blades and outlined buttocks arched to rigid legs stood like a large boulder, shouting, "You shall not pass! You are not wanted! We don't need you here!" Would this man do or say something even more insulting if I continued to stand there? It was time for me to leave.

I walked out of his office into a daytime nightmare. Suddenly I was a nobody. I did not know which way to go or what to do. I was numb with the knowledge I was not going to teach in Canton. A ringing echo in my ears resounded over and over again. "I shall never hire a colored teacher as long as I am superintendent of these schools! Go South!"

Mr. Mason would banish me to a foreign land, among strangers more alien and more depressing than living with the Joneses in Kent had been. His words created feelings I had never known before. In no way could I describe my humiliation, my defeat, my shame! I had spent the greater part of three years completing a two-year college curriculum in elementary school education. I had lived off campus in the most unpleasant of living arrangements. I had made few friends, seen few movies, stayed away from dances and had no dates, no boyfriends.

For all of this, a Caucasian man of European stock, one of Canton's most respected citizens, had scorned me as the most detestable of human beings. He, a civic leader, a well-educated, university-degreed proponent of academic preparedness wielded the power to destroy me, a native born American of African extraction.

How was it possible this man could make me feel so worthless, so undeserving, so full of guilt? What was my crime? I had been caught with my "color" down. I had no business being in a white man's office. I should still be a slave. I should return to Africa or live within the white man's "freedom" limits. How long would it take and by what methods would

I learn the "freedom" message to Negroes? You are free to go to school, free to live in certain neighborhoods and free to follow your religion. So stay in your place!

He, that man, <u>one person</u>, perhaps with the approval—even the directives—of his institutional superiors and the Board of Education, could deny me the right to participate and contribute as a full American citizen. <u>It wasn't fair!</u>

The walk home was a trial run for the nightmares that began disturbing me and would for years to come. I was completely submerged in darkness at 10:00 a.m. on an autumn morning. I was hemmed in by tall buildings rising from muddy waters and lost from view by menacing clouds. The people I passed were faceless shadows. I walked down High Avenue Northwest, past Sixth Street, Fifth Street, Fourth Street, Third Street, Second Street, and stood for awhile at the corner of West Tuscarawas Street. Then I crossed over to Second Street South, proceeded to Fifth Street South, and walked the twelve blocks west to home.

My sleep had never been disturbed by a nightmare as a child. I had never awakened screaming because monstrous creatures were pursuing me. I had never been in a maze of futile wanderings trying to go somewhere, but that morning—that morning—I was lost and frightened. I was wandering in a world where hate directed toward me could have given birth to hate in retaliation. Is hate born when one cannot discern a religious, moral, political or philosophical rationale for what is happening to one's very soul? What actually takes place when one is unfairly rejected and brutally demeaned?

"Hate no one," Grandpa had taught me. "Hate no one ever!"

Not to hate another was only half of my family's teachings. I had been taught to like myself. I was reminded to think well of myself. I was told to keep my self esteem positively intact. I, along with others in our family, had adopted the slogan, "If we can always see ourselves as somebody, no one can ever make us a nobody." With this high goal in mind, little energy would be left to spend on hate, our family had reasoned.

When I arrived home, the wooden swing on the front porch was a welcome sight. The colorful cretonne cushions embraced my strange, hurting zombiness. Sitting there, I had three or four hours to pull myself together before Mom came home from work. My brothers would be caddying. It never dawned upon me to wonder where my sisters were.

In telling Mom I was not hired to teach—the hardest, most humiliating task of my life—she offered no encouragement, no sympathy, no advice, no alternative suggestions, no nothing. I sensed an "I could have told you," attitude. I felt her unspoken words: "The Lord has a way of punishing daughters who turn their backs on their mothers by going away to college and forgetting family priorities. So come down to earth, realize who you are, where you are, and do what you can to help me rear and support your brothers and sisters."

Whatever the message, spoken and unspoken, real or imagined, there was a deep gulf between Mom and me. It began when as a high school senior I felt Mom was not developing the kind of interest in my teen-age thoughts and feelings which she had so often expressed when I was a little girl. There had been moments when I felt sad about outgrowing my small child dependency. On this day I envied the carefree existence of my youngest sister, Virginia. Age seven was an age of innocence with no complications.

Before Mom could detail her financial obligations and her expectations of me, I made my own commitment. I would search for a cooking job where I could return home evenings. I did not want to live in the "help's quarters" confined and cut off from the outside world. I would pay Mom room rent, not one-half of my salary as I had in the past. I had decisions to make about my future.

I did not tell Mom that maybe I would consider going South to teach, perhaps to Raleigh, North Carolina, my father's birthplace. Neither did I tell her (now was not the time) that while in college I had written to the police departments of several large northern cities, asking them to search for my pop. The picture that I had mailed of my pop standing outside the "Snipes Bar and Grill" was returned from New York, Chicago, Cleveland, Boston and Philadelphia with a notation that "no such person" resided in their city. Did Mom suspect the feelings I had for my pop? Could or would my father have understood my situation, my yearnings, my ambitions any better than Mom did?

At the next meeting of the Canton NAACP, I was eager to relate my experience with the school superintendent and to seek the organization's intercession. Surely they would intercede for me in my attempt to teach. They could let Superintendent Mason know that the colored community supported me. They could challenge the legality or the ethics of his refusing to hire an applicant because of skin color.

The ten to twelve members listened and then discussed my problem in tones of confused annoyance. Annoyance at me? After nearly an hour of discussion, questions and out-of-order rulings, revealing frustration, fear, ignorance, bewilderment and surprise, the NAACP president expressed an opinion with the rest of the members nodding their heads in agreement.

"Really, a smart girl like you should have known the white man is not ready to hire colored teachers in a town the size of Canton. Maybe in large cities like New York or Chicago where there is a large colored population you would have had a chance. We will check around in other Ohio cities like Cleveland, Columbus, Dayton, Toledo and Cincinnati and see if colored teachers are being hired there. We know your mother would like to have you remain here as you are the oldest, but maybe you ought to consider going South. You are just a bit ahead of the times and you have to realize the race situation as it is today."

The race situation as I understood it was that Negroes had been leaving the South in great numbers in recent years. In 1906 when my parents were married, there were fewer than four hundred Negroes in Stark County, three hundred of whom lived in Canton. By 1920, with an influx of Negroes at the start of World War I, their population increased to two thousand or 1.6 percent of the total. With so many southern migrants coming to Canton in part because of job opportunities and in part to escape the racism of the South, why should I, a fourth-generation native Ohioan, migrate to a disadvantaged "Jim Crow" Southland? I had no inclination to be a missionary in a foreign land. I wanted to be a vital part of the town of my birth.

This migration suggestion came from the husbands and relatives of some of Canton's leading colored citizens. A few were former co-workers of my father. I recognized some of the church members who had stood by at the Sunday school picnic nearly eight years earlier and had seen nothing wrong when the Sunday school superintendent offered two dishes of ice cream to be shared by four Snipes children. Neither was it wrong now for them to imply I had no entitlements to pursue my chosen career in my hometown. I felt I did not meet their social, economic or physical standards. I came from a large family. Our father had abandoned us, and my skin color was too dark to mobilize their "advancement" concerns.

Several fair-skinned mulatto girls who had not completed high school had been hired as elevator operators because of the NAACP intervention. That was a monumental advancement. They were employed at the First National Bank Building, the Renkert Building and the Stark Dry Goods Department Store. Many Cantonians visited those buildings and rode the elevators to the top floors just to get the thrill of witnessing a colored girl in a job which did not require a mop and bucket.

The time had not arrived to advance the dark-skinned girl in a white collar or professional capacity when she could easily obtain employment as a cook, housekeeper or cleaning woman. Louise Beavers was being extolled in the movies as the lovable, accommodating, humorous, dark-skinned Negro house servant. Hollywood was educating all of America with their stereotyped portrayal of Negroes.

My own mother had been denied a day cleaning job which included the outside scrubbing of the porch and washing windows, because of her fair skin. "My neighbors will never know I have colored help if I hire you," a would-be employer told her. "I prefer a much darker woman to do my work. I hope you understand."

Miss Clotild Ferguson, job placement and career counselor at the Canton Urban League, spent a great deal of time investigating careers with me. She was a tall, attractive octoroon who seemed to sense deeply my hurt and my dilemma. We reviewed some of the better jobs open to Negroes. All were unappealing to me. The list included janitors, secretary, window trimmer, dressmaker, alterations in a tailor shop or dress shop and nursing. We began to consider social work as a professional alternative to teaching.

"With your two-year college background, you could train for a social worker in a welfare agency in at least six months, one college semester. You could enroll in an economics and a sociology course at Temple University and study at the Armstrong School of Social Service, an institute conducted by the Philadelphia Urban League. Wherever there is unemployment, there will be job opportunities for trained social workers," she advised.

Miss Ferguson's suggestion only added to my confusion. I wanted to say "yes," and to board immediately the next train to Philadelphia. But should I? I had never considered living outside Canton, Ohio. I would travel some day, all around the world, but Canton was home. What about my desire to remain in the town of my birth? I was experiencing again that yo-yo feeling I felt in high school when one teacher treated me one way and another reacted towards me in a far different manner. The superintendent's job denial, the NAACP's lack of concern, and my own mother's retreat from her optimistic encouragement were hard to accept, harder to understand. The social work career alternative gave me a ray of hope, but I did not know how or when to get started. Today? Tomorrow? Next year? I could not decide what to do next.

The private family cooking which I had done from the late summer of 1926 to January of 1929 to earn my college diploma was one thing. It was by all comparisons to my peers a commendable accomplishment. Still I did not want to continue this work much longer. I was beginning to dislike cooking very much. At seventeen, a kind of pioneer spirit moved me into this strange, uncharted pursuit. Maybe because my Aunt Clella was such a good cook I was challenged to say, "I can do it, too!" I did it! It was a challenge because college was a goal. I wanted to be the first in my family to move beyond the restraints and limits of a class, or a race of people, all by myself. Cooking had been my vehicle for moving beyond high school to college.

To cook for the rest of my life, however, just to pay for the privilege of eating and sleeping, to cook for the rest of my life, looking forward to a half day off every Thursday and a day off every other Sunday, would be living the life of a slave. I was not cut from the same cloth as the dozens of foreign-born and Negro women I had seen board the city streetcars daily on the public square. Like invisibly chained slaves, they left their homes at dawn to be household servants. They were cleaning ladies and laundresses for the well-to-do families in the north end of town. At night they returned home weary to give their families the residue of their physical energy. They shared few words of hope and encouragement.

Yes, Mom was now one of them. She had put aside her home laundry, now that all of her children were in school. She cried many mornings as she locked the doors of her modest home to clean the homes of other women. But she was willing, even insistent, that I work as a cook. She would help me put aside my dreams, rearrange my life. She reasoned that to be a cook for the wealthy purported a prestige superior to those who cleaned the houses of "half-strainers," people who put on the appearance of being socially and economically elite. Many of the people Mom worked for were just fifty dollars in the bank richer than she.

A career as a social worker was definitely more appealing than that of a private family cook. Yet I panicked at the thought of going as far away from home as Philadelphia. I remembered too vividly the hungry, moneyless days at Kent. What would happen to me if I were penniless and among strangers? Cooking assured me of room and board and wages, but suppose I lost my job? To whom could I turn for help?

I had overheard a group of women at a bridge club say, gossiping about a family scandal, "You can never tell about these kids who have been reared so strictly and nicey-nice. When they get out on their own, they change. Some of the fanciest prostitutes in the underworld have come from goody-goody, religious homes. You know this girl they call 'Goldie' . . . ?"

I needed to think twice about going that far away from home alone. I had been tempted to steal a dollar from a college professor's purse. Could I ever be tempted to sell my body for a dollar, just to survive, just to have a place to sleep?

It was not exactly a temptation, but an incident occurred that I never mentioned to anyone. A prominent businessman, husband of one of the women for whom I catered a wedding breakfast in June of 1929, came into the kitchen and made this remark, "I hear you are finishing two years of college and have done it all by yourself. Anytime you want to go for your bachelor's degree at a large eastern college, let me know. It won't cost you a cent. I could use a girlfriend like you when my business trips take me to New York. Think about it and get in touch with me."

His sensuous mouth and dripping pink lips recalled to mind my grandmother's account of the judge who had defiled her innocence. A new fear entered my heart as I thought of being easily accosted as a live-in servant in a wealthy white home. I might not be as safe three hundred miles away, among strangers, as I had been just a mile or so away from family and acquaintances. With this new apprehension, I felt pressured to seek a job as a cook immediately. I could think of no other alternative.

Work was not easy to find. By October of 1929 the stock market had crashed. Many maids, cooks, day-workers and chauffeurs were out of work. When I eventually obtained a fifteen dollar a week job, I felt most fortunate. I gave Mom five dollars a week. I was lucky to save ten dollars a month while attending to my personal needs. I continued to teach a Sunday school class and to sing and play for the church choir. I usually had a date Sunday afternoons and went to the movies. Yes, I began dating at age nineteen years and nine months.

VI

A Friend's Proposal

After my rebuff by the superintendent of schools, I went to Richman's and told Percy I needed his advice. He suggested I have dinner with him at a new restaurant he frequented. We had many dinners together that September. Percy became my friend. I began to admire him as a big brother, kind of pal and protector. He was also the father-conversationalist for whom I had always longed. We talked about everything, hour after hour.

Percy made his debut to my family as a home-calling escort late that fall, along with a number of other Sunday movie-going dates. I never considered him a date. He escorted me to out-of-town dances at which neither of us danced. Throughout the evening he hovered as close to the bandstand as he could, entranced by the musicians and their instruments. I wandered aimlessly among the non-dancing guests. Now and then I consented to a dance request from a stranger by saying, "I don't know how, but I'll try." In time, I learned to dance the two-step quite well and sat out fewer dances.

Percy was the handsomest figure of a gentleman when he was togged in his Sunday best. Having seen him for nearly three years in only work clothes, wielding a long-handled squeegee as he washed Richman's windows, I had no idea what a striking appearance he made. He stood six feet tall and weighed one hundred thirty-five pounds. He was slim, but not skinny and gangly like an Ichabod Crane. He added to his tailor-made suits from Richman's all the accessories for highlighting his gait, his stature, his slenderness, and his self-confidence. He wore buttoned, suede spats, in season, over Florsheim shoes, which accentuated his size ten, narrow feet. With well-gloved hands, he carried a cane and wore a derby hat made especially popular by Al Smith, the presidential aspirant from 1923 to 1932. My father was a meticulous dresser, but Percy's dress was "dandyish!"

After sharing my rejected teaching application with my mom, the Urban League, the NAACP, and Percy, I settled down to a routine of private family jobs. A half dozen weekly hours Percy and I shared between church, a movie or two, and an occasional evening at a public dance. Perhaps, given my career problems, my confusion about my role at home and my daring to associate with other young people from less favored backgrounds, I moved too fast into a world that alarmed and disgusted Mom. She was concerned about which way I was going.

"Mom, you have to trust me," I insisted one evening. "I cannot get to know young people my age by working clear across town all week long and sitting here at home on Thursday afternoons and my Sundays off."

"But who are they? Who are their parents? I do not know where they live. I know nothing about any of them. They are disgusting, the way they look and act," Mom sneered accusingly.

"They are my people, my race, my generation," I answered. "I never had a close colored playmate or classmate in grade school, high school, or college. How am I to know how they behave? The only gauge I have are the few kids I met at St. John's A.M.E. Zion church, and they were not really friends,"

I explained. "All of the colored kids we ever met at St. Paul's were a bunch of color-conscious snobs. There is no way that I can meet their qualifications for acceptance and friendship."

"Is it that important to choose friends who have no social etiquette, no good manners?"

"Mom, I think you believe all white kids have high standards, but do they? I could tell you a thing or two about some of the white girls who worked as maids where I have cooked. You would not believe the dirty jokes they tell and the things they do when they go out on dates. The only high standards some whites have is avoiding me because I am colored. The white kids who went to school with me for twelve years never speak to me when they meet me on the street. I cannot live by myself! I want friends the same as anyone else!"

"Just anybody for a friend?" Mom challenged.

"I know, you have always told us that if we cannot walk with the best to walk alone. But I shall never know who is best or worst, good or bad, unless I walk with them and talk with them and maybe dance and play cards and we go to movies and hayrides and barbecues together," I continued.

"But the kids you attract are trash, just like the kids you invited to your high school graduation party. They have no manners, no training, no nothing; and they look like the devil!" Mom said, becoming angry.

"Mom, I realize we Snipes are different. You have raised us with standards unlike many families, I know! I am glad for my upbringing. I am proud I have been taught right from wrong. I do not, never have, and never will do some of the things other kids do. I think I can walk among them part of the way long enough to see and judge for myself."

"One bad apple can spoil a barrel of good apples," Mom remarked acidly.

"I am not in the same barrel, Mom. Quit worrying!"

"Why is it they come here in bunches, as if you were the

hottest thing in town?" Mom shouted at me.

"Mom, I resent that!" I said in as firm a tone as possible, without the volume of a shout. "I am not a canine in heat. I am a human being. I am a person who can consent or object, say yes or no, be good or bad, do right or wrong! That is my choice, my territory. No one can invade what is my business!" I walked away, tearfully angry.

Theodus Curry, George Claybourne and Alvin Jones had collided with each other on an unconfirmed Sunday afternoon visit. Mom's last remark was in reference to that incident. Mom thought it was disgusting that three gentlemen wished to escort me to a Sunday matinee at the Palace or Loew's State Theatre. I thought it was funny, and I was flattered.

Mom was not entirely alone in her apprehensions. I had some young adult misgivings about moving outside the circle of home, school and work. I had no sexual desires, no physical yearnings as yet to get involved in boy-girl, male-female relationships. Dating was a temporary interlude between where I was and where I wanted to go.

It was a disquieting experience for me to discover how many young men had no manners and knew nothing about dating etiquette. They would drive up to the house and honk the horns of their missing muffler-treated cars, alerting the usually quiet neighborhood they were there. They had never been taught to knock on the door, announce their arrival, introduce themselves to their date's parents, and escort their lady to their car.

There were several one-time movie dates with young men who were rude and crude. Their eagerness to pay the theater price of admission had nothing to do with the screen's attraction. The darkened theater was to them a legitimate place to paw and fondle their date's anatomy. I knew how to pinch in a sensitive spot or go to the ladies' restroom and leave the eager beaver stranded in the theater, while I slipped out and ran all the way home.

Still, I had to learn about my peers. I had to learn about the advantages and disadvantages of single-dating, double-dating and the pull of collective behavior. At any given time in appropriate seasons of the year there were hayrides, picnics, and carloads of young people driving from one home to another, eating, drinking and partying. At almost all home gatherings, after the couples paired off, the lights were turned down low, the shades were drawn, and the petting began. There was never any adult supervision or planned evenings of games and entertainment. I made it a rule never to give my date a second chance to subject me to an unsavory situation.

One weekend a girl acquaintance invited me to join a caravan of cars going to Cleveland to attend a night club. Would I go along? Her older brother, who was home from college, would be happy to be my escort. I did not know then, but I later learned with Percy's warning and closer attention to other invitations, that I was only invited to cover up the group's intended mischief. Some parents were inclined to give their daughters permission to go somewhere, commenting, "If the Snipes girls are there, I know there will be no hanky panky."

By the time the three-car caravan had assembled, it was nearly midnight. When we arrived in Cleveland, the drivers could not find the night club. I was not so naive as to believe a legitimate entertainment spot had a show beginning at 2:30 a.m. There was something eerie about giggling, excited young people driving around traffic-abandoned, dimly lit streets, inviting something to happen.

Eventually we headed for a "relative's" home on the East Side. We were graciously welcomed and served plenty of food. The young men shared and emptied their flasks with their particular brand of bootleg liquor. I knew fewer than six of the nearly twenty people gathered in that crowded living room and dining room.

Close to 4:00 a.m., the mistress of the house was dispersing couples all over her upstairs to "catch some shut-eye and sober up" before driving back to Canton. Eight couples had vanished up the thickly carpeted steps to the second and third floors. Four of us remained in the living room. George, my escort, Alberta, a daughter of one of Mom's friends, her date and me. Alberta lay sprawled on a cushioned chair after drinking a small glass of wine. I attempted to make her comfortable. She was insensibly drunk.

Her escort announced vehemently, "Take your hands off her. She is mine for the night, drunk or sober! I'll take care of her." At that he picked Alberta up, slung her unconscious body over his shoulder and headed up the stairs.

George and I were left in that gaudily furnished room alone. He looked at me and said, "We're the last couple. What are we going to do?"

"I am sitting right here in this chair until it is daylight. I can phone a taxi to take me to the train station tomorrow morning," I announced.

"Don't you think you need some sleep, like the others?" he asked.

"Not the kind of sleep they are getting. And if you brought me here for your enjoyment, you are going to be very disappointed. I do not do things like that. Even if I did, it would never be in public like this. No, I am sitting right here, and you stay where you are, over there."

"I wouldn't think of touching you," George said. "I expect to be asleep in no time. Don't let my snoring bother you. I'll see that you arrive home safely tomorrow."

George settled himself in two overstuffed chairs and went to sleep. I was not afraid. Grandma had told me what to do in case of an attempted rape. Even the meanest critter would not want a house full of peers to hear an outcry that would advertise his rejection. When I shared with Percy how we sat there until daybreak and nothing happened, I realized he was the only person I knew who would have believed either of us.

Percy explained, "You literally spent the night in a bootleg brothel. There are women who are not madams of houses of prostitution, but they make their money the same way. They don't own the women who sell their bodies, but they rent rooms to any couple who can pay the price. It matters not who the customers are or whether it is for one hour or one evening.

"Take another look at your friends and know where you are going and with whom before you go out of town again. You must have a guardian angel looking after you. You were sure in a dangerous situation."

George and I became fairly good friends after that night. I think I could have developed a fondness for him except for his drinking. After a few drinks, and he drank heavily, he was a charming, good-natured humorist. Mom liked George in preference to all my dates. He had attended Wilberforce college, and he was "Northern" born.

It was next to impossible to find a group of young people who knew how to gather socially for clean fun, parlor games and intellectual conversations. The Negro teen-ager had no access in the twenties to roller skating rinks, swimming pools, the YMCA and the YWCA. The segregated movie house, the public dance hall and the dimly lit, lights-out front room or speak-easy residence set the stage for intimate illicit relationships. I remember hearing about the lovely recreation room Dr. and Mrs. J. B. Walker had in their Broad Avenue home. I began to dream of the house I would live in some day where young people would be invited to engage in activities I had never experienced: darts, pool, chess, bridge, ping pong and all kinds of exciting thought-provoking games.

Looking for moments of enjoyment with my peers meant that I ran into several situations that had the potential for disastrous consequences. I became good friends with Vera Spencer, an only child. She was short and stocky and I was tall and thin, but we were both "wall flowers" and had similar personalities. Her parents were divorced and her mother had remarried. Vera and I felt a similar father loss and shared to some degree our feelings about our predicament.

One Saturday, she and I decided to hire "Buster" to drive us to Akron, Ohio, to hear the Mills Brothers in concert. "Buster" was one of the most popular, personable young men in town. Had we been sophisticated, boy-crazy, young ladies, we would have made a play for him. Our only reason for hiring "Buster" was that neither of us wanted to be bothered with a jealous, possessive date, or a companion who required boxing gloves or a nail file to fend off an assault. "Buster" called for us at our homes and agreed to return us to our door for two dollars apiece.

Vera and I sat in the back seat of the Model T Ford while the driver, "Buster," with another male companion, sat up front. They stopped to get gasoline at a filling station in Greentown and then proceeded to Akron. We had a delightful music-filled evening and were driven home close to 2:00 a.m. Sunday morning, grateful for our uncomplicated safety.

About 8:00 a.m. that Sunday morning, as I was trying to convince myself that sleep would be more enjoyable than church, Percy phoned. He announced he wanted to see Vera and me right after church services. "Be there!" he demanded.

As we emerged from the morning service, Percy walked with us down Cherry Avenue and up Thirteenth Street in the direction of Housel Avenue where Vera lived. He said seriously, "Anytime the two of you want to go to an out-of-town affair, dance, night club, concert or whatever, get in touch with me. Don't you ever hire that fool 'Buster' or anyone to take you anywhere again!"

Percy was furious. "Do you know how close you came to being in jail this morning or even shot to death? Last night your chauffeur and his friend robbed the filling station where they stopped to get gas. I know you had no idea what was happening, but no judge, no court in the land, would believe you were not accomplices, or decoys, to distract the victims as to what was going on!"

From that time on, Percy escorted Vera and me to all out-of-town events. Mom had to admit she was impressed with Percy, his dress, his manners and his courteous attention to her. She never mentioned his color or the skin color of any of my dates, but I sensed an unspoken criticism of my male companions. My tastes lacked discrimination. None of my dates met the standards befitting a young woman who had graduated from a Normal School College.

Percy always brought Mom a box of chocolate candy or a flower when we went to a dance, announcing he would have her daughter home by such-and-such a time. He was also lavish with the corsages he gave me on special occasions. Our favorite flower was the fragrant white gardenia.

When I asked permission to invite Percy to have Thanksgiving dinner with us, Mom had no objections. There was no need to explain he was a long way from his family in Mississippi and that I was grateful for the many dinners he had treated me to, not to mention his being my only dance escort.

After papering the dining room and buying a tablecloth and some dishes at the Atlantic Tea Store, I felt comfortable about inviting Percy to sit down to our dining room table. Ethel and I even urged Mom to invite presiding Elder Leftwitch of the A.M.E. Zion Conference to have dinner at our home the following Sunday. My sister and I discussed at length how we could get Mom to go out more and how to invite members of the Zion Church to our house. We wished Mom would remarry.

If Vera's mother, a short, heavy-set, dark-skinned woman, could get a new husband, surely Mom could, too, as pretty as she was, we reasoned.

That beautifully exciting Thanksgiving Day in 1929 combined celebrating my twentieth birthday, which had occurred a month earlier. In the air was a disturbing premonition of some new beginnings. It was the first time I had planned and prepared a formal four-course dinner at home. It was the first time for the Snipes family to have a gentleman guest to dinner. It was the first time for all of my sisters and brothers to be together around the dining room table since my senior year in high school, three years earlier. Mom sat at the head of the table. Eugene, then sixteen, sat at the other end. Percy sat opposite me with Virginia and Carl on either side. Ruth and Ethel sat on my side of the table. I had no way of knowing this would be my last Thanksgiving dinner at our dining room table in my childhood home.

After dinner, Mom and Percy and I lingered at the table in less than a relaxed atmosphere. Mom was asking Percy such questions as, "How old were you when you left home? Your father is a minister? How large is his congregation? Did you graduate from high school? Will you go to college some day? You say that your sister is a nurse in Brooklyn, New York. Is she married or single? Do you plan to move back to Mississippi?"

I interrupted. I was embarrassed by the tone of Mom's questions. I rattled off nervously. " Maybe we could go to the piano and sing. I can play 'When the Red Red Robin Comes Bob Bob Bobbin Along' and 'Among My Souvenirs.' Mom sings soprano, I sing alto. Mom, you ought to hear Percy whistle 'My Blue Heaven'."

We sang a song or two, but I played clumsily. The three of us returned to the now-cleared table, courtesy of Ethel. The box of chocolates Percy had given to Mom had been placed on the table waiting to be opened. Mom ignored that rare delicacy. She appeared to be distanced from us in deep thought.

Percy broke the silence. "Mrs. Snipes," he began, "I've known your daughter for nearly three years. She reminds me of my sister Alberdeen. She's a very smart girl and she knows what she wants out of life. You must be commended for that. A few weeks ago, I told your daughter that she's the kind of girl I would like to take home to introduce to my parents. I don't think she even heard me, and I'm not surprised because she has heard me say more than once I never intended to get serious about a young lady. Seeing you and your family today, a thought's been going around in my mind. It's this: What would you say if I asked permission to change your daughter's name to mine, some day?"

Without a pause, without time to think as though she had been anticipating this moment, Mom stood up. She pushed her chair to the table with a bang. With her hand on the back of the chair, she barked, "I would rather follow every one of my daughters to their graves than see any one of them get married! That is what I have to say!"

She left the room and went into the kitchen, slamming the two hall doors behind her. Percy and I, speechless, sat at the table for a moment and then walked to the deserted front room. Where had everyone gone?

"Gee, I never expected anything like that," Percy remarked.

"Me neither." I did not know what else to say.

"I'd better go," Percy announced, adding, "Let's forget about the movie tonight. Maybe I'll phone you later. You know how to reach me. Thanks for the best dinner I've ever eaten."

He left.

The rest of that day is blurred. I think everyone headed for a movie. I wished I had maid's quarters to return to. I wanted to scream. I left the house. I may have walked over to visit Grandma and Grandpa. I do not remember.

I do recall I was as stunned at Percy's proposal as Mom was angered. He liked me well enough to marry me, but how was I supposed to ever suspect? He had never put his arms around me. He had never kissed me. He was my big brother friend. I was planning to tell him I had been writing to Catholic convents for information about becoming a nun. There would be security there, and I could pursue a teaching career. One reply from a distant convent had advised me to talk to the priest in my parish. I had no parish priest. I was not even Catholic. But marriage? No! It had never been on my agenda.

Mom might not want me to marry, but my future would not become a part of her agenda. My life was not hers to manipulate or control. She had no right to say what she had said to Percy and me. At twenty she had prayed to God, beseeching a long life to rear her babies. How could she dare speak of me, going to my grave, at age twenty? The parent-child bond between Mom and me was broken. I ceased being a child. I would no longer be subjected to parental tethering.

Nella Rosella Dorsey Evans
1851-1937

Evans Family Album

Grandpa Robert Evans
1841-1933

Eugene Robert Evans

Clella and Ida Evans

**Nora Evans Smith
1907**

Clella Evans (1920s)

(1950s)

90

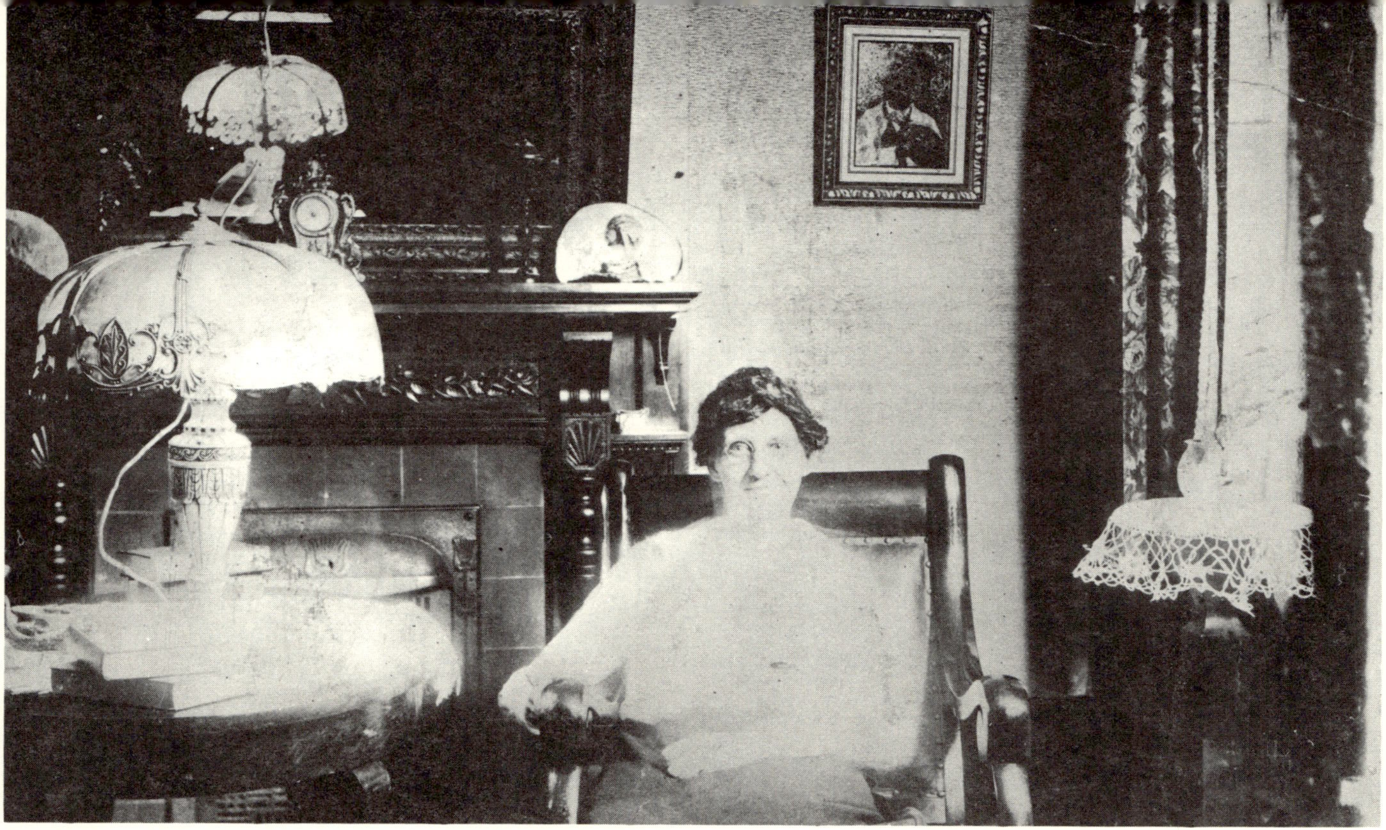

Grandma Evans, 1920s.

Four Generations 1933
Back: Norma Marcere 25, Ida Snipes (Shuggie) 45
Front: Norma Jean Marcere 2, Clella Evans 82

Shuggie and Great-Grandma Evans.

My Working Life

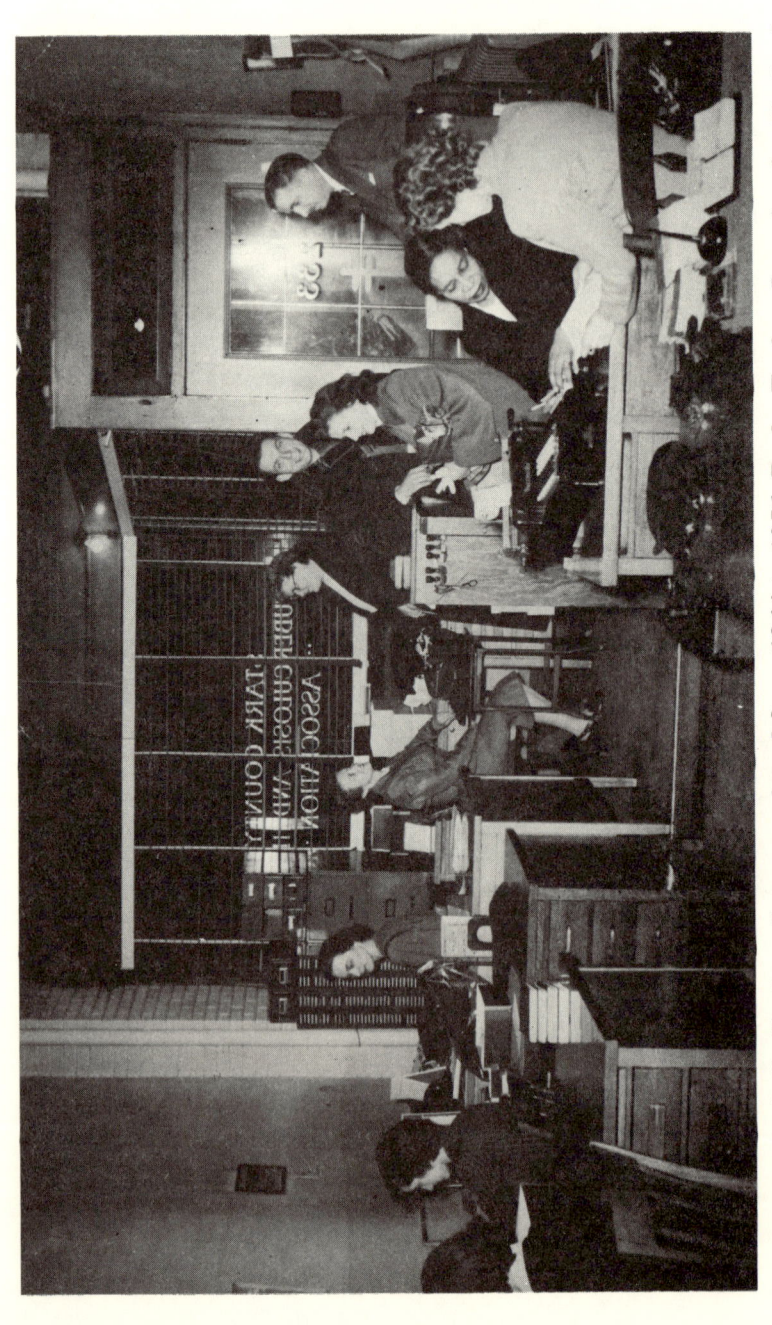

The Tuberculosis Staff where I was employed from 1944 to 1956. Becky Taylor, June Austin, Katharine Worley, Kay Meiner, Wanda Lewton, Harold Tope, Norma Marcere, Margaret Collison, L. L. Taylor.

Jones Junior High 9th grade class, 1958.

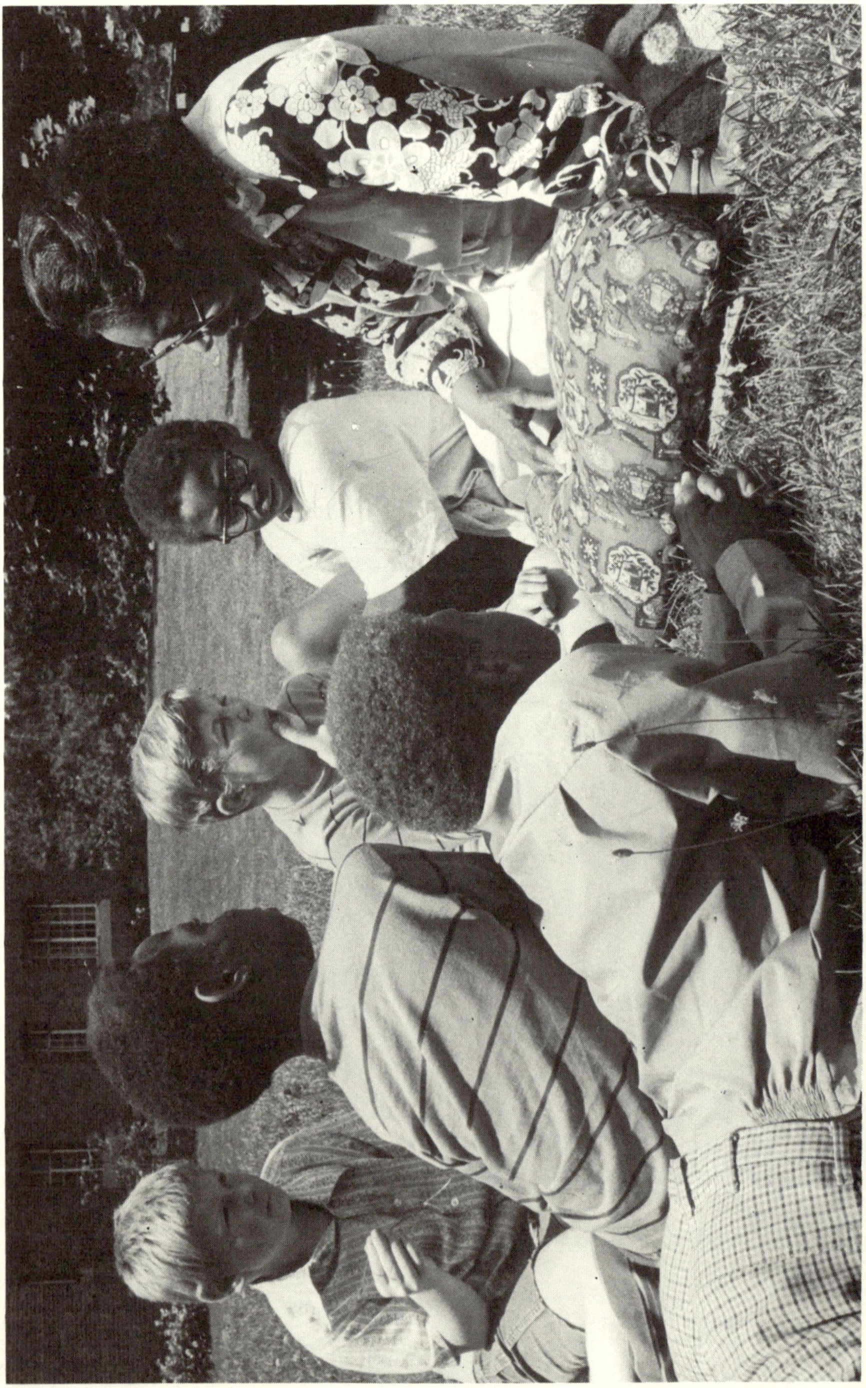

97

Youngstown Diocesean School Board Meeting. Sister Mary Grace SND, Mrs. Frances Garcia, Norma Marcere, Msgr. William Fitzgerald, John Augustine.

District Presidents of the Ohio Association of Colored Women's Clubs.

Catholic Interracial Conference. Percy Marcere, John Garner, Mr. and Mrs. Emmett E. Cooper Jr.

VII

The Most Educated Cook In Town

I continued to work as a cook during the holiday season, which followed my catastrophic Thanksgiving dinner. I was restless and uneasy when I spent my evenings and Sundays at home. Mom confused me. We did not seem to know how to converse. My sisters and brothers would give me a polite "Hi, Norm," and then disappear to study, to do their chores, or to go to a movie.

I knew how Mom felt when her world fell apart. Why couldn't she try to understand me? Did Mom ever stop to consider what was going on in my mind? Did she know how much I cared for her, revered her? How long did she expect me to remain living halfway between her world and my temporary world of domestic service? For three years, from September 1926 through December 1929, most of my time had been spent in the kitchen and servants' quarters in a variety of upper-class homes. I wanted a lifestyle far different from the role my aunt had played, being "Santa Claus" and the "good fairy" to nieces and nephews. I did not even want Mom's world of motherhood. I wanted a career.

Being referred to as the most educated cook in town provoked me. I quit a job in early January 1930 when I was asked to take a fifty percent cut in salary because of the Depression.

After a silent treatment at home, I quickly took another job as cook for the Weir family. It was a daytime job from 7:30 a.m. to 7:30 p.m. with Thursday afternoons and Sundays off.

The Weirs had five children from ages three to thirteen. To begin the day, preparing breakfast became a scene comparable to a brood of chickens, scratching and pecking to eat from one hen house dispenser. I was as pecked over as if I had been in the middle of the dispenser! Even though Mrs. Weir planned the breakfast menu, each child exercised his own veto power to demand something else. If a hot cereal was on the menu, one child wanted Farina with dates, another wanted Cream of Wheat with raisins, and still another wanted a dry cereal or no cereal at all.

Preparing eggs resulted in a messy assemblage of yellow and white glutinous consistencies that ended up in the kitchen sink before being scooped up and tossed into the garbage can. Soft boiled eggs, sunny-side up, scrambled—they might not have heard of eggs Benedict or omelet—no two children wanted their eggs cooked the same way. They seemed to take delight in their whimsical specifications as they pushed their eggs aside. Somewhere from the midst of yelling, squabbling, unruly children, a voice would complain, "You don't know how to cook anyway. You never do what you're told!"

Pancakes and waffles fared somewhat better, but there was always spilled milk, spilled sticky syrup and untouched food. I was a strange kind of toy to be bounced around by unrestrained children. Their father rushed out the door at 7:30 a.m. on his was to the Timken Company and their mother returned to bed after swallowing a cup of coffee. The children were deposited at the breakfast table in my care. The noon meal was less chaotic because Mrs. Weir was there. The evening meal was controlled by Mr. Weir's authoritative, in control demeanor.

There were evenings when I salvaged for my brothers and

sisters at home half gallons of milk, oranges that were not juicy enough and dry cereal that was being discarded because it had been on the cupboard shelf for two weeks. I was paid a good salary at the Weirs, but the food that was thrown away more than doubled my weekly earnings. The Weirs had not yet been hit by the Depression.

One morning the nine-year-old lad yelled at me accusingly, "You should know better than to put raisins in my oatmeal. Don't you remember what I told you the last time? Raisins remind me of flies!" He walked to the kitchen sink and emptied his bowl.

"No, my dear young man, I do not remember. But you remember this: Those were real flies. They were dead, but once in your stomach they all come alive again! Now run upstairs and tell your mother I just quit!"

I had enjoyed catering for special occasions when the hostess sat down with me, planned the menu, discussed portions, decorations, color schemes, place settings, and then left me like a professional to carry on. From the Weir experience, I developed a strong aversion to working for families with children. In looking for my next job, I began to consider only those homes with one or two high school-aged children. I was even prepared to issue an ultimatum about breakfast preparation when I heard about an office job that paid ten dollars a week.

Clay E. Hunter, a young Negro attorney, was opening his law office on Third Street Southeast, a short distance from Market Avenue and across from the McKinley Hotel. His ground floor office was just a block away from the corner of Walnut Avenue and Third Street where my father had operated a billiard parlor from 1906 to 1909. My Pop's goal was to be an attorney some day.

Attorney Hunter employed me as a receptionist. I was to answer the phone and schedule appointments. I could not have been a typist even if my employer had had a typewriter in his miniscule two room office complex. I did not know how to type. The receptionist's office was a far cry from a cook's kitchen. A large display window, the width of the room, gave full view to the outdoors.

It was not in my job description, but because the days were not hectic with an abundance of customers, I dusted the furniture, washed the windows on the inside and kept clean and sanitary the small single commode washroom.

I was thrilled with this job. I was treated with respect by those who phoned for an appointment and the clients who came for consultation. Listening to intelligent exchanges of information was invigorating. I was fascinated by this purposeful environment. Even the people moving about on the streets outside had direction and purpose.

I read newspapers, magazines and glanced through the law books, similar to those I had observed my father pore over so studiously. An office like this was what my father wanted. The shingle outside could have read, "Attorney Norman S. Snipes" instead of "Attorney Clay E. Hunter," or both. They could have been partners.

Working in an office required clothing in no way comparable to a cook's uniform or the one or two plain dresses in my wardrobe. I needed business clothing badly. Working for an attorney was most prestigious. The nearest job approximating contact with the public was that of a downtown elevator operator. Her salary was also ten dollars a week. Attorney Hunter had assured me he would like to pay me more, but he was just starting his practice. I wondered what the elevator girls contributed toward their room and board at home. They came from small families, their fathers had not deserted their mothers, and they had no younger siblings at home with myriad needs.

If I planned to remain on this job, I ought to learn to type,

I reasoned. How could I afford to go to night school, buy nice dresses and pay room and board at home? As much as I enjoyed this charged atmosphere of legal decisions and personal involvements, I realized I might not be able to remain. I would have to look for a more lucrative job. In the meantime, this work setting provided an excellent opportunity for inquiring about other job opportunities.

Within a short time by skipping several lunch breaks, I had contacted City Hall, the county commissioners and the post office civil service department. I left resumes and job applications with Mayor C. C. Curtis, Louis Elsaesser, the postmaster and the Stark County commissioners. My downtown excursions as a preteenager, handling business transactions for Mom, put me at ease in this newest of ventures.

Although I was received courteously, nothing was happening. I made a second appearance to the city recreation office to inquire about a playground supervisor's job. Did they still have my application from last year, or did I have to submit a new application for this summer of 1930? The shock of that revealing interview angered me and turned my world upside down.

"I am so sorry," the director began in answer to my question about my application status. "We cannot hire two people from the same family. We hired your sister, Ethel, last summer when you did not respond to our letter of your appointment. You were attending Kent Normal School last summer. Is that right?"

"Yes, I was. I decided to remain during the summer session to graduate in August," I explained.

"We phoned your home and spoke to your mother recently. In fact it was just a few days ago. I can look up the date if you wish. She told us you were already employed, so we have hired your sister, Ethel, for the second summer," I was told.

"Could you answer one question?" I asked.

"Surely, surely," I heard.

"Is the salary the same as you quoted to me last year?"

"Yes it is," I was informed. "It pays sixty dollars a month."

"Thank you. Thank you very much." I left the office.

This revelation hurt me even worse than the denial of a teaching job by the superintendent of schools, Mr. Mason. I would not have taken the playground supervisor's job the summer before and postponed my graduation, but it would have been encouraging to know I had been considered a qualified applicant. It would have pleased me to know my sister was hired, maybe partly due to my application and interview. I did not even know! No one had said a word to me!

With Ethel earning sixty dollars a month and Eugene and Carl caddying on the golf course, living must have been easy last summer. Last summer when I had written home explaining the difficulties I was having meeting graduation expenses, not a cent was mailed to me. Not a member of my family attended my graduation! It smacked of dishonesty to have kept me in the dark about Ethel's lucrative and prestigious three-month summer job.

Here I was trying to get up enough courage to explain to Mom how much I liked this job with Attorney Hunter, and that I might not be able to give her more than ten dollars a month for my room rent.

After allowing myself several days to simmer down, I explained to Mom I needed some clothes and could only give her two and a half dollars weekly.

Mom protested without a moment's hestitation, saying, "I think you should forget trying to look cute in a lawyer's office and get back to a job that can pay you three times what you are earning there!"

"There is a depression you know, Mom, and many wealthy homes have reduced their help's salaries to almost nothing.

They are also working everybody twice as hard," I explained.

"Yes, and if you only pay me what you suggest, you will be taking food out of the mouths of your younger brothers and sisters. Have you thought of that?" Mom asked accusingly.

I did not answer. I was thinking maybe I was too hasty in dismissing the idea of studying at Temple University in Philadelphia. Maybe what I had learned about the playground job should have put Philadelphia in closer focus. Mom used to speak of her children as birds who should leave the nest upon high school graduation. Maybe I had no business remaining at home. Maybe when I had gone to Kent, I should never have returned after finishing my studies.

As a teacher, I could not marry. All the teachers I knew lived at home with their parents or a close relative. No single woman lived in an apartment away from home. Such an arrangement would have invited speculations as to a woman's morality and respectability. So my remaining at home was the only choice I had. It was important to protect my reputation as long as I planned to teach.

"Did you hear what I said?" Mom shouted at me. "Get yourself a decent-paying job and think of someone beside yourself. You are even more selfish now than you were as a child."

"What responsibilities do I have for your kids?" I shouted. "They are not mine! No law in this land can make me support anyone but myself!"

"Do you think that two dollars and fifty cents is supporting yourself?" Mom countered.

"Have you forgotten that I have given you half of every cent I have ever earned up till now?" I challenged. "Have you forgotten that when I was giving you twenty-five to forty dollars a month and not eating a meal and not sleeping at home, I was doing more than my share in supporting this family? I hardly have a decent dress to my name and you call me selfish!"

"Now, don't get sassy, and don't talk back to me!" Mom shouted.

"I am not sassy! I only want you to know I am not a child! I would like to be treated as a twenty-year-old," I retorted.

"Well, you are a child as long as you remain in this house, and you will always have responsibilities," Mom announced.

"Maybe this is the time," I fired back, "I should let you know that I learned how you and Ethel stole that recreation job from me. You should talk to me about responsibilities and loyalties! All you see in me, yes, and maybe the boys and Ethel as well, are dollar signs!"

Mom reached over and slapped me in the face. She lunged at me again, all two hundred and twenty pounds against my one hundred and five pound body. I raised my arms to ward off the next blow. Mom called Eugene. "Hold her," she screamed, "so I can give your sister the beating she deserves!"

When Eugene grabbed my arms, it was as if he was getting even for all the childhood fights, when I had been the winner and he the loser. I fought away from him. Mom turned to Eugene, "Get the gun and hold it on her. If she attempts to strike me or defend herself, pull the trigger!"

All of the rage Mom had allowed to build up in her forty years of life was spent on me. Mom had seldom spanked us kids. She and Pop never came to blows with all their quarreling, but a mad woman was unleashed that night.

It was as if she was driven to destroy that which she had created. Like the artist who slashes his canvas to pieces or the writer who crumples his manuscript and tosses it into the wastebasket, this incensed creature lunged at me wildly. In the little four by four foot hallway leading to the kitchen, bathroom, dining room and stairs to the second floor, Mom punched me this way and that, shouting angrily, "So you think you are old enough to give me your sass, do you? I will show you! After all I have sacrificed and slaved for you! Is this the thanks I get? You, telling me what you will and will not do? I'll kill you first! You ingrate!"

I prayed that my teeth would not be knocked out. Dr. DeWeese, the medical director at Kent, had alerted me to the fact that I had a perfect set of teeth. They were so beautiful. I could not lift my arms to protect my face. Eugene was standing just a few feet away, holding the gun Pop had purchased in 1918 to protect us from frightening, abusive neighbors.

Someone (it might have been ten-year-old Ruth or fourteen-year-old Carl) began screaming, "Leave her alone, Mom! Mom! Please leave her alone! Come over here and sit down! Please leave Norm alone!"

After awhile, I fell face downward on the bathroom floor and lay there, silent and motionless till dawn. Strange that no one had to go to the bathroom that night. Strange, too, that this incident was never referred to in the years that followed. There were no apologies, no explanations. It was as if it had never happened.

VIII

An Unexpected Happening

As children we chanted a little verse every time the warm spring rains announced that the season of winter was departing. "April showers bring May flowers." Three family members very dear to me had birthdays in May: Mom, my Aunt Clella and my sister Ethel. On this cheerless May morning after the beating of the evening before, I was not thinking of May flowers or May birthday greetings. I was thinking of distancing myself far away from Mom and Ethel.

Ethel had not come downstairs to the bathroom to console me last night. Why not? We were so close as sisters. Our family chores were generally coordinated peacefully. We traveled together to the movies, to church, to our friends' homes. We sang in a church quartet. Ethel sang soprano, I sang alto. We shared confidences about the events we liked and the things we disliked, the books we read, the things we wanted to do, the events we wanted to see, and the places we wanted to visit.

Our life goals of service were similar. I wanted to be a teacher to feed the mind. Ethel wanted to be a doctor and heal the body. Paradoxically, Ethel spent more time with the little ones' studies and I was the family physician. It was I who made the steaming hot onion and mustard poultice when Mom had her severe bronchial colds every winter. It was I who squeezed a splinter out of a finger and coaxed a cinder out of an eye.

Maybe Ethel only said she wanted to be a doctor because no one would have paid any attention to her had she said teacher. That was her older sister's choice. Maybe I needed to move on, so Ethel could come into her own.

Big sisters have a tendency to hog the whole show, to dominate the landscape. With me out of the way, Ethel could be the big sister, the number-one daughter, for awhile. I was angered at not knowing about Ethel's playground position, but I did not envy her. I would have shared her playground incidents as she had shared with me a happening in an employer's kitchen.

Maybe Mom had a point when she said I was selfish. I was the one who was given the Menelick Culture Club College Scholarship. I was the one who played the piano at church, taught a Sunday school class and directed the youth group. I was the one who won a third-place art prize at the Ohio Theatre for a pen and ink drawing of Abraham Lincoln. I was the one who was most often called on the phone for special cooking and catering jobs. Yes, it was time for me to leave home, to get out of the way, and let Ethel . . . But why had she not attempted to see how I was? She could have said something to me to let me know she understood. How would last night's incident affect our future?

On this May morning with a pronounced post-winter chill in the air, I wept an agonizing farewell to Mom and my sister. I had already said a glad farewell to my aunt upon her marriage a year ago. Long before dawn I slipped noiselessly out the back door, down the porch steps, into a foggy gray mistiness. The moisture-laden atmosphere was holding back the torrential rains eager to drench the retreating night blackness. I walked through the back alley and across several streets to Grandma's house. My sore, aching and bruised body rebelled at carrying the nearly empty suitcase taken from its hiding place behind the piano. It was always there for the next trip to my live-in quarters as a cook. This morning my suitcase and I were leaving the springtime of my life behind.

Grandma was an early riser, but no one was stirring when I arrived at her house. I sat on the back porch steps for an hour, half hidden and uncomfortably protected by a tall lilac bush and a fully leafed pussy willow tree. I waited for some sounds that would tell me Grandma had awakened and was putting the kettle on the stove for a cup of tea. As she unlocked the kitchen door in response to my light tapping on the window, I shoved my suitcase in ahead of me, saying rapidly, "Grandma, I want to leave my suitcase here. When I get off from work tonight, I want to talk to you and Grandpa about my staying here for awhile. Thanks, and bye."

If I had said another word, I would have burst into tears. I did not want that to happen. The chilling rain began its torrential descent. I draped my coat over my uncovered head and hurried limping in pain towards town. I let myself in Attorney Hunter's office.

My coat was soaking wet. I was shivering. I went directly to the little lavatory to tidy myself a bit. My lips were swollen twice their size and my eyes were narrow slits of blackness. My teeth were intact.

I repeatedly submerged my face in cold water hoping to shrink its size. I tried combing my uncontrollable hair a different way, bringing it down over my forehead. I dabbed layers of powder and rouge on my face to cover the black and blue bruises.

With as much composure as I could muster, I left the office and walked the three blocks to Richman's store to await Percy's arrival. When he walked into the foyer, with water pail and squeegee, I greeted him in as calm a manner as I could.

"Can you see me alone on your lunch hour today? I want to show you something. Can you please?" I pleaded.

"I guess I can," he replied. "I'll meet you in front of that new restaurant below my apartment. What's the mystery? Are you all right?"

I could not answer other than to say, "I am in a hurry to get to the office. I'll be there at noon."

Back in the office there was an hour and a half wait before Attorney Hunter would arrive. I did not want him to see me and question what had happened. How could I explain my appearance? I could never concoct a believable fabrication.

"I tripped over my little sister's roller skates and fell down the steps. . . ." "I was hit by a swing from my brother's golf club. . . ." "I bumped into a door. . . ." "I fell out of bed. . . ." "I . . . I . . . nothing happened."

I would never reveal my estrangement from my family. I just prayed Attorney Hunter would phone in, as he sometime did, to ask whether there were any messages and to say he was going directly to court and would contact me later. It almost happened that way. At a quarter to nine, Attorney Hunter opened the office door and hurriedly said, "I am glad you are here, Miss Snipes. I am on my way to court and will return after lunch." He reached for the morning newspaper, tucked it under his arm and left. He never looked me in the face. He never saw how strange I looked.

That morning on the stroke of nine, my phone call to Miss Clotild Ferguson at the Canton Urban League was her first of the day. It set the stage for my departure from Canton. I asked her to follow through on all the particulars for my move to Philadelphia. I sought details for enrolling at Temple University in September. Would she contact the Philadelphia Urban League and the Armstrong School of Social Service? Would arrangements be made for a place for me to stay? The only assurance I gave Miss Ferguson was that I had time to earn enough money for train fare, tuition, and three or four weeks' room rent. As an experienced cook I could take on a part-time job in Philadelphia.

"Smart girl, Norma. I am glad to know you are not letting that job denial here destroy your determination to train for something else, just as good or better," Clotild said. "I shall get started on arrangements immediately. It is not too soon. Do not worry about a thing."

I nervously busied myself about the office until 11:30. Then I placed a note on Attorney Hunter's desk, telling him I was not feeling well and could not remain for the rest of the day. I locked the office and hurried to meet Percy. He was waiting for me outside Hutchinson's Restaurant. He rather reluctantly invited me into his one-room apartment on the floor above.

"What's the big surprise you want to show me?" he asked with some concern.

Without any embarrassment, any hesitancy, I removed my dress to show him the cuts and bruises on my back and arms and legs. "Look," I said.

"Who did this to you?" Percy asked in disbelief. "I'm taking you to Dr. Walker's office right away. Come!"

"No," I said. "No, I will be all right, I think! Not Dr. Walker," I protested. I put my dress on and sat dejectedly in a nearby chair.

"Why not? He's my doctor and the best in town," Percy bragged.

"I know. He is Mom's doctor, too, and one of her fondest friends. He is the only person who can make Mom really smile when he tells her she is a great woman for having a large family. Dr. Walker is the thirteenth child born to his parents, and he respects Mom as if she were his own mother. I could never go to Dr. Walker and say, 'Look at what my Mom, this wonderful mother, did to me' or have him ask me what I did to cause these injuries," I explained.

"What *did* you do?" Percy questioned.

"I talked back to Mom. That is an unforgivable sin! But that is not why she beat me while my brother Eugene held a gun on me!" I began crying. I stood up and started to leave the room, but I had to talk to someone, and there was no one else I trusted to hear what I was going to say. I sat in another chair and continued talking. Percy was somewhere in that room, pacing slowing back and forth, but he did not come near me.

"Mom and I have always been close, very close. Something happened between us when I went to college. I have been replaced to some extent by Ethel and Eugene, but Mom does not ever want to lose me. You heard what she told you. She would rather follow all of her daughters to their graves than see them marry. If we girls marry, me in particular, she will have lost us all because, as the oldest, I will lead the parade of the others' departure from home.

"She lost Pop and his leaving hurt her deeply. I know. I felt her pain. I think she wishes she had fought back, put him in jail for inadequate support, sued for a divorce, revealed his faults to his lodge brothers, punished him in some way. So Mom's beating me, to keep me in line, was her way of releasing all the anger, all the humiliation, all the frustrations she has carried for years. Somehow, something about me, my color, the ambitious plans I have, the things I say and do, touches a very sensitive chord associated with Pop. I think she realizes or suspects how much I love my Pop and she feels betrayed." I burst into tears again, but I had more to say and had to control my emotions.

"I just want you to know I have left home. I will be staying with my grandmother until I get enough money to go to Philadelphia. I have reconsidered the Urban League's recommendation to go to Temple University to train for a job as a social worker. School starts in September. I am scared to death." I tried to force a faint smile. I stood up and paused, uncertain about saying the words that followed.

"You asked Mom, last Thanksgiving, if you could change my name some day and she said 'no.' If you ask me, I will say 'yes.' I want you to marry me. I do not love you. I do not know what love is, but I like you a lot. You are a real friend. I trust you."

"Come now," Percy said, and he quickly put my damp coat over my shoulders. "I think that a doctor, any doctor, should see you right away. We must hurry downstairs. My landlady, who saw us come up here, I am sure, might get ideas and start a fancy rumor about me and you. Now if you can walk with me back to Richman's, I'll get a taxicab to take you to any doctor you're willing to see, and then take you to your Grandma's."

"I think I want to go to a movie and sit there all afternoon and then go to Grandma's much later. I want to be alone for awhile. A good soaking in a tub of hot water this evening will help heal my wounds. I won't need a doctor," I said.

Two days later I sat at dinner with Percy in a dimly lit corner of Hutchinson's Restaurant. I thought there were no more tears in me, but not so. One look at Percy and the floodgates opened wide. Never in my life before had tears flowed so profusely. I could not explain why I was crying. I was not angry, but I did hurt all over. Every physical movement was painful. Inwardly I was numb and terribly afraid.

The first time Percy ever touched me with a gesture of affection and tenderness was in that restaurant. He pressed my hand firmly in his, pleading, "Don't cry, please. Crying won't change a thing. You have shared a great deal with me. Now let me tell you what happened to me when I was just a fourteen-year-old boy. I'm a man and you're a woman, it's true, but I think I know how you feel. I went through almost the same experiences you're going through now. Let me tell you something I've never shared with anyone else before.

"Your mother reminds me of my father. They're both strong, determined people who think things must be done their way. My dad beat me with a bridle bit from my pet horse when I was fourteen. He beat me because I spoke to him in a manner which no son should ever use when speaking to his father. I told him not to make my mother cry anymore, or I would tell Grandma, his mother.

"After that whipping, I ran away from home and I've been on my own ever since. I changed my last name from Marcy to Marcere to deny my father. I hopped freight trains from one state to another. I made stops in New Orleans, Louisiana; Houston, Texas, Los Angeles, California and dozens of cities in between. I avoided small towns. I've worked at all kinds of jobs on the railroads, in hotels, on farms, and in orchards. Now I'm a porter in Canton, on my way to New York.

"I love my mother very much, and I keep in touch with her and with my sister in Brooklyn. You'll love them both when you meet them some day. I've been helping Alberdeen complete her nurse's training because I don't want her to be mistreated by, or totally dependent upon, any man. Blame my dad for my concern about my sister. My dad's a Baptist preacher, and he thinks he's God's ambassador to make people, especially his children, do what he wants them to do. He's a small-framed, light-skinned man of African, French, and Indian heritage. He's a hot-tempered person. I've been struggling for twelve years not to harbor hard feelings against my dad. Try not to build up a hatred toward your mother. It's hard learning how to 'unhate,' " Percy gently concluded.

I sat there awhile as his every word penetrated my consciousness. How little we know about the incidents in the lives of those whose paths cross ours.

"My Mom is a great woman," I confirmed, tasting the salty tears as they ran down my face and seeped into my mouth.

"She is wonderful with small babies and little boys and little girls. For some reason she cannot transfer her image of me from an obedient, unquestioning, ten-year-old to a decision-making, self-willed responsible adult. I have tried to understand how she feels as an abandoned wife and worried mother. She has no adult to talk to, no one who understands her thoughts or needs, no one to share her responsibilities. Pop should be by her side. I think I am angry because he is not with her. If Mom had someone paying attention to her, she would lean less on her children.

"What Mom wants from me I cannot deliver. She cannot punish me for the pain my Pop has caused her. She cannot expect my labors to compensate for her husband's neglect. That is not why I was born. That is not the way I want to live my life. I could never hate my mother. I respect her too much. She is a great lady, the greatest; but I will not be tethered to her or to anyone!" I burst convulsively into fresh tears.

"Come, let me take you home before you flood this place," Percy coaxed. "You've shed enough salt water to fill a small aquarium. Come!" He walked me to Grandma's house and met my grandparents for the first time.

The fifth or sixth night at Grandma's, as I was about to retire in Aunt Clella's single bed, Grandma stood in the bedroom doorway, eyeing me from head to foot.

"Your Mom was here today," Grandma began. "She insists I refuse to allow you to stay here any longer. I think she feels it is my responsibility to see that you go back home. There was very little sense to all that your Mom said. She was in a bad frame of mind. She was a nervous wreck! At my age I want no part of a family dispute." She paused and asked, "Since you will have to leave here, will you go back home?"

Her remarks, just uttered, dried up all my unshed tears and

fired up a fresh energy to do the impossible. It ignited a determination far more intense than any resolve I had made in my efforts to survive at Kent State. Mom could not force me to go back home. I resented her attempt to keep me and Grandma apart. Well, I would show her.

"No, Grandma, I shall never spend another night at home again for as long as I live. I have left the nest. I shall never return."

"Where will you go? Where will you stay?" Grandma probed.

"I cannot go anywhere on the small salary I am making now. I could afford to stay at the YWCA, but my face is not white like yours. No Negro is permitted in the YWCA, except as a cleaning lady, and even she cannot sleep there."

Was I trying to hurt Grandma? Was I trying to make her feel guilty for not urging me to stay? Was I attempting to remind her of all the things people with white skin like hers did to people with brown skin like mine?

"I can look for a job tomorrow as a 'live-in cook' for room, board, uniforms, and twenty dollars a week. I shall find a place. I will leave in the morning," I promised.

Grandma continued to stand there and then asked, "How well do you know this Percy fellow?"

"So that is why you are looking a hole through me," I began. "There is nothing wrong with me, Grandma. I am still a virgin. Do not worry about Percy and me. I won't ever sleep with anyone until I am married."

It dawned upon me that when I asked Percy to marry me, he had not said yes; he had not said no. He had said nothing.

"Well, take care of yourself," Grandma warned. "Make sure that neither your Mom, nor anyone, can say 'Look what she's done.' "

Sleep eluded me that last night in Aunt Clella's bed in Grandma's house. I was spared those recurring nightmarish dreams of trying to find my way out of a midnight blackness surrounded by tall windowless buildings. Where would I go in the morning? Should I contact one of the highly reputable church people at St. John's or St. Paul's? They would not consent to my spending one night in their homes without Mom's approval. After all, I was treated well and respected because of Mom, not because of me. I might as well go back home as to try to lean on Mom's friends. No, church people were out.

I could sleep on the floor in Attorney Hunter's office for a few nights, but should I tell him or just slip into the office after dark? Mrs. Lattimer, a white neighbor, mother of six little ones, lived a couple of blocks away. Maybe she . . . Oh, there was Mrs. Tabbs, a fairly new neighbor just around the corner from the Lattimers. I sat beside Mrs. Tabbs many mornings when I boarded the streetcar at Sixth and Shroyer on my way to the Square. We were the only Negroes on that crowded streetcar, and we sat together because no whites ever sat beside us. I think we both went out of our way to exhibit an attitude of close friendship for the benefit of the white passengers. Our dramatic message was, "Look how much we enjoy each other's company. If you think you are too good to sit beside us or stand too close to us, who cares? See how happy and friendly we are? We like each other."

Mrs. Tabbs had two children who occasionally joined the younger Snipes children at the neighborhood McKinley Theater and the Strand Theater uptown. Lucille was sixteen, four years my junior, and Dan was about twelve, two years younger than my brother Carl. It was rumored that Mrs. Tabbs' two mulatto children had been fathered by a prominent white businessman.

I did not want a town gossip, a free-for-all about me and my Mom's differences. I did not want to humiliate Mom. I did not want to hurt my chances for professional employment some day. Perhaps Mrs. Tabbs was in the least plausible position to question another's character or motives. She was the sister of Sadie Cook, Canton's most notorious underworld madam, who operated the largest house of prostitution in the red light district. Why not stay with Mrs. Tabbs for a few days?

The next morning early, before the neighborhoods became alive with children leaving their homes on the way to school, I headed for the Tabbs' home. It was just four blocks west of Grandma's house and two blocks south from our house. Tonner Court, where the Tabbs lived, was a short, two-residence street, between Sixth Street and a number of meandering alleys leading to Ninth Street Southwest.

In answer to my timorous knock, Mrs. Tabbs came to the door and greeted me warmly. She insisted I have breakfast with Lucille and Dan. When they had departed for school, Mrs. Tabbs and I walked to the corner to await the streetcar. Whatever the unemotional, uninformative tale I gave to Mrs. Tabbs for wanting to live away from home for awhile, she accepted without question, without prying. I was welcome to stay at her home and share a room with Lucille.

Within a week, I obtained a job as a cook for the Barricks. This very fine aristocratic family lived west of Cleveland Avenue within a comfortable walking distance from the Public Square. I was delighted. There were no children to contend with and I would live on the premises. Attorney Hunter was given just three days' notice of my departure. I never phoned anyone at home. I stopped going to church because I feared running into Mom or Ethel. Every Sunday, Percy and I had dinner at a restaurant and went to a movie.

After those early weeks of May when our talks were about family hurts, conflicts and loyalties, Percy and I shared our dreams of what we wanted from life and how we perceived the world we lived in.

We talked about politics, sports, religion, travel, history

and philosophy. Strange how conversation reveals one's beliefs, one's values, one's code of morality and decency, and one's concern about justice and fair play.

"What do I want out of life?" Percy repeated my question one evening, and answered, "I'm not too sure. A year ago, I would've told you I might consider a smart wife, a good job, one or two children, and a little house somewhere."

"And now?" I urged.

"Now I'm not sure. I just wonder a lot. Dr. Walker told me this past winter, when I was so sick with the mumps and the flu, that I may never father any children. That narrows my marriageability. Maybe I should remain a bachelor. What woman would knowingly marry a man who couldn't father children?"

"I would!" I announced light-heartedly. Somehow the subject changed.

Our philosophical discussions grew weightier and sometimes ridiculously absurd. It was as if we were tossing ideas, like rubber balls, against the side of a house to see how far they would bounce. Could either of us catch the ball, or would it be lost?

One evening I blurted out, "You know, Percy, I have been having second thoughts about love. I cannot believe in love. I do not think there is any such emotion. I believe love is a catch-all word that has no singular quality."

"All of today's popular songs are about love, and there's a saying that love makes the world go round," Percy declared.

"It is not love that makes the world go round, it is goodwill. I am not sure I could, or would, want to love everybody; but I can and must have goodwill towards everyone," I explained.

"Don't you love your family, your relatives?" Percy asked.

"I have a deep affection for them. You see," I continued, "words like admire, respect, trust and like describe a specific quality of feeling toward another. Love may be a combination of the above attributes. My point is, what is love? Family affection, a tender feeling of loyalty, may be present without the qualities of trust, respect and admiration. Is loyalty love?"

"Whoa!" Percy interrupted. "You're too deep for me. Do you really want to tell me that you can't believe in love, just when I'm getting up enough courage to tell you I love you?"

"D-Do you-? W-Were you? Uh, are you?" I stuttered.

"I loved you the moment I was introduced to you by Mrs. Premmer in her restaurant in 1926. But you don't believe in love, so maybe I'll have to call it something else. I heard this definition the other day: 'Love is a ticklish feeling around the heart that says a certain individual is very special. The person with the ticklish heart wants to be as close to that individual as possible.' "

"That tickling around the heart could just be a case of heart palpitation. I had that when I was twelve years old, and I am sure that was not love!" I laughed.

"Now you're trying to be difficult. I'll say no more. Let's change the subject," Percy suggested, and we did. The days and weeks tumbled over each other, and I was ready to leave Canton. I shared the minute details with Percy.

"Did you know Richman's Store has been trying to get me a job with one of their men's furnishing stores in Philadelphia?" Percy remarked as we walked up Cleveland Avenue to the Barretts' residence. "I had plans to leave Canton with you, but there are no jobs in Philadelphia. The Depression is much worse there than here.

"Your school in Philadelphia is from September to December. By the first of the year, I'll have some place for us to be together. You see, I should say a 'no' or a 'yes' to your proposal of marriage of last May. Remember? Yes, I'll marry you whether you love me or not. I don't want to lose you. You're still the girl I want to take home to my parents

AN UNEXPECTED HAPPENING

and say to them, 'Congratulate me for being so lucky.' I'm going to marry you! Did you hear me? We're going to get married! All you have to say is when."

I could not believe my ears. "If we are going to get married," I almost shouted, "I am going to do something right now that we have never done before." We were standing on the back porch at the kitchen entrance to the Barrett home. Grabbing Percy by the neck, I pulled his face toward mine and kissed him.

"Is this a sign that you're falling in love?" Percy asked as he drew me toward him and gathered me in his arms.

"No, I just wanted to know what a kiss is like, and I wanted to say 'Thank you.' " I was overwhelmed with gratitude and filled with a comforting sense of security by our first meaningful embrace.

"We'd better plan when, where and by whom we're going to be married," Percy suggested.

In less than ten minutes we had decided. We would be married by a justice of the peace in Pittsburgh, halfway between Canton and Philadelphia. I also decided to tell Mom I was leaving town, but not that I was getting married. "I could never do to her what Pop had done," I explained. "She should know where her daughter is."

Mom surprised me by wanting to come to the Pennsylvania train station to see me off. Percy and I could not board the train with a "Why is he going along?" We had to change our departure plans. I was to get on the train in Canton, then get off the train in Massillon and wait for Percy to join me there. Then together we would board a train for Pittsburgh. After our exchange of marriage vows before a justice of the peace, Percy would return to Canton and I would continue to Philadelphia. I insisted that neither Mom nor anyone else be told of our elopement. It was to be our secret.

Our departure was as planned. Percy, Mom and Ruth stood

at the station, waving unemotional goodbyes. An hour later Percy and I were on our way to be united as one.

Our two-day sojourn in Pittsburgh was almost a tragedy. I made a half dozen attempts to call the whole thing off . . . to back out of the marriage. I literally panicked. I was fearful of an impending intimacy which would change our relationship from friend to lover. I was giving up forever my virginity, even my back-burner "wish" to become a nun, for the respectability of "Mrs." Was this too big a price to pay just to travel several hundred miles from home as a respectable woman?

My mindset and my behavior would have angered the devil, but not Percy. He was a paragon of gentleness, patience and endearments.

When my husband escorted me to a seat on the Philadelphia train, he kissed me with the plea, "Write me every week. Promise."

I was not to have a care or a fear in the world. What had he told me? "We're one now. I am you, and you are me. No matter where you go, no matter how far apart we are, we are forever one. I love you, I love you. I will always care for you."

My husband was my security, and yet I had an adventurous and rebellious thought. If everything went well in Philadelphia, school, work and a place to live,—maybe, just maybe—we would never see each other again. Percy had better try to come to Philadelphia. I never wanted to return to Canton!

IX

Philadelphia

Philadelphia, the city of brotherly love, caught my fancy from the moment I alighted from the train at the huge Pennsylvania Railroad terminal in the center of town. A staff worker from the Philadelphia Urban League met me and spent the greater part of that August day introducing me to the main streets, the large department stores, and the subway systems. By midafternoon a very weary newcomer from Ohio checked in at the Central YWCA and was assigned room 205. I remember the number because some time later I played the three digit combination on the illegal numbers lottery game for a penny. I hit and was paid five dollars.

After scanning the newspapers for a job as a cook, I reneged upon a promise to work for a Jewish family in Germantown and took a job as a salad girl at a very select tea room.

It was a perfect arrangement. I could go to school half days. I received room and board in addition to seventy-five dollars a month.

Miss Jeanette Leatherman, the energetic owner, had been a former home economics teacher in a small town in western Pennsylvania. I had never before known a single woman who owned a business, and she intrigued me. She lived in a charming apartment on the third floor. The dining room, with its large plate glass window overlooking the endless traffic on Locust and Thirteenth streets, was really on the second floor. The first floor, slightly below ground level, was for storage and supplies and the employees' rest room.

Miss Leatherman's clientele were retired men and women of means who lived in one of the many apartment complexes within a short walking distance. The Mayfair tea room, known for its cuisine, also attracted many business executives for the noon meal. Lunch was served from 11:00 a.m. to 2:00 p.m. Dinner, always with linen napkins, tablecloths, and fresh floral arrangements, was served from 5:00 p.m. to 7:00 p.m. The atmosphere was one of serenity and elegance.

My classes at Temple University were from 8:00 a.m. to 10:00 a.m. three days a week. Often I was in the kitchen at 5:00 a.m., preparing all of my noon salads and desserts before catching the 7:30 subway to school. I was back by 10:30 to finish setting up my lunch plates, start my yeast for the dinner Parkerhouse rolls and complete the dinner dessert and salad menu. We served approximately one hundred patrons each meal.

Cooking in mass quantities was quite different from the six to eight portioned family dinners I had prepared in a private home, but it was exciting. Preparing gallons of mayonnaise, boiling dozens of eggs, and washing and sorting bushels of fruits and vegetables for savory salads provided a real challenge. I baked pies, cakes, plum puddings, fruitcakes, and cookies for desserts and prepared all kinds of fancy breads.

Quality was never sacrificed to quantity. Every heated or chilled dinner or salad plate was artistically proportioned and served as if it were the only special order on the menu. Before long, I was getting compliments for the attractiveness and tastiness of my salads and desserts. The meat and vegetable cooks already had an established reputation for their culinary expertise.

I learned how to manage my tea room hours according to the menu and the time needed for food preparation. Whether my day began at 5:00 a.m. or 7:00 a.m., I tried to keep out of the way of the two cooks and kitchen aides. Kitchen traffic could be a problem, affecting tempers and dispositions. The all-Negro staff fascinated me. They were hard working, generous, fun loving people. I was amazed at their optimistic philosophy of life and the accounts of their off the job activities.

Later when I was introduced to the Urban League staff and fellow trainees, I realized that for two nights a week I would be studying with an exceptionally professional team of social workers and dedicated individuals. Part of my training at the Armstrong School of Social Service was to gain first-hand experience with the impoverished. We were to work with neighborhood groups of from five to ten families. The Great Depression had created a society of unemployed citizens. None was hurt more than the rural-oriented, southern migrant, with less than ten to fifteen years in the urban North. Now unemployed and confused, they gathered hopelessly in small groups on street corners, in barber shops, and pool halls. They played cards, staked a penny or two on the numbers, and waited for something to happen.

I was in charge of organizing a Swain Street neighborhood unit of six families. We met once a week, rotating from one neighbor's home to another. I was to teach, demonstrate, and counsel these families, mothers in particular, about basic adjustments to their environments. The preparation of food, housekeeping hints, handicrafts, the care of children, and the return to school to update their education became our major emphasis.

From September to December I had the rare experience of a genuinely personal contact with the class of people I had heretofore observed at a distance. It was a welcomed challenge. I was bursting with a wealth of skills and experiences to share with my families. My cooking responsibilities at home and the knowledge I had gained as a cook in private families and now at the tea room made it easy for me to set up practical and economically nutritious meals. The Industrial Arts classes at Kent made it possible for me to teach parents how to build tables, chairs, cribs and storage closets from orange crates and the wooden containers that once housed refrigerators, stoves and household furnishings. My Child Development courses, not to mention being the oldest in our family of six, were a help in suggesting games and activities for the young children. One of my more popular gatherings was the knitting and crocheting class.

Years earlier when my Pop had worked for two months or so at the Timken Roller Bearing Company, he brought home a pair of steel knitting needles. He taught me, an eleven year old, how to cast on and how to do the simple knit stitch. When I taught Mrs. Tomalet, the Rumanian immigrant next door to us, how to speak English, she taught me how to crochet doilys, mittens, hats, and scarves. Every woman on Swain Street completed a jiffy knit sweater or a crocheted doily in record time.

It can be an erroneous and unscientific practice to make generalities about individuals and groups of people. Still, I was surprised and a little annoyed by some of my conclusions based upon what I was observing time and again. There was always an abundance of food on the tables of the most needy families, and soft drinks (almost like an addiction) took precedence over milk. In a corner of the most poorly furnished house, there would be a clothes rack with the neatest, latest styled clothing. These same people at church on Sunday could make me feel underdressed, an out of place intruder. Nearly every home had a "number" playing addict, hoping to "hit" and become wealthy all at once.

As a young adult, I was repulsed by these observations. An abundance of food, expensive clothing, and faith in lady luck were so unproductive. I wondered what field of endeavor, social work, religion, education, or psychology could help these people reach for more meaningful, long-range goals.

I postulated other generalities perhaps just as unfair and just as lacking in insight. I was willing to attribute to these poor southern migrants such worry free and irresponsible stereotypes as fun-loving, carefree, indifferent, uncaring and unambitious. How was I to know then that fifty years later the children of the people with those labels would have the highest death rate and the shortest life span due to hypertension, strokes, and heart disease? These conditions are attributable to the unobservable presence of concern, frustration, worry, malnutrition, stress, and tension.

Notwithstanding my work relationships and professional interaction with the tea room staff, the Temple University classmates, the Urban League staff and the Swain Street neighborhood families, I was generally alone. Being alone was a most enjoyable portion of my day. I was getting to know myself. I was enjoying my own company.

Many evenings and Sundays I walked up and down Broad and Chestnut to Lombard and streets in between, taking in the urban sights. The strange houses joined together as one for a whole city block—each with the same four-storied architecture, separated only by their roof tops—created mixed emotions in me. They were such a contrast to the Ohio neighborhoods of sprawling, two-storied homes surrounded by spacious lawns. I wondered how many people must have climbed those stone steps only to have mistaken their house for someone else's with an identical front door entrance. I wondered how people could maintain their own identity living so close to their neighbors.

The display windows in the downtown stores were decorated

to please both those who had money to spend and those who were content to enjoy the beauty of color and artistry. It appeared to be the season to feature live mannequins doing mechanical gyrations before their viewing audience. Spectators would gather and themselves make facial and body contortions in an effort to distract the actors behind the plate glass window. The actors were not distracted.

The poor man's boulevard was not too many blocks away from the Broad Street shopping area. The businesses along South Street for several blocks had their own style of physical gyrations to attract the passer-by to their wares. Late into the fall season, the merchants hauled their commodities outside the store to coax and coerce customers.

Friday and Saturday evenings in particular there was increased activity in that area as patrons of the theater wended their way to the weekly amateur hour shows. The Earle Theater was in the vicinity of South and Ninth Streets. If I was late because of my fascination with the street merchandise, there would be theater standing room only. I saw my first movie with Negro actors at the Earle Theater.

It was strange how a feeling of racial pride could fill my whole being when I watched the young and adult musicians, dancers, singers, and comedians compete for amateur awards. It was while I was in Philadelphia that I saw the Blackbirds' stage performance.

There were other attractions. The Philadelphia Amusement Park, Father Divine's famous dining room for feeding the unemployed, and a Catholic church with a Negro priest excited me. I was never afraid to walk the streets alone, regardless of the time of day or night. No one ever followed me, whistled at me, or yelled out an obscene phrase. I felt free and safe.

On my twenty-first birthday, I realized I was late in my menstrual period. In a way I was glad because it had always been a painful experience. Dr. O. DeWeese, the Kent Normal School physician and health director, told me he had known only one other young woman who suffered as I did.

The thought of being pregnant never entered my mind. Percy had been explicit and apologetic that he could not father a child. Dr. Walker insisted Percy explain this fully to me. I married, assured we would be childless. Childlessness, the absence of children, would enhance my educational and career pursuits.

I went gaily about, enjoying my new life. I began thinking adventurously of studying for a Bachelor's degree, of getting an apartment of my own, and of remaining in Philadelphia. I seldom ever thought of Percy, my husband. I was not the least bit excited that he was coming to visit me on Thanksgiving day. A week before his intended arrival I received a postage-covered, special delivery letter from him. He asked me to phone Richman Brothers store on a certain day, at a specific time and to reverse the charges.

When I phoned he said, "Hello, Wife. My, how nice it is to hear your voice. I miss you. And by the way, why are you keeping secrets from me?"

"It is wonderful to hear your voice, too. What kind of secrets are you talking about?" I asked.

"You're pregnant, aren't you?" Percy began.

"Of course not! How could I be? Why would you ask? You said you could never . . . ."

"Well, I know you are; and everybody here at the store knows that you are, too. Catherine, Jack and Louie are standing here beside me. They want to say hello. The whole store has been cracking jokes on me."

I could hear voices, and they were asking, "What is she saying? Is she? Tell us!"

Percy continued, "I should've gone to a pay phone and avoided the invasion of our privacy, but the whole outfit here has been telling me for weeks that you're pregnant. I've lost weight. I can't eat. I'm miserable. How are you?"

"Fine! Nothing is wrong with me. I have never felt better in my life. I have a super job as a pastry and dessert cook. I go to school. Philadelphia is great. I love it here!"

"Listen, sweetheart, don't you . . . ? Wait a minute. . . . Scram, all of you! Everybody go! The rest of my conversation is private."

The voices in the background that had been whispering, "Is she? What did she say?" vanished.

"Don't you know that you're pregnant? It has to be you. I don't know any other woman but you, and I can't live without you much longer. Are you putting on weight? Do you realize what's happening to you?" Percy questioned.

"Gee, maybe I am pregnant. . . . It never crossed my mind. . . . Dr. Walker had said . . . ."

"Listen," Percy urged, "when is school out?"

"A week before Christmas," I answered.

"Good. Now pay attention. I had planned to visit you on Thanksgiving, the anniversary of my first proposal to the girl who is my wife, but . . . I think I had better stay here and look for a house. I want you back here as soon as school is out. Do you understand? Do you need anything?"

"I think so. . . . But I do not want to come back to Canton. No, I am not in need of a thing."

It slowly dawned upon me that maybe the total freedom and independence I thought was within arm's reach, was not just ahead for me.

"If you need anything, let me know. I'm going to look after you. I'll phone your mother and tell her we're married and that you'll be coming home around Christmas," Percy explained.

"I cannot come home then," I said. "It is the busiest season for the tea room. I have already planned to do a great many things over the holidays. A very unusual Mummers' Day parade takes place on New Year's Day, so I will see you sometime after. Do you think I should see a doctor?"

"Yes, why don't you?"

"All right. I shall."

"Write me please, every day, will you?"

"If I can."

"I love you, Norma. I want you here with me. Do you understand?"

"I guess if what you say is true, I have no other choice, do I? How fortunate I am to have a husband with mental telepathy who knows what is happening to me even before I do."

"Have a happy Thanksgiving and write to me."

"I will."

"Goodbye, my love."

"Goodbye."

The holiday season was a time of investigating the changes in my body, analyzing my immediate situation, and living one day at a time. There was no point in dwelling upon what was happening or becoming concerned about the unknown future. This was the present. I had a husband. We were going to have a child. I was completing my requirements as a qualified social worker. What did I have to complain about?

Three days after a freezing cold January first, with my curiosity about the famous Mummers' parade fully satisfied, I boarded a train back to Canton. My farewell thoughts of Philadelphia were filled with excited memories. The sight of hundreds of half-clad male marchers in the Mummers' parade amazed me. They cavorted down Broad Street openly consuming alcoholic drinks from their flasks, while their frosted flesh took on various hues of red, blue and purple. Their cavorting and drinking antics reminded me of witch doctors dispelling the influenza and pneumonia virus which threatened to enter their reddened, chilled bodies.

The tea room staff gave me a warm farewell party. I had made more friends in Philadelphia than in all of Canton and Kent combined. I was sorry to leave it all and was helplessly annoyed to be returning to the town I thought I had permanently left behind.

Percy was so happy, so full of excitement, as he helped me alight from the train. He grabbed me in his arms with a show of emotion I had never known before. A taxi drove us to the house he had rented at 1405 Fifth Street, Southwest, across the street from my childhood home. He walked me through the six-room house. Only three of the rooms were furnished with the typical newly married couple's specialty. I counted exactly seventeen pieces of furniture. They were: in the living room, a couch, two chairs, two end tables, and two lamps; the kitchen had a stove, a kitchen table and four chairs; the bedroom with its double bed, dresser, dressing table and night stand was large enough to add a rocking chair and a baby crib a couple of months later. The dining room and the second and third bedrooms were empty of any furnishings.

Linoleum rugs covered the floors. We would haunt the Salvation Army and the Goodwill Union Industries for bargain pieces of furniture, item by item, in the weeks that followed.

Before I unpacked, we decided to cross the street and say hello to Mom. I tried to prepare myself for our meeting. Not once since May of 1929 had I directed my thoughts toward home. I had sent no letters from Philadelphia. Those first twenty years of my life were a closed book I really did not want to reopen.

"So you ran off and got married and now the secret's out. You are back in town. You have rented the Jordan house across the street and I suppose you are pregnant, even though you don't look like it," Mom announced accusingly. There was no hug, no embrace, no smile.

"Yes, we're going to be parents," Percy added quickly. "And I expect to honor your daughter, my wife, and cherish her the rest of my life. I hope you understand why we did things the way we did. That Thanksgiving you made it plain that you'd never give us your consent to get married, but we're looking forward to your blessing."

"I still do not approve of my daughter's marriage and never will!" Mom insisted. With a glance in my direction she added quickly, "You have made your bed. Just realize that you have to sleep in it."

I felt no anger, no faulting, only a strange sadness as if a once-cherished mother-daughter relationship had deteriorated beyond our grasp. I was looking at a very angry, vindictive woman and I could not understand why she was so disturbed. I could only assume that she, whose early years of marriage were totally involved in the pleasurable role of a nurturing mother of infants and small children, could not make an emotional transference to her adult offspring.

As once she had inspired me as the prettiest, most wonderful mother in the world, she now frightened me. I wanted to go far, far away. Why did Percy rent a house across the street from her? Why did I come back to Canton? Why was I having a baby when I had been told this could not happen?

As we left her house, Percy put his arms around me, "You don't ever have to go back to that house again," he began. "You're the queen of our little house across the street. You may come and go and do whatever pleases you there. You're a free woman, no strings attached. Your working days as a cook and a maid are over, and I'll insist upon that.

"My parents are two thousand miles away, and I want you to think of your family as just as far away or farther. If you allow your mother to push you around in any kind of manner, I'll step in and put a stop to it. You're my wife. She has no claims on you anymore. Do you understand? None whatever! No matter how bad things get, this Depression and all, you're never to go to her for anything, and I pray God that your family never asks us for anything. We've been told to sleep in the bed we've made and that is what we'll do, for better or for worse."

I cried that first night in our new home, trying to put into perspective my family relationships. Distancing myself from my mother could be justified scripturally, "leave parents to cleave to one's husband or wife." But what about my sisters and brothers? We were of the same generation and would be facing problems and challenges never faced before. Suppose they found themselves in the same situation I was now in, to whom in the family could they turn?

We Snipes children had no cousins, no uncles, only a forty-one-year old aunt in Pennsylvania. Grandma and Grandpa were eighty and ninety years old, respectively. My thoughts became resolves that night. I must prepare myself to be the big sister when (and I really believed it would happen) our mother could not deal with her other children's young adulthood. Whatever had happened between Ethel and me (her secrecy about the summer playground job) and Eugene (his holding a gun on me while Mom beat me), I must hold no ill will toward them. We might not be close, but I must not desert them. They must have a "Percy" to turn to as I had that night. I would reach out to them as their big sister.

X

Fenced In—
By Our Own Four Walls

January 1931 was cold and sunless and our moods were influenced by a nation submerged in the Great Depression. That is when Percy and I began the process of becoming one, husband and wife. Neither of us knew what that really entailed. Percy had lived independently of intimate family relationships since the age of fourteen. With thirteen years of carefree habits, he, at twenty-seven, was well inside the door of unburdened bachelorhood.

For four years I had been making my own decisions and assuming responsibility for my full support. Plans for linking my life with another had never entered my thoughts. There had been no daydreams of a Prince Charming, or a Romeo, in my waking or sleeping fantasies. The choice of a teaching career in the 20's and 30's, requiring an unmarried commitment, denoted an "old maid" mentality. Due to circumstances initiated by an aborted teaching opportunity, Percy and I had promised to share our lives, "for better, for worse, till death do us part." It was not going to be easy; the adjustment could be insurmountable.

The most favorable virtue about our relationship was that we were friends. We liked and respected each other. Percy called his "like" love. I called my "like" trust. My husband was sexually mature and patiently restrained. I had to be awakened to the desire of sexual intimacy and closeness. A second positive factor of our marriage was that our families were not likely to interfere in our affairs.

Our marriage demanded a continuous series of adjustments, of learning and unlearning, of changes and adaptations. I felt imprisoned as a housewife. I resented the dependence of looking to my husband for my personal needs. I felt locked in by a house subject to me for its maintenance. I never relished the monotonous routine of keeping a house clean and orderly. My duties as a child maximized cooking, budgeting, shopping, and sewing. I performed a minimum of household tasks.

My work as a cook was enjoyable because I was not responsible for the drudgery of bed-making, dusting, sweeping, scrubbing, washing, and ironing. Only one room in the house was my responsibility—the kitchen. It was mine to organize in such a way as to create culinary masterpieces. I could cut flowers from the garden and arrange artistic centerpieces. I could scrutinize the cleaning lady's thoroughness, spotting an overlooked cobweb on the chandelier or an undusted piece of antique furniture. The laundress could be reminded to iron and fold the table linens just so. That was it!

There was some thrill during those winter months of our first year when slowly, piece by piece, we began furnishing our house with the necessary items that would make it a home. A house is just a structure of wood and glass and brick. It takes gadgets and furnishings to make it habitable. I became a gadget procurer, stretching a dollar or two from Percy's weekly salary as far as it would go.

The Salvation Army outlet store had a wide selection of pots, pans, skillets, dishware, silverware, laundry tubs, and pails which I purchased. The "Ten Cent" store was a fertile source for the other household items and toiletries. The finishing touches of curtains, draperies, linens, and the baby layette were last on the list of essentials and called for a full price, cash outlay. I shopped at the large department stores such as Zollinger's and McKenzie and Jones'. I must have been a sight, carrying packages from town to home, sloshing through the snow covered sidewalks in the January and February cold.

Grandma came to visit me in February. It was one of those rare sun-pierced mornings that fulfilled the Groundhog's Day prediction of continued cold, and awakened a yearning for a Valentine's Day of brighter promises. Dispositions are elevated by the parting of the heavy blanket of winter clouds signaling that spring is just around the corner. I was standing on a ladder hanging curtains in the living room, when Grandma knocked on the door.

"Come in, Grandma," I called out. "Gee, I am so glad to see you! Just a minute. Give me time to hook this drapery pin and I . . ." I started to descend, and fainted as I touched the last step.

Grandma helped me to a chair and began patting my face gently, commenting as I stirred to consciousness, "You know, pregnant mothers should not climb ladders. You must use common sense and be careful. Can I get you a drink of water?"

"No, no. I am fine," I assured her.

"Are you happy about having a baby?" she asked a few minutes later, eyeing me up and down as only Grandma could.

"I guess so, Grandma. I am not sure how I feel. I keep thinking that I should feel different somehow, but I don't! This fainting is the first thing to happen to me," I confessed.

"Do you mean the baby's movement, mother love or what?" Grandma asked.

"The baby moves a lot. I think we are going to have a ballet dancer or a long distance runner. On the other hand, I am waiting to feel like I imagine an expectant mother should feel. I am disappointed," I tried to explain.

"The moment your baby is born, something beautiful will happen to you, I know," Grandma said reassuringly. "I had twelve children. Every baby has its moment of letting out a cry that says, 'Look at me. I love you for bringing me into the world.' Then you will know the meaning of becoming a mother."

Changing the subject, she commented, "You have a nice place here. Looks like Percy is a good provider. I only saw him once, but he seemed like a real nice fellow. Kind of a shame he is so dark though. Dark fathers make dark babies."

I made no attempt to reply to her remark immediately. I had to weigh my words carefully. Grandma was always outspoken and never made any pretense about her honest feelings. I had often wondered about her skin color feelings. How must she feel, being white enough to be mistaken as white and yet designated as a Negro because of an infinitesimal infusion of African blood? Grandma had felt the lonely, degraded curse of looking white and being rejected, just as all Negroes had felt the repulsion of their blackness. She knew the feeling of being looked upon as loathsome and inferior.

Grandma commented more than once that she was ashamed of the eighty percent Caucasian blood that flowed through her veins. She never mentioned her feelings about the twenty percent Negro blood from her beloved father.

Grandma's Caucasian mother abandoned her family when her mulatto husband (who was the freed son of a white plantation owner and his slave mistress) died in the Civil War. Authorities placed Grandma in the home of a pure blood African woman. It was from this environment that Grandma met her husband-to-be, a colored Civil War veteran of mixed Afro-Caucasian genes. All but four of their twelve beautiful mulatto children died in infancy and early childhood. Only one daughter, my mother, had married a full blooded Negro and brought brown children into the world. Grandma had never embraced a grandchild with her characteristics of fair skin, luxuriant auburn hair, or blue-green eyes.

One's religious upbringing can encourage the love of peoples of different races from afar: the Eskimo, Indian, Chinese, African, Philippino, and Polynesian. How does one acknowledge as one's own kin, one's own flesh and blood, offspring with no resemblance to one's own likeness and skin color? Was Grandma thinking that now her first great grandchild would be even further removed from her likeness than her grandchildren?

"Things are not like they were just after slavery, when you were growing up, Grandma. Negroes have almost the same freedoms and opportunities as whites. Things are a lot better now, and each generation will find equality and justice closer for everybody." How could I make such a statement knowing that my condition was a result of racism.

"It will make no difference whether a person is white, black, brown, red, or yellow; have curly, wavy, or straight hair," I emphasized. Did I really believe that?

"I intend to see that my child has every opportunity to get the most out of life, the most out of being an Afro-American!" I meant that as a promise.

Grandma said, "I hope you are right." The expression on her face told me I was young and idealistic. I would grow up to learn the realities of life pertaining to racial attitudes.

In the meantime I had other concerns. Alone in my own home, with the arrival of our baby just three months away, I indulged in a privilege heretofore unknown to me. I lounged in bed every morning for as long as I desired. I indulged in this luxury as if there was a biological need to remain supinely inert till noon. I had never realized that a part of me harbored a fantasy of languid uselessness.

I had always scrambled out of bed at 6:00 a.m. for as long as I could remember, never even indulging in an extra five minutes of extended pleasurable idleness. Before this pregnancy, an illness (even a feigned illness) could have been a legitimate reason for staying in bed, but such eluded me. There were no days with propped up pillows, a good book, meals in bed, and cheerful visitors or peaceful solitude. In my mid-teen years, with school to attend and job responsibilities, I had to get about the duties of the day. Now was my chance to indulge in lazy, useless rest; and I did. I remained in bed until rest became tiresome.

Percy never wakened me in the morning on his way to work. He was not a breakfast-eating man. If I stirred, he would say, "You lay there and go back to sleep. I'll be home at noon and eat lunch with you." Then he would walk the mile to his work.

He returned at noon to a lunch of soup and crackers and one of Reel's homemade pies, fresh from the bakery just a few blocks away. Percy was not as dutiful about coming home in the evening. He would head for the busiest, most popular pool hall, on the corner of Sixth Street and Cherry Avenue Southeast. There he would join his bachelor and married buddies who made it their business to always stop by the pool hall after work. They joked, they used careless, uncensored language, releasing the frustrations of constraint proper to their smothered, subordinate functioning in a dominant white environment. They seemed to create an euphoric illusion that helped them escape the negative realities of their existence.

Our dinner became a delayed, warmed-over, dished-up-from-the-stove, kind of smorgasbord meal. I did not like it. It was a far cry from the conventional, on-time, three-course dinners I prepared as a cook in private family and the tea room. Only on Sunday did we bask in the luxury of formal meals and shared relaxation.

We took turns preparing the ten o'clock brunch that consisted of steak, rice, eggs, and biscuits. Percy taught me how to make biscuits the way his mother and most southern women baked them. Then he taught me how to make white, unsweetened cornbread. We had always eaten yellow, cake sweetened cornbread in our home. My husband insisted upon biscuits or cornbread at every meal, claiming he never ate white, store-bought bread.

After a mid-afternoon dinner, reminiscent of dozens of restaurant meals we had shared for three years of our unrecognized courtship, we read the Sunday newspapers, talked a lot and sang. We had a small radio and listened to some special programs; but most of all, we enjoyed our singing and whistling duets. In the evening we went to a movie. Sunday was our day of enjoying one another's company and growing closer to each other.

We chose Dr. Mantle Burt Williams to be the physician who would deliver our baby. He was the second Negro doctor to practice in Canton. He was such a warm, reassuring individual. No one will ever know the encouragement, the hope that welled up in me when I met Dr. Williams. It was my first opportunity to see, to talk to, and to shake hands with a highly trained physician with dark skin. My thoughts abounded with the awareness that Negroes could achieve and become. As a race we did not have to point only to our white blood connections to believe we could be somebody.

Because I was still covered by a Metropolitan life Insurance policy, one that had been taken out upon my birth, I was entitled to free home nursing service. Dr. Williams had advised, "With a professional nurse, plenty of bed linens, hot water and newspapers, I would recommend you have your baby at home. Neither Aultman Hospital nor Mercy Hospital can provide the atmosphere and attention that your family and neighbors can give you."

On a Friday evening, two weeks before the anticipated birth of our first child, I waddled alongside Percy on our way to the McKinley Theater. It was just four blocks from home and located on Tuscarawas Street and the B & O Railroad crossing. We walked down the railroad tracks, stepping over the railroad ties and being on the alert for any moving cars. Freight cars, sometimes called boxcars, were still being shifted to sidings leading to a coal yard, the Schneider Lumber Company, Brumbaugh Lumber, and the Climalene Company.

The proprietor of a small restaurant and confectionary that hugged the tracks just west of the theater knew just when to start the popcorn machine and turn up the hamburger grill to entice the theater patrons. I had had no pregnancy yearnings for strange food in unheard of combinations, but a hundred feet away from the source of the food odors I was determined to have one of those heavenly smelling hamburgers. Percy purchased one for me.

Fifteen minutes into the movie, I was seized with severe abdominal pains and an upset stomach. Percy accompanied me back home, taunting me in a humorous manner. "First of all, you had no business eating that hamburger. You are always telling me you never eat meat on Friday, and I caught you in the act. Now with your discomfort you know what I went through those first three months and didn't know why. It's your turn now, ha ha."

"Oh you, you meanie, you! You should have reminded me today is Friday," I exclaimed in exasperation. "Anyhow, I lost it all back there. It was not nearly as good as it smelled."

All that night I walked the floor in pain. I was in labor and did not know it until noon the next day. "I am not in labor," I protested as Percy, home on his lunch hour, insisted upon phoning the doctor. "The baby is not due for two weeks, May 5th. It was just that tainted old hamburger. It has my stomach all upset."

When the doctor and nurse arrived, the contractions were just minutes apart. Dr. Williams said to Percy as he ushered him out the door, "We will not need you around here for awhile. You will only be in the way. Kiss your wife and go back to your job. Come straight home after work." His instructions to me were, "Get into bed and do as you are told."

The snow fell persistently that April 25, 1931, and richly robed every tree and shrub and greening blade of grass. King Winter was determined not to let an impetuous spring maiden, heralded by tantalizing beams of sunshine and soft fragrant breezes, dethrone him of his wintry reign.

Percy wrapped a scarf around his neck and headed back to work. I turned from the snow pelted window to allow the nurse to properly prepare me for this new venture. The doctor handed me a small wad of cotton saturated with chloroform to sniff every time there was a labor pain. The pains did not concern me. I wanted to see all that was happening because this, I thought, would be a one-time event.

"Lie back down there and push when you are told," the doctor scolded.

Our daughter came into the world that evening with an air of determination similar to the weather. It astonished me to look upon an infant squirming with such vitality, so alertly intelligent and so resolutely independent.

That strange, miraculous emotion did not well up in me as Grandma had promised it would. Still, when Dr. Williams placed our eight pound little girl in my arms, I wanted to hand the world to her on a platter. This eagerness to get moving must have shown, because Dr. Williams had a few words of caution.

"Remember, you are to remain in this bed for ten days. After that, you are not to walk up and down the stairs for a month. Have Percy carry you up and down the steps or move your bed downstairs. You have a beautiful little girl here. Now get some sleep. I shall see you in the morning."

When the doctor left, I began to cry. Lying beside me in

the large double bed was a new life. I was awed by my motherhood. I gazed upon a beautifully formed, bald-headed infant, with all of her ten little fingers and ten little toes. I wept a prayer of thanks. Percy should be home soon. I wondered how he would express his feelings toward his infant daughter.

Upon his very late return from work, Percy bounded up the stairs, came to the bed, and asked, "Are you all right?"

He was shaking with fear and relief. All afternoon he had recalled whispered accounts of childbirth deaths he had heard about in his childhood. He glanced at his daughter, but made no effort to pick her up. "She's so small. I'm afraid to touch her," he said.

I began to cry afresh, and Percy suspected I was angry at him for his late arrival. I was. For a brief moment, I saw a picture of my father who never fondled or held us, and I panicked. Would he love this child of his?

"You must hold her," I sobbed. "Grandma told me a story once which explained that father love and mother love must be shared evenly. It only happens when the father holds the baby before it is six hours old and kisses its little hands and feet and forehead."

"I never heard of such nonsense, but if that is what you and your Grandma believe . . . . I'll hold her whenever you say and I'll kiss her because no one knows better than I do that she's mine. I love her because I suffered for her as much or more than you did," Percy remarked proudly.

The kissing ritual over, Percy announced, "Why not name our baby after you? Norma is a pretty name. Two talented movie actresses, Shearer and Talmadge, carry that name. What do you say?" We had not discussed a name earlier, so I said, "Why not?"

Before Norma Jean was a week old, she let it be known that she wanted no cuddling, no fondling, no closeness. She seemed to accept that it was essential to be bathed and diapered and fed; but once her comforts were attended to, she pulled herself away from me as much as to say, "Leave me alone and do whatever else you have to do."

Lying there in that bed for ten days, I saw myself as a prisoner, a slave, a servant for the next eighteen years. My life, I feared, was no longer my own. I would have to be cook, nurse, laundress, seamstress, teacher, playmate, doctor, chaperone, everything. Even my child's guarantee of having a father to cherish her depended upon my ability to create and maintain a husband-wife, father-mother relationship that fosters a father-daughter, mother-daughter family bond. It would be a challenging, difficult role. I feared the ability to establish a home or to provide the ingredients so necessary for a full life.

The young children I knew in well-to-do homes where I had worked were given piano lessons and dancing lessons. They rode their ponies, went on ocean voyages, and took trips to the mountains. They had many supportive relatives and peers. We had no bevy of relatives or peer support. We were near misfits in the culture to which our skin color assigned us. My husband's salary of twenty-five dollars a week was a poor man's salary. I no longer saw myself supplementing our livelihood. My state teacher's certificate hung on the living room wall, but no school board would hire me for two reasons. First, I was a Negro, and second, being a married woman disqualified me. Few systems hired married women.

From some source and for many reasons, I wanted our child to have the best. But how was it to be done? She would be smart and become a scholar. Her father and I had already helped her by passing on to her good genes from past generations. Few of America's immigrant Caucasians had any better gene inheritance. I did not wish for her dolls and ponies and toys. I did not wish for her a childhood of plenty and fun. I realized that discipline, responsibility, study and labor were well-learned requisites for a meaningful existence. I would make her beautiful dresses and outfits so she could walk proud, knowing she looked "somebodyish." She would go to a good school, Catholic perhaps, where God and academics had a meaning and purpose. At home she would be introduced to all kinds of books (from the library, of course), and we would spend hours upon hours of reading and dramatization. Our daughter would be taught many household skills, and she would learn to earn, to budget, to save, and to plan for her wants. I saw the two-score years of child rearing that lay ahead for me as an endless series of responsibilities.

Our daughter entertained herself endlessly with the toys and playthings we supplied for her pleasure and her intellectual development. When she had amused herself to her satisfaction, she contentedly fell asleep making no demands of me, her mother. The rocking chair Grandma had given me saying, "This will be just right for you when you rock your baby," never was. I brushed aside my disappointment at not having a cuddly baby daughter and accepted her on her terms. From the very beginning we were young adult equals, my daughter and I. I talked aloud to her continuously. Before long I felt she enjoyed the tones and inflections of my voice with some understanding.

A typical one-way conversation filled with the thoughts racing through my mind went something like this: "I read in the paper this morning that the opera season is opening in Cleveland next month. It would be so nice to attend my first opera. I would love to see and hear Faust, Lohengrin and Aida, but it is impossible. Maybe some day your daddy and I will have a car to drive to Cleveland and back in an evening. We will need money, too. I do not even have an evening gown.

"Can you imaging what a handsome couple your daddy and I would make walking into the opera house? Your daddy would be stunning in a most expensive tuxedo from Richman Brothers Men's Store. My gown would be fashioned in sky blue satin, complemented with a long silver cape, silver slippers and elbow-length gloves. It would be nicer than anything I ever had before. For my junior and senior high school prom, my evening gown of pink lace was so cheap and tacky I was embarrassed and left the prom before it was over. I would show it to you, but I burned it in the coal stove years ago. Maybe I can draw you a picture of that hideous gown some day. It will make you laugh." I laughed, recalling the ugly dress.

"The next formal gown I wear will come from a store like Stern and Mann's. Believe it or not, I have never been inside that store. From the outside display windows, Stern and Mann's looks so exclusive and fashionable it is almost frightening. Some day I shall get up enough courage to go inside. I could buy a very pretty linen handkerchief just to look around. I may take you with me. Would you like that?

"Now where was I? I was talking about the opera, was I not? You are too young to go with us, but your daddy and I shall tell you all about it. I know what you and I can do. The public library has all kinds of books about operas. I can read the stories to you, and we can imagine that we are sitting in box seats at the Hannah Theater in Cleveland. Better still, we can imagine that we have taken a train to New York City and are way up in the third or fourth balcony of the Metropolitan Opera House."

As long as Norma Jean seemed entertained by my voice, I continued. "Would you like to go on a train ride some Sunday? I have been on a train two or three times, but you have not. Oh yes, you have—once. I was returning from Philadelphia, and I did not want to believe you were on the way. Do you remember that trip? I shall never forget it. I did not want to come back to Canton, ever. Canton had hurt me very, very much when I was denied a teaching job. I would not be married, I would not have you if I had been allowed to teach. But here I am with you, your father and a house of our own. I think your daddy is happy. I am not so sure about myself. Your daddy is always singing or whistling, 'Just Molly and me and baby makes three. I'm happy in my blue heaven.' He loves us."

I began to sing a verse or two and then stopped. I could never sing as my Mom had sung for so many years. Singing would not be my means of prayer or of releasing my frustrations. I was programmed for expressions of a different sort.

My monologue continued. "Now let's see. . . . I must get the housework done before your father comes home for lunch. Maybe you would like to have him feed you. Would you? Of course I shall have to nurse you first. He cannot do that. He can feed you some mashed vegetables, maybe spinach, the kind Popeye likes. Shall I prepare some? After lunch you must take a nice, long nap so I can get some other work done. When you awake around three o'clock, I shall dress you in one of your prettiest little outfits and we shall go to town to borrow some books from the library."

We had no baby buggy or a toddler's cart, so I carried Norma Jean on all of my excursions. I conversed with her while pointing out and describing dwellings, street names, conveyances, animals and people. When our daughter was two years old, she had a perfectly enunciated vocabulary of more than two thousand words.

XI

Shuggie

It was nearly a week after our daughter's birth when my mother came to our house to greet her first grandchild. She came alone as if to survey the premises—to see if my place was fit for the other children to enter.

I felt unclean, impure. I did not know whether to welcome her graciously or to tell her she was not welcome. For three months and three weeks, she and my sisters and brothers had daily passed on the other side of the street and never glanced in the direction of our house.

I could not have been more ignored in death. It hurt that my siblings had been forbidden to have anything to do with me. If during Mom's visit I behaved unseemly, I could invite a permanent alienation from my sisters and brothers. Cognizant that words once spoken of hurt, bitterness, anger and unforgiveness can never be unspoken, I bit my tongue and was discreetly polite.

Mom's ten- to fifteen-minute visits about once a week helped to narrow the gap between us. One by one with a small toy the other children came to see the baby.

Mom held Norma Jean in her arms and whispered over and over, "You are such a darling. You are just as sweet as a lump of sugar. What a precious little sugar plum!" I could not believe my ears.

Listening to Mom's endearments as she hugged and cradled my baby, who seemed to enjoy her attention, I pictured myself as her infant twenty-two years earlier. She must have held me in her arms and uttered the same endearments. If she could express such affection for my baby, she cared for me still. A cautious, but comforting, sort of warmth began to develop between us.

She called her granddaughter "Sugar." What better way to proclaim that the sweetness in her life had come through her babies. For some unfathomable reason, Mom was, and maybe always would be, a baby's mom. She did not know how to transfer to her young adult sons and daughters, so filled with confidence and determination, those same magnanimous expressions of caring, protection, teaching and accepting which she had so generously lavished upon her babies and growing children.

When Norma Jean first attempted to address her grandmother, the sound she uttered was "Shuggie." She could not distinctly say "Sugar." Amid peals of laughter we all called Mom, "Shuggie." The name "Shuggie" initiated a new relationship between her and me and between my sisters and brothers and me. As if by magic the new cognomen, uttered somewhat jestingly and gleefully, stripped her of her "momness" and created a new person. Her teenage sons and daughters politely, but purposefully, removed themselves from her central focus. They directed her loving attention to her grandbaby, who coined the endearing term "Shuggie." Progressively the hurtings between Mom and me began to heal.

My first meeting with my brother, Eugene, since that unfortunate spring morning a year and a half earlier came the day he wheeled the Singer sewing machine to my house saying, "Mom wants you to have this." We met as casually as if we had been seeing each other daily.

Eugene was a serious, almost sad, young man. At seventeen he looked so much like the father he never knew too well. In stature, in body build, in skin color, he could have been his father's clone. Eugene, however, lacked the sparkle and the hopeful anticipation that his father evidenced in his stride and bodily motion. I was greatly disturbed when I learned Eugene was quitting school in the eleventh grade.

"I have been working at Brookside Country Club as a caddy, groundskeeper, and odd-job man since I was nine years old. I have taken this job as chauffeur for this wealthy industrialist. He has been a fairly decent man on the golf course and around the club. I have never heard him swear or curse. He doesn't tell jokes and he has never referred to me as Sambo or boy," Eugene explained. "I have always been Mr. Eugene to him."

"You have always been a good student, too. Don't you think you should graduate from high school?" I hesitatingly inquired.

"A high school education can hurt more than help when you are a Negro. I don't need to have studied high school mathematics, science and foreign languages to drive and wash automobiles or mow the lawns on some huge estate. Neither is it necessary to work as a laborer in the steel mills. If I had the education you have, high school and two years of college and could not get a suitable job, I would kill myself or kill the person standing in my way."

Eugene's voice was filled with hurt, anger and pessimism. Was he trying to tell me he was sorry for my situation?

"You should not talk like that," I rebuked. "No one is keeping me from anything! Just wait until our baby is older. I shall do the kind of work I want to do, and nobody will stop me."

"Well, maybe. You always did have a lot of guts. I just don't see that much good in the world right now."

"You will, and I hope you will like this new job. Your Uncle Eugene enjoyed his work as a chauffeur. You will look just as handsome in a uniform as he did. How well do you remember your Uncle Eugene? I guess you don't. He died when you were about eight years old." What more could I say?

Eugene came by the house once in a while looking dapper in his chauffeur uniform. Sometimes he played with his little niece. At other times he chatted with his brother-in-law. He never had much to talk about, however. In that respect, he was very much like Pop.

A year later, Carl was thinking about leaving school before graduation. Brookside employed him after school and on weekends. He assisted the caddy master. He was learning to mix drinks at the bar, and he was called upon to wait tables. Carl, somewhat taller than his older brother, had a disposition very much like his Uncle Eugene and his Grandfather Evans. The little "lover boy" of infancy and early childhood was a self-confident, self-assured young man who could smile his way into the hearts of all who glanced at him a second time.

Carl had dreams of owning a business of his own. "I want to go into business as soon as I can. I favor a golf course environment and have visions of a plush dining room and bar somewhere, some day. Even the idea of a restaurant is exciting. The courses taught in high school have very little relevance to my work interest," Carl reasoned.

"I need to know how to cook. There is a lot for me to learn about foods. Brookside has taught me that there are more foods than hamburg and chicken and boiled potatoes and gravy. I want to learn about the choice cuts of beef and a variety of vegetables. I need to know the nutritional value of foods and how long they can be stored and at what temperatures. People are still talking about the poison olive episode at the Courtland Hotel in 1919 when seven people died of food poisoning. Handling food is not for amateurs.

"There are some hotel and restaurant management training schools in New York and Philadelphia. If I quit school,

I can work full-time and begin to save the money to go East. There is plenty of work at Brookside, and I am not too picky about doing whatever needs to be done."

Carl picked my brains about my job at the tea room in Philadelphia. Would I give him the names of people I had met? Would some of the people who worked with me be willing to rent him a room temporarily? "You know," he said one day, "you have had some darn good cooking experiences. If you never get to teach, or even if you do, why not consider managing a first class dining room with me? It could be a family venture—you and me, and Eugene and Percy. If Percy is as good with figures as you say, he could be the treasurer, accountant and paymaster. I would want to handle the golf course and golf promotion. Eugene would manage the lodge and you, the dining room. We should plan on it, big sister. Dreams do come true, they say."

Ethel was never mentioned in Carl's dreams of becoming a business tycoon. Ethel's plans had other directions. Mrs. J. B. Walker, the founder and executive director of the Phyllis Wheatly Association, became Ethel's friend, role model and part-time employer.

The wife of the first Negro physician in the Canton area was a most impressive community minded socialite. More Caucasian in appearance than Negro, she championed the cause of the neglected working girl by establishing a residence on South Market Avenue, just seven blocks from the public square. She worked with an influential board of wealthy whites and respectable middle class Negroes. Within this impressive resident structure, Etna T. Walker's program provided training in job skills, personal counseling and exposure to social graces. Some community gatherings had access to the meeting room facilities at the Phyllis Wheatly Home.

From her job as a city playground supervisor, Ethel was sought to be in charge of some youth activities under Mrs.

Walker's guidance. Ethel organized a Negro History Club of nearly twenty high school juniors and seniors. "It is a shame that not only I, but the teachers who taught us, know so little about our history," Ethel would lament as she told me about the books, plays and poetry her eager club members literally devoured.

Ethel had had fewer experiences as a servant for white families. I attributed a certain dignity she carried as not having been conditioned to the restrained compliant demeanor of a cook or house servant. Ethel was less assertive, less spontaneous than me. She was selective, proper and dignified. She appeared to be more cooperative, more anxious to please Shuggie than I had been.

She took advantage of her affiliation with the Phyllis Wheatly Association, however, to break away from home gradually. She spent many nights at the Association, making herself available to chaperone a youth gathering, assist at a dinner meeting or substitute for the night matron. She would explain to Shuggie that it was best not to walk home alone late at night.

My relationship with Ethel consisted of polite, superficial salutations. "Hello, how is my little niece? I brought her a little gift I hope she enjoys. What do you think of this? Just read the most interesting book on Negro history. Would you like to borrow it? Mrs. Walker is a fantastic woman. Some people label her as a little snobbish, but I see her as a real lady. She is teaching me so much about a great many things. I like her!"

I had a feeling that, to Ethel and to Mrs. Walker, my marriage to Percy placed us outside the realm of approved, promising Negro couples. We could never make the Negro "400." I had goofed. I had not married a college man. I had married a porter from the dreaded state of Mississippi, no less. In just a matter of time it would be seen how badly I had goofed.

Ethel was preparing to depart for Howard University in Washington, D.C., the alma mater of Dr. and Mrs. J. B. Walker. She had been assured a job at Catholic University which would provide room and board in exchange for her services. Like me, she had saved enough money to cover two semesters of tuition and books. Eternally optimistic and determined, she hoped some opportunity would present itself to take care of the second year's tuition.

Ruth, eight years younger than Ethel, was the one child who wanted to be like her mom. She declared she would marry some day and have twelve babies. Ruth could describe in detail the large brick house, with two bathrooms, which she planned to live in. She pored over magazines and the Sears and Roebuck catalog to visualize her fantasies. Ruth was a pleasant, docile girl until someone rebuked her or got in her way. Then she could become as stubborn as a mule and as immovable as a brick wall.

She was approaching her thirteenth birthday. The valvular leakage of her heart caused her to complain of tiredness and shortness of breath. Doctors Hart and Walker warned Mom that the onset of Ruth's menses could cause her death. "She ought not to continue at Lincoln High School, climbing up and down stairs every hour of the day. Her heart condition already appears to be worsening. She is literate enough to get along in this world. She can do light work and help you around the house. She must never consider marriage, should she reach maturity. A pregnancy would be fatal."

Mom immediately withdrew Ruth from school at the beginning of her ninth grade. Ethel and I had some apprehension about this diagnostic arrangement that Mom welcomed so readily. I foresaw that Ruth would become Mom's permanent baby girl. Mom could make sure that one of her four daughters would never date, never marry and never leave home.

Virginia, the youngest of the Snipes children, was an

excellent student. Albeit she reaped the harvest of a "good family" reputation, she had some qualities her older brothers and sisters did not demonstrate. She was more spontaneous and less inhibited. She was outgoing in making friends and expressing her opinions. Unlike her older brothers and sisters, who paired off, two boys and two girls, she and Ruth were never close. Being alone as she was, Virginia was delightfully self-assured. I rather envied her independence and self-confidence. I wished I had had a chance to know her better. I was the oldest, she the youngest. With twelve years between us, we had not shared the same experiences in our growing up years in the same family.

Ruth and Virginia seldom came by the house. When they did, it was a ten-minute visit to fondle the baby. I never asked them to baby-sit, never asked them to run an errand to the store, or help me with a household task. Part of "sleeping in my own bed" was not to ask any favors and not to accept even the least assistance from any member of my family.

I had resolved after that first encounter with my mother upon my return to Canton that no situation would ever persuade me to return to my childhood home or to ask for help. No financial problem, no emotional marriage situation, no disillusionment, no physical distress or boredom would change my mind. I would never return home to ask a favor or to hear the words, "You asked for it." "It is your problem, solve it!" It was Percy and me against the world. We would make it together or we would go our separate ways alone.

My resolve to be a friend to my sisters and brothers was off to a good start. A comfortable warmth was developing between us.

Shuggie had put aside her washtubs and the paraphernalia connected with her nearly ten years of home laundry. She had also given up her day work customers for several evening office cleaning jobs. The evening work hours were shorter, the jobs more dependable, and the pay scale nearly double that of the day worker's fifty cents an hour wage.

Forty dollars from four regular office jobs of approximately twenty hours a week was twice the salary of a day worker for five eight hour days. Mom found that three evenings a week from 6 to 9 or 7 to 10 p.m. could net her a substantial income. With her day hours her very own, she was experiencing a freedom she had not known in nearly twenty-five years.

Shuggie opened a small neighborhood convenience store on the northeast corner of Eighth Street and Liberty Avenue Southeast. The store room, which had been a shoe repair shop attached to a residence, measured about eight by fifteen feet. Shuggie's limited stock was canned goods, fresh bread, soaps and house cleaning items, some Watkins products of medicine, spices and toiletries, and a large supply of candies, gum and trinket toys such as balloons and windmill twirlers.

Between the two candy cases to the left and the right of the center aisle, there was just enough room for two people to walk abreast to the serving counter. It was an attractive, inviting little store even with its half-filled shelves. The cash register was a wooden cigar box that Shuggie carried home daily to count the day's receipts. She stopped by my house early one evening, ostensibly to cuddle her granddaughter, but in reality she had a burning comment to make.

"Look at this," she began, lifting the lid of the cigar box cash register and displaying hundreds of pennies, an equal number of nickels, a few quarters and several one-and-two-dollar bills. "I am glad I taught you kids not to spend every cent you put your hands on at the corner grocery store.

"Morning, noon and afternoon, my little store is jammed with kids, little kids hardly big enough to reach the candy counter. Eagerly they point to their candy preference clamoring, 'I want this. I want that one. I want two of these.'"

"Your business is going well, I gather," I interjected cautiously.

"Oh, yes, except that ninety percent of my customers are children. Their parents go where they can get credit. They pay cash for junk, but they expect to be given credit for bread and milk and eggs and potatoes. I just do not understand poor people's spending habits. These are poor kids. Their parents make the lowest wages when they are employed. Many of them are on relief. I feel guilty taking their pennies."

"That is why you are in business, Shuggie, to make money, hopefully lots of it," I offered.

"I did not expect it to be like this. The parents of these kids encourage their children to enjoy themselves and have fun. They hand over to their offspring pennies and nickels to spend right away. They have no plans for tomorrow or next week or next year, and that is sad. I get no pleasure from my day's work when I feel I am contributing to the continued poverty of the colored family."

"Do you think that Charlie Strausser or Cohens or Maggiores feel that way? Business is business." I tried not to speak argumentatively.

"You may be right. I may give up my store one of these days. I think it would be nice to move to a place such as Cleveland. There ought to be some decent jobs there for a woman my age," Mom concluded.

I wanted to expand upon her last remark and tell her how beautiful she was and how all of her children would like to see her get married again. She should be taken care of like a queen. She should not be leaving her home to go to work. I did not express any such thoughts. Shuggie kissed her grandbaby and crossed the street to home, to count her pennies and nickels and to wonder about the spending habits of poor people.

XII

Like Father— Like Daughter?

Months before our daughter reached her second birthday, I was bored to tears with my confinement to the house and its routine duties. The only weekly diversion was an occasional Sunday service in one of several different protestant churches, and a Sunday afternoon movie. I did not have the wardrobe to feel at ease in the churches. It was humiliating to walk to the front of the church, procession like, to place a clanging quarter in the collection plate while others noted your Sunday apparel. For a twenty-five cent theater admission, no one looked at my clothing. I could keep in touch with world events and view other cultures.

Almost daily I carried the baby over to Grandma and Grandpa's house to give them the pleasure of holding their great granddaughter. Mrs. Tabbs, the neighbor who befriended me prior to my trip to Philadelphia, came by our home occasionally. Each time she generously offered to baby-sit for us. "Any time you and Percy want to go out for an evening, let me know. I'll be happy to care for your little one." That invitation was stored away for a later acceptance.

My husband and I knew no young married couples our age. Shuggie and my sisters and brothers were still keeping their distance from me and me from them. I never crossed the street for an afternoon or evening visit.

I recall one evening I was particularly lonely. Night after night I sat at home waiting for Percy to come in from the pool hall. It was nearly ten o'clock. The houses on Fifth Street, already darkened and silenced, proclaimed that decent, respectable, hard-working family people retired soon after nine o'clock even on a warm summer night. I was alone and so unfulfilled. I became angry. If my husband could not come home to me and his baby, we would go to the pool hall that fascinated him so.

Careful not to awaken Norma Jean from her sleep, I threw a lightweight blanket around her and headed for the corner of Cherry Avenue and Sixth Street Southeast. The deserted street and the calm of the night tempered my anger somewhat, but I would not return home to wait. Even carrying a twenty-five pound, fifteen-month-old child in my arms, I walked that mile in ten minutes.

Once in the area of Walnut Avenue and Sixth Street, the near-midnight activity was that of high noon. Autos and limousines cruised lazily from one street, one alley to another. I passed little groups of men and women giggling and whispering on corners and on porch steps that hugged the sidewalks. They came from other areas of town. They did not belong there. Neither did I. I was too angry to worry about that.

As I approached the pool hall, I resolved not to create a scene. I would not walk in and surprise my husband with an embarrassing confrontation. I stood outside and knocked. Nothing happened. I knocked again, this time much louder, hoping to pierce the noise within. A wizened five-foot gentleman, whose name I later learned was Crip, came to the door. He walked with a pronounced limp.

"Is my husband, Percy Marcere, here?" I asked, peering into a friendly dark brown countenance.

"I will look and see, ma'am," he politely answered, leaving

the door half ajar.

Loud noises shrouded behind dense clouds of tobacco smoke began to quiet down and I heard Percy say, "This is it for tonight, boys, my wife is outside and it's time for me to head home. Can't keep the little lady waiting. See you later."

Percy greeted me with a "Hi there" and closed the pool hall door. Fifty feet away he said, "You know, you have no business being out on the street at this time of night. It's not safe!"

I did not answer. The situation was ripe for a quarrel, the kind that I had heard between Mom and Pop. Mom would have said, "Why don't you come home like a decent husband and father? You never pay any attention to your family. You don't care about anyone but yourself!"

I kept quiet. We walked up Cherry Avenue to Third Street and from there, west to Market Avenue. Why were we taking such a circuitous route, I wondered. Maybe it was to avoid the pimp and prostitute activity on Fourth, Fifth and Sixth Streets, some of which I had unknowingly glimpsed on my way to the pool hall.

I was carrying our daughter. She had stirred and she was heavy. As we crossed Market, I said to Percy, "Here, you take the baby. She is heavy and I am tired."

"You carried her to town and you can carry her back. It will teach you to stay home where you belong."

Oh, how I would have liked to have quarreled, but what would I say? Something to hurt him? I could insult him because he was not a college graduate, a professional man. I could call him a pool hall bum. I could ridicule his small paychecks. I could slander his southern background, but words once spoken could never be unspoken.

I had overheard Mom call Pop a "dirty, black nigger" once and I never forgot it. No matter how much she lectured to us about being free of prejudice, I wondered. She must have had some reservations about dark skin in order to verbalize her thoughts with such venom. I had been hurt deeply by her remark, and Pop must have been, too. I made a vow that night, as a child, that I would never hurt a human being with a criticism over which he or she had no control. I kept my mouth shut.

In my marriage relationship, I was still reluctant to use the expression "I love you," but I liked my husband too much to demean him.

We crossed Cleveland Avenue and were approaching McKinley Avenue. I pleaded, "Percy, your daughter is awfully heavy. Take her. I can't carry her any farther."

"You heard what I said. No!" he declared firmly.

The Washington Hotel was on the corner of McKinley and Third Street. We passed it and were approaching Leahy's Grocery Store. I walked hurriedly ahead of Percy and deposited Norma Jean on the two-step entrance to this cozily abandoned store shadowed by the hotel and surrounded by porch-to-porch two-story rooming houses. When Percy came within ten feet of the entrance, I shouted, piercing the silence of a deserted street, "There is your daughter! Pick her up or leave her there. I don't care!"

I then ran faster than I had ever run in my life. I ran south on High to Fourth Street, then over to Fifth Street, across the B&O railroad tracks and home at 1405. Once inside the unlocked house (we never used a key), I rushed upstairs breathless and panting to the unfinished middle bedroom and hid in a corner.

Percy came in the house five minutes or so later. I could hear him as he and his daughter retired. I slept on the floor in that empty room. Early the next morning, I tiptoed downstairs. I was preparing breakfast when Percy appeared, carrying our daughter.

"Well, look who's here," he began, as he placed his daughter in her high chair. "I thought I'd have to fix breakfast and take Norma Jean to work with me this morning."

Cooing tenderly to his daughter, he continued, "Mommy has a nice breakfast for you, so like the little baby bear, 'eat it all up.' Be good for Mommy while Daddy's at work."

He turned to me and announced, "I won't be coming home at noon today. I heard last night that Mr. Lefkovitz at the Parisian Clothing Store is looking for a porter. I'm going to apply for the job. Wish me luck."

He left. There would never be any serious quarreling in our home. I was convinced of that. The incident of the evening before and a combination of circumstances and feelings gave birth to a revelation and a resolve. I needed a job. I had to get out of the house several hours each day or keep exhaustingly busy inside of the house. How many times could I turn around in a six-room house with just three of its rooms furnished and keep busy? Besides that, I had no money. It was a useless, helpless feeling. I thought of opening a day nursery in our home.

If I was to be entrapped with the care of our daughter for an indeterminate number of years, if my husband was not going to share his companionship with me in the evenings after his work day, then I needed to do something. If I worked to the point of physical exhaustion and mental stimulation, that would make me indifferent to whether he came home or not.

My college courses in child development made every activity with my daughter meaningful and purposeful. Not only could I earn some money with my education, but I could help teach and train other children whose parents were rearing them by instinct only. I could easily care for as many as ten children in our house.

The still unfurnished dining room and the two empty bedrooms on the second floor would provide adequate space for a nursery school. Working mothers earning four dollars a day in domestic service ought to be willing to pay fifty cents for the professional care of a child, one year to five years of age.

Percy was most cooperative. He brought home orange crates from the uptown fruit and vegetable markets. He added to my list of bright colored paints and enamels the necessary construction tools I needed. I built tables, toy chests, benches, and even a cradle for the anticipated children for my nursery. Sleeping pads were made from two bath towels sewn together with cotton batting inside.

Woolworth's Five and Ten Cent Store was the purchasing center for a variety of practical and inexpensive supplies. Story books, coloring books, crayons, rubber balls, blocks, harmonicas, baby rattles, two little teddy bears and several baby dolls were stored neatly in the orange, green, yellow, blue and red toy chest compartments.

The Urban League executive enthusiastically announced the opening of my nursery and preschool program by passing out leaflets in the Southeast vicinity. In September of 1933, I waited for days for a gratifying enrollment. Three mothers each brought a child, one time. That was it! The let down was disappointing. I was defeated.

Percy explained my colossal failure. "If we lived in the southeast section of town instead of the southwest, your nursery would have had a better chance of getting off the ground. Your 'would-be' customers must pay two bus fares to ride from their home here, back to the square and then to their jobs. To leave their homes with squirming children at least an hour earlier and arrive home that much later in the evening is too inconvenient. Most working mothers have grandparents close by who can watch their babies. They're not like us. Remember? Our parents are a thousand miles away, or at least we function as if they were.

"Your nursery school was, and still is, a good idea; but it won't work. Not just now. Forget it as long as we live in this section of town and the kids you want to serve live in another section of town."

For weeks after the nursery school failure, I floundered around like a chicken with its head cut off. My loss of direction was heightened by the Depression which was still with us. Percy was only working part-time and earning fourteen dollars a week. He was working out the twenty-five dollar a month rent with four days of work each month at the Schneider Lumber and Storage Company, our landlord. He enjoyed this new work experience. Still there were food, clothing, gas, electric, coal heat, medical bills and an unpaid furniture bill to meet. Our income would not stretch.

My flounderings pointed me in the direction of the postmaster and the county commissioners for job possibilities. Postmaster Elsaesser gave me information about federal civil service examinations. The Stark County commissioners gave me state civil service forms for juvenile court jobs.

In between submitting applications and taking civil service examinations, I heard about a three-dollar-a-week child care job and took it. A young mother engaged in a sales job needed a young adult to care for her fifteen-month-old son from 9:00 a.m. to 1:00 p.m. I could take Norma Jean with me. Aside from preparing a noon meal, there was very little housework to do. I was back home by 1:30.

On the pretense of going to the library, I kept this job rendezvous from Percy for nearly a month. When he became suspicious of the daily library visits which left him to his noon meal alone, he came to the library looking for me. He was upset to learn I was not there. When he questioned my whereabouts, I revealed my baby-sitting job.

Percy scolded me soundly. "My wife is never to go to work in a white woman's kitchen. Remember that! You shame me!

You rob me of my dignity as a man. Things will get better in time. I shall never object to your doing the kind of work for which you are trained. Please be patient. You have a whole lifetime ahead of you. Don't be in such a hurry! Now phone this woman immediately and tell her she must seek other help."

I did so and continued my agency rounds. The Family Service and Children's Bureau eagerly accepted my application for foster home care. Immediately we received into our home a three-year-old girl, one year older than our daughter. My husband agreed because as he said, "I have a foster father role to play as important as yours."

With the twenty dollars a month from the Foster Care Agency, I was able to spend at least half toward much needed furniture. The large middle bedroom shared by our daughter and Ella Mae became the prettiest room in the house with its junior-size twin beds and children's furniture.

We began to search for furniture for the third bedroom when Percy's cousin, Eva Burwell from Meridian, Mississippi, came to live with us. Unemployment and marital problems caused Eva to look to his favorite cousin for help and advice. If he could find employment in Canton, an industrial city, perhaps he could entice his wife to bring their two children north and start a new life together.

Eva, a congenial soft-spoken gentleman, was a pleasant addition to our home. Daily he walked from one end of Canton to another, applying for work and offering to do odd jobs for as little as twenty-five cents an hour. He generously gave me a portion of his meager earnings toward his board and related expenses. From his contributions, I was able to purchase a yard of pretty material now and then to make a dress for my daughter. I designed all of her clothing and took great pride that she had a morning and afternoon outfit for every day in the week. Between the garments the social agency supplied

Ella Mae, and the dresses I made for Norma Jean, the outdoor clothesline looked like a style show preview of what the best-dressed two- and three-year old little girls were wearing. I laundered three times a week and spent hours over the ironing board transforming starched dresses and petticoats into garments of unwrinkled perfection.

I never pedaled my treadle sewing machine during the day. My daylight hours with my daughter and foster child were preciously devoted to reading, games, trips to the park and supervised play activities. My sewing began after the children retired at about 7:30 in the evening. I sewed often until nearly midnight or until Percy came home. I could make a complete outfit in one evening. I consoled myself that I knew where my husband was, that he was not having an affair with another woman and that the Depression was creating frustrations that birthed aberrant behavior.

One evening Percy brought home some winnings he had made in a game of chance at the pool hall.

"Here, take this," he said. "Buy yourself something nice. I wanted to buy you flowers, your favorite gardenia, but I know you have other needs."

I refused it. "We can't live by chance!" I told him. "If you think I am going to get excited about a ten dollar or a fifty dollar winner's payoff, you are mistaken. No money comes into this house which is not the result of honest labor. So take your money back to the pool hall and leave it there! Now, who is impatient? Have I ever complained about your earnings? Just bring your paycheck home. I shall manage, no matter how small it may be."

I was sure Percy continued to gamble and play the numbers after he had given me his pay minus his share, but I never questioned him about his winnings or his losses.

With two built-in baby sitters, my husband and his cousin Eva, I announced I was enrolling in a Kent State Extension course one night a week at McKinley High School. It would be another step toward that bachelor's degree in education.

"You go to the pool hall for a change of scenery, to rap with the boys and to relax," I told Percy, and then continued, "I have a right to go to night school for a change of scenery, to rap with classmates and to relax my style." There was no dissent.

The money for my tuition and books came in part from the five dollars a month Grandma was paying me for doing the daily bed linens that Grandpa soiled. Grandpa was now 91 years old and had taken to his bed. I would go over to the house early in the morning, gather up the soiled articles and take them home for laundering in my recently acquired Maytag washer.

The next morning I would return carrying fresh linens. I would help Grandma bathe Grandpa, settle him in a chair and feed him. Then I made a fresh bed. Often I shaved him with his straight razor before hurrying home to be there before the children awakened.

Whenever I took Norma Jean with me, Grandpa would hold her on his lap and thank God he had lived long enough to know the third generation of his seed.

Grandma was in perfect health at age 81. She and I continued to have a talkative relationship about world events, race relations, morality and sex. She made a statement once which I, at 23, was too naive or too young to comprehend. "A young woman, if she is wise, would be better off to marry a man ten years her junior, instead of ten years her senior. A woman is forever young, and if she is not, she can pretend. An old man is good for nothing, nothing at all!" she declared.

While Grandpa spent many solitary hours in bed, broken only by visits from Shuggie, his grandchildren and two or three faithful neighbors, Grandma made jellies and preserves, knitted, quilted and read the Bible. She enjoyed a good discussion about the judgment of a sinful nation and the coming of the end of the world.

"It is such a wicked world. It is not only the divorces and crimes I read about in the newspaper," she would say. "The things which go on up and down this little street are a disgrace. When I read the book of Revelation, I think the end of the world is near, very near."

As I listened to Grandma enumerate her observations, I would comment, "I hope not, Grandma. I do not want the world to end. I am just beginning my life and there is so much I want to do."

But life came to an end for two people in our family in 1933. Grandpa died at age 92. Grandma greeted me one morning and told me Grandpa was breathing heavily and that he would leave us before the day was over. I rushed to tell Shuggie and to make sure the children, Norma Jean and Ella Mae, would be cared for. Grandma and Shuggie watched the departure of the last Evans in the family. There had been no sons of his sons to carry on the family name. We, his four granddaughters and two grandsons, the only offspring of one daughter, bade farewell to the dearest image of a father, our grandfather.

Grandpa had instilled patriotism and pride in our heritage by his stories of our freedom before the Civil War. He made us proud that, as a freed man, he fought against slavery and to preserve the nation. "One nation indivisible, with liberty and justice for all," he reminded us. He taught us to love our fellow man, all men. "Hate no one ever!" he had told us. "Never hate!"

Virginia relates how she begged to spend the night sleeping on the floor alongside Grandpa's casket in the little living room. It was a tearless, reverent farewell to a man who had been a giant of a man, a father substitute to his grandchildren.

Aunt Clella and her husband came from Sharon, Pennsylvania to attend the funeral. They insisted Grandma return with them. Before leaving, Grandma signed her little home over to Mom.

It was a warm summer evening a few months later when Ruth and Virginia came to my house and announced, "Shuggie wants you to come over right away. She has a letter about Pop!"

At home Shuggie had gathered those of us who were still in town around her at the dining room table. "This newspaper clipping," she began, "came in the mail today. Your Pop is dead. He died in a Detroit hospital. I do not know who sent this notice. There is no name or address. I do not know when he died. The newspaper clipping has no date. His age is listed here as forty-five, which is not exactly correct."

What could any of us say? Shuggie had always hoped, even prayed, that Pop would return some day and express his pride in his children. One sentence before he died, "Ida, you did a good job rearing our children," would have repaid her for all her toil, her sacrifices, her celibacy, her loneliness. In their twilight years, they could, Mom and Pop, have reviewed what went wrong with their marriage and tried to make amends.

I had witnessed Mom's Gethsemane some ten or eleven years earlier. This final separation would not be as severe. Her husband had removed himself from her life and she had prayed to God to remove the hurt, the pain, the embarrassment and the emptiness from her. Still she had to feel cheated. I felt for her. The youngest, Ruth and Virginia, had no memories of their Pop. Can one miss a parent one has never known? The boys, Eugene and Carl, had three or four years exposure to their father when they shared a working environment at Brookside Country Club. I never knew how Ethel felt about Pop; but as for me, I was angry about his death.

He had no right to die before getting in touch with his children, me in particular. He must have known I thought a lot of him. I was his oldest. I had been named after him. I used to walk beside him on the way to high school. I went to the country club to beg him to come back home when he left us during my seventh grade in school. Did he ever know he had a granddaughter named after him and me? "Why, Pop?" I wanted to scream aloud. "Why?" But I said nothing.

None of us said a word. What could we say? There was that shock and disbelief that accompanies the realization of a permanent loss. Shuggie would write to the hospital, ask for some information and request a death certificate. Life would go on. There were still two teenaged daughters to rear with the same intensity and devotion she had expended upon her other four children.

Life does go on and something I had not thought about was a second pregnancy. By mid-winter I was aware our second child was on the way. I was so busy trying to keep our heads above water that I did not really care one way or the other. The nine-month gestation period was uneventful. I was disgustingly healthy. As before, there was no morning sickness, no discomfort whatever. For all that Percy had bragged about his "father-to-be" signals with my first pregnancy, he was not so inconvenienced this time.

In an effort to distance myself from captivity, I grasped at every thought-provoking activity I could find. From dawn till midnight I was on a treadmill of motion. I entered every competition that promised dollars for a skill. I solved puzzles, wrote poetry, made up recipes, designed budgets, created short stories and used my art skill in drawing pictures and magazine covers. I sought every outlet of expression that would assure me I was intellectually alive and optimistic about the future. I even sewed, crocheted and embroidered a complete layette of baby clothes.

One week before the birth of our son, all of our furniture, the three-room package deal for newlyweds that we had purchased in 1930, was repossessed. I surveyed our hapless plight, wobbling with my misshapen body from room to room. My swollen feet were encased in my husband's house slippers, the only foot covering large enough for them. I was a prisoner of mother nature and all of the societal forces that declared, "No job, no income, no future, no nothing!"

The living room furniture was gone and our bedroom was empty. The kitchen stove had been removed and only a capped gas line protruded from the floor. A kitchen table and two chairs stood accusingly in the middle of the kitchen. I had quickly hidden these three items under some trash in the laundry room telling the repossessor they had been broken and discarded nearly a year ago. This furniture, missing two chairs, seemed to shout at me, "Thief! Liar!"

In addition to the children's well-furnished bedroom and Eva's cot surrounded by nursery school furniture, our possessions included Grandma's rocking chair, Shuggie's sewing machine, an ice box and a washing machine. What we needed immediately was a double bed, a cook stove and a couple of chairs. Now both the living room and dining room echoed thunderously the hollow sounds of emptiness.

Percy and I slept on the living room floor. He was humiliated and apologetic. "I never thought we'd come to this, but we'll make it. Our second baby won't be born on the floor. Eva and I have a few more back alley stores to check out tomorrow. I can't get any credit from a regular store. I've tried them all. The word of repossessed furniture goes out and all credit is cut off. What angers me is that our furniture was taken with only thirty dollars unpaid. For three years they smiled in my face when I regularly made the twelve dollar a month payments. We won't ever buy another piece of furniture on credit again. Everything we buy in the future will be an out-and-out cash deal or we'll do without."

If the Foster Children's Agency had known we were in such

straits they could have removed our foster child, thus eliminating that twenty-dollar-a-month remuneration. I hoped neither the caseworker nor Shuggie would decide to call. How would I explain a living room and dining room both with no furniture? I shuddered at the thought of someone making a comment or asking questions about our plight.

My worry was unfounded because no one from home had been near the house since my second pregnancy became obvious. It was distasteful for a pregnant woman to exhibit her condition in public or for an unmarried miss to be seen in the company of a woman in a "family way." There would be no family visitors until a respectable time had elapsed after the baby's birth.

On August 8, Percy and Eva could be seen walking down Fifth Street behind an old fellow hauling a brass bed on a junk hand cart. It was a ridiculous and embarrassing sight. They approached the house noisily and unloaded everything—bedposts, coiled springs and mattress—on the front porch. I inspected the mattress and springs minutely. I was so afraid of bed bugs that I would have sent the outfit back and continued to sleep on the floor had there been any evidence of that bloodsucking insect.

The brass bed, thoroughly scrubbed, was set up in the still unfurnished dining room. Properly adorned in fresh linen, it became a pretty sight. A coverlet over the sewing machine made it appear as a night stand. The very next day, on August 9, the ugliest looking rusted kerosene stove was delivered by the same old man. He deposited this two burner monstrosity in the middle of the kitchen without my inspection. I wanted no part of it. As long as the weather was warm, we could live on canned baked beans, tomatoes from the garden, bread and butter and milk.

After such a meal, I went into labor early in the evening of August 10, 1934. As I walked the floor taking count of the spasms, Percy and Eva tried frantically to heat water on a stubborn, smoking, rusty kerosene stove. I heard Eva say, "Damn, there's no kerosene in this thing. Where can I get kerosene this late at night?"

"Down on Cherry Avenue on the corner of Sixth Street or Tenth Street," Percy answered.

"I've only a dime. Better give me a little more change and a container of some kind," Eva begged. He then hurried to town.

I wondered why we had to heat water. There was already hot water in the tank. Dr. M. B. Williams and the same Metropolitan Insurance nurse of three and a half years ago arrived simultaneously. Assured my labor pains were minutes apart, Doctor announced, "I have another expectant mother also about to deliver. I must go to her. I shall return in time. Your nurse is here. You are in good hands."

With a word or two to the nurse, Dr. Williams left. I could hear and smell a pot of coffee boiling away on the reluctant smoking kerosene stove. Eva had gone upstairs to watch the three- and four-year-olds in case they stirred.

Percy remained with me during this birth. I thought of the scripture, "Yea, though I walk through the valley of the shadow of death, I will fear no evil for You are with me." I held onto Percy's hand and was overjoyed that his grip was so comforting, so reassuring. Birth was no mystery complicated with curiosity this second time around. I was only too willing to "push" and get it over with. I ignored the nurse's urging to "relax and hold back until the doctor returns."

Our eight-and-one-half-pound infant son was born ten minutes before Dr. Williams returned. My husband had shared the valley of the shadow with me and revealed a loving tenderness I was embarrassed to witness.

It took us nearly a week to name our son. I was the stubborn one, suggesting every name under the heavens to which Percy said, "No." Finally, with a note of annoyance, he questioned, "If our daughter is named after you, why can't our son be named after me? I know you think 'Percy' is a sissy name and that the owner of such a name is likely to be teased and taunted. A man is a man. A name cannot change that. Am I less a man because my name is Percy? Look at my cousin, Eva. Is he less a man because his name is also a woman's name?"

"You have an uncanny way of reading my thoughts when not a single word has been spoken. How did you know?" I conceded.

"Well, you don't hide your thoughts very well. The expression on your face shouts every thought you are thinking. Suppose we put my middle name first and let 'Percy' be our son's middle name. How does Alluren Percy Marcere sound to you?" my husband questioned.

"That is perfect! So distinguished, so unusual. I like that. Both of our children have beautiful uncommon names," I concluded.

We called our son Al for short and for nearly three years he was also known to our immediate family and friends as "Jew Boy." Al had a head full of black curls and he looked as much like a brown-skinned Ethiopian or Israelite as an American Negro. Some years later we tried to analyze why we had nicknamed him "Jew Boy." We saw the Jew as a despised individual who was never defeated, never conquered. He was indestructible, brilliant and resourceful, one of God's chosen people. Subconsciously I wanted our son to have all of those Jewish qualities: dignity and the determination not to be subdued. "Jew Boy" embodied a role model and an endearment.

In the '60s, Percy and I might have attached the letters M. L. K. to a son or grandson. Martin Luther King and his determination to overcome in a spirit of nonviolence became a contemporary Black role model and hero. Martin Luther King changed the term black from a lower case adjective to Black, a proper noun designating a race of people. Where once we cringed at the name-calling black, we could now hold our heads high and say with pride, "I am a Black."

Our son was the warm, cuddly, snuggling baby I had missed in our daughter. Grandma's rocking chair went into overtime activity making up for three and a half years of neglect. At feeding time, nap time, bedtime and for many minutes after, I could hold Al in my arms. I could rock as softly as though we were gliding on the soft waves of a pond, or rock as though we were soaring high in the air on a garden swing. I experienced joyfully that closeness, that trust, that total dependency of one human being upon another. I needed every moment of this shared communion, for disturbing thoughts and feelings were beginning to stir within me.

I had handled my second pregnancy as calmly and as resignedly as my first pregnancy. Both were unanticipated and, therefore, to a degree, unwanted. I would not have drunk a glass of water to undo what was begun; but I was thinking, and thinking hard. The result was a very determined decision.

I would never bear another child. No longer would I depend upon diagnostic predictions about my husband's sterility. My husband would have to protect me from any more children or release me from our marriage. I subscribed fully to the Catholic church's teachings that sex was for the procreation of life, so I was faced with a choice.

My willingness to consider forfeiting my marriage was not a declaration of selfishness, but a fear of poverty. I was becoming convinced the society I lived in was unjust to its Negro citizens. Society wanted to see its ex-slaves re-enslaved, underemployed, underinvolved, and on the periphery of society.

I was looking over a fence, seeing white Americans

achieving goals and knowing that even my former classmates, neighbors and teachers, did not believe their goals should be for me. I could not stay in a marriage and have babies just to fulfill their prophecy that Negroes were breeders and wanted nothing from life except sex and babies. I was beginning to hate sex.

With the birth of our second child, we were experiencing poverty such as I had never known before. Our rent was in arrears. There was no money to pay the doctor for the delivery of our son. We had no furniture in the living room. I would not return home to live with Shuggie. I would not move into the slums. I did not know which way to turn. Beginning with the teaching job denial and the lack of jobs due to the Depression, it appeared I was being controlled, submerged and discarded by limitations and denials. I was trapped behind insurmountable fences erected according to dominant Caucasian mores.

My husband's salary as a porter, with frequent layoffs and part-time scheduling, would always be in the lowest income category. It was not too bad when he was single, but now he had married responsibilities. When he applied for a job at the steel plants, he was told they were not hiring because of the Depression. They always added, "Anyhow, you are much too skinny to do heavy work around the steel furnaces."

My husband and I were being told that neither we nor our children were going anywhere. I wanted no part of it. How could I remain married? How could I birth more children into such a world, such an environment?

The sociology course at Temple University had impressed me with the class divisions in our society. Doctors, lawyers, industrial tycoons and people born to wealth comprised the upper class. Teachers, tradesmen and owners of businesses had an opportunity to move into and maintain a middle class status. Middle class people were the backbone of a progressive, stable society. They set standards and values, had a voice in politics, were identified with religious groups and had high standards of morality. Lower class people barely made enough from their service labors to meet their basic needs of food, clothing and shelter.

My childhood years had inculcated not only middle-class, but upper-middle-class values and strivings despite our limited income. If we were poor (which we were), we never knew it. We believed in ourselves and the ability to control our destiny. My husband's upbringing in a home where his father was a minister and his mother an inspiring homemaker had given him a middle-class mentality. If (notwithstanding his pool hall addiction) we must continue to exist at a lower class level, how would it affect our personality, our social status, our health, our children's future, our place in society and our usefulness to others?

In my education courses at Kent State, we had been taught a theory of the distribution of intelligence. There were three divisions. The intellectuals, geniuses and high achieving individuals comprised the upper bracket, about fifteen percent, of society. They controlled the political and economic destinies of nations and the world. The middle group, about seventy percent, were the dependable, conscientious, average solid learners. They understood, they performed well and they could be depended upon. They were the backbone of society. At the lower end of this curve was the nonacademic, disinterested and disabled learner. Many were physically, as well as intellectually, inadequate. They were on the receiving end of life's blessings. They were expendable.

There was no reason for me to be poor, to be a part of that lower class. Neither should I be considered intellectually incompetent. I was well educated. My speech and diction were void of vulgarisms, colloquialisms and ethnic dialects. I was a well formed human being. I was pleasing to look upon, brown skin notwithstanding.

I could teach, I could lecture, I could be a leader if the white man would permit me. I wanted to minister to others, my people, all people. I did not want to be ministered unto. I wanted to serve my country and the world. I did not want to be served by some individual, some agency, some social welfare organization which slapped an inferiority label on me and treated me as less than a first-class, high-type human being.

In the back of my mind, as I nursed my infant son and reviewed our situation, the faintest of resolves was forming. If I could not break out of this economic trap by getting a job in Canton, my home town, my birthplace, commensurate with my talents and formal education, I would do something drastic. I would disappear as my father had done. I would leave my husband and two children and go out into the world in search of personal and professional fulfillment. Norma Jean and "Jew Boy" would be in good hands. Their father loved them as I had never imagined a father could love his offspring. He could care for them.

My father must have felt the same way about the love his wife had for his children. He knew we would always be well cared for. My father dominated my thoughts. I tried to understand the feelings, the resolves that led him to desert his wife and the six of us children. My Pop as a young man had dreams of becoming somebody. He left the Southland convinced the North was the land of opportunity. He married a beautiful mulatto girl believing she would be a supporting life partner. He ventured in his own business and it failed because of the dishonesty of his partner. He was recognized as a leader in several fraternal lodges. He wanted to become a lawyer. He pored over his law books in preparation for admission to law school. Law school was always distanced by the routine demands of a growing family of more babies than he ever wanted.

Pop wanted to be in life's driver's seat. Instead he was being driven by forces that said, "Get back! Wait! Why can't you be content as a servant waiter for the wealthy white folks?" "You cannot do that, until you do this!" "Pay this month's rent!" "Buy six pairs of shoes for your children." "And above all else, pay the gas and electric bills!"

I had always tried to understand how Mom, an almost perfect mother, reasoned and felt. Now I was beginning to analyze how Pop must have felt. Maybe he was more right than wrong. Maybe he had to do what he did. He had to leave his wife and children to try to fulfill his heart's desires. He escaped.

The feelings I was having must have been like those Pop experienced. I, too, should escape this chronic frustration; this restrictive nature of my world, caused by racial exclusion and injustice. I could head for Philadelphia or New York or Washington, D.C. or even London as my Aunt Lib's only daughter, Ruth Fisher, had done. Somewhere in the world there should be the opportunity to become a professionally employed woman of color. Soon I must escape this bondage!

Before I could detail this determination, a number of things happened. Percy lost his part-time job to a permanent layoff. He was assigned a WPA job in January, building a road in frigid weather. Two weeks later, he became ill and had to quit. In February our son Al, who was six months old, became critically ill with double pneumonia.

Dr. Williams, our faithful family physician, attended Al as if he were his very own son. A couple of nights when an overworked, fatigued doctor should have been at home in his own bed, he phoned his wife to say, "I plan to get some shut-eye here at the Marceres'. Their little boy is still very sick. His fever has not broken and I am needed here. Phone me if there is an emergency call."

No infant received better care. Our son survived to suffer two more pneumonia attacks before he was two years old. When Al was nine months old, on a bright May morning several days after we had celebrated Norma Jean's fourth birthday, I received an unexpected phone call. Mr. John W. Crawford, the executive director of the Canton Urban League, was talking excitedly.

"If you can come to my office right away, I would like to talk to you about an adult education teaching position through the WPA." One hour later my life was headed in a new direction. A form of escape was within arm's reach.

Snipes Family Album

September 1906
Norman Sherwood Snipes and Ida Rosella Evans
Wedding picture

Norman Sherwood Snipes (1888-1935) outside his tavern at 3rd and Walnut, S.E. (1907).

Ida Evans Snipes (1890-1966).    **Virginia and Ruth**

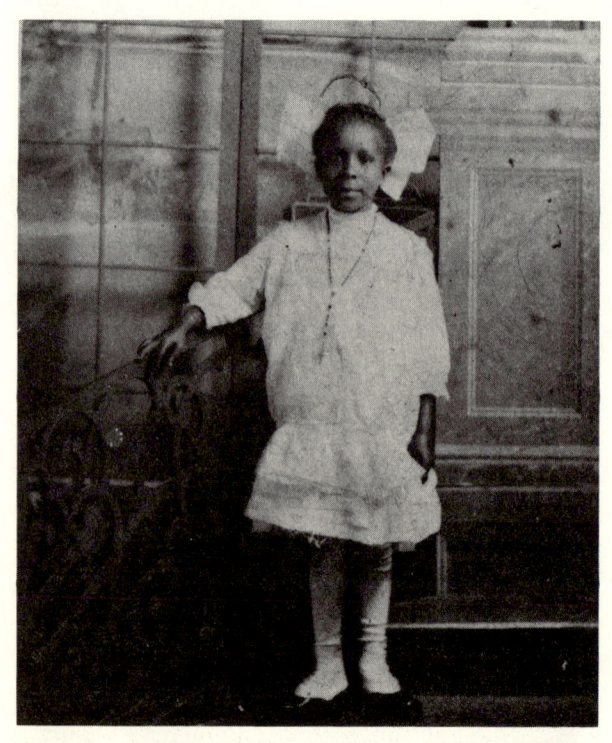

Norma, age 7, dressed for Forty Hours (1915).

Eugene Robert Snipes (1912-1957)

Carl Evans Snipes (1914-1959)

Norma Irene Snipes Marcere, 1944.

Norma, 10 months old.

Virginia Mae Snipes Powe.

h Doris Snipes.

Ethel Rosella Snipes Turner.

Dueber School—8th grade (1928)   Eugene

Norma 15   Ruth 5
Virginia 3

Shuggie at 70.

Al, cousin Kate, Norma Jean.

**Standing: Ruth, Norma, Virginia, Ethel.
Sitting: Norma Jean, Percy (1970).**

XIII

A 1935 Working Wife And Mother

Mr. John W. Crawford, the second executive director of the Canton Urban League, greeted me courteously. When he stood, his muscular frame was barely two or three inches above my five-foot-four-inch height. Seated behind his executive desk, he had the appearance of a broad-shouldered six-foot athlete. His keen piercing eyes, like beacons from his dark-skinned countenance, seemed to flash the intellectual processes at work in his brain. His scholastic astuteness intrigued and piqued me all the while he explained the teaching position he had mentioned on the phone.

He detailed the recently initiated Federal Works Program for adult education with as much dignity and seriousness as if he were launching a battleship or pleading a case before the Supreme Court. He lauded the program, which would dissipate illiteracy. In 1920, at the peak of the European migration to America and the trek of the Negro northward, the United States illiteracy rate was 6 percent for whites and 22.9 percent for Negroes. In 1930 at the height of the Depression, the non-reading, non-writing rates for whites and non-whites were 4.3 percent and 16.03 percent respectively.

For many years, due in part to the debates of Booker T. Washington and W. E. B. DuBois, which began in the late

1890s, groups such as the National Association for the Advancement of Colored People (NAACP) and the National Urban League began to express concern about this literacy disparity. It was recognized that the inadequacy of schools in many rural southern areas, along with the demand for unskilled laborers in the industrial North, contributed to a disregard for formal education. Strong-bodied laborers did not need to read or write.

The Canton Urban League would be one of several community centers providing classroom space for the WPA adult education classes. I was elated. Since I had not been allowed to teach little children in the Canton Public Schools, I could, I was being told, teach their illiterate parents.

Mr. Crawford outlined the eligibility requirements. One had to be the unemployed head of a household with a state teacher's certificate. I had the latter, but I was not the unemployed head of my family. My husband was. His educational qualifications limited him to outdoor WPA construction work only. He became nearly as ill as his pneumonia-stricken six-month-old son after just two weeks on a WPA road job. I would never consent to his return to outdoor construction work.

Percy was a speedy, accurate mathematician. When we went to market, he could tell the check-out clerk the exact cost of a wagon full of groceries without the use of pencil or paper. If he had been a teacher, his students would never have feared arithmetic or called it hard. To me, he made it seem so simple, so easy. My husband attributed his mastery of oral addition, subtraction, multiplication and division with the word "drill."

"If you'd been taught and drilled," he would say, "by the teachers I had in the fourth and fifth grades of our little one-room school in Mississippi, you'd be good with figures, too. Gee, how those teachers could teach! One of my cousins, Louise Burwell, was the greatest. She was mean and she was strict, but everybody learned. She meant business."

Percy was not trained to teach. I was. How could I claim a job priority? Nearly a year before Al was born, Percy had begun to explore job possibilities that would improve our financial situation. Together we surveyed the job opportunities for a Negro man. There was an abundance of porter/janitor jobs in the downtown furniture and department stores. The two large hotels had waiters, porters and bellhops. The train station and the bus terminal had redcaps and a shoe shine attendant. There were as yet no political jobs open to Negroes in the city or county. No policemen, firemen, bus drivers, garbage collectors, street cleaners or mailmen of color had been considered for hire.

Ruling out the top professional careers of law, medicine and dentistry requiring college degrees, there were only three directions to consider. Percy could open a small business, take a civil service examination for a federal job or continue to submit his application for a laboring job in the heavy steel industries.

The thriving Black business entrepreneurs had special skills and services directed to the personal needs of Blacks. At Z. A. Hunter's Restaurant, Hutchison's, and Premmer's, "down home" foods dominated the menu. Even with my upper class Caucasian cooking skills, I enjoyed an ethnic meal of collard greens, pickled pigs feet, black-eyed peas, corn bread and sweet potato pie. The Powells had a thriving grocery on Eighth and Lafayette, Southeast. One block south, Nathan and Marian Doyle operated the South Side Confectionary.

Page's Bakery was known for its tasty breads and pastries. The Webster, March and Matthews funeral home catered to the lengthy, elaborate and emotional funerals with an "it's all right" attitude white undertakers did not exhibit. George Scott was a plasterer, Owen Barnes a paper hanger. Percy had no skills nor business inclinations in any of the above mentioned directions.

I urged him to study for a civil service job, specifically, a mail carrier or a postal clerk. We prepared a card table full of geography and history books from the public library. At some hour during the day or night, we concentrated upon historical dates and events likely to be included in a civil service examination. We began our sessions with enthusiastic high hopes, but our teacher/pupil relationship was short-lived.

One afternoon Percy tossed the books to the floor and shouted, "I've had enough of this! Don't try to make me over! Just take me as I am! You knew all about my book learning before we married. You knew how old I was when I ran away from home. I can't make up for all those lost school years by studying at this card table twelve hours a week. Why should I want to work in a post office reading names and addresses on letters and packages day after day? I'm not trying to make you over. Just forget about making me over. I know what you want out of life and I'll not interfere one way or the other, but for God's sake leave me alone!"

I respected his demand. Never again was any mention ever made of his schooling or his job skills. Percy was an avid newspaper reader. His knowledge of current events, politics and sports put me to shame, but kept the main arteries of communication open. We had soul-searching discussions on topics that reached into the areas of science, sociology, psychology and philosophy.

My husband's speech was good. He spoke with no accent or colloquial drawl. He had one expression that sounded strange. He would say "hope" for "help." "I'm going to hope Eva with that job he has Saturday. He hoped me a lot when we were kids in Mississippi."

I never told him the word was help. He never cursed or swore, and he never used street or pool hall slang at home around me, the children or the people who came to our house.

I had a right to respect him for the man he was, not the formal education he had or did not have.

Once after a hilarious debate, I conferred upon him a MW and CS degree (Mother Wit and Common Sense). He then surprised me with a SDDYP degree. Holding me in his arms he taunted, "SDDYP means 'so damn dumb you're pitiful.' Book learning—yes! But you know so little about the real world out there!"

Now talking to Mr. Crawford I knew that I faced a dilemma. How could I become eligible for the one-hundred-and-six-dollar-a-month, fifteen-hour-a-week teaching job? How could I disqualify my husband for the sixty-dollar-a-month, forty-hour-a-week outdoor laboring job?

"You will have to prove your husband is incapable of working on WPA, disabled or . . . ?"

Mr. Crawford's voice hung in midair. I felt he was hesitant to offer any specific alternatives. My thoughts were many. Percy had applied for a number of jobs after those harshly spoken words during that last tutoring session. If Republic Steel refused to hire him . . . ? If the two weeks on WPA had caused him to become ill . . . ? Would or could his doctor write a statement . . . ? If I was unmarried . . . ? If I was planning a divorce . . . ?

The 1930s saw the beginnings of all kinds of excuses, lies, deceptions, concoctions, arrangements in an attempt to better one's living conditions. I was on the verge of using any strategy, however dishonest, to put my training to use to improve my economic security and independence.

"If you could get a statement from your doctor, I could go to work right away," I announced to Percy that evening. "I am not sure how willing you are to do this for me, but I must get this job. This is my chance. Please do something to help me. Don't tell me there is no way, that you cannot or will not help me."

"When did I ever tell you I didn't want you to work? I just don't want to see you at work as a servant in another woman's kitchen. That's all. I'll see Dr. Walker or some doctor and see what can be done. I know what you need."

"Thanks, thanks a lot. You may have just saved our marriage." I began dancing around the room. "Believe it or not, I was willing to do something desperate to qualify for this job. I was even willing to claim we were not living together, that we were getting a divorce."

"Don't think I haven't known what's been going on in that brain of yours. I know you better than you know yourself and a lot better than you know me. I'll never stand in the way of your doing what you want to do. Just don't ever embarrass me or make me feel cheap. I'm behind you one hundred percent."

"You really mean that? You do, don't you? What do you mean, embarrass you?" I asked.

"I guess I'm afraid I'm leaving myself wide open for an 'I told you so' laugh some day. That's what love does, I guess," Percy spoke hesitantly.

"What in the world are you talking about?"

"Some of the boys downtown, most of them in fact, have bets that our marriage won't last. They predict your education will give you the big head. Some day you'll look at some educated big shot and say I'm not good enough for you. You'll realize I can't ever give you the better things of life. You wouldn't believe some of the jeers I take for having married a college girl like you."

"Any brother who sends his sister to college deserves a college wife," I remarked. "You are entitled to a girl like me."

I glimpsed a little boy taunted by his neighborhood peers because he had the nicest ball and bat or something special that they did not have. They would threaten, "You will never keep it. Someone will steal it from you the minute you lay it down. Then you will be no better off than the rest of us."

The little boy, in fear, does not know whether to enjoy his treasure to the fullest or to blame his treasure for his insecurity. I embraced my husband and spoke as reassuringly as I had ever spoken.

"Our togetherness is for keeps. Never, ever worry about losing me to someone else. I have some concerns about whether our marriage will last, but it will never fail because I have been to college or because I have switched to another man. There are times when I think your preoccupation with your downtown buddies is a form of wife neglect. I fear neglect. You could lose me quickly that way. My Mom was neglected and that is not for me," I explained with some firmness.

"I also fear poverty very much. I have never wanted to be rich, but I cannot stand being poor. Something in me will not allow me to be worthless. I cannot sit helplessly by waiting for a ship to appear on a distant horizon laden with silver and gold. I want to dig my own gold and silver mines with an active life. I want to do for you and me, our children and everybody, things which have never been done before. We can be helpmates! Your MW and CS can help me, who is SDDYP. Understand?"

Our embrace was a renewed vow to each other. It was more meaningful than those utterances made before a justice of the peace five years earlier. With a renewed sense of partnership, more than dependency on each other, we headed for that first decade of marriage, a day, a week, a month at a time.

The next day my husband handed me a doctor's statement indicating he was temporarily unemployable. I attached it to my college transcript, my teacher's certificate and my application for WPA employment. It was approved by the Canton Board of Education. I went to work immediately.

It was difficult entering the school administration building with my time sheet and class schedules that first week since my encounter with the superintendent in 1929. I felt that everyone knew I had been denied a teaching job. Did they know the real reason why I had not been teaching? When on subsequent report days and staff meetings there were no cues to nurture my uneasiness, I entered the building weekly with head held high. I was undaunted by that past memory.

Mr. Oscar Ritchie from Massillon, Ohio, a handsome, intelligent gentleman whom I met at a teacher's meeting, was an unemployed, certified teacher, too. I experienced strange emotions of anger and a oneness when I realized I was not the only qualified Negro teacher bypassed because of race. Several had been rejected, discriminated against by other school systems in Ohio. There was another awareness. I discovered that my partners in rejection, not crime, had superior qualities of personality, integrity, intelligence, determination and positive thinking.

What had my Mom said when I was a little girl? "Maybe you are destined to be 'extra special' . . . 'superior individuals' . . . 'quality par excellence.' " Mr. Ritchie, among others, was one of those people. He became a source of inspiration to me then and when he became a professor at Kent State University several years later.

There was much to learn from the theories and points of view Mr. John Crawford put forth during the months I taught at the Urban League. He had deep-rooted convictions that women, biologically, were predisposed to being treated royally. "They should," he remarked, "have elite status in the home. They should be shielded and protected from the world."

We had many debates that could have created deep wounds had they not been held to a high level of intellectual premise and interpretation. Sometimes I felt that he was intimidated by women. I was grateful for my husband's acceptance of his sisters, his mother and me as special women. He was not intimidated by the threat a woman could outdistance a man. Getting into a work routine presented no problems. Percy continued to share the household chores. I delighted in the affection and attention he gave his daughter, his son and our foster child. When I left the house in midafternoon to walk the mile and a half to teach my adult students, I carried with me no fears, no anxieties and no guilt about leaving the children. Their daddy was with them.

The anticipatory excitement of leaving the house to go to work caused me to tackle the household tasks of washing, ironing, cooking and cleaning with a swiftness far outdistancing the ordinary volume of work generally performed in a sixty-second minute and a sixty-minute hour. Work outside the home was play for me. It was a form of recreation combined with adventure, excitement and challenges. Tireless energy and creative ideas propelled me from one activity to another. I never realized how much I wanted to teach and how natural it was to interact with my students.

My oldest and most enthusiastic student was an eighty-year-old great-great-grandmother. Anne Alexander's expressed wish was to write her name before she died. She struggled laboriously to move her arthritic fingers in the thirteen-letter formation of her name.

The thrill of a dream come true was experienced when a forty-year-old Republic Steel worker signed his name to his paycheck instead of an X. He invited me to accompany him to the George D. Harter Bank and witness the signing of his check in the presence of the bank teller. With a glow of self-esteem such as I had not here-to-fore witnessed, John bragged, "This is the teacher who taught me how to write my name. I am going to learn a lot more, too. Lots more."

These were not stupid, brainless people, my students; but individuals who had never been inspired to use their intelligence in disciplined, purposeful pursuits before. Somehow, at no time in their youth had they been rewarded for using their intellect. Their focus was on their physical strength, their natural talents and their personal pleasures, including sex. For most of them, fun and basic survival needs had been their main goal. No one had taken time to explain the meaning of life. They had not been shown a world beyond their family, their neighborhood, their church and their peers.

Like travelers without a road map, they as children had left their marbles, their toy soldiers and their backyard and street corner ball games headed for nowhere. At the onset of puberty, little girls put aside their baby dolls. They stopped their pretending play, wearing their mothers' and grandmothers' high-buttoned shoes, long dresses and floppy straw hats to assume the role of adults. Young boys fathered children before they had fuzz to shave from their upper lip. Young mothers nursed babies before they had outgrown little girl games of double dutch and hopscotch.

They had been too unsophisticated as teen-age adults to realize how illiterate and unprepared they were to function in a predominantly materialistic industrialized society. Maturing with ever-increasing obligations, many had wasted half a lifetime beating at straws before they understood that they were out of step with the world in which they lived.

Now in the adult classes they cherished their books in the belief that this belated WPA education was the key to something they needed. Some, not all, hoped something would happen without exerting the discipline they had never become buddies with in their early childhood.

My childhood indoctrination had been to study hard and to get a good education so I could support myself honorably and be of service to others. At last I was in a position to do just that. I was well prepared. I could now honorably supply some of my needs from my teaching income. I would never become so engrossed in monetarily feathering my own nest that my pupils would leave my classes little, or no better off, than when they entered.

My first resolve was that I must never become so overwhelmed by the oppressive condition of their environment, health and poverty that I would forget or negate their hopes. A parallel resolve was that I was not to feel sorry for my people, not to pity them, not to entertain and waste precious moments with them. Neither was I to encourage minimum efforts, but excite them to maximum performance. With these resolves I experienced periods of high success. My adult students learned. We learned a lot about each other and the human potential.

The teaching position ended when the WPA informed me that my husband's part-time job, proving he was employable, made me ineligible for the government job. Mr. Crawford hired me as girls' work secretary at sixty dollars a month for five irregular eight-hour days each week. The title "secretary" had nothing to do with clerical duties. I conducted a half day forenoon preschool program for four-and-five-year-olds. Adult handicraft classes in sewing, knitting, crocheting and quilting were taught two afternoons a week. I directed a teen-age drama class one night a week. Another group of high school girls were taken on tours weekly that combined career guidance and recreation.

The women attended their handicraft classes faithfully. They were anxious to learn and just as eager to share some unique hand skills of their own. Their pleasantness surprised me. They never complained, never gossiped about others. There was always something humorous to laugh about. They were generous and gracious, revealing a royal dignity from some long forgotten ancient heritage.

The teen-age boys and girls in the drama club had a variety of artistic talents. They could transform themselves as if touched by a magic wand to be the character in their one-act classic plays. They helped me experience with them the joys of play-acting and the abandonment of reality to a world of make-believe.

The major phase of my work at the Urban League was the preschool program. It was really a forerunner of what later was known as a Headstart program. I had no toys, no vehicles, no manuals or procedural guidelines; but I had space and ideas. I had the use of a large lobby, a huge gymnasium and a full-scale stage. Seated at small tables and often on the floor, the children worked with pencils, paper, crayons, paste, scissors and alphabet building blocks. We made life-size papier-mache animals from chicken wire, paste and newspapers.

During that half-day children's program, the emphasis was on strengthening listening skills, motor skills, finger dexterity, group and individual performances, verbalization and vocabulary building. We had a story hour, a calisthenics and organized play period, a talent hour during which every child was taught to memorize a poem, sing a song, dance and pantomime. They all sang in the children's choir.

It was a joyous experiment. I was never quite sure what parents expected to happen to their little ones. Their parting words to their darlings as they entered the lobby were "Behave yourself!" and to me, "If he (or she) doesn't mind you, let me know."

At the close of the school year, the gaily decorated gymnasium became the setting for the children's fairyland performance. The flower garden choir, wearing headdresses of roses, daisies, sunflowers, pansies and tulips, became the stage background. Their colorful crepe paper and net costumes were created by their parents, volunteers and members of the sewing and handicraft classes. The older boys and girls paraded throughout the garden scenery doing special acts. They sang, danced and recited as bees, butterflies, rabbits and fairy tale characters.

Our foster daughter, Ella Mae, who came to our home at age three with a speaking vocabulary of less than fifty recognizable words, was one of the performing stars. She stood before a packed audience with a fishing rod over her shoulder and a pail in her hand and sang "Gone Fishin'." Her clear tones had the promise of a budding vocal artist.

Each child in that preschool program had learned three things: how to listen, how to memorize, and how to perform. Each experienced the miracle of accomplishment. They would remember for the rest of their lives (as I would my six-year-old stage debut at St. Mary's) the feeling of pride and self-esteem. Walking on stage, performing and hearing the applause of the audience would be an indelible remembrance. More than that, the satisfaction of personal achievement would take root as a tiny seed destined to sprout to excellence.

When the funds for this position vanished, I became a job-seeker again. During this period of waiting for replies to a number of job applications, tragedy visited our home. One early summer day when many parents who had combatted the discomforts of measles and chicken pox among their young children, were worried about the approaching polio season, my three became ill with upset stomachs, fever and diarrhea.

A day and a half of caring for a two-year-old, a five-year-old and a near-six-year-old wore away the sheen and dimmed the rose-patterned design on the linoleum carpeting. I was apprehensive and fatigued. From the living room couch where Norma Jean and Ella Mae lay at either end, and the crib where Alluren rested, I made a steady march through the dining room to the bathroom adjoining the kitchen. As soon as I had cleaned up one explosion of abdominal discharge, there was a hurried trip to the bathroom for each to eliminate their intestinal waste. An insistent thirst for water and orange juice meant that another volcanic eruption or intestinal expulsion would follow momentarily.

When Ella Mae's fever escalated, our family doctor, who had generously attended all three, requested that the Children's Bureau physician be consulted immediately. Within a few hours, Ella Mae was admitted to Aultman Hospital. The diagnosis was tuberculosis (TB) meningitis. Ella Mae died a week later.

The public health nurse explained how Ella Mae had from birth to age three lived in the home of a close relative who had died of tuberculosis. During her infancy, Ella Mae understandably had many exposures to the TB bacillus. Sources such as crawling on the floor where sputum may have carelessly been expectorated, eating from the same plate as the infected adult, and being kissed by the carrier, were explained to the bereaved mother and Percy and me. My fears for the health of our children counteracted the grief over Ella Mae. It was devastating to look upon the corpse of a young child and envision what her loss meant to the world. An immediate imperative was to assess our children's vulnerability for a similar fate.

Had Norma Jean and Alluren been exposed to the bacillus during those vomiting seizures? Was Dr. Williams examining them thoroughly with every diagnostic procedure? I knew from my Mom the devastating history of tuberculosis-related deaths in her family. I did not want that tragedy to return in my children's generation.

After losing Ella Mae, my husband and I decided we had better not keep any more foster children the ages of our own. It was a short-lived resolve. Little Johnny, a four-year-old, came to live with us for several months. It was an emergency. There were few licensed foster homes, and it was impossible to persuade the county home to care for Negro children. To make matters worse, Johnny was a disturbed child. We were assured he was not a carrier of any contagious diseases.

I did my first child study on Johnny. The results were helpful in making recommendations to the agency for the kind of foster home he needed for maximum adjustment and development.

One of the high school girls active in the Urban League drama club was saddened by the death of her mother. When I learned that the nine children were to be divided among relatives, I asked to be allowed to take the oldest girl. Marcella Oliver came to live in our home. She became a big sister to Norma Jean and Al and a mother's helper to me. She graduated from high school and was married from our home. She was the fourth in a succession of ten foster children to become a part of our lives. Unaware I would for a period of eight years be called upon to care for foster children, I doggedly sought a work career. I was resolutely determined not only to be a full-time professional employee, but also to be a full-time caring and concerned mother and foster parent.

Mary Quinn Stanton, the director for the certification of WPA workers, interviewed me for an investigator's job. It was our second meeting. "I am impressed with you," she began. "I want you on my staff. In my enthusiasm, I tried to impress the county commissioners about your education at Kent State and Temple University. I may have done you more harm than good because the commissioners rebuked me in these words, 'A college education doesn't mean a damn around here. This is all politics.'

"I want you to become a volunteer worker in this office. I also want you to attend every political meeting held in the wards and precincts throughout the county. You must become a member of the League of Women Voters and the Democratic party. Are you a registered voter?' "

"Oh, yes. I registered when I became twenty-one. I have voted in every election. My mother works at the election booth and is a presiding officer."

"Good! Now with you as a volunteer I have a plan. When

there is another opening, I can point to you as the commissioner's political plum. I can say, 'Norma has been a trusted volunteer. She knows the job. She is already trained.' " Mrs. Stanton paused. "Are you interested?"

I was. Mrs. Stanton, a petite woman, perhaps in her early forties, was graciously dynamic and persuasive. With a hint of theatrics, she revealed an Irish wit polished with charm. It was whispered she could hold her own in any board room filled with male chauvinistic politicians and executives.

For eight months under the watchful eye of Mrs. Stanton, I was assigned duties in every department of the WPA Certifying Agency. This was my initial experience as the only Negro professional on a county agency staff. The fifty or more employees were Irish, Italian, Greek, Syrian, German and many other less ethnically identifiable Caucasians.

At the Urban League the all-Negro staff consisted of the executive director, a male and female activities supervisor, an office secretary and a custodian. There were perhaps a dozen part-time employees and volunteers. The Urban League atmosphere was friendly, informal and non-competitive. It became the yardstick by which I measured all agency staffs.

I was aware, but not uncomfortably so, that my ability to get along with the all-white staff was being watched and evaluated. Mrs. Stanton alerted me to the highly prejudicial attitude of one of the members of her staff. "Do not let any of her inflammatory remarks upset you enough to cause an outburst. Her beliefs are not worthy of recognition," she advised.

This staff person was a very devout Catholic girl who hoped to become a nurse. She worked as a volunteer at the Mercy Hospital emergency room every weekend. On Monday she took great delight in detailing the incidents of Negro violence and the victims admitted to the hospital. "They're disgusting animals," she blurted out more than once across the coffee table in the staff lounge.

Avoiding her became an art. When our paths crossed, it was easy for me to pretend she was nowhere near or that I was stone deaf. She never spoke to me. She would look past me, pour a cup of coffee and corner someone in the room with "Did I tell you about this real big black man who slashed this guy to ribbons last Saturday?"

There might have been some therapeutic satisfaction if I could have sworn at her, but swear words were not a part of my vocabulary. I could not blush. My pigmented complexion would not blanch white. Any verbal protest on my part revealing an inner turbulence would not change her. My anger could justify a volley of hate-filled curse words if I wanted the feeling of immediate, personal gratification. But I had a goal. There was a professional career ahead for me. She, this insensitive, ignorant, hate-filled girl, was not about to topple me from my pedestal. I was a lady. I ignored her, walked out of the room and left her facing the coffee pot and brown-stained, half-emptied coffee cups. Others, too, walked away from her.

Eight months as a volunteer without pay called for optimistic patience and fortitude not only on my part but that of my husband as well. Many an evening we questioned whether I should quit and start looking for something else. Was I being taken advantage of? Were other young women being asked to work for nothing? What if a staff member or a citizen registered a complaint about a Negro being employed in the agency? I could be fired before I was hired. Suppose the commissioners continued to be adamant about their choice of political appointees?

When Mrs. Stanton learned my husband's salary was only fourteen dollars a week, based on the NRA minimum wage scale, she suggested I was eligible for partial assistance. "I shall never stand in a welfare line for any kind of assistance,"

I told her.

"Who said anything about welfare or standing in line? Come to my office and pick up a fifteen dollar check every two weeks. It will be a partial reimbursement for your expenses of lunch money and some odds and ends."

Finally the day arrived when I was hired as a full-time investigator for the WPA Certification Office under the auspices of the Stark County commissioners. I was happy to get away from the intake clerk's desk and the file room with its tissue paper thin, multicolored triplicate copies of all of the applicants and workers on WPA. My new task was to determine the work eligibility of those who applied for WPA. Not every WPA worker was on welfare, but every able-bodied, unemployed head of a household on or off welfare was eligible for certification. I visited the applicant's home to interview the wage earner, record the names and ages of the household members, list all the places of employment for the previous five years, itemize their overhead living expenditures and note the condition of the home.

That portion of the day spent in the homes of my clients provided rewarding experiences of human interaction. Each family had its way of letting me know how happy they were with the prospects of a job and an income. They also had a way of letting me know how proud they were of me. There was an abundance of trust and cooperation.

I vividly recalled the social worker who came to our home when I was twelve years old. She said and did everything she could to demean our dignity. Without so much as a "May I please," she parted the draperies between our dining room and front room. Seeing the beautiful upright piano, she announced her decision. "We can sell the piano and get enough money to support your family for several weeks or even months."

She inquired about our insurances and asked for the policies to be given to her. She would move us to a cheaper rented house in the slums and take me out of school at the end of the seventh grade. She saw me, a little brown girl, as a potential maid in some well-to-do Caucasian home.

I was never able to understand why in the presence of that nameless caseworker I wanted to become a social worker. Now as a WPA investigator, I knew why. Subconscious resolves had taken root in my psyche. I would treat my clients with respect. I would not snoop into their personal affairs. I would not cheapen their dignity by insult, by belittling their aspirations or by ridiculing their errors in coping with misfortune.

"Being out of work and having to accept relief is hell," one man commented as I gathered the many sheets of paper for his case folder, "but seeing you at work in a job like this takes some of the heat out of the fire. Some good comes out of the worst of things. You help us hold up our heads a little anyway. All of us are proud of you. You are a beautiful Negro woman."

One day I received a call requesting, "When you are in the neighborhood, stop at my place." When I knocked on the door of this Rex Avenue residence, I was greeted by a very well-known madam of the Red Light District. Mamie Franklin, a gray haired matriarch of the underworld family, began, "I just wanted to tell you something personally. It is this: You have nothing to worry about as you walk up and down the streets here in the southeast end of Canton. No one will ever attempt to harm you. We know your mother and father, your husband and all about your family. This section of town is not like the neighborhoods where you have lived, but never worry. Word has gone out that no one is ever to bother you. We are watching out for you. We are proud of you."

All of my life I had thought of underworld people as sinister sinners, the scum of the earth. Somehow and for some reason, they did things outside the realm of decency and fair play. Kindness, thoughtfulness and caring were the attributes of saints, not sinners. As I uttered a rather startled "Thank you, I appreciate your assurance of safety," I had to smile. Maybe it was more of a controlled uproarious laughter because of the visual image that was flashing before my brain. My guardian angel was being assisted by pimps and prostitutes to deliver me from evil.

There was never an instance of fear or any hint of danger as I walked up and down the streets and alleys all over the southeast and northeast sections of Canton. Never was there a curse word uttered in my presence. Neither was there ever an insulting remark nor a sensuous look. I was treated as a royal lady everywhere I went.

A home call was just one phase of my work as an investigator. A second phase was to verify the most recent work history by phone or mail. Most emergency cases were given phone call priorities. A number of employers revealed their prejudicial hang-ups over the phone. Most of the work reference remarks made by the employers of porters, janitors and low-skilled maintenance workers were meant to disqualify them for WPA employment.

"Yeah, he worked for me; and like all damn niggers, he was no good. I fired him because he could never get to work on time. There's plenty of people looking for work. I didn't need him. I hired this dago and he can't speak English, but he's a damn good worker."

The employer never knew he was speaking to a Negro woman. He continued, "You sound like a pretty smart cookie. I'd like to meet you sometime. I don't know why the government wants to give a WPA job to those shiftless niggers. You know the kind of people they are. Don't you? I hear there's a couple of nigger bitches working in some of the downtown relief agencies. I hope none of them ever phones this office.

They'll wish they hadn't. I'll give them a mouthful."

I learned a fact of life on this job. For every negative, prejudicial, jealous, vindictive individual, there was a positive, fair-minded, supportive, encouraging person among my clients and my co-workers.

In five short adventuresome years, I had made it into the work world. I was a wife, a mother and foster mother. I had successfully taught adult education classes, conducted a preschool program and learned the office routine of a county agency. The full-fledged career I envisioned ahead of me need not suffer because of my role as wife and mother. There had been many periods of doubt and discouragement, but things were different now. I was on my way. I had never felt so confident of what lay ahead.

XIV

My Hand To The Plough

It was not until we celebrated our daughter's sixth birthday in April that I began to think seriously of selecting a school for her education. September was just five months away. We still lived in the Dueber School district where I graduated from the eighth grade. We were also within the St. Joseph Catholic School parish boundary where Monsignor Treiber had refused to enroll me as a fifth grade pupil in 1918. Wanting so very much for my children to have the same religious and educational experiences I had had at St. Mary's, I was prepared to become a Catholic so no refusals, no rejections, no limitations could be placed in my daughter's or son's way.

St. Joseph's church, school, rectory and convent covered a city block spread between Second and Third Streets, bounded by Bedford and Columbus Avenues. Like little chicks nestled close to the mother hen, the surrounding neighborhoods absorbed some of the grandeur and dignity of the religious fortress. The two-story framed homes with well-kept lawns proclaimed the strong middle class values of an industrious working class. They seemed to draw strength from their Catholic citadel and each other.

Although there was a predominance of second generation European ethnics in St. Joseph's membership, they were as strongly committed to an English-speaking American Catholic culture as the Mayflower aristocrats who lived in the northwest neighborhoods and patronized the downtown Lutheran, Episcopal, Methodist and Presbyterian churches.

Many of St. Joseph's parishioners owned businesses and many more were skilled mechanics and laborers in industry. In the vicinity of my own neighborhood, there were numerous Catholic-owned small businesses. There was a shoe repair shop, a shoe store whose co-owners were a father and his two daughters, a family hardware store, a tavern, a bicycle shop, barber shop, restaurant, lumber company, confectionery and drug store. Dueber Hampden Watch Works, Timken Roller Bearing Company, brick companies and construction firms employed many of the parishioners. They were also well represented in politics.

I had been inside most of the business establishments from the 1200 block of West Tuscarawas to Dueber Avenue, but I had never been inside the church where many of the residents worshiped. How would these people react to Negroes worshiping in their church? What would happen when I came face to face with the priest in charge of this vast domain? What courage my Mom must have had to walk up to this red brick rectory in 1918, I was thinking. At the age of ten I understood that Mom was coming here; but now that I was twenty-seven, just ringing the doorbell unnerved me with fear but unwavering determination. I was trembling as I waited for someone to come to the door.

The buxom housekeeper, decorated with a white starched apron, ushered me into the office. Within seconds a tall, imposing Monsignor Kotheimer entered the room and greeted me. I explained I wanted to take instructions and to enroll my daughter in the first grade. His first comment was, "And your address?"

"Fourteen-O-Five Fifth Street, Southwest," I answered.

"Is that this side or the other side of the B&O tracks?"

"This side." (Just inside the boundary) I could have added, but I did not.

"I just wanted to make sure you were not in St. Peter's or St. John's parish," he explained.

"I understand," I acknowledged.

I also understood I was once again in the wrong neighborhood as when nearly twenty years earlier Mrs. Broomhandle had shouted, "Let's run these niggers back to where they belong. We don't want them in our neighborhood."

"Out of sight, our of mind," was an old adage which seemed to explain the white man's nearness and distance philosophy. The Negro by reason of his complexion visibility revived the imagery of slavery and exclusion. As long as the Negro was confined to certain neighborhoods, behind the warehouses, on the other side of the tracks, the white community could go about its business free of personal contact and conscious involvement.

A homogeneous grouping of European ethnics within certain parish boundaries could restrict the flow of residents unlike themselves from entering their neighborhoods and attending their schools. They could live their own lives free of the challenge, freer still of the reminders to love one's fellow man of physical, religious, racial and cultural differences. So isolated, they could succumb to half-truths and racial myths. They would become the chief creators of a socioeconomic disparity within the land their parents chose for liberty, the pursuit of happiness and freedom. I could be seen as invading their turf.

Back in 1920 or 1921, my Mom and a Mrs. Ida Bluford had a lively discussion about the neighborhood in which we lived. I was perhaps twelve or thirteen years old. Mrs. Bluford was an effervescent, short and stocky, medium brown-skinned woman. She was an active member in her church and an officer in the Eastern Star and Elks Lodge. Her outspoken manner qualified her to be respected as a civic leader. As a race advocate, she was impressed with Marcus Moziah Garvey and his followers. There was a growing sentiment among many leaders that Negroes should consider returning to Africa. They could never be free and equal citizens of dignity in America surrounded by racist Caucasians. Returning to their African homeland, they could build a nation free of the white man and his Ku Klux Klan terrorists.

"Ida, I don't know how you can live way out here in the southwest end of town with no colored neighbors. All I saw coming down the street were white-faced, red-necked folks everywhere. We are a majority in the southeast end of town and I like that. Who do your kids play with?" Mrs. Bluford asked.

"No one," Mom retorted. "No one. They have plenty of brothers and sisters."

"Your children should be with their own kind. The white man don't want you out here. The way the people stared at me as I passed their houses, coming over here, told me volumes. They don't want us anywhere near them," Ida Bluford insisted.

"Maybe they don't. But since when and by what right do they restrict my movements? I am a free woman. Slavery is over. If we willingly segregate ourselves, the time will come when they will erect legal barriers, fences if you like, to keep us where they want us to be," Mom said defending her position.

"Do you know that when Mr. Snipes and I moved here there were perhaps two dozen colored families living wherever they desired. On Bedford, Harrison, Prospect, Logan, Maple, Dueber, Park, Belden, Henrietta and Brown Avenues one and two miles distance from downtown, there were colored families. Now I understand the banks and realtors deny

Negroes access to certain neighborhoods by refusing to approve property loans or to show their homes. They chant the refrain, 'You will be happier among your own kind.' "

"I think we are happier among our own," Mrs. Bluford insisted.

"Speak for yourself, Ida. Do not speak for me," Mom remarked and launched into a lengthy comment. "People should live where they want to live. The southeast end of town was a good place to start. The immigrants of a variety of European tongues and most Negroes migrating from the South got their start in the crowded melting pot of Cherry Avenue and surrounding neighborhoods. Does that mean they should remain there forever?

"My family came here from Bellevue, Ohio, in 1900. We lived for a short time on Cherry Avenue. My children are second generation Cantonians. They, I, we, have a right to live in a better neighborhood than the newcomers who arrived last week or last year. I did not move out here just to live in a white neighborhood. I moved out here to live in a neighborhood of well-constructed homes with neat lawns, paved streets, a park close by and very good schools. My children do not have to pass saloons, gambling joints and houses of prostitution on their way to and from school.

"When families work hard, save money and want to move across town to something better, why shouldn't they? That is progress. That is what America is all about. My little daughter tells us at story time that she is going to live in a large brick house with twelve rooms for the twelve babies she wants some day. A child, even a Negro child, should be able to dream dreams for which we, their parents, will set an example and say, 'It can come true.' "

"That's the white blood in you talking now. I guess with skin color like yours, you can think that way. Remember, though, your children are not half-white like you. I think you're throwing them to the wolves. They'll be misfits. You'll see," Mrs. Bluford warned.

These thoughts almost crowded out the purpose of my appointment with Monsignor. Was I throwing my daughter to the wolves enrolling her as the first and only Negro student at St. Joseph's Catholic School? I doubted for a moment the wisdom of my being in the rectory office.

When I was just six years old, I had sat in Father Hassel's office at St. Mary's. There had been a minor school disturbance on the playground. Two other children and I had gone to Father's office to complain about the commotion. I was in tears because someone had called me "nigger." Father Hassel rather brusquely remarked, "You can't cry every time someone calls you a name, Norma," which gave me no comfort.

Peter Kintz and Hortense Schario, both in the first grade, were more friendly to me thereafter. I shied away from Father Hassel whenever I saw him on the playground. I never liked him. I felt he thought I had been the cause of the disturbance. If I had not been in his school, nothing would have happened.

I looked at Monsignor with a bit of apprehension. He was seated so assuredly in his swivel chair. There was stirring within me a predisposition to dislike his authoritarian manner. I hoped my daughter would never have to come to his office in tears. My brothers had spoken of Monsignor disdainfully. Eugene remarked often, around the dining room table when he was eleven and twelve years old, "I don't know how a priest can spend so much time on the golf course getting a suntan and then hurt the feelings of people with naturally dark skin. He and the men he golfs with are always telling jokes about Jews and darkies and the Irish. Pat and Mike and Abbie and Sambo are always in trouble. They act as though I am blind and deaf and have no feelings. I would never go to his old Catholic church. He would think I was coming to steal something . . . like Rastus stealing chickens."

Here I was, my brothers' oldest sister, enrolling my daughter in this offending golfer's school. I was no longer nervous. I looked him straight in the eye. I spoke with confidence. I was proud of my English as I enunciated every word clearly and politely. The ten-minute interview ended pleasantly enough. Our daughter would be officially enrolled in the first grade the first week of June. I could begin instructions immediately or wait until school started in September. I decided to wait. I walked home, satisfied. My mission was accomplished. All of those mixed-up feelings were hanging in limbo somewhere. What was I to do with them?

As sort of a parting look at all of the Protestant churches I had attended since age twelve, I began visiting practically every Negro church in the city of Canton. In part it was to convince myself I was ready to identify permanently with the Catholic church as soon as our daughter was in school.

Percy and I visited many churches together. The largest denominations were St. Paul's A.M.E., Mount Calvary Baptist, People's Baptist, Jerusalem Baptist and St. John's A.M.E. Zion. There was also a Seventh Day Adventist church with nearly twenty-five members and Elder Finney's Pentecostal Congregation, but these we bypassed. Walking throughout the city as an investigator for the WPA, I counted close to twenty storefront churches with congregations ranging from twenty-five to fifty worshipers.

Sometimes the insipid, toneless hymns of the Catholic church and the calm instructional homilies delivered by an unemotional priest contrasted sharply with the resonant songs of a jubilant choir and their minister's emotional sermons. I knew I was making mental notations of what I liked and did not like. I was cataloging what was emotional and intellectual, meaningful and meaningless, acceptable and unacceptable; but I did not know that my negative feelings showed on my countenance.

I was seated one Sunday afternoon in what might have been Jerusalem Baptist Church. The choir had been performing in a soulfully melodious manner from their position behind the pastor's pulpit. Finally they approached the congregation. The singers shouted and swayed in the aisles. I was seated on an aisle seat midway in the church. I was wearing a navy blue straw hat that coordinated well with my navy polka dot dress. As one of the singers reached me, she let out an emotional shout, raised both hands in the air and with a gesture of complete loss of bodily control, lowered her right arm and struck me in the face. My hat went flying off my head into my husband's lap.

With my dignity bruised, I retrieved my hat, adjusted it jauntily and left the church. My husband followed. Once outside, he began to laugh.

"How dare you!" I accused. "How dare you! None of this is funny. My face hurts."

"It serves you right," he said. "You should have seen the expression on your face. I was watching you. Your hat couldn't hide your feelings. Forgive me. I'll never insist upon you going with me ever again to a Protestant church. I never knew how uncomfortable you felt. I'll go with you to your Catholic church when you want me to, but I'll go alone to my Baptist churches hereafter." His understanding and that incident moved me closer to the Catholic form of worship.

The opening day of school was an event of high expectancy. Norma Jean was excited. She looked like a little princess in a Shirley Temple styled dress that I had sewn. Perhaps fifty or more of the first grade parents, like me, were there to dispel those last-minute fears about leaving our young children in the care of others. I prayed I would be assured that my daughter and I were where we should be. I cried that day, fearful of all the unknowns that could happen to her to assail her self-esteem. She was such a confident, self-assured child.

With his statuesque German frame complimented by his priestly robe, Monsignor began to address the student body with authority and dignity. "I want to welcome each and every one here to our school." His words rang out loud and clear.

"We pray that you will be blessed with good health so you will be in school every day and on time. There is to be no tardiness. Some of you will carry your lunch because of the distance you must travel to and from school. You will eat in one of the classrooms, and you are not to leave the school grounds at noon. You will have many rules to obey.

"We will not tolerate any misbehavior on or off the school grounds. You are to behave as good Catholic ladies and gentlemen always. There is to be no fighting and no name-calling here at St. Joseph's. There will be boys and girls here who look different and dress differently from some other children you know. You are to treat every boy and girl the way you want to be treated. Study hard, pay attention to the sisters and have a good school year."

I quickly put aside my negative suspicions of Monsignor. He was sincere in his desire to have a good school. He would be fair. He had already created an atmosphere of fairness. I found myself standing in the church vestibule, chatting with a group of parents. With each introduction, a comment was made about our first-grader. The untying of an apron string had not been as painful as we had feared. I walked home with the resolve that this was a good school. I must do all I could to make our daughter as acceptable as any other child in that school.

My catechism instructions were every Monday evening. The months went by. September, October, November. I finished my instructions but did not set a date for my baptism or reception into the church. Then followed January, February and

March. Easter would arrive in April. What was I waiting for? There would be time. Norma Jean would not be ready for her first communion until the close of the second grade. I could wait until fall of the next school year.

My employer, Mary Quinn Stanton, announced to all of her staff at the beginning of Lent that we were invited to attend a Lenten service with her at St. John's.

"Some of you are Catholic and some of you are not. I have always invited my staffs of whatever religious persuasion to see how we Catholics commemorate the forty days before Easter. You are welcome to my apartment afterwards for some light Lenten refreshments. Just let me know which Friday you are coming so I can get an extra chair or two from the custodian to seat everyone."

When the weeks had passed and I did not appear, Mrs. Stanton remarked one Monday morning, "Norma, I hope you have not intentionally ignored my invitation to go to a Lenten service with me. You are the only member of the staff who has not yet given me a 'yes' or 'no.' You will have to say 'yes' today because this coming Friday is Good Friday, the last Friday of Lent. I shall call for you at your home at seven, so be ready."

That Friday, like the Sunday of my almost-first communion twenty-two years earlier, was to be a memorable one. St. John's Catholic Church was filled to capacity. Mrs. Stanton and I managed to crowd into a space for two, seven or eight rows on the right rear of the church. I was just a part of the congregation straining my eyes to see the priest and altar boys moving up the aisles carrying the crucifix. The congregation chanted the Stabat Mater.

MY HAND TO THE PLOUGH 225

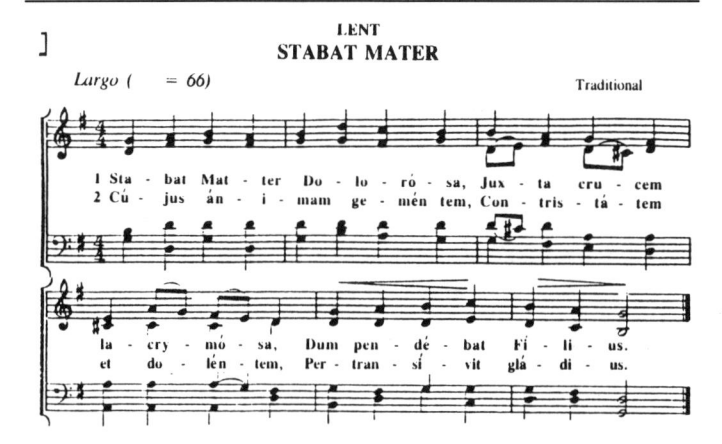

LENT
STABAT MATER

Largo (♩ = 66) — Traditional

1. Sta - bat Mat - ter Do - lo - ró - sa, Jux - ta cru - cem
2. Cú - jus án - i - mam ge - mén tem, Con - tris - tá - tem

la - cry - mó - sa, Dum pen - dé - bat Fí - li - us.
et do - lén - tem, Per - tran - sí - vit glá - di - us.

The Latin words, which I had not heard in years, heightened a nostalgic awareness of Christ's journey to Calvary and His crucifixion. The procession passed by me continuing to the twelfth, thirteenth and fourteenth stations of the cross.

I recalled from my Bible history, learned in the third and fourth grades, how two people came close to Jesus. Veronica reached out to wipe the face of Jesus and captured His image on her veil. Simon of Cyrene, who lived in Africa, eight hundred miles away, was a part of the crowd watching the procession to Calvary. The Roman legionnaires forced him to carry Jesus' cross. He did.

I knelt and made the sign of the cross. I was touched. Suddenly tears filled my eyes and my bosom heaved with noiseless sobs. I felt the holiness of this place. Somehow I sensed the power of God. I knew I was being called to become a follower of Jesus in the Catholic church. I was to love Him, to serve Him and to live a life that would glorify Him.

Mrs. Stanton placed an arm around my shoulder as Sister Mildred had years before. We walked silently to her apartment. Over a cup of coffee, Mrs. Stanton remarked, "I noticed that you knew the songs, when to stand and kneel and how to make the sign of the cross. Are you Catholic?"

I explained in detail my four years at St. Mary's, my near acceptance in the church while at college, my attraction to the church in Philadelphia and my recent completion of instructions at St. Joseph's. "For some reason I keep putting it off, becoming Catholic," I explained. "I want to and yet I am uncertain whether it is the right thing to do."

"We shall think no more about it. Your journey is over. I shall be your Godmother. On Monday morning with Holy Saturday and Easter Sunday out of the way, I shall phone your pastor and arrange for your baptism immediately," she promised.

"I knew there was something special about you when I first met you. I am so happy for you. Welcome into Christ's holy church."

After the children and I were baptized, I phoned Sister Mildred to tell her the good news. "Yes, Norma, it is twenty-two years since I invited you to attend St. Mary's school. Remember this, Norma. You have not chosen God, God has chosen you. Never doubt why you are where you are."

I was thinking of another scripture I had read: "He who puts his hand to the plough and turns back is not worthy of the kingdom of heaven." I had made a lifetime commitment. No matter <u>what</u> . . . <u>this</u> was forever.

XV

My Expanding World Of Many Circles

Percy was a whistler. He could whistle melodious tones such as I had never heard before, and rarely since. Rain or shine, early dawn or high noon, good times or bad, Percy had a tune on his lips which came from the heart. Sometimes he would vocalize the lyrics with his rich tenor voice. One of his favorite songs was "My Blue Heaven."

> Just Molly and me, and baby makes three
> We're happy in my blue heaven
>
> When whippoorwills call and evening is nigh
> I hurry to my blue heaven
> A turn to the right, a little white light
> Will lead you to my blue heaven
> You'll see a smiling face, a fireplace
> A cozy room
> A little nest that's nestled where
> The roses bloom
>
> Just Molly and me, and baby makes three
> We're happy in my blue heaven.

Home was our haven but I felt smothered, restricted. Like most young married couples our little nest pre-empted all but the most basic of human interactions. A polite non-intimate relationship continued with my family. The job-employer-employee interchange provided little fraternization during or after the work day.

In the first seven years of our marriage we had invited no guests to our home. Neither had we been invited out. We knew of no married couples in our age group. The commerce of daily living provided some polite interchanges. The paperboy, the milkman, the iceman and the store clerk became extensions of the family with their greetings of "Hello," "Good morning," "Thank you," "How are you today?" and "A good day to you, Ma'am." My world was much too small. I was ready to sail forth.

Having joined the Catholic church which forbade its members to worship in a protestant church, I had distanced myself from the social and cultural gatherings of the Negro community. I felt no special affinity, no craving need to be in the midst of dark-skinned people. Neither did I feel any uneasiness about being the only brown-skinned woman in a white gathering. A few times when I received a strong nonverbal message of "Gee, I didn't expect you to be here," I wondered what it would be like to be one of the majority instead of the only minority.

I attempted to find out. I observed Negro people up and down the street, in their N.A.A.C.P. meetings, beauty shops, lodges and wherever two or more were gathered. I became more confused and disheartened than inspired.

What did being a Negro mean? Did it consist of a magnetic pull towards people of multi-hued skin colors? Did it mean feeling comfortable with individuals who had been hurt, frightened and intimidated by whites to the point where they were reluctant to venture forth? Did it mean being surrounded by those who had lost their self-esteem, lost the will to fight and backed away from challenges? Did it mean huddling with those who yearned to be pitied and comforted because of "the troubles I seen?"

I observed a number of homogeneous groups out of touch with the vital challenges of life. Even the professionally elite Negroes, with their well-furnished homes and recreational rooms, had established exclusive gatherings based upon education and skin color.

Their race isolated them from the white professionals. They could not golf, swim or become Rotarians with their Caucasian equals. They isolated themselves from the common Negro, who embarrassed them. A very thin line separated them from their impoverished brother. An act of racial injustice resulting in the loss of their job could nullify their status, rob them of privileges and plummet them to the same economic level as the lowliest unlettered, unskilled Negro. They were insecure and powerless.

Most of the people and groups I observed were outside the mainstream, going around in circles, creating their own little worlds. I did not want to be excluded in any manner from the majority culture. That skin color could limit my coming and going anywhere in the land of my birth filled me with rebellion. I was angered by the restrictive nature of the Negro world.

I would fight to the death not to be excluded from the Caucasian world nor to be confined to the Negro world. Neither would I be pushed to the bottom of the heap. I would make every effort to climb over those barriers that fenced me in or fenced me out. I might not have the genes to be a Mary McLeod Bethune, a Sojourner Truth, an Eleanor Roosevelt or a Marian Anderson. I might not surf the highest wave on life's seas, but somewhere in the middle I could make a big splash. My whole being shouted, "Hello, world, white, black, yellow, red and brown. Here I come!"

Mary Quinn Stanton had no idea of my resolve when she invited me to go with her to Akron, Ohio to hear Dorothy Day, a New York writer and publisher of a one-cent tabloid, *The Daily Worker*. Dorothy Day championed the poor and downtrodden Negro and white from a Catholic Christian conscience. Houses of Hospitality, soup kitchens, clothing centers in urban ghettos, and farming communes in rural areas were being operated in response to her expose of the poor's needs and the workers' plight in the 1930s.

Only a portion of what Dorothy Day said that evening registered because I met two women to whom I was attracted with a fascination I had never experienced before. They were Mrs. Iola Ellis and Mrs. Margaret Davis from Cleveland. They were the first Negro Catholic women I had ever met. Mrs. Ellis was opening, in response to Dorothy Day's appeal to help the poor and to evangelize, a Blessed Martin DePorres Catholic Service Store. It was located on the ground floor of her apartment home on Cedar Avenue and East 79th Street. She invited me to come to Cleveland for the formal opening a few weeks later.

"I am a convert to Catholicism, quite a few years ago," she stated. "How about you?"

"I have been a Catholic just a little more than a month," I answered.

"Then you haven't been confirmed yet?"

"No, my confirmation will not take place for another two years."

"My dear, you should not wait another two years. The Lord has work for you to do. You must be confirmed very soon so you can bring others to Christ's church."

"I have already brought someone into the church," I announced. "I was godmother to a young lady just last week."

"Evidently no one has told you," Mrs. Ellis remarked in

a jestfully scolding tone, "that you should not be a godmother before you are confirmed. We can do something about that. There is to be confirmation at St. Agnes, which is my parish, in just three months. Why not come to Cleveland to be confirmed? Ask your pastor to give you instructions. I shall alert my pastor that you will be here. I shall be your sponsor." I did, and she was.

My husband and Mr. Joseph Ellis became very good friends. Neither was Catholic, but both were agreeably supportive of their wives' chatter covering every phase of the Catholic church. When they tired of our discussions, they would retire to Mr. Ellis' study to listen to the Sunday sports.

Both Mr. and Mrs. Ellis were old enough to be our parents. They had no children. Margaret Davis had a son and daughter the ages of Norma Jean and Alluren. Mrs. Davis was all of twenty years my senior. She had married late in life, bore two children and was deserted by her preacher-husband less than four years into their marriage. Mrs. Davis sought solace in the Catholic church and converted. Our three families formed a close bond of friendship which continued for many years. Percy and I, with the children, drove to Cleveland nearly every two months to hear Mass at the Blessed Sacrament Church on East 79th and Central Avenue. Negro worshipers were in the majority with a dozen or so white ethnics sharing in the celebration of the Mass.

Perhaps for the first time I felt a kinship with Catholics throughout the world. I saw pride, confidence and reverence on Black countenances. I sensed the soul stirrings of a people who saw God as the majestic deliverer from their oppressors, once as slaves and now as freed men. Their soul-stirring, resonant choir made meaningful the Gregorian chants and the hymns they sang.

Upon leaving Mass I sometimes felt the urge to go out into the street and stand in front of a storefront church and invite the people—like the Jehovah's Witnesses did as they went from door to door on Sunday—to step inside the Catholic church and look around.

I wanted to say, "You will like it here. This church has meaning. This is where you belong."

First impulses are discouraged as impetuous and unwise. Who can say how barren this world is or how beautiful it might have been if more of us had given in to our virgin impulses?

Mrs. Ellis was an impulsive, spirit-filled activist in the church. She was outspoken in her concerns for social justice. As an advocate of integrated involvement, she exhibited a religious devotion such as I had never previously witnessed in a lay person. She was a daily communicant and she urged me to go to Mass daily.

"You have to stay close to the sourse of grace or else all your efforts will be powerless and without meaning," she counseled me.

She explained the Rosary, the Divine Office and introduced me to novenas, retreats and gatherings of the Council of Catholic Women. She took me to Bishop McFadden's office and challenged him to make use of my services. At that time, Canton was a part of the Cleveland Diocese.

To me she explained, "The Catholic Church has operated for hundreds of years only thinking of us as heathens, a people to whom they toss their rags and give a loaf of bread. We have been tolerated to varying degrees. We have not been viewed as advantageous to their causes. They have not always taken us seriously. Their seminaries and convents are closed to us. Their documents proclaim justice, equality and opportunity, but they are seldom challenged to deliver by practicing what they preach. Some of America's most serious racial incidents can be laid at the door of devout white Catholics. They are insensitive to our needs and to our feelings.

"Norma," Mrs. Ellis continued with a graciousness and dignified bearing uncommon to such fervent enthusiastic remarks, "we must become involved, not as the poor looking for a handout, but as responsible first-class Negroes paving and paying our own way. We must be seen in their organizations making decisions and carrying our fair share of the load, evangelizing the world and helping one another. If the Catholic church is to be a universal church, it must include us. We must be there, everywhere! We must work tirelessly in the vineyard to produce a harvest which will please God and benefit all of mankind. We have so much to offer."

Over the years Mrs. Ellis saw that I made an annual retreat in Cleveland and as far away as Katharine Drexel's Monastery of the Blessed Sacrament on Red Lion Road, Philadelphia, Pennsylvania. At the very first women's retreat Mrs. Ellis and I attempted to attend in Cleveland, we were not permitted to stay.

"I am sorry," Sister said. "We don't have any space for you. You can't stay here. We didn't know . . . We weren't told . . ."

"Do you mean," Mrs. Ellis asked, "that we are not allowed to pray here? You would refuse to allow me to pray to Jesus? You are his bride, are you not? Have you confessed your feelings about my dark skin to your Jesus?"

Sister stood there with her arms folded on her stomach. The dark habit accentuated the pink and white flush underneath eyes that carried a scowl of determination. Other women were arriving. Sister sought to dismiss us. "I am sorry," she repeated. I, I . . ."

Mrs. Ellis interrupted politely and calmly, "Please don't be sorry. My friend from Canton and I intend to stay. You do not have to feed us or give us a cot to sleep on tonight. We shall stay in the chapel where our Lord is perpetually exposed and pray to your spouse."

We stayed on our knees all that day. I doubt if the retreatants who came in to adore the Blessed Sacrament ever saw us. It was after dark when Mrs. Ellis and I stepped out into the Cleveland downtown traffic and hailed a cab to East 79th and Cedar. We spoke not a word. The next morning my knees were swollen twice their size with water blisters so painful I could hardly walk.

Did I pray during those twelve hours on my knees? I doubt it. I questioned the meaning of Christianity. I had to hold on firmly to my childhood images and the saintly memories of Sister Mildred, Sister Hortense, Sister Gertrude, Sister Bernardine and others. I did recall my grandfather's command, "Never allow yourself to hate . . . ever!" I tried to recall the words of a poem I had read at one time without serious reflection. It was about two brown boys.

Upon my return home I went to the library to look up the poem, then I went to the bookstore and purchased a book of Negro poems. I read over and over again the poem by Frank Horne, who was born in 1899.

On Seeing Two Brown Boys in a Catholic Church

It is fitting that you be here,
Little brown boys
With Christ-like eyes
And curling hair.

Look you on yon crucifix
Where He hangs nailed and pierced
With head hung low
And Eyes a'blind with blood that drips
From a thorny crown. . .
Look you well,
You shall know this thing.

Judas' kiss will burn your cheek
And you shall be denied
By your Peter — And Gethsemane . . .
You shall know full well Gethsemane.

You, too will suffer under Pontius Pilate
And feel the rugged cut of rough hewn cross
Upon your surging shoulders —
They will spit in your face
And laugh . . .
They will nail you up twixt thieves
And gamble for your little garments.

And in this you will exceed God
For on this earth
You shall know Hell —

O little brown boys
With Christ-like eyes
And curling hair
It is fitting that you be here

Whenever there was a tendency to feel otherwise, I recalled the line, "It is fitting that you be here."

The next time Mrs. Iola Ellis entered this monastery on a Catholic women's retreat, there was no incident. Iola frequently offered to pay all or part of my fare or expenses to retreats and Catholic gatherings. She was generous in assisting others in a variety of ways. She took Mrs. Davis off welfare by paying for her training as a cosmetologist. Then she opened a beauty shop and placed her nieces and Mrs. Davis there as full-time employees.

"Now Margaret," Mrs. Ellis told her, "let the church and the community know you are paying your own way. You can beg for others, but never for yourself again."

The Blessed Martin DePorres Service Center operated by Mrs. Ellis and many Cleveland volunteers from all walks of life was a beehive of activity. Mrs. Ellis, a devotee of Dorothy Day, saw her as a Joan of Arc of the poor and lauded her for her concern of the working classes and minorities. She mailed me copies of the *Daily Worker* or loaded me with armfuls of back copies and Catholic literature when we visited her.

Because of Mrs. Ellis' enthusiasm, I decided to get a closer look at Dorothy Day by visiting her center in Harlem. The trip to New York, ostensibly to visit my brother, Carl, his wife, Betty, their young son, Raymond, and to congratulate Carl upon his new position, placed me within a few streets of the Dorothy Day Hospice. Carl was manager of the Theresa Hotel, the largest hotel in Harlem patronizing the Negro tourist and the theatrical stars playing at the Cotton Club.

Carl, the little brother who had begun caddying at age seven, had made good his desire to manage a first-class establishment. After three days of sightseeing and watching the fabulous nightlife of famous Negroes, I announced I would spend perhaps a week lending a volunteer hand at Dorothy Day's Hospice and then return to the hotel for an extra day or two before going home.

Dorothy Day was a dynamic, determined, aggressive, purposeful individual. She had gathered her spiritual, physical and intellectual energies to combat the thoughtless, blind and deliberate injustices heaped upon the powerless. She was less feminine in appearance than a garbed religious, but she had none of the insipid, spineless, apologetic insensitivity of the prim nuns who had not welcomed a Negro Catholic into their chapel to pray. I had not been permitted to sleep on the antiseptic plain cots in a holy convent, but at Dorothy Day's I slept on a canvas cot in a crowded tenement hallway. Our co-volunteers of many mixed skin colors and of religious and irreligious persuasions had a friendly acceptance of everyone. We arose after a near sleepless night interrupted by discordant street noises and the adventurous scampering of rodents up and down the dark hallways. We became the hide-and-seek victims to winged and crawling insects that dispatched their calling cards of little red welts the moment we flung the tattletale-gray sheets off our bodies in search of a comforting, cool breeze.

Before dawn I was anxious to join the crew that prepared the breakfast for those who would be in the bread line. The hungry marched into the combination dining room, meeting room and office all day long. There was always coffee and bread being dispensed.

As the eager hands of the unfortunate held chipped bowls of many shapes and sizes for their ladle of food, they were served with a smile and a cheery word. Standing there in Dorothy Day's soup kitchen, gazing at the homeless poor of every size, age and ethnic appearance, I felt pity for white persons.

Generally in my home environment whites had everything. We had been taught to be like them. Somehow in some way we learned to envy them. Here at Dorothy Day's I looked into white faces where eyes, once brown, blue, green and gray, looked like opaque, unseeing marbles peering from sockets drained of hope and direction. I felt decidedly superior to them, and, yes, repulsed. Who would want to be white and be like them?

After two nights and three days, I left the multifarious environment of disturbing sights and smells and sounds to return to the plush setting of the Theresa Hotel. Even that paled, and I returned home ahead of schedule.

A year or two later, I decided to visit one of Dorothy Day's farms in the Cincinnati area. Real guilt followed me as I walked away from the Harlem Hospice. Maybe on a farm I could redeem myself. I could handle ministering to the poor, breathing fresh air in the great outdoors, I reasoned.

Alighting from the Greyhound bus in Cincinnati, I was greeted by two young women perhaps in their late teens or early twenties. It was midafternoon when we arrived at a large farmhouse in the middle of nowhere. The house had the barest of furnishings on the first floor. There was an abundance of tables, chairs, books and magazines. All were an invitation to study, discuss and reflect. The ten to fifteen volunteers were at their respective farm duties. "Just make yourself comfortable until the crew comes in from the fields about sunset. Then we shall assign duties, prepare dinner and have our evening prayers," I was told.

That first evening, as the setting sun was casting shadows hurrying to embrace the darkness, I was assigned with a young man to go to the barn and milk one of the two cows. I was being shown how to squeeze the udders and direct the white flow into what had been a gallon Karo syrup container. The cow moved. I slid off my stool and one hand landed in a warm pile of freshly dropped manure. I picked myself up, walked to the house, rinsed my hand at the pump outside the kitchen door, walked inside and begged to be taken to the bus stop.

"I must go home at once!" I begged. I was on the verge of tears. People who surrounded me understood and urged me to wait until morning. They gave their reasons. They did not relish driving the long distance into Cincinnati. They were tired. They had been on their feet since 4:00 a.m. It could be dangerous for me to be sitting in a bus station, alone, all night; and supper was about to be served.

"Let's spend an evening together talking about ourselves and Dorothy Day's mission," someone suggested. We talked until 2:00 a.m. With minimum sleep, I was driven to town as the sun in the eastern sky was pushing the darkness out of sight. Somehow Dorothy Day's disciples had convinced

me I should feel no guilt about my discomfort at the Harlem Hostel or the Cincinnati farm.
"This mission is not for everyone. Don't be too hard on yourself. Except for a few married couples, we are all single, widowed and retired loners. We need this challenge. You don't. You have a husband and children. How fortunate you are. You can, and probably are, doing things we could never do."
Urban hostels, soup kitchens and farms were not for me. Still Dorothy topped my list of God's special people. She was a person who possessed intellectual persuasion. She challenged the powerful through her newspaper. She could mingle with the poor and not diminish their dignity. She could hold the hands of the most hapless wretches, touch them and not turn up her nose at their appearance—appearances that could upset one's stomach and produce vomiting. She never recoiled at the human smells emanating from their person.
I could not choose her path of service. I could only bless her and pray for her from afar. I would choose to work with people before the blood poison of unemployment, detachment, defeat and hopelessness made putrid ulcers of their lives.
My economic status was just a thin thread away from the hungry, homeless and disparaged. I yearned for an experience with luxury, beauty and plenty.
Had I not relished for a time the wealthy homes where I worked as a cook? Was I not drawn in part to the Catholic church because of its beauty, grandeur and solemnity?
I recalled the luxurious, secluded suburban paradise of Mother Drexel's retreat house in Philadelphia. It was a world away from soup kitchens and rescue centers. Perhaps I should return there for a spiritual uplift. Perhaps, there, I could be inspired to find my niche for service.
On my way home from that Dorothy Day trip to Akron, where I had first met my Cleveland friends and before any of the above came to pass, a new friendship was about to form.

Father Thomas Heimann, a new assistant pastor at St. Peter's, was in the car on the return trip from Akron. With the car filled with passengers, I had not noticed this young priest. There is no recollection of the content or quality of the conversation on that ride back to Canton.

The next day I received a phone call from Father Heimann. "I wonder if you would come by St. Peter's Rectory? I would like to talk to you and get to know you. You are the first intelligent Negro I have ever had the opportunity of meeting. May I have the pleasure of knowing you better?"

I hoped my response was polite. A thousand thoughts can pass through one's mind in seconds. Intelligent! What did he mean? Was he surprised I did not talk or behave like the giddy-headed house servant portrayed on the movie screen or the black-faced comedian seen at St. John's minstrel shows held every year?

I had never seen a minstrel and had only a vague idea of the images in jest or seriousness that portrayed the Negro. From NAACP meetings I heard that minstrels portrayed Negroes as bumbling, ignorant, thieving buffoons. Intelligent? Not likely.

A polite curiosity was a high level component with both of us as we conversed in the spacious visiting room at St. Peter's a few days later. It was Father Heimann's first assistant pastor assignment at the huge cathedral-like German parish. He was a native of Massillon, just eight miles west of Canton. He was educated at John Carroll, St. Mary's Seminary in Cleveland, Ohio, and Innsbruck, Austria.

He was about five years my senior and as German as I was Negro. I envisioned him as the kind of family member my grandfather must have grown up with in his childhood. His nordic, whiter-than-fair skin contrasted pleasantly with his deep blue eyes and his black priestly robe. He asked many questions about my family and how I became interested in the church. He wanted to know how the parishioners in general received me. Were they friendly? Did they ever move away from me when they found themselves seated beside me in a pew? Would I feel free to contact him any time there were questions?

I came away from that half-hour visit convinced he was genuinely concerned I should feel welcome and comfortable in the Catholic church. I must have shared my appreciation of a really sincere and caring priest to my mother. Without my knowledge, she, my brother Eugene and my sister Ruth began taking instructions from Father Heimann. Six months later they were received into the Catholic church as members of St. Peter's congregation.

Coincidentally, many things unexpected and unexplained were happening all around us. Our baby sister, Virginia, was attending Bennett College, North Carolina. Upon high school graduation she had received the same Menelick Culture Club scholarship (now one hundred dollars) that I had received. Like Ethel and me, she would hope to find work to pay for all additional expenses and remain in school.

Mrs. Broomhandle, the neighbor who objected so vociferously to our moving into "her" neighborhood, was sending Virginia a dollar a week, four dollars a month, so she would have some spending money while in college.

In the meantime, Aunt Clella, recently widowed, had written from Sharon, Pennsylvania that she planned to return to Canton as soon as Grandma was able to travel. She and Grandma had been taking instructions to join the Catholic church. When Grandma became ill, the priest baptized her and came to the home to give her communion. Then we got a call that Grandma had passed away. Aunt Clella was bringing her body home. Father Heimann read the funeral prayers at 743 Union Avenue Southwest in the home Grandma had begun to purchase when she was sixty-three years of age. At age eighty-six,

she was laid to rest beside Grandpa at Westlawn Cemetery.
   The unexplained spread of Catholicism in our family continued to happen. Ethel wrote from Howard University to say while working part-time at Catholic University she began taking instructions and was soon to become a Catholic. Virginia wrote that she was taking instructions at a Catholic church in walking distance from Bennett College. All of these events happened over a period of two years.
   Carl congratulated us over our new faith and lamented that because he had married a divorced Catholic, he could not be one with us. At that time, Percy gave no thought to the church. His only comment now and then, made with a great deal of pride and respect, was, "My dad is a Baptist preacher. I must remember that."
   He frequently attended Sunday Mass with me and the children. Norma Jean had only to comment, "Daddy, it's not any fun when you are not with us. You must come, too." Her evening prayers always ended with, "Make Daddy become Catholic some day, God. Please."
   Marcella, our foster daughter, took instructions from Father Heimann. She was married to Bill Powell from St. Peter's Rectory. When it became known I was Catholic and that my daughter was in a Catholic school, many people contacted me for further information about the faith. They asked to accompany me to church to witness a Catholic service. One of my friends, Georgianna Umbles (Mrs. Howard Page) sought advice about enrolling her four children, Howard, Marva, Twila and Alan, in Central Catholic High School. "My children are smart, but I am concerned about a better-than-average academic performance combined with a concept of ethics and morality," she avowed. "Can you help me get them enrolled?"
   There were perhaps 40 Negro children in six Catholic grade schools at that time. A small but growing number of Negro

Catholics became the source of a spiritual and psychological fellowship.

In July of 1939, nearly a year after Mary Stanton had stood at the baptismal fount with me, she called me to her office and invited me to accompany her to the home of a welfare client. I had been hired full-time as an investigator/caseworker just days after that memorable Easter weekend. Mrs. Stanton, who had always been most friendly and supportive, took an even greater interest in me after she became my Godmother. Sharing the faith with almost as much fervor as my Cleveland friends, Mrs. Ellis and Mrs. Davis, initiated between my boss and me a sincere bond of caring.

Mary Stanton encouraged me to become involved in many activities as one of her staff. She would invite me to be present at a meeting of agency executives and political gatherings. She urged me to attend the monthly meetings of the Social Workers Institute. At a state meeting of social workers in Columbus, Ohio, Mrs. Stanton registered me as a delegate. I spent my first night at the Deshler Wallick Hotel at a time when it was impossible for a Negro to be assigned a hotel room. We shared a double room without incident. The Negro bellhop smiled first awkwardly and then victoriously as he carried our bags to our room.

This morning's invitation to a welfare client's home was just another in a series of unexpected ventures into strange, uncharted territory. "We are going to see a client whom I visited when she was a patient at Mercy Hospital. I hardly know how to explain this except to say that a woman who was dying is now well," Mary remarked. "Her name is Rhoda Wise."

We drove to the eastern limits of the northeast section of Canton. The small white-framed bungalow was characteristic of the lower socioeconomic level of what I described as a struggling, poor, white neighborhood. It was the kind of residential area I preferred to avoid as an investigator and caseworker. I feared their reaction to a Negro woman stepping on their front porch. Poor whites, I had heard many times, were the Negro's greatest enemy. They saw us as some kind of threat or embarrassment.

Because Negroes were also poor, they and the poor whites were frequently thrown together in low-paying, hard-labor jobs. Living in rented houses on dirt streets and back alleys, it was their children who were taunted about going to school with "niggers." They were not tradesmen or skilled laborers. They had no money in the bank. They were too poor to move into well-established middle-class neighborhoods.

They could, however, and did, buy cheap plots of land in unzoned, unrestricted areas of the townships outside the city limits. Small settlements developed just two and three miles from the city square. They built three- and four-room, cabin-like homes and added an additional room every few years. They did all they could to glorify their status as "poor, but white." Many voiced their contempt for Negroes.

We ascended the porch of a neat, unpretentious bungalow and were admitted by one of the many neighbors who literally became attendants to the Wise family. Mrs. Stanton and I entered the bedroom of Rhoda Wise. She and Mrs. Stanton became engaged in an animated conversation. Then, with me not knowing all that had been happening to Mrs. Wise, I heard her say, "Let me show you my abdomen. You can see for yourself, it is completely healed."

As we approached her bed, she lifted her negligee and exposed her abdomen. Mrs. Wise was a large woman. I gazed upon a smooth, waxy-looking area about three inches in width and ten to twelve inches long in one direction and several inches shorter in another direction. It looked unreal. She proceeded to detail how the Little Flower and Jesus appeared to her on June 28, 1939, and how she discovered her healing early the next morning.

On our way back to the office, Mrs. Stanton detailed her knowledge of Mrs. Wise's stay at Mercy Hospital, her request to take instructions and her conversion to Catholicism. She had been sent home to die of a cancer which drained continuously, keeping her open abdomen raw and sore. Mrs. Wise was convinced of the reality of Jesus. He was alive and deeply concerned about the least of His little ones.

I became a frequent visitor at the Wise home and spent many a first Friday night from 10:00 p.m. until dawn of the next day watching with several hundred curious people for a light or some sign that our Lord had entered Rhoda Wise's room and was speaking to her. On these visits, I met Catherine Barthel, Mae Francis and her teen-age daughter, Rita Francis (Mother Angelica).

Many cures were reported. Rita Francis told of her deliverance from an annoying stomach and back condition. She may have been inspired to enter the Poor Clare's cloister at Sancta Clara Monastery from her association with Rhoda Wise and some of the beautiful people there. I became a close friend of Mae Francis, Rita's mother. For a period of ten years, Mae and I joined each other at a morning Mass before going to our respective jobs.

Mrs. Wise spoke to me in the spring of 1940 about a message Jesus had given her. "Norma, Jesus wants people of your race to come here, too! He is concerned about all of us. He loves us all." Mrs. Wise experienced the stigmata and I was privileged to see the blood that flowed from her forehead, hands and feet.

Still there were moments when I wondered, doubted, questioned. On the first Friday crowds, on Rhoda Wise's lawn, where two hundred or more people gathered to pray the rosary expectantly, only one, two or three Negroes were to be seen. There were occasional warm smiles. No one pulled away from another. The crowds—men and women, young and old, short and tall, believers and skeptics—were body to body, hip to hip, arm to arm, waiting expectantly for a miracle. Hands clasped rosary beads, lips moved in prayer. From downcast eyes, furrowed brows and taut cheeks, I could sense fear, hurt, sorrow, pain, hope and expectancy in their silent waiting.

The next day, away from the covering of the star-studded night, away from the momentary expectation of something eternal and good, I would see other feelings in white faces. It would begin when I got on the bus in the early morning, headed for downtown, and dropped my fare in the box. The bus driver's indifferent attitude, the look of hate and revulsion when I sat beside a passenger on the bus, the nonverbal messages of a dozen patrons, "Why do we have to put up with your kind." All of this would hit me with a force covered up in the presence of holiness.

I was discovering that second only to the comfort, security and peace of one's home was the inspiring, accepting atmosphere of a Catholic gathering. Maybe that was reason enough to nourish the idea to form an Interracial Council. In 1945 I organized a small group of active, enthusiastic, sincere Christians. We met twice monthly, became sponsors to new converts and studied the doctrines of the church. Its main purpose was to strengthen the relationship of Negro Catholics and Negro converts with their white godparents and sponsors. I recall one woman telling me that the priest who baptized her had called the custodian to stand as her godfather. She never knew his name, never saw him again. She was in the church without a human connection.

It was through this Catholic Interracial organization of thirty members that I took seriously the commitment to remain an active evangelizing Catholic. Those who expressed an interest in Catholicism were invited to attend the Christmas Eve midnight Mass with my family. The fast-breaking breakfast that followed became an annual affair. Over a period of time, I became a godmother and sponsor to more than fifty converts. For nearly ten years, we held a Day of Recollection at Sancta Clara Monastery within the octave of August 15, the Feast of the Assumption of the Blessed Virgin Mary. It was always a joy to plan this event with Sister Juliana, the extern nun. Busloads of people come from Akron, Cleveland, Detroit and Pittsburgh to meet other Negro Catholics, to listen to inspiring talks and to pray. Bishop McFadden and the O'Dea's, upon whose estate the monastery was built, were supporters of this gathering. The day began with a beautifully celebrated outdoor Mass with the Knights of Columbus in formal regalia, giving full honors to the Bishop and his flock. We affirmed the universality of the church.

The first Negro priest in the Youngstown Diocese, Father Allen Simpson of Ottomwa, Iowa, was a regular celebrant, assisting at Mass, giving the homily, a midafternoon talk or leading the Rosary. He was a handsome mulatto gentleman who caused our hearts to swell with pride and thanksgiving. The older Catholics saw hope in Negro vocations. Young children and teen-agers who had never seen other Negro children in their church or school met these young people and become pen pals.

One of the last speakers to attend our gathering was Father LeFarge from New York, the national head of the Council for Interracial Justice. Between four and five hundred people were in attendance. The local priests were conspicuously absent. Some time later, as I was making plans for the next year's event, I was politely informed in a most unusual, roundabout manner by a most faithful supporter, that the new Bishop Walsh, who had never acknowledged the letters I mailed to him, disapproved of the annual interracial gatherings.

"You are not permitted to invite a priest from another diocese without the Bishop's approval," I was told. "He disapproves of this gathering."

I wondered if the Bishop disapproved of the annual minstrel shows sponsored by numerous Catholic organizations and patronized by devout Catholics throughout the country. The NAACP was actively involved in a nationwide protest of the black-faced musicals that fostered prejudice through laughter inciting racial insults.

If Bishop Walsh disapproved of a fully Catholic celebration of the Mass, with timely discussions about Christ's love, shared by whites and Negroes together, I must attend a minstrel composed of an all white audience. How did the black-faced, white-lipped star performers caricature the Negro? What was the good or the harm of this fun-poking ridicule of pigmented human beings created in the image of God?

Shuggie invited me to accompany her to St. John's minstrel show. "It is highly publicized and I would like to hear some good old fashioned music," she explained.

Mom had sung as many tunes about Negroes, colored and darkies while we were growing up as she did the Irish and German tunes and the ballads that appealed to everybody. The "Dark Town Strutter's Ball," and "My Gal is a High Born Lady" were as beautiful with their catchy phrases as "My Wild Irish Rose" and "Bill Bailey Won't You Please Come Home."

The basement auditorium of St. John's Catholic Church was filled to capacity for the Sunday matinee performance. I thoroughly enjoyed the music, the attempts at a buck and wing dance and even the uncoordinated tap dancing. I was not too offended by the black faces, blacker than any midnight or any Negro alive. Their antics were not personally offensive for they were unreal caricatures like the false face comedians of Halloween.

The Irish jokes about Pat and Mike were interspersed with

a preponderance of jokes about Rastus and Sambo. Pat and Mike had one too many beers, got into a discussion about heaven and hell and won a battle of words without landing a punch. Rastus and Sambo engaged in chicken stealing and running from ghosts in the graveyard. Their imbecilic, childlike behavior portrayed a mentality of lying, stealing, laziness and cowardice.

Even these traits, I reasoned, not knowing whether to laugh with the audience or not, could be the antics of any group of people. I must not become overly sensitive or read into a situation that which did not exist. Were they making fun of the Negro? If they had painted their faces green or purple or gray or blue or orange or paper white, no particular race could be demeaned. No particular ethnic group could take offense.

The last act of the minstrel show was a performance by a group of St. John's school children. It left no doubt in my mind! They were most certainly ridiculing the Negro. Twenty children singly and with a partner came on stage dressed in native costumes. They identified themselves as Irish, German, Italian, Swiss, Polish, Rumanian, Hungarian, English, Indian and American. Adorned in colorful garments, crocheted and embroidered shawls, wooden shoes, Scottish kilts, beaded moccasins and every accessory accentuating artistry, grace and beauty, they gathered around an American girl dressed in a red, white and blue uniform. At the very close of this extravaganza, Topsy ran on stage and asked, "Why you all ain't invited me to yo' party? Jest b'cause I jest growed doan mean I doan want to bees with yo' all. I'se an American, too, I is!"

Topsy, with a patched and ragged dress, wore size twelve men's shoes that flopped when she walked. One stocking of one color was up, the other stocking of another color hung over the other shoe. Her wig of black kinky hair had little braids tied with a dozen red ribbons. With her shoe polished black face and huge red lips, she was as ridiculously caricatured as the others were gloriously portrayed. I wanted to run screaming from the hall. Topsy was a real slave-born Negro in Harriet Beecher Stowe's Uncle Tom's Cabin. That whole audience could laugh at this great American tragedy. Did they thank their God they were not born with black skins? How can a Negro man or woman, boy or girl, walk with dignity and maintain his or her self-esteem when the majority population sees black and brown skin as an object of ridicule?

Without saying much to each other, Shuggie and I returned to our homes. Within the hour I was back at St. John's Church. I knocked on the rectory door and asked to speak to a priest.

"Any particular priest?" the housekeeper asked.

"No, anyone will do."

"Father Barrett's here. I'll tell him you want to speak to him."

A most handsome, personable young priest entered the office. He listened attentively while I spoke. The gist of my concern was this. "If you are going to show all of America's ethnic groups in their best light, then I object strenuously to your minstrel portrayal of the Negro child as a party-crashing buffoon, a 'just-growed' organism short of resembling anything the least bit human."

Father listened. There was no anger, no accusations. I voiced my remarks as an offended individual to a young priest who had not the faintest idea an offense had been committed.

"I have two children going to a Catholic school," I explained. "I assure you I am not sending them there to develop an inferiority complex. When my children's classmates, parents, teachers and every family in the parish feeds upon this kind of racist inferiority portrayal, what chance do I have as a Negro parent to convince my children that they are somebody?"

I continued. "How can your parishioners be expected to see Negroes as human beings deserving of justice and equality when the only Negroes most of them see or hear about are portrayed through your highly publicized, yearly entertainment. You are teaching them that my people have none of the honorable qualities you respect. We are liars, thieves, dirty, cowardly, illiterate and shiftless. You know, of course, that the NAACP is waging a national campaign against this kind of racial defamation. I believe in doing my own fighting. Until the day comes when Negroes have total equality with all other Americans, I shall protest the lynching of the Negro through humorous entertainment."

I left. When, an hour later, I returned for the evening performance, Topsy was not there. A few years later, the minstrel show, along with Amos and Andy, became history. The great wrong was not just in the jokes and antics of the performers. Consciously and unconsciously the viewers and listeners transferred the denigrating characteristics to America's most identifiable minority and sullied our self-image. My expanding world of many circles held quite a few surprises. I welcomed the challenge and the new involvements.

XVI

My Work Place, The Slums

Most professions dealing with human needs dispense their services from environments that are very different from the daily habitats of the people receiving their administrations. A school teacher, physician, hospital nurse, judge and merchant generally teach, prescribe, medicate, dispense justice and serve clients from their politically approved and culturally accepted bases of operation. Too often they have only a faint understanding of the poor and the less fortunate living in those other worlds outside their own status circle.

From time to time a student of the humanities, a newspaper reporter, a novelist or a scientist researches a segment of society and its variable lifestyles. Sometimes these studies appear to enlighten the reader and benefit the client, but often they tend to justify the gap between the haves and the have-nots.

In the 1950s, the city fathers of a thousand depressed urban areas saw the ugly inner city sights and their inhabitants as expendable. With an emphasis upon renewal, they sought to eliminate the eyesores and the incidents they claimed were hurtful to progress. By tearing down old, even landmark dwellings, building innerbelt thoroughfares and zoning industrial parks, they changed their cities' images, their skylines and their priorities. Considerations, if any, for the displaced residents assumed the new topography would conceal, if not eliminate, socioeconomic disparities.

It was the social worker and the public health nurse of the 1930s, 1940s and 1950s who knew the slums and its inhabitants. They walked the disordered streets and entered the multifarious dwellings where lived the lowest strata of society.

Cherry Avenue, Piedmont and Robin Courts, Walnut, Liberty, Rex, Lafayette and Madison Avenues were some of the beautiful street names in the slums of Canton. From afar one's imagination could envision colorful fruit-and-nut scented orchards, a bird sanctuary in a forest of gracious trees and marble statues of patriotic heroes adorning a parkway boulevard.

Such was not the case. One entered the southeast section of town by way of Cherry Avenue, a main thoroughfare stretching north and south and paralleling Market Avenue two blocks to the east. Appearances had changed from my sixteen-year-old, wide-eyed, entranced picture of the multiethnic melting pot of 1925. That whole area, caught in the stranglehold of the 1930s Depression, began a downward trend.

In the dead of winter the area took on the appearance of a ghost town. The heavy pall of formless clouds in somber skies wrapped the brick and wood framed dwellings in anonymity. There was little to reveal who or what stirred beneath its funereal shroud. In the summer, like bed bugs escaping a smothering mattress, humanity poured into the streets seeking some comfort and some anticipated excitement. The ugly four- and five-storied commercial buildings glowered over the deteriorating two-story residences like a Frankenstein about to annihilate his victims.

Sightseers, politicians, investors and do-gooders made their warm weather excursions to assess the condition of the area. One of the women I cooked for used to drive her children down Cherry Avenue to show them how happy-go-lucky (lazy) the poor people were, how cluttered the streets and how dirty the windows. There were other intruders and adventurers who saw "gold in them thar slums." They swooped down upon the poor with carnivorous intent.

Salesmen with portable commodities of every kind descended upon the hapless to make their door-to-door sales pitch. They sold brooms, brushes, encyclopedias, shirts, ties, aprons, pictures, wall coverings, cooking utensils, spices, food seasonings, cough syrups, beauty aids and more. Word had gone out that the slum dwellers were eager spenders. All a salesman needed was to smile pleasantly, give a penny to a small child and convince the buyer his product was indispensable. Most merchandise was not.

At all hours of the day, small groups of unemployed men stood around or sat on orange crates in front of abandoned businesses and empty store front entrances. If they were not gesticulating in a heated discussion, they were playing cards or checkers. Others went behind the building to roll dice. They stayed respectfully clear of the businesses that still attracted paying customers, namely the restaurants, the pharmacy and the barber shop.

The barber shop was never a place for loitering, just for lingering. Regular, generous-tipping patrons could linger as long as there was an empty chair awaiting the next customer. The barber shop of the '20s, '30s and '40s was the forum for the town's philosophers. The doctor, lawyer, dentist, preacher, steel worker, porter, chauffeur, custodian, county employee, business operator, numbers player and pimp shared their views openly.

They engaged in heated discussions about the emerging Black consciousness, how to move into the mainstream, the world depression, Negro patriotism, African liberation, religion, science and social justice. The nature of these discussions were leaked to the general community by a husband, father or brother who had been inspired or annoyed by the comments they had heard. The determination to move forward as a viable force in the community was attributed to the opinions of such men as Frank Beane, Clay Hunter, L. L. Slaughter, Albert Joyce, A. A. Andrews, Howard Page, Robert Hughes, Bud Smallwood, John Archer, Z. A. Hunter, George and James Titus, Floyd Umbles, Moses Powell, George Webster, Charles Frazier, James Calhoun, Rev. S. E. Gibson, Rev. Donald Jacobs, Nathan Doyle, William Warren, Baldwin Harris, the Powe brothers, Henry Pearson and others. They were pioneers in new careers, new jobs and business ventures. They were in tune with the pulse of Negro America and sensitive to the needs of Black youth.

The vocalizations of the debates could be compared to a Chamber of Commerce deliberation. The activists solicited shareholders to build The Pathfinder Roller Skating Rink on Liberty Avenue, a recreation site for youth.

Tolerant, yet adamant, the debaters researched their philosophies. They read William Monroe Trotter's "Guardian," DuBoise' "The Crisis," Robert Abbott's "The Chicago Defender" and O. W. Walker's "The Cleveland Call & Post." They gathered data from the library, encyclopedia, legal precedents and "hand-me-down" gossip from chauffeurs, waiters and house servants who had heard and seen what historians might never record.

The debaters' treatise would never be broadcast afar. Unless a seed of inspiration took root in a quiet listener's psyche, it was as if no one had spoken. The President of the United States would never know the thoughts of Negro America. A university professor could not add a new concept to his lectures. Neither the United Nation's Assembly nor the Pope of Rome would ever know the Negro's concerns for an understanding and caring world.

The barber, never drawn to take sides or referee, discreetly snipped his customers' hair, lathered their whiskers, shaved them, brushed them off and gave them a mirror to see their image.

Women were seldom seen between the hours of 8:30 a.m. and 4:00 p.m. Those fortunate to have jobs walked those streets long before they became alive. They would return with the teen-agers on their way home from McKinley High School. Occasionally an ephemeral female figure slipped into the drugstore, whispered to the druggist and, just as unobtrusively, left. She disappeared around a corner to enter one of those mysterious houses of ill-fame. A happily burdened old lady with a bag from the vegetable market or a newspaper wrapped fowl from the poultry store (slaughtered while the customer waited) received polite salutations from the male sidewalk brigade. "Good maunin', ma'am." "How you be today, ma'am?"

Small children frequently ventured through the narrow passageway between buildings to listen to the sidewalk loiterers and assimilate the colorful street language. In due response to an elder's call, "Sammy, Lilly, where are you?", they would return to their backyards cluttered with uncontained rubbish.

The social worker and public health nurse walked through those dark passageways in search of their clients. They saw little children playing with half-starved, flea-infested kittens and puppies. They learned to suppress their fears of the bold rodents wending their way in and out of debris, unmindful of humans, large or small.

For fifteen years the slum was my occupational territory. Working with people was one glorious banquet feasting upon the different personalities with whom I came in contact. They were so unique, so intriguing and so lovable. Who were some of these people? Composites of many of my clients, altered to protect their identity, follow.

Mrs. Anderson was the widowed mother of nine children

ranging in ages from six to twenty-two. With the five infant grandchildren from three of her oldest, there were often fifteen people seated at the dinner table. Mrs. Anderson had issued a standing invitation for me to stop at her home for lunch any day I was in the neighborhood. Several such invitations from other clients were most appreciated. Engaging, attractive restaurants were not in the area and others did not welcome Negro patrons.

Mrs. Anderson's statuesque Watusi-gened body never tired of cooking, washing, ironing or tending the little crowded five-room house, with its small vegetable patch at her back door. The garden extended to the rear of another two-story dwelling that fronted on Liberty Avenue. The front porch jutted out toward the alley on Thompson Court as a four-by-ten-foot barricade, defying the alley debris from encroaching any closer.

In the summer and fall, the narrow unpaved alley sought to undo the cleanliness of which Mrs. Anderson was so justly proud. Clouds of dust settled on the porch, came through the windows and splattered the garments on the clothesline with a misty sand. In the winter and spring, the snow and the ankle-deep mud clung to shoes and boots and left clods of dirt on the newspaper-strewn kitchen floor.

I recalled how as a child we had played "Baker's Man" and shaped little mud cakes from the sandy soil under the grape arbor. After the mud cakes had "baked" in the sun for awhile, we would each taste our imaginary confection and courageously swallow a small morsel with the comment, "Everybody has to eat a bushel of dirt before he dies."

We just knew, my sister and brothers and I, that we would live to be a hundred. We never thought of the dirt in our backyard as unclean. Soil from which sprouted lilies of the valley, morning glories and asters was clean. Even so, we had no plans to consciously consume a bushel of dirt.

The dirt in the slums was not clean. I knew how many tuberculosis victims lived within a two-block radius of this and other homes. Some thoughtlessly spit their germ-laden sputum anywhere. I had seen the dozens of dogs, alley cats and even a homeless tramp defecate in these polluted alleys. Many bacilli and other germs were carried into these homes by muddy feet, to lay in wait to invade the body of an infant crawling on the floor. Was dirt ever clean in the slums?

Mrs. Scott was the mother of six children. At some period of each of her children's early childhood, they had been patients at Molly Stark Tuberculosis Hospital. Because Mr. Scott was in and out of the hospital with a chronic, but not immediately life-endangering disease, the family was on and off welfare. The Scott children were intelligent. They showed great stamina of mind and spirit. This patient, long-suffering mother confided to me once that if ever another caseworker spoke disparagingly of her large family, she could easily land in jail for assault.

"I am legitimately married," she cried, "and I take good care of my children. I hate being on welfare. I only ask for the barest of our needs. If I were an unmarried tramp with one or two bastards, they would give me everything I would ask for."

She paused in an attempt to calm her feelings and predicted, "Welfare is dragging some of our people down to levels beneath the dignity of human beings."

Mrs. Handley, an ebony-hued, gangly woman in her midtwenties, had a most attractive fair-skinned son about to enter school. She had no verifiable work history. She claimed to have been married in Georgia and moved to Canton when her husband deserted her. Her unpromising world centered around her child whom she worshipped affectionately. She would have done anything (and it was rumored that she did) to give her son the little pleasures that a welfare existence did not provide.

There was a period of time when it appeared the Negro community disapproved of extra-marital sex and illegitimate offspring. Rape, promiscuity and bastardy, a dehumanizing condition of slavery, was frowned upon. It was unbecoming of free persons. At the same time, the immediate families accepted and supported their infrequent out-of-wedlock grandchildren, nieces and nephews. They asked no one for financial assistance. It was an extended family responsibility the relatives assumed.

With subtlety some Negroes extolled the dark-skinned woman who was cunning and resourceful enough to birth a child by a white man. A dark-skinned woman was applauded for populating the race with a good looking mulatto child. Being "kept" by a white man gave a woman and her child a status envied by the struggling wife of a low-salaried Negro laborer. This was a carry-over from the slavery and post-slavery era when the white man indulged in two households, his beautiful "lady wife" and his "black mistress" lover.

Mrs. Hadley was without a man, white or black, and the social agencies dogged her every step. They practically made her beg for the minimum assistance they gave her. They suspected there was a white man in her life somewhere. Mrs. Hadley tried to hide the fact she and I were becoming friends. I donated two pints of blood when she lay in the hospital for months as the result of a serious accident.

"Pretend you don't know me, and please don't come by my house. It will only hurt your reputation if we are known as friends," she told me as she left the hospital.

This unfortunate woman literally became a bag lady before the age of thirty-five. She walked the streets picking up trash to redeem for a little cash. She became ineligible for even minimum welfare assistance when her son was killed at age fifteen. He was shot while, with a group of high school students, he peeked through a second story window of a house of prostitution.

Another mother known to be the mistress of a well-known white businessman was not a particularly engaging young woman. She never ventured in public further than a block or two from her second-story tenement at the rear of a pool hall. Her two attractive, well-dressed mulatto children were the darlings of every gambler, prostitute and pimp in the area. Their European father contributed generously to their support and sent them to college. They started life anew in a distant state.

Mr. Jonathan had spent ten years in the penitentiary for murder. A condition of his parole was to apply for WPA employment. He had a fourteen-year-old daughter and a twelve-year-old son. His wife abandoned him and the children, saying that she had suffered enough while he was in prison. His children feared and hated him. Twice his daughter attempted to run away from home in search of her mother. The father wept unabashedly, begging me to help him. He came to my office for counseling for nearly a year.

Just around the corner from Mr. Jonathan lived an eighteen-year-old mother with three children whose ages ranged from two months to three years. They lived in a one-room dwelling just a few feet away from the owner's own modest home. There was no running water, no toilet, only a small shelf with a canned heat burner and a few plates and cooking utensils. The owner permitted the young mother to empty the contents from the pot or slop jar once or twice a day in his toilet. She could get water from the garden hose faucet on the side of the house.

Two of the babies were crawling on the floor in an array of potato peelings, crackers, pieces of bread and spilled milk. I had never seen humans wallow in such filth before. The suckling infant she held to her breast was almost smothered in the folds of voluminous body fat. This inept, slovenly, teen-age mother had nothing to say when I told her I would have to notify the health department and have her removed to another facility. She only looked at me with eyes that were indifferent but telescoped the message, "What do I care?"

The ten people who lived in the attic of a multi-purpose business dwelling, were protected and endangered while escaping the outdoor elements. They used candles for light and canned heat for warming canned foods. Two little attic windows allowed some cool fresh air to breeze through on hot nights. Weather permitting, most of their cooking took place on an old rusted barbecue grill in the backyard. They had access to a toilet and wash bowl in a hallway off the empty first floor business area. The three adult members of this gathering were certain WPA employment could help them pay rent in better surroundings. The seven children, from three to ten years of age, sat on mattresses and made not a sound as I observed their crowded abode.

The principal of Liberty Avenue grade school asked me to visit the home of two of his pupils. The teachers and classmates were upset about the odor emanating from the six- and eight-year-old brothers. An attractive middle-aged grandmother hesitatingly ushered me into her neatly arranged sitting room. She eyed me suspiciously. "The principal sent me a note tellin' me to 'spect you," she said.

"He wanted to make sure you would be here," I explained.

"I'se heard bout you but I doan think I'se eber see'd you b'fore. What church you'se go to? Wha's yo memba'ship?"

"I am asked that question a lot. If I belonged to every church recommended to me, I would have membership in at least twelve churches," I sidetracked. "Let us talk about your grandsons. I hear they are well-behaved boys in school, but they smell up the class. Can you tell me why?"

"Meybe it be's dey und'wear. I gits a smell f'om dem, too.

What's I to do? It too cole to tek dem off til it waum up a bit." Grandma revealed she was fearful of Ohio's cold winters and had not taken off the first pair of long johns she had put on her grandsons in October. What she had done with Christmas just a week away was to have sewn two additional pairs of long underwear on top of the first pair. Between an occasional bed wetting, other soilage, and the lack of a soap-and-water body bath, two boys sitting in a warm classroom with thirty other boys and girls were most offensive.

Tactfully but firmly I advised the grandmother, "Unstitch the underwear, put them to soak and give the children a bath. Put the children to bed while at least one pair of laundered underwear dries overnight. Keep one pair for night sleeping, like pajamas. You must bathe the boys and change their underwear every week. I assure you they will not get pneumonia. They will not get sick and die, and their teacher will never have to complain that they smell."

Both young men grew up to be handsome fine citizens. I wonder if they ever knew what I knew about their underwear. It might be good for a laugh, but it was really no laughing matter in the late '30s.

Families suffered temporary hardships because of the loss of employment or the inability to work because of ill health. A work relief job and welfare provided them with the wherewithal to exist with some dignity. There were families living in abject poverty even when the head of the household was healthy and gainfully employed. The wives and children of the gambler and the alcoholic suffered unnecessary poverty, neglect, fear and humiliation.

There were those families also in the slums, but generally a half mile or more distant from the main drag, which filled me with hope and pride. Even with their loss of saving deposits when the banks were closed by F.D.R. in 1933, they escaped the devastation of the Depression. They sought as a last resort minimum temporary assistance. After a few weeks on WPA, a job they never fell in love with, they obtained other employment and took steps with new resolves never to be without again.

For a decade and a half, my clients in the slums helped me develop some real ministering skills. Empathy, identification and understanding headed the list. I gave them my full attention. I listened to them and I treated them as I would have wanted to be treated were I in their situation. I never pitied them nor was I ever upset to tears over their plight. Pity is so degrading, tears so unproductive.

My clients were trusting, respectful and honest. They told me things I did not need to know, little incidents and situations which in no way nullified their eligibility for assistance. I never cluttered up my records with this information. It was like their confession. I was the one who had heard their innermost secrets. I could never record their remarks to reveal to another what they had voluntarily shared with me.

With the exception of a few families, I came to the conclusion, rightfully or wrongfully, that people living in the slums were not overly ambitious. They were certainly not envious, not subversive nor covetous. Most were easily hurt, easily defeated and easily discouraged. They had lost the will to cope with challenges. They tended to practice an avoidance behavior by retreating from difficult situations. They were often labeled as lacking initiative, when in reality their wants were minimal. They were fun-oriented and seldom desired more than their fair share of life's necessities.

How different was my outlook on life. Would living where my clients lived have made a difference in my philosophy, my aspirations? And I saw only the daytime picture. I was warned that it was very important for anyone living outside the slums to finish his or her work before dusk and leave. "Go home before the real funning and whoring begins." My husband had said to me, "When you see the kids walking down Cherry Avenue from McKinley High, you finish your work and head for the office or come home."

Since my high school years, the Negro enrollment at McKinley had increased from ten and fifteen students to more than two hundred. Many of the boys and girls who lived in other sections of town would trek down the Avenue in small groups, wide-eyed with curiosity. Sometimes they hoped for a glimpse of a well-known pimp in a flashy Cadillac or a Walnut Avenue prostitute in a black lace peek-a-boo chemise peering through a window. These role models gave them more hope of a prosperous future than any formal education where the downtown offices and the city fathers would say, "We're sorry. There are no jobs for you here."

As the students living in the area disappeared around the courts and alleys into homes of every imaginable variety, other figures appeared. Strange, illusive, phantom-like creatures called from open windows or stepped outside their doorways to ask, "Did you heah what de number be today?"

"Seven fifty-two on the stocks."

"I play that for a month and change it today. Damn."

"I hear Jim-Jim hit for two hunred bucks."

"No, you doan say!"

"Yeah he did, an I be on my way to collect ten dollahs he owe me."

"Good luck. He neber pay nobody nothing. He owe us all."

"I gets mine or else. Be seein' you all."

I finished my investigative house calls at the end of the day, tired but invigorated. I never worried about my clients and never took my work home with me. When I closed my briefcase, I walked out of that world to enter my own.

Feeling good about the accomplishments of an eight-hour day, I could put in another six or seven hours enjoying my home and assuming the role of housewife and mother. I found what I called "quality" time to read to the children, to teach them and to converse with them. After dinner and the children's early retirement, I was free to recharge my batteries by reading, sewing and studying.

This was possible because as soon as I was employed, I enlisted the services of a 6th, 7th, or 8th grade girl from the neighborhood. Two afternoons after school and on Saturday mornings the routine chores of dusting, sweeping, mopping and cleaning resulted in an orderly home.

Study, soft music, sleeping children in a tidy house in a peaceful neighborhood was so rejuvenating. If I retired before my husband came home, I would awaken upon his midnight arrival and we would share for a half-hour or so some of the day's events in our extremely different work worlds.

One early June evening in 1937, when the newspapers headlined the Republic Steel strike, Percy shared with me a rather frightening plan. "I'm going to enter the Republic Steel plant this weekend as a strike breaker."

I sat upright in bed and exclaimed, "You must be crazy!"

"Just listen to me," Percy coaxed. "I've got to get work in the steel mill where I can make a decent salary to support you and the children. Don't talk about this to anyone. Once inside the plant, I'll stay until the strike is over. It may last for weeks. Now don't worry about me. If I can phone you, I will. I've got to get a decent-paying job. It's impossible for me to raise a family on a store porter's salary. I don't mind you working, but I do mind you using your money to make ends meet. If there's to be two salaries in this family, mine should be equal to yours, not less. A job at Republic Steel is the solution."

Percy entered the plant the next day and remained throughout the strike. When the strike was over, around June 30, Percy had a new job.

XVII

Seeking Employment—After Pearl Harbor

The Christmas display window at Kobacker's Department Store on the corner of Market and Fifth Street Northwest held our attention on that Sunday afternoon, December 7, 1941. We were on our way to Loew's State Theater just across the street. As excited as we were to see Greta Garbo and Melvyn Douglas in *Two-Faced Woman*, we were fascinated with every detail of the animated characters of the yuletide season.

I was reminded of the unfulfilled Christmas wishes of my childhood when there were no dolls, no electric trains and no velveteen dresses trimmed in fur. We had been told many times that Santa was sick or that he had to visit some very poor children hundreds of miles away. We were grateful for our popcorn ball, orange, candy cane, one or two to-be-shared games and a personal item of clothing, but it would have been so nice to have had more.

As adults Percy and I allowed ourselves the joy of watching an animated Santa, his North Pole elves, dolls, teddy bears and rocking horses come alive amid falling cotton snowflakes and joyous Christmas music.

"Look. Look at this. How clever! Did you see that? Now watch when that train comes through the tunnel. Isn't that neat?" We were behaving like little kids.

Our concentration was disturbed by loud excited shouts up and down the street, "X-tra, X-tra! Read all about it! Pearl Harbor is bombed by the Japanese!"

Newsboys were everywhere waving the Sunday papers and adding an extra word of advice. "Listen to your radio for details."

We gave the newsboy a nickel for the three-cent Sunday paper and entered Loew's Theater, our reason for being in town. We paid special attention to the newsreel shown before the movie, but it was too soon to detail Pearl Harbor. War could be the Great Depression's death knell. For months prior to this catastrophe, there had been some rejoicing that the American economy was on the upswing mainly because the Lend Lease Act provided seven billion dollars in military credits to Great Britain, revitalizing our industries. Jobs were on the rise and our Depression-weary nation rejoiced. It was too soon to fully realize what it would mean to be at war.

Industry began employing every able-bodied worker. Only the ill and the indigent aged continued on welfare. On Tuesday, December 9, this ad of nearly a half page appeared in The *Canton Repository* newspaper.

> We're in the War
>
> All of us from this day on have but one task. That is, to hit with all of our might— on sea, on land, in air and in the shop—to protect and preserve the American freedom that we all hold dear. More bearings and more steel are badly needed. Let's give them all we can.
>
> The Timken Roller Bearing Co., Canton, Ohio

In my agency there had been frequent cutbacks in staff for several months. We moved from a three-story office complex to a four-room office suite. This bulletin was on my desk one day. "All caseworkers must be able to type their own case load reports or be replaced by a caseworker who types. Please advise your supervisor of your typing competencies before the next staff meeting."

I could not type. I had never inserted a sheet of paper into a typewriter or tapped a key in curiosity to locate a letter, a number or a punctuation mark. I was not ready to relinquish my job for the lack of a typing skill. That evening, I stopped at Stebbins Typewriter rental store on Fourth Street Northwest and arranged to rent a typewriter for two weeks.

Within that two-week period, I learned to type by my own method, a hunt and press technique. In my piano playing, I had to see the notes and then play. So, too, with my typing. I never memorized the keyboard. I hunted and touched with both hands. It looked somewhat more professional to be using all of my fingers than having a one-fingered hand hopping all over the machine. My speed was satisfactory and my accuracy was perfect. I was one of five caseworkers who continued working. My job had never been more vital to our livelihood.

With two incomes, our needs escalated rather than diminished. My investigative calls required a car. Schneider Lumber Company planned to tear down our house to enlarge their lumber storage space. They gave us a three-month "relocation" notice. We began looking for another house. I feared leaving the Southwest section of town.

With less than forty-eight hours to vacate our home, I appealed to Mr. and Mrs. James Titus II of 1215 Third Street Southwest, just six blocks away, to rent us two rooms "until we can find a place." I never came so close to begging. I was ecstatic when they said, "We'll do our best to share our home with you temporarily."

I don't know what I expected living in someone else's home, but I was miserable. We had the use of one room in the attic, one bedroom on the second floor and we cooked our meals in a very cluttered basement. The Tituses were in the process of elaborately remodeling their first floor kitchen.

Two months later, after watching the newspapers and straining my eyes for empty houses in a nine-block stretch from McKinley Avenue to Dueber Avenue, I spied a three-room apartment. It was above the office of the Brumbaugh Lumber Company at 1400 West Tuscarawas Street, an area where we already lived.

I never expected Mr. Brumbaugh to rent the apartment to us. I had run into so many "no"s I expected him to say "sorry" with some quickly concocted excuse. With six rooms of furniture plus the piano Shuggie insisted we take for Norma Jean's piano lessons, we had less space to move from one spot to another than a canned sardine.

The next job layoff was directed to women whose husbands were employed. I was in that bracket. The WPA office had folded; the welfare staff was reduced to three, the director, a secretary and one caseworker. Since my work had brought me into contact with the staff and executives of other social agencies, I decided to explore this field further. I re-applied for a civil service job as a Juvenile Court worker and took the next scheduled examination. My grade was the third highest, but nothing happened. I was never interviewed.

Soon after Pearl Harbor, my brother Eugene enlisted in the Navy. We were so proud of him. To me, Uncle Sam's "I need you" seemed to shout above the deafening sounds of cannon fire, tank explosives and aircraft bombings that we saw and heard during the Sunday movie news briefs. The psychological impact upon me was to arouse deep feelings of love of country and allegiance.

My grandfather had fought in the Civil War to preserve the nation. My husband's work at Republic Steel was defense-related. Percy's venture as a strike breaker, four years earlier, had not caused any difficulty. He enjoyed his work as a laborer. He held his own with the largest and brawniest men on the pool gang.

The newspaper and radio called its readers and listeners to "Work in a defense plant." "Help our allies." "Support our soldiers." "Save the world for democracy." I wondered what I could do as a true American.

One day I ventured into the Employment Services Office on West Tuscarawas Street at High Avenue to apply for a defense job. The interviewer recorded dutifully my work history as cook, adult education teacher, WPA investigator and welfare caseworker. When she had asked some other questions about education, family and dependents, she commented, "It seems that jobs in the areas where you have worked recently are no longer plentiful."

"I realize that. That is why I am here."

"Would you consider a job as a cook?"

"No. I am specifically interested in a defense job in an industrial plant."

"I'll see what we have." There was a long pause as she shifted papers on her desk. "We have nothing just now."

"On the radio this morning there was an announcement that Westinghouse General Electric on Raff Road needs machine operators," I informed her and added, "They are willing to hire women."

"Let me check." She left her desk and quickly returned. "I'm afraid I can't help you. I'll look into this Westinghouse radio ad. Industry is pretty specific about requirements. They also prefer not to hire married women with young children. Yours are eight and eleven years old, I see. Please return at this time next week. We may have better news then."

I went immediately to the Urban League hoping to learn more about the Westinghouse plea for machine operators. Their call to the plant confirmed that referrals were coming from the employment office. I was not the only person to seek the Urban League's help. Miss Sadie Clark, a recent graduate of Howard University, had been told by the employment office that she had too much education for the types of jobs available in industry. "Besides you are much too tiny to be around machinery and you have no factory work experience," she was told.

Returning to the employment office the following week, I met a very attractive woman in the waiting room. Soon we were conversing. "I intend to sit here until I get a defense job," she shared with me. "They have been giving me the run-around in this office for the past two weeks."

She was a trained nurse, married with no children. I told her my story and what I had heard about Miss Clark. We decided the three of us should get together and forthrightly left the employment office to locate Miss Clark.

The employment counselors had concocted every conceivable premise to disqualify the three of us for employment. Were these managerial directives? They tried to logically define our unemployability because of our married state, motherhood, single state, childlessness, height, weight, over-education and under-experience. They emphasized the need to have competencies in algebra, geometry, chemistry and physics. The only thing they did not mention was the obvious color of our skins, distinguishable as they were.

We ranged in age from twenty-two to thirty-five years, in weight from one hundred to one hundred sixty pounds. Our education was two years of normal school training, three years in nurse training and a four-year college degree in liberal arts. We each had advanced mathematics and science courses and strong verbal skills. We were in color, black, brown and yellow

. . . quite attractive women.

The next day, without regard for our regularly scheduled weekly appointment, we entered the employment office together and politely insisted upon a joint interview. We were poised for a confrontation.

"Each of us standing here," I stated in a most controlled voice," has been given contradictory reasons for not being eligible for a job in industry. Please call the managing supervisor because we plan to stay here until your reasons for not referring us to a job make sense." Surprisingly nothing happened. The receptionist greeted us graciously and gave us referral cards after hurriedly consulting our files. We were all hired by Westinghouse that day and became the first Negro women machine operators in any of Canton's industries. I worked on a lathe, the other two worked on various machines.

Shortly thereafter, Mrs. Esther Archer was hired by the Timken Roller Bearing Company, the first Negro woman in their Savannah plant. She later became Canton's first councilwoman.

Within six weeks, more than a dozen Negro workers were hired as machinists. Most had no high school diploma and not the faintest knowledge of algebra or geometry. Neither did seventy-five percent of the white machinists until instructed by their foreman. Almost immediately there were racial incidents. Whites made insulting remarks, and the blacks retorted with derogatory street language. There was near panic when one worker threatened to toss another worker into a revolving lathe and reduce him to mincemeat.

The anger I had suppressed in the employment office surfaced. When such high demands had been made of the three of us, why did the company reduce its standards so drastically?

The blacks aroused within me dual emotions of empathy and disgust. I was one of them, and yet I disapproved of their attitude. I saw the kind of person I could have become. "There but for the grace of God go I," I uttered many a day. The whites protected by the structure of institutional racism infuriated me. I envied and hated my co-workers.

One moment I was secretly urging the blacks to "scare the hell out of the whites." The next moment I was praying that like the three little monkeys, they would "hear no evil, see no evil and do no evil."

This new, highly skilled technical job for which I would have gone to jail, demonstrating my right to be hired, became a place of fear and embarrassment.

Toward the end of an unusual year, I was informed of an opening for a health educator at the Stark County Tuberculosis and Health Association. The position called for a Negro with a minimum of two years of college. I applied with confidence. I was overjoyed at the thought of leaving Westinghouse.

Mr. Delmar Serafy, the executive director who interviewed me, was a young man in his early thirties. Recently recovered from a bout with tuberculosis, he decided to dedicate his life to the eradication of this white plague. He was slight of stature and as straightforward as any gentleman I had ever met. He explained why he favored my application and then detailed my duties.

"Mrs. Marcere, I am impressed with your work history. You're not allowing grass to grow under your feet, are you? You completed a two-year normal course at Kent, but I see you continue to take other courses now and then. You are evidently hoping to get a bachelor's degree. Right? Fine! A scholarship at the University of Michigan is included in your new position. You will need some basic health courses to function adequately in this new job. The scholarship is total: tuition, books, dormitory residence, board and travel. You can add between nine and twelve quarter hours of college credits to your transcript.

"One more thing," he explained, "I have had to convince

the Board of the seriousness of tuberculosis in this community. I have further had to insist, with the help of some people from the state level, that only a Negro educator can be effective in conquering this dreaded disease.

"The newspaper publicity may appear as if you were a Negro worker serving only the Negro population. I want you to understand, however, that there are no limits to the scope of your work. The entire community, with special attention toward the Negro, is your territory. You will work with whites as if you were white as well. I have every confidence you can do a superb job. You are beginning as a part-time worker; but by the end of the year when our Christmas Seal sale returns come in, you will be placed on full-time. Our job is to so effectively eradicate TB that we shall work ourselves out of a job." We exchanged a vigorous handshake, a promise and an understanding.

I recall that immediate plans had to be made about the care of the children that summer. We were still living in the three-room apartment above Brumbaugh's Lumber and Storage office. We had just taken a one-year-old foster child in our home with plans to adopt him. Percy arranged to work a straight night shift from 11:00 p.m. to 7:00 a.m. for six weeks so he could be with the children daily. Aunt Clella spent her nights with the children. Norma Jean became a twelve-year-old mother substitute for little Carl and her brother Alluren.

Once on campus, I remember how thrilled I was to be living in the dormitory of a well-known university. That which I had missed at Kent State in 1928 and 1929 was savored to the fullest at the Michigan campus that summer. The courses in *Communicable Disease Control, Race Hygiene* and *Public Health* increased my knowledge of the factors that can shorten or lengthen one's life. I learned about the public health structure for ensuring a healthy community.

That summer I relived my grandmother's account of their

seven children who died before the age of nineteen. I remembered my mother's graphic recall of the untimely death of her beloved twenty-nine-year-old sister, Nora, and how her seventeen-year-old brother Charles breathed his last in her arms. I was twelve when my twenty-nine-year-old Uncle Eugene died from galloping consumption.

I understood that some, perhaps all, of the other four or five early childhood deaths of my aunts and uncles, attributed to whooping cough and high fevers, could well have been tuberculosis-related. I learned that with early detection, proper nutrition, proper home care or sanatorium treatment, Grandma's children might have lived to become for me and my sisters and brothers the aunts and uncles we never knew. Because of their early demise, we had only one cousin, a Helen Smith, whom we had never seen. Her widowed father ignored his wife's family.

I returned from the University of Michigan eager to begin a new adventure. A missionary entering a foreign land to bring the message of Christianity to the heathen could not have tackled his or her job more enthusiastically than I did mine. Carrying the message of health to my community would be most rewarding. It was, but I had no idea of the environmental terrain ahead. I was like the missionary who in saving the pagan souls of exotic natives is ill prepared to cope with the tangled jungle of wild beasts, pesky mosquitoes and slithering snakes. I was totally unprepared for the deliberate annoyances on my job that would acquaint me with the jungle of unmitigated racism. Before I recount the next twelve years of my professional career, join my brothers and sisters and me at one of our Thanksgiving gatherings at my dining room table.

XVIII

Around My Dining Room Table

I recall a Thanksgiving or two, not only in my childhood but also in the early years of my marriage, when the menu on that Thursday holiday was no different from any other day. There was no stuffed turkey, chicken, duck or roast pig to enjoy. There were no Thursday leftovers that became forbidden meat, not to be eaten on Friday.

We followed the Catholic practice of meatless Fridays. It fitted our modest food budget. Mom reminded us, as our high school circles of friends taunted and questioned us about not eating hot dogs and hamburgs on Friday, with these words: "If you can say 'no' and proudly walk away from your friends who tempt you to eat meat on Friday, you can say 'no' and walk away from sex or any other temptation your friends or the world puts in your path."

There had been times when I was a child that the designated fatted hen for Thanksgiving or Christmas had been eaten many weeks earlier. The spring batch of fifty baby chicks would be incubator-hatched in March or April. While they were developing into fryers and egg-laying hens, hamburg and canned salmon were our main source of meat. We seldom ate pork, wieners or lunch meats. Once in a while, a piece of smoked bacon or a slice of ham would season a pot of beans. There was always a soup bone for flavoring soup or vegetables.

Friday temptation or not, there was one Thanksgiving before our children were of school age when I really wanted to savor a delicious, juicy turkey with a rich sage dressing. I had the ingredients for the stuffing—sage, onions, celery, bread crumbs and butter—but not enough money to buy a turkey.

From the newspaper I learned that the Salvation Army had free turkeys for needy families. I phoned the agency and took advantage of the fact I could speak like "an aristocrat" to recommend myself.

As I approached the Salvation Army that Wednesday afternoon, a long line of people waited beside the building. Each held a grocery bag for a turkey and supplementary food. I could not join them. From across the street I walked away with that same determination Mom had felt when she said, "Welfare, no!" I was not that hungry and "Please, God, never ever let me get so hungry that I have to stand in line for free food," I prayed. Was it because I did not want to be labeled "those people", "those poor", "those so-and-so's"?

Gratefully I went to a food market on East Tuscarawas and Walnut Avenue to purchase two pounds of hamburg. Our "turkey" was a rolled meat loaf stuffed with sage dressing. Percy reminded me, "Don't be in too big a hurry. Things will be better for us up the road a piece."

Up the road a piece! Norma Jean and Alluren described their daddy and me in these words. "When Mother got an idea, she was ready to take off. It was Daddy who would say, 'Have patience. Don't be in such a hurry. Slow down. There's a lot of tomorrows ahead. Cool it. Wait awhile.'"

What none of them knew was that I planned anywhere from weeks to years in advance of my stated wants or intentions. Announcing my intentions meant I was ready to get started. All the mental calculations of ifs, ands, and buts had been fully explored.

As we approached our twelfth year of marriage, I was anxious to purchase our first home. I needed a house where I could invite guests and have space for our growing children and their friends. Brumbaugh's three-room apartment with the children's closet-sized double deck bedroom, the dining/kitchen area and the crowded living/bedroom space made me feel unbearably claustrophobic.

"Percy," I began, not alluding to my real feelings, "you know it won't be long before our daughter will be approaching womanhood. This apartment on this busy street is not safe for a young Negro girl. You should see the bums who hang out across the street. We need to look for a house in a decent neighborhood."

I did not expect my husband to take the initiative: watch the newspapers, contact a realtor, monitor our savings. That was my job. It went with the territory of knowing how far and how fast to make a move.

Economically and matrimonially we were in peril. Percy was in that sea of unskilled workers in the steel industry. Sometimes wooed and sometimes confused by the labor unions, he was uncertain about his future. My professional career seemed secure. Without both of our jobs, there would be no opportunity for socioeconomic stability.

While we walked a thin line between economic security and the threat of welfare, we faced another danger. One misstep by either of us because of misunderstood role performance could topple our marriage. Was I feminine and dependent enough as a married woman? Did my husband display the attributes of a decision-making, upwardly mobile husband and father?

In my fantasy I envisioned my husband as a masterful general who understood some strategies for escaping racial bondage. He already knew when he was paying for his sister's education that the Negro woman was more favored in job pursuits. He chose to love and marry a woman with education and ambition to help him do the things he could not do alone.

Together we could be victorious. Together we could keep our heads above the poverty line and raise an honorable family. I was cautious not to say or do that which would make him feel I was taking over. He must see himself as the pilot even while I steered.

Three months after my "need a house" announcement, we moved from our little apartment. We purchased a one-hundred-year-old, eight-room house on the corner of Prospect Avenue and Ninth Street Southwest without a peek at the inside. The Jewish broker who arranged the sale took special pains to show us the exterior without attracting the neighbors' attention. Whenever the traffic light turned red, we got a longer glimpse of the house. The realtor arranged (at our expense) to have curtains and draperies hung at all the downstairs windows before moving day.

The draperies and the interior spaciousness drew our attention away from the deplorable condition of the interior. It was only after I had skipped and danced from room to room with out-flung arms to embrace distance and freedom of movement that I saw the task ahead to make this disaster a habitable home.

Rats had gnawed through doors to scamper from one room to another. The plumbing, the electrical wiring and the furnace were in alarming stages of disrepair. The flooring in the bathroom was so weak from rot we feared to sit heavily on the toilet for fear it would fall through to the dirt basement below.

When a week later a family attempted to get our closest neighbors to sign a petition for our eviction, we jokingly suggested we give it away. The petition failed.

Over the years we spent more than fifteen thousand dollars in improvements to a five-thousand-dollar home in a four-thousand-dollar neighborhood (1958 costs). We dug out the dirt foundation to construct a cement basement with an enclosed garage. We put in a furnace, added a kitchen and bedroom, modernized the windows, paneled the walls, built a wood-burning fireplace, installed two new baths and separated the second floor for an apartment. It became one of the most attractive homes in the area. Inviting guests to our home was a delight.

I had kept my resolve to be a big sister to my siblings. All my brothers and sisters, except Ruth, shared the hospitality of our home. They stayed with us on Fifth Street, West Tuscarawas and on Prospect every now and then.

"Norm, can I stay here a day or two? . . . Shuggie and I don't see eye to eye just now . . . and . . . well it won't be for long. I'm on my way back to . . . ."

They were on their way back to school, in between jobs, on their way out of town. First it was Carl at seventeen, then Eugene, then Ethel, then Virginia.

I was sure I could have choreographed the situation at home, but I never commented, I never questioned. Perhaps we all knew how difficult it was for Shuggie to allow her children to pass through the separation canal of emancipated adulthood.

Percy never remonstrated when I announced my intention to visit a sister, brother or in-law. I visited Ethel when she was a student at Howard University. Eugene and Carl were on my itinerary when they were in Philadelphia, Buffalo and New York City. I wrote to Virginia when she was at Bennett College, North Carolina. Having kept in touch and gone to see them on their home territory, I could urge, "Why not come to my house on Thanksgiving for a family get-together?"

They came and there was an annual succession of family gatherings with Percy and me at our home. This gathering became a healing, inspiring experience. All of the misunderstandings while growing up vanished in the challenging excitement of adulthood.

Percy was a charming host. I was a little jealous of the way my family greeted me with a "Hi, Norm," "Hello, Aunt Norma" and then gathered around Percy. Uncle Percy was a big brother to everyone. His congeniality created a joyous atmosphere. His dignity commanded a respect akin to reverence. Those moments of jealousy convinced me that Percy's personality was the bonding force in our family.

Ethel's husband, Everhart Turner, was a native of Mount Vernon, Ohio. His effervescence seemed incompatible with his introverted career as an electrical engineer. I was always fascinated by the gadgets and machinery he had in the basement of their Columbus home. To me, Ethel and Everhart headed a perfect household with their three sons and one daughter, Everhart II, Robert, Kenneth and Diana.

Everything was done on schedule: meals, play time, piano, ballet and violin lessons, study and bedtime. I wondered how I would have run a household if Percy's income had made it unnecessary for me to seek employment outside my home. My answer; "I was not born to be a housewife. I was a career woman, and I was an excellent mother to my children and foster children."

Shellie Powe, Virginia's husband, had made headlines in the *Ebony* magazine as an outstanding insurance agent for the Supreme Liberty and Life Insurance Company. Shellie's first wife died in childbirth with their third child. Virginia's ready-made family of two boys and a girl, Gary, Lindsey and Myra, made her a candidate for sainthood. Their son Carl evened Ethel's family of three sons and a daughter. I admired my baby sister greatly.

Shellie and Percy, born in Mississippi, shared many recollections of their childhood "down home." Carl and

Eugene seemed somewhat awed in the presence of brothers-in-law who had made unannounced entries into the family. Each of us girls slipped quietly away to be married. Percy and I hosted a small wedding reception in our home for Shellie and Virginia. It was the only public announcement of a Snipes girl's marriage.

Eugene and Mary met and were married in Philadelphia. They were employed as a chauffeur and cook. They parented a son, Robert Eugene, and a daughter, Carole. Carl's first wife, a very pretty mulatto girl from southern Ohio, had difficulty adjusting to Carl's meteoric successes. Jealously and possessively she joined him at his work every evening and became embarrassingly drunk. After their divorce, Carl married a Caucasian divorcee. Her family disowned and disinherited her. All of Mom's six children with their five spouses and thirteen grandchildren, and our lovable Aunt Clella, ate well and feted the family matriarch, Shuggie, on our Thanksgiving Day gatherings.

With pride I prepared the meal without assistance and sat at the table to enjoy every family member present. After the blessing, the turkey with sage dressing, mashed potatoes, giblet gravy, candied sweet potatoes, scalloped oysters, peas, cranberries, parkerhouse rolls, strawberry jam, tossed salad, mince pie and pumpkin pie disappeared between nostalgic remembrances.

Listening to accounts of current family incidents, Shuggie seemed amazed that her daughters' husbands went grocery shopping, changed the babies' diapers, cooked a meal, washed the dishes and allowed us freedom to do pretty much what we wanted to do. Pop had done none of these things. We were all part-time college students working toward a bachelor's degree. Ethel, Virginia and I had only completed two years of college at the time of our marriage. Carl and Eugene's wives never mentioned their schooling.

After dinner the youngest grandchildren were taken by Aunt Clella upstairs to nap. The others joined in word games and crossword puzzles, compared their skills at the piano or just got to know their cousins better.

Shuggie's children remained at the table to host her and to tease her a bit. "Here's to Shuggie," someone would begin, "who was and probably still is absolutely, positively the world's worst cook."

We laughed good naturedly and clicked the glasses of my homemade elderberry and dandelion blossom wine made from Grandma's recipe.

"Her biscuits and corn bread were just like rocks," another would recall.

"Mulligan stew had nothing on Shuggie's homemade soup. Everything went into the soup kettle, except meat and a bar of laundry soap. Those things would have added flavor and color, and we would have lost our appetites."

Shuggie would restrain her comments for the moment while she basked in our attention and devotion. Her graying hair, like a halo, highlighted her fair skin, as smooth as a baby's, without a blemish or a wrinkle. Her clear brown eyes sparkled, revealing her pride in her children. They also revealed a sadness. We knew she wished our Pop was there.

"Look at my beautiful children," she would retort, disclaiming the "worst cook" accusation. "You have sound teeth, no cavities; you have straight limbs, no rickets; you have clear skin, no blemishes. None of you are wearing glasses. You have perfect vision. You have sound minds, good intelligence. There must have been some nutrition in those soup bones from whence came the soup.

"I have seen Percy and Norma with groceries in larger quantities than I ever purchased raising my family. I never bought a five-pound quantity of anything. With Mr. Snipes' one dollar seventy-five cents a day to feed six children and take care of all household needs, I bought one pound of this, one half dozen of that, one can of something and so on. God in heaven performed the miracle of the five loaves every time I called you to supper. Even so, I never heard any of you complain that you were hungry."

"We were afraid to. If we were hungry," one of us explained, "we kept quiet. We did not want more of what it was we had been eating.

"Oh, come now, you are much too hard on Shuggie. There were some good meals," Ruth and Virginia said, trying to soften the attack.

"You may not remember the lean times. You came along when times were a little better. We always had plenty of chicken that we could not eat." I remarked. "One day I would be praising a hen for laying an egg every day and then I would be asked to wring its neck, clean out its innards, cook it and eat it. Imagine eating a pet!"

"Every family in town had the same experience until an ordinance forbade raising chickens within the city limits," Shuggie reminded us.

Carl interjected, "It's fun now to look back to those days at 1424 Fifth Street. When Gene and I lost our chicken coop cleaning job because of a city ordinance, no two kids were happier. Civilization marches on!"

"Good! Let's change the subject," someone suggested.

"What shall we talk about?"

"Shuggie," Eugene began one Thanksgiving, "why did you raise all of us kids to be such misfits?"

"Misfits?"

"Yes. You have already said we have no bad teeth, crooked bones and so forth and so forth; but neither do we fit in with others of our own race. It's hard to take sometimes. Worst of all, there's no one to talk to who seems to understand," Eugene tried to explain.

"What are you trying to say? What is there that you want to understand?" Shuggie asked.

"We don't talk like Negroes, we don't walk like Negroes. We don't eat black eyed peas and chitterlings and all those greens and salt pork like others with skin colors like ours. We don't act like them. We're misfits. Even our religion, Catholic, makes us different. I look Black, people point to me as Black, but I can't act Black!"

"Why are you so concerned about your color, and since when do you refer to yourself as Black?"

"That's the new term being used now. I'm always being reminded by others who I'm supposed to be."

"What others?"

"All the others, whites and nonwhites. The whites we went to Dueber School with don't want to have anything to do with us. I can't walk into Seiser's and get a glass of beer with any of the boys I played ball with at the Shroyer Field. I can't get a job where they work. I can't get a haircut at their barber shop. I can't eat in the restaurants where they eat or shoot pool with them on West Tusc or the YMCA.

"When I go among people of my own color, they make fun of me. 'Man, why ain't you like us? Why you talk so proper? You ain't no better than us with all your high falutin' English and polished manners. The white man ain't a goin' to let you get no further than any of us, so Man quit actin' and talkin' white, and be one of us. Be what you is!' they say to me."

"Has it been that bad, that hard to take?" Shuggie questioned.

"You'll never know what I went through in the Navy. I had a streak of patriotism and love of country a mile wide because of what Grandpa had said about serving his country in the Civil War. I wonder how much he hid about the bad things that happened to him. Maybe times were different then.

"I was 'nigger' this and 'black man' that when sailing the high seas, saving the world for democracy. On board ship I was the darky slave, flunky for the white sailors and treated with disdain. If I went ashore to stretch my legs, I was reminded of my limits. I could not go here, I could not go there. To protest, to complain, meant I stood a chance of being court-martialed, beaten up or even lynched. I learned to hate the white man, and I detested myself for being so helpless and so vulnerable."

"And you blame me?"

"Yes, in a way. It might have been better to have been raised in a black neighborhood, gone to black churches and black schools and stayed away from everything white. I might have had some identity."

"You are saying I helped to make you a misfit because I did not use the color of your skin as a recipe for raising my family?"

"You never taught us how to be a Black. You would not even give your permission for me to play sports in high school. That is one of the reasons why I quit. Teachers and the one or two friends I had were always asking, 'When are you trying out for the team?' " Eugene revealed for the first time.

"You are right. I did not rear you as a Black any more than I would have reared you as a Chinese, Eskimo, Indian, Italian or African. I taught you as I believed all humans should be taught. I taught you not to concentrate on color, yours or anyone else's. Color is only skin deep. The world is full of brown and black, yellow, white and red people. There is no way we can all be alike. My standards were universal, without limits."

Shuggie shifted her position at the table, determined to justify her philosophy. "I suppose I did raise you differently than a lot of mothers rear their children. I did not let you roam the streets day and night. I taught you how to study and work and save. I taught you boys not to impregnate a girl, and you girls not to have sex before marriage. You come from a family of high moral and ethical standards. I confess I am an old fashioned mother as was my mother before me. I never asked of you what I did not prescribe for myself. I lived the life I preached about. I could have lowered my standards and had affairs after your father left. I could have been the hottest yellow abandoned wife in town. I had my offers, but I was your mother.

"You complain, and I did not know this before, about high school sports. You have a right to know why I disapproved of them for my sons. You are not a giant. You would never physically have been a Ben Johnson or a Dan Motley. I did not want you to be known as a 'jocko, a chimpanzee or South African ape.' Whites, jokingly, in their country clubs and private gatherings, have been telling lies for years (your father told me this) about the super sexual prowess of Negro athletes.

"He said to me once, 'When I become a lawyer, I shall see that my sons never become the talk of the town for their physique or athletic strength.'

"Neither your father nor I brought you into the world to have people gaze upon your bodies and fantasize as to your sexual endowments and beast-like strengths. I am sorry about your Navy experiences, but I still say you should not allow circumstances to make of you a lesser person than you wish to be."

"But does it work? What has it done for me? Do you see me getting anywhere in this land of the free and this home of the brave?" Eugene questioned.

"How can you question that progress is not being made? Look at what each of you has done? Carl here is manager of the East Aurora Country Club in Buffalo. Do you think he was hired because the owners liked the shade of brown of his face and hands? Do you think they were making amends for some slaves their ancestors whipped in the 1800s? No, it was because of his manners, his speech, the experience he had at Brookside and his family's reputation.

"Eugene, would the millionaire family you chauffeur trust you with the responsibility of managing their estate when they go on extended travels if you murdered the king's English and had no gentlemanly traits? I know you dislike being a servant, but until you find something else, you have a job few, very few, Negro men hold.

"Virginia is a social worker. Norma holds a professional job never held by a Negro in Canton before. Ethel has decided not to go to work just yet, with her young children; but she held commendable jobs before her marriage.

"Now you, my children, are grown. You will have to decide whether to turn your back on your inheritance, so different from so many Blacks, as you wish to be labeled. You can raise your children, those beautiful, intelligent grandchildren, thirteen in all, just now, the same way you were raised or you can throw them to the uncultured Negro masses.

"I have thought of you, my children, as being what W. E. B. DuBoise describes as the 'Talented Tenth' of the Negro race. You were trained as best I knew how to be leaders of people and missionaries to the underdog. Leaders and missionaries serve their constituents for the good of all mankind, not a select few. They do not look for buddy-buddy friends and smooth sailing. They are honored to be considered a misfit. Now if you will excuse me, I am going upstairs to enjoy my grandchildren."

She left us sitting at my dining room table. It was our next-to-the-last gathering as an intact family unit. We sat there somewhat overwhelmed. We would spend the rest of our lives pondering how Shuggie, like a Sarah Bernhardt, had taken on the star role of inspiring six poor, brown-skinned, semifatherless sons and daughters to aim in the direction of the talented tenth.

Within five to seven years of this gathering, Eugene and Carl had departed this life. Eugene and his wife Mary returned to their jobs as chauffeur and cook in Philadelphia. Eugene enrolled in a radio and TV repair school. Upon the completion of his training, he returned home to live with Shuggie. He worked in a steel plant to earn the capital he needed to open a small repair shop and salesroom. Mary continued as a cook with their long-time employer. Generous living arrangements were offered her and the two children. Shuggie was elated to have Eugene home and to note a more positive outlook on life. Eugene was pulling steel from one of the furnaces at the Ford Motor Plant in Canton on March 5, 1957, when he suffered a massive coronary occlusion and expired. I recalled his words to me just days before.

"I have been to the Ford personnel office several times to request work in one of the fine parts assembly lines, but I hear only 'no openings' and I see 'no Blacks.' Look at my hands. They have been trained to work with fine calipers and tweezers and thread-like wires. Now I must develop hard muscles in my arms and wrists handling hundreds of pounds of hot steel. When I have saved the money to go into business, my hands, my fingers shall have lost their agility, their sensitivity, their delicate touch.

"You and Shuggie and even Carl have glorified ideas of what the real world is like out there. We're asked to compare ourselves with the lowest in our race and to feel lucky. We're never given the opportunity to enter the arena of those who have power and influence."

Eugene, the sensitive little boy afraid to fight back at the name-calling he heard at age six; Eugene, whose emotion-filled heart caused tears to roll down his cheeks unbidden at the slightest insult to his person; Eugene, angered because his questions of "Why?" had no right answers, was released at age forty-five from fear, pain and wonderings.

Carl's reputation as an efficient, affable, charismatic gentleman landed him the position as manager of the Theresa Hotel in Harlem, New York. When with the urgings and approval of all of her children Mom was married to Ed Hardy, a bachelor, in 1957, Carl provided the honeymoon suite for them at the Theresa and gave them a royal holiday.

Shuggie at seventy-two saw sights she had never dreamed she would see. In addition to the Negro movie stars, the jazz bands, the Statue of Liberty and Macy's Department Store, she insisted upon seeing St. Patrick's Cathedral and the Metropolitan Opera House where Sarah Bernhardt had performed.

When Carl's health began to fail at age forty-three, he was advised to give up the strenuous demands of the Theresa Hotel. He took over the management of Paddy's Restaurant on Eighth Avenue. I visited him, his new wife, Betty, and their son, Ray, several times.

Carl and I had many serious talks about life, religion and ethics. He still hoped he and I could own and operate an elite restaurant some day. "You know," he said on one of my visits, "I often wonder where Mom got her wisdom and the stamina for rearing the six of us. I have met, seen and observed all kinds of women, white, black, mixed, rich, poor and in between, Christian, Jew and whatever; but for decency, honesty and courage, Mom tops them all." We were in unanimous agreement.

Carl died in his sleep two years after his brother's passing. He, too, was forty-five. Betty, his widow, followed him one year to the day. Their orphaned son, Raymond, came to live with Percy and me, at least temporarily.

Two generations of men, my father and his two sons, had succumbed, in their mid-forties, to heart disease. Was there an added life-destroying stress for the American Negro male who sought to achieve?

It did not happen rapidly or easily, but eventually Shuggie saw her children as we were, very much like her. We were determined, goal-oriented, independent and honorable. Once Shuggie said to me, "Do not forget your sister, Ruth. The rest of you girls have husbands, careers and children. She has nobody. She may need each of you some day."

Ruth never dated, never married, never had the twelve babies she dreamed about as a child. She was faithful to her Catholic beliefs and to her devotion to Shuggie and Aunt Clella. She remained, as her sisters knew she would, Shuggie's baby girl.

XIX

Racism, Pure And Lethal

Six months after I was hired by the Stark County Tuberculosis and Health Association, Delmar Serafy accepted a position in Omaha, Nebraska. He was replaced by Mr. L. L. Taylor from Wapakoneta, Ohio. When the staff was introduced to Mr. Taylor, I sensed a reaction I could not immediately discern. A man somewhere in his forties taking charge of a new agency in a much larger city than his home town was bound to be a little nervous, but should it be so obvious?

There was more than nervousness in the eyes that looked at me and turned away. He seemed almost agitated when my professional duties were being detailed by the President of the Board. The first comment made to me a day after his private conferences with the other three staff members explained his "nervousness."

"I think I should tell you that I am very upset," Mr. Taylor began. "I cannot understand why the Board of Directors would hire a Negro woman on the staff in your capacity before hiring a white woman. You have a position which rightfully belongs to a white person. The white population of this town is ninety percent, the Negro population is ten percent. There is no way you can effectively deal with the majority population. It is impossible!"

I stood there in his little eight-by-ten-foot office stunned, shocked, insulted and angered by his remarks. I did not know what to say. I had no words in my vocabulary to respond in an equally insulting manner to a grown white man. It was important to me not to appear upset. I needed a few seconds to observe my adversary and plan an appropriate response.

On my second visit to his office in St. Peter's rectory, Father Heimann had asked me point blank, "Are you experiencing any prejudice in the Catholic Church?"

"None that I can describe as overt," I had replied. "No one has moved away from me. There are not many smiles. Some people try to stare a hole through me, that is all."

Now this keen-featured, dark-haired Caucasian was overtly (without any pretense of subtlety) telling me I was an unwelcome member of his staff. I could sense his intense feeling of repulsion toward me. It was based upon his aversion to the difference in our race and my skin color.

He was saying that it was proper for a white person to benefit from the condition of the tuberculous-ridden Negro, but that I as a Negro must not, for compensation, help my own people, much less presume to tell a white community of the contagious nature of this disease.

Was that the reasoning behind the school system's refusal to allow me to teach? A white teacher could teach a minority Negro child, but a Negro teacher could not teach a white child? How close I had come in the past ten years to being as impoverished from underemployment as the least educated slum dweller because white people believed and practiced what Mr. Taylor had just spoken.

He must be told that I intended to remain in my present employment, and the time was now. I looked him straight in the eye and began, "As I understand it, Mr. Taylor, the majority of the TB victims are Negroes. There is evidence to support the belief that the disease is epidemic because whites have paid no attention to the conditions aggravating the problem.

"A Miss Jane E. Hunter from Cleveland, President of the State Association of Colored Women's Clubs, has mandated the Governor of Ohio to appoint Negro health educators in its six largest cities. She has some forty-two affiliated women's clubs supporting her. I am a member of a local women's group named after our state president. I have been properly trained with five other Negro educators from Cleveland, Akron, Columbus, Cincinnati and Toledo. I am not alone. I am here because there is a job that must be done, and I can do it."

Mr. Taylor looked at me and dropped his eyes. His face alternately flushed red and turned ashen gray.

"I shall expect a written report of your activities daily," he commented.

"Yes, sir," I replied and left his office.

It is not easy to relate even a portion of the many insults and discourtesies I endured over a twelve year period working under L. L. Taylor. I record them to refute the claim that racism ever died and that Negroes are over sensitive and read into situations meanings that were never intended. I do not record these incidents to defame or discredit a well-known, highly respected executive, but rather to illustrate racism as I experienced it and felt it.

Racism is insidious. Sometimes it is practiced with such craftiness and trickery, such cunning and underhandedness as to be questionable. Sometimes it is blatantly overt. Apart from denying an individual liberty and the pursuit of happiness, it demoralizes the victim by stripping him of an essential life force—his self-esteem. I felt its unadulterated onslaught repeatedly while an employee of the TB Association.

Agnes, a high school graduate, joined the TB staff as a secretary in mid-June. She was an attractive Catholic girl whose Slovak parents could barely speak or understand English. Agnes introduced me to her family when I drove her home one evening after work. It was refreshing to meet Europeans with no prejudices and no aversions to people of color. She and her parents were in that category. We became friends. Agnes and I ate lunch together at the Woolworth lunch counter on South Market and Third Street.

A short time after Agnes had been on the job, she came to my desk and asked if she could speak to me privately in the basement storeroom. I had never seen a more agitated young person.

"Mrs. Marcere," she began, "I cannot go to lunch with you anymore. Mr. Taylor told me it is improper for a Negro and a white to eat together in public. I am so sorry. I like you, but Mr. Taylor is my boss. I don't know what else to say."

"There is nothing you can say," I assured her.

"Whatever work you assign me will be my best," she promised.

"So this is how racism is perpetuated," I uttered to myself as Agnes ascended the stairs to her desk.

During her eighteen years at home, she had escaped prejudicial indoctrination. Now on her very first job, her boss was teaching her the difference between white-skinned and brown-skinned employees. Eating with Negroes was taboo. She was young. She was a first-generation ethnic, new to American mores. She could be intimidated.

Mr. Taylor frequently ate at Bender's Restaurant on the corner of Court Avenue and Second Street Southwest, within the same block as the TB office. I wondered what he would do if a Negro walked into this highly acclaimed dining room and sat at a table close by. Would he protest and tell the management he would go where Negroes were not allowed? What would he say to other business executives, his peers? If he were the manager, would he do what the manager did to a customer my grandmother had cooked for in a railroad lunch counter years ago? Would he throw the steak on the floor, spit on it, stomp on it and say, "Now serve this to that nigger"?

I wondered. White managers and customers had ways of discouraging Negro business when it came to eating out. When a Negro couple seated themselves at the soda fountain of a drugstore, their order was filled. They were, however, charged an additional fifty cents. The couple paid the bill and picked up the menu revealing the true cost of the confection. The next morning the druggist received a call from an attorney informing him that he was liable for a lawsuit. The druggist sought his pastor, Father Heimann, to ask if what they had done was a sin.

"We feared that we would lose business if we began serving niggers,—Negroes," he and his wife explained. "Now we are threatened with a lawsuit and unfavorable publicity."

"I think you are overreacting. Your business will not suffer the loss of a dime by serving Negroes," Father remarked.

"Do you really believe that, Father?"

"So much so that I am willing to reimburse you for every dollar you lose."

It was then that Father Heimann phoned me, related the incident and asked, "How much do you think this is going to cost me, Norma?"

"Nothing!" I assured him. "Not a red cent! But would you back down if it cost you money, all of the fifty dollars you are paid as salary each month?"

"No, right is right and wrong is wrong. It is never right to treat others in a way that we would not want to be treated."

I was beginning to appreciate this young German priest's naive but fair assessment of human rights and obligations. Next to my grandmother, now deceased, he was the only white person I knew to whom I could express my feelings about the injustices his people of white skin inflicted upon mine. Since considerable publicity had announced the opening of the Tuberculosis Association, the avalanche of requests for a free speaker came as no surprise. The remarks I heard Mr. Taylor make over the phone one afternoon shocked and angered me.

"Yes, we do have a staff person who speaks to groups. You should know, however, that she is a Negro. If your group should prefer not to have a Negro speaker, I can make other arrangements."

That evening I phoned a young woman whom I had heard speak at interracial gatherings. "It is embarrassing to hear him refer to me as some kind of an incompetent freak," I blurted out, humiliated to acknowledge my helplessness.

Gladys listened attentively and then took the initiative. "What we need, Norma, is to have some of Canton's leading men and women remind your boss of the meaning of true Americanism. This is not Germany, and he is not Hitler. Give me a list of some of your friends. I shall gather a list of my own. We shall phone your office and request a speaker. If he gives me that refrain about color, this is what he will hear: 'I don't give a damn about the speaker's race or color. I am concerned about eradicating this contagious disease. Germs are color-blind. If you are so obsessed about the color of the person appointed to educate the public, if you are more concerned about catering to people's prejudices than healing the sick, maybe you are the wrong person to be associated with this agency.'"

She continued, "I am a Jew. I know what prejudice and badgering is. I am on your side."

Gladys never reported to me how many calls were made to the TB office or who made them, but the succeeding telephone comments I overheard were decidedly different. Mr. Taylor recommended me in superlative terms. I became the envy of many who said, "I wish my boss spoke as highly of me as your boss speaks of you."

Neither my co-workers, my friends nor my husband suspected there was anything but a perfect employer-employee relationship. In the presence of others, Mr. Taylor was polite and courteous. In the privacy of his office, he was demeaning. I worked in the environment of a Dr. Jekyll-Mr. Hyde.

I fought to be professional, to be a lady and to hold onto my self-esteem. I tried to subdue the turmoil of anger and confusion. On a scale of one to ten, my emotions bounced from a zero depression level to a super-energized pitch of work activity just short of exhaustion.

My activities were fast becoming full-time, but I was still on a part-time salary. One day instead of handing my weekly report to the secretary, I took my report to Mr. Taylor and explained my full-time hours. Would he recommend to the Board full-time status and a comparable pay increase that had been promised me?

Mr. Taylor assailed me immediately. "You are never to walk into my office unless I send for you. As for full-time, I might consider hiring a white person to relieve you of some engagements. I shall review your work schedule. As for a pay raise, never! You are making more money now than the average colored woman."

"But I am not an average colored woman, Mr. Taylor. I am considerably above the average woman of whatever race or color. I could not put my foot in the front door of this agency if I were average." I was trembling when I left his office.

The day after the next month's Board meeting, Mr. Taylor called me to his office. He was in a bad mood. "The Board has approved your full-time status, but I did not press them for a salary raise. I have been authorized to search for a male public relations director. You should know how frustrating—and I cannot repeat it often enough—it is having you here on this staff. There are so many things a white woman could do that you cannot. I would like to conduct a Nurses' Institute, bringing together all the nurses in the district to acquaint them about the newest methods in the treatment of TB. This you cannot do."

"If you will tell me what you have in mind, I would like to try."

He went on to detail the highlights of a full-day seminar with one or two outstanding speakers, exhibits, films and a catered lunch. While he was speaking, I was visualizing a magnificent program. It took weeks of detailed time, but less than a year later the first of several annual Nurses' Institutes took place at the Mercy Hospital School of Nursing on Cleveland Avenue at Eighth Street. The Institute attracted as many as one hundred nurses and a score of physicians and surgeons specializing in chest diseases.

Despite Mr. Taylor's attitude toward me, I admired his efficiency as an agency executive. He was a businessman. His ideas were creative and productive. He demanded high performance from all of his staff. He had efficient, time-saving and cost-curtailing methods for each agency function. His salesmanship qualities with the public were an asset. The agency flourished under his direction. He was a handsome, personable gentleman; but to me, an annoying individual.

Once during the preparation for the first Nurses' Institute, Mr. Taylor called me aside in the basement storeroom where the staff could not be a witness to his temperament. "It just will not work," he bellowed at me. "This is not something you can do. We had better call a halt to it now. Just stop everything! Stop!"

My response is indelibly etched upon my brain. "Mr. Taylor, I know you do not want me here. You are hoping I will do a poor job so you can fire me. Let me tell you something. If I am not the damnedest, bestest health educator in the state of Ohio, I shall quit. You will never have cause to fire me. Do you hear? Never! I repeat, the damnedest, bestest." I was creating a new vocabulary to express my determination.

"Lower your voice," he said to me and walked upstairs to his office.

While attempting to perform beyond normal limits on the job, things were getting out of hand at home.

As a working wife and mother, I knew the value of time. There was a "today" time and a "ten-years-hence" time. I learned how to budget activities and how to increase the pace of my tasks without appearing hurried.

I anticipated events of the future with a "looking-ahead" watchfulness. Teen-aged children required a different kind of attention from that given to the infant, preschooler and ten-year-old. I had concerns. I was on the alert for the preventable. I wanted no surprises, pleasurable or catastrophic.

Our son and daughter needed a great deal of attention. I was concerned about both. Al had a disposition similar to both of my brothers—the warm, friendly personality of Carl and a timid, easily hurt temperament of Eugene. The three and a half years difference in our children's ages was enough to create and maintain a distance between sister and brother.

Al joined Boy Scout Troop Number 16 at St. Joseph's Catholic Church. Mr. Larry Harbert, a scoutmaster of the highest order, took a special interest in Al. He conducted his troop in a well-disciplined, hard-working, project-oriented program; but he was also warm, compassionate and inspiring. I recall Al insisting that I listen to his Scout oath and laws.

Dressed in his uniform, hand over his heart and standing as erect as a soldier, he repeated:

Scout Oath and Promise

On my honor, I will do my best
To do my duty to God and my country
And to obey the scout law.
To help other people at all times
To keep myself physically strong
Mentally awake and morally straight.

Scout Law

A scout is trustworthy, loyal, helpful,
friendly, courteous, kind, obedient,
cheerful, thrifty, brave, clean, reverent.

I listened to his serious declaration and had few fears about his future.

Our daughter's entry into high school was an unsettling experience in peer rejection. Remembering my own high school years was of no help in coping with my daughter's need for peer acceptance. With other mothers I became involved in the Junior Jane Hunter Club. We chaperoned many teen-age social and recreational activities.

I wanted so very much to maintain a relationship with my daughter that had vanished between my Mom and me in my mid-teens. I had not fully recovered from the emptiness for never having cradled, rocked and hugged my daughter as an infant. I was, however, delighted with her intelligence and the conversations we shared on an adult level.

Now at fourteen, Norma Jean was becoming evasive and critical. "Oh, Mother, how preposterous! You're so old-fashioned!"

Percy's comment, "Leave her alone. She's just going

through a phase," annoyed me.

I could not cope with my boss, my daughter and my husband all at once. I wrote to Bishop McFadden and sought his advice about sending my daughter to a Catholic boarding school.

Bishop McFadden answered my letter promptly. He highly recommended St. Francis DeSales Academy in Virginia and added, "Have all of her tuition bills sent to me."

When Mr. Taylor learned that my daughter was away at a Catholic school, he called me aside.

"Am I hearing things correctly? Why are you sending your daughter to a private school?"

"My hours here have been such that I was not able to spend as much time with her as needed."

"How about your son?"

"He is still in grade school. He is very active as a Boy Scout and finds plenty of things to keep him busy."

"You are a very foolish woman," I heard. "Why can't you live like the rest of the colored people in this town? I watch them when I drive down Cherry Avenue. They know how to live. They are happy and carefree. They laugh and joke and play. They are content with what they have. They are not trying to be like other people. You should be more like them. You want too much out of life."

What was I to say? How was I to feel? Why was he saying these things to me? Another human being was telling me to my face that I should be content to be a nobody, wanting nothing. I had no entitlements!

Not because of something I had done wrong . . . lying, stealing, murder . . . .

Not because I was unkempt, slovenly, obese, reeking of body odor from an unwashed body or dirty clothing . . . .

Not because of a foul mouth, dirty language . . . .

Not because I was uneducated, illiterate, imbecilic . . . .

But because of the five colors of humankind, God had not created me white, but black. I wondered what his feelings were toward the brown-, yellow- and red-skinned people in this world?

I walked out of his office speechless. I wanted to hate him with every fiber of my body. I did not know how to hate. It was so frustrating to not say anything, to not do anything. My first thought was to run to church, to turn to God in prayer; but I was afraid. I was afraid that my prayer might be blasphemous, for there were times when I wanted to be angry with God for surrounding me with hypocritical Christians.

What precipitated the following remarks from my boss sometime later, I shall never know. It might have been his witnessing, as we all had, persons who passed by our agency window. It might have been a handcuffed Negro prisoner being taken into the city jail across the street from our office. It might have been the boisterous laughter of teen-agers on their way home from high school. It could even have been the elderly woman who entered the office to contribute a dollar for Christmas Seals because she saw me working in the office. "I'se so proud of you," she glowed.

"I am being very honest," Mr. Taylor announced after a series of similar attention-getting incidents. "I could endure anything in this world except that of living with a black skin. I think it is the worst curse God could put on anyone."

"I have never thought of it as a curse. I like who I am. I am sound of body and mind. I am richly blessed," I replied.

"Be that as it may, I could not live with a black skin. I could handle anything in this world but that!"

This time I did go to church.

I stopped by St. Peter's that evening before going home. I knelt before a large crucifix of Jesus in agony on the cross. I felt feelings I could not label and could not understand, rolling like a tumultuous storm in every fiber of my body. I wanted to tear them from me before they took root and destroyed me. I was feeling what no one could see . . . the pain of a crucified, abused spirit.

"You ought to know how I feel," I spoke to the depicted tortured body of Christ on the cross. "You were hated, you were despised, you were spit upon and scourged. Look at what is being done to me. I am giving everything that happens to me back to you. I cannot handle it. My boss is saying these hurting remarks to you, not to me! He cannot stand your creation. He cannot stand you. He hates my brown skin. He hates your tan skin. He hates me because I am a nigger. He hates you because you are a Jew!

"You are not through carrying the cross you carried to Calvary. You are carrying mine now. I am transferring everything, his every thought, word and action toward me, over to you." I was crying.

I continued going to Mass nearly every day, a practice that began at the time of my acceptance of the Catholic faith. I felt drawn to "lay my burden down" and pray "not to hate."

Later, perhaps a year or two after Mr. Taylor expressed abhorrence of my race and color, he announced to his staff the birth of his first grandson. Then he added, "We are very saddened. I am leaving for the East immediately. We have been told that the baby is terribly deformed. It is believed he is mentally sound, but he may be a helpless cripple for the rest of his life."

I wanted, oh how I wanted, to stand up in that little office crowded with the five staff members and shout, "You asked for it! You told God you could take anything—anything in this world—except a black skin; and He heard you! He heard you because I told Jesus, suffering on the cross with nails in His hands and feet, what you said to me. Now you will know, and your innocent grandchild will know, what it feels like to be looked upon with pity and scorn for something over which he has no control."

But I said not a word. Nothing! Margaret Collison, the Christmas Seal Chairman, and Catherine Minor, the office clerk, were offering their condolences, asking questions and assuring L. L. the office would run smoothly in his absence.

Had I committed a mortal sin just then and earlier—not in word or deed—but in thought? I had prayed daily for the grace not to hate. I had not asked for revenge. How could I think for one second of wanting to gloat over a child's misfortune. By nature, my first thought should have been to grieve for a faultless, misshapen infant.

Were my feelings so wrong? Is it natural to feel hurt because of ridicule and rejection and then wish to inflict that same hurt upon another? The victim then is just as evil as the persecutor, is he not? If my mother had hated and wished evil upon Mrs. Broomhandle, would she not have been just as wicked? Mom forgave and forgot. She was responsible for leading Mrs. Broomhandle back to her white, Irish Roman Catholic Church some twenty years later.

I needed to talk to someone. Why was I so agitated? Had I by thought done anything that required confession? My mind turned to two people on the Tuberculosis Board of Directors who I might talk to. Dr. J. B. Walker, a prominent Negro physician, and Monsignor Habig, pastor of St. Peter's Catholic Church, were active, influential persons. If I detailed the unpleasantries on the job to Monsignor, he could give me spiritual guidance and absolve me of my sinful thoughts. If I spoke to Dr. Walker, he might prescribe some medication for my increasing impatience, my irritability and moodiness. I had a fear of becoming embittered and full of hate.

It was a heavily paneled, high-ceilinged, austerely furnished reception room where Monsignor Habig and I sat. He was a personable, mild-mannered man with the graciousness of a prince of the church. "I need to talk to someone. I cannot keep all of this inside me," I began. Monsignor listened to me, questioned a few of the unbelievable happenings and then said, "I don't know why you are telling these things to me, What do you expect me to do?"

"I need to talk. I am not asking for anything specific. I just wanted someone to know, someone to be aware of what goes on behind closed doors and someone to advise me."

"I must admit I am stunned. Will you give me time to do some thinking?"

"Of course," I said and left without asking pardon for my sin or asking for his priestly blessing.

Two weeks later Monsignor Habig mailed a letter of resignation to the TB Board. He stated he was too busy to devote as much time to the agency as it deserved. I felt deceived. He either thought I was a liar, or he was in accord with the racist attitude of Mr. Taylor. If I had been a white Italian, a German, an Irishman, a Slovakian supported by an ethnic parish of some three hundred, five hundred or a thousand members, would he have thrown the weight of his office-pastor, monsignor, vicar general—behind me? Would he, could he, have let the offending boss know that such attitudes toward ethnic minorities were unchristian, wrong? Could he have said something? Perhaps not, because his own house was not in order. Discrimination was present and tolerantly "understood" in the Catholic church. I was between the devil and the deep blue sea.

One of the few Negro families we had known as children was the Gardner family on Shroyer Avenue about three blocks away from our home. Mae and Eva Gardner were friends of my Aunt Clella. They were part of the summer picnics and the winter sleigh rides Aunt Clella and her crowd enjoyed. Mae Gardner, a fair-skinned mulatto girl, married Andrew Perry, a Portuguese gentleman from the Cape Verde Islands. The newly married couple moved across town in the vicinity of the Republic Steel Corporation.

The Portuguese resembled the American Negro in appearance, but they spoke their native language and they were Catholic by birth. They resented the American segregation tactics practiced toward them. If they entered a theater or restaurant downtown and were denied service, they began to speak agitatedly in Portuguese and were immediately served, seated and treated with deference. They wanted no part of the American Negro's second-class status. In their country, I was told, there had been no skin color differences between white-skinned and black-skinned Portuguese.

Mae Perry shared with me the growing anger and discontent of the Portuguese men toward St. Paul's Catholic Church. The ushers directed the Portuguese to a few side aisle pews at the rear of the church. So obviously isolated, they felt the uncaring stares of the white parishioners and returned home angered and demeaned. Their Protestant wives could and did return to their Baptist and Methodist churches, but their husbands vowed to remain Catholic. In many cases, the practice of their faith became minimal: baptism, first communion, marriage and burial.

I called at St. Paul's rectory to talk to the pastor. I asked him why he felt obliged to divide his congregation according to skin color. "The city of Canton is above the Mason and Dixon Line, and we are no longer slaves," I remarked.

This European immigrant with a decided accent argued with me for nearly an hour justifying the separation of his congregation. He was convinced that the descendants of Africans were so far behind the Caucasian that it would be hundreds of years and a half dozen generations before the barbarian Negro could call himself civilized. I listened to a priest tell me to my face that only by watching and copying the white man's ways, from a distance, could I or any member of my race be regarded as an equal.

Father Stephanic's viewpoint was equally as abusive as L. L. Taylor's. How could Monsignor Habig remonstrate with a white Presbyterian executive when a fellow priest only "amen'd" the white racist's viewpoint? Could I respect and abhor at the same time? Could I respect the office of cleric, superintendent or executive while abhorring their racist use of power, authority and misguided wisdom?

I continued working on my job with an unreal determination. There were no other professional opportunities in Canton. I worked as if this were the first, last and only job on earth. Within five years my work had taken me into every segment of the community. The Black churches, Rosary and Altar Societies of the Catholic Church, PTAs, clubs of all kinds, ethnic civic groups, Missionary societies, lodges, United Fund agencies and schools made use of my services. Often my field work kept me out of the office seventy-five percent of the time.

Every Sunday required my appearance at a Black Protestant church service for a five-minute announcement about the importance of a chest X-ray. Every week meant two or three nights at a Grange or PTA, lecturing and showing a film. My husband drove me to all of my night appearances.

I was active in a dozen organizations. I became president of the Jane Hunter Civic Club, secretary to the Social Workers' Institute, president of the Catholic Interracial Council, active with the Council of Catholic Women and the Negro Citizen's Council.

I became acutely aware of the reality of nonverbal communication. I could walk into a PTA group, a church Rosary and Altar Society or missionary unit and know if I was facing a negative, positive or indifferent audience. I was frequently challenged by the questioning countenances in the many gatherings.

"Can she do the job?" "Will the audience be upset?" "Gee,

I hope everything goes well. We have never had a Negro speaker before. I wonder what she will be like."

I began to relish the game of changing my audience from an "Oh my God, no" to a "Gee, this woman is okay." Some changes were no more than a thirty-degree angle, others made a complete turn of one hundred eighty degrees.

For twelve years my TB Association contacts with fifty or more public and parochial grade and high schools in Stark County brought me in touch with each principal, the school nurse and the English or journalism teacher. Annually I conducted a school newspaper contest. Students told their own message about disease control. As a reward for research and excellence, I took an average of thirty student journalists to the Cleveland Health Museum during their Easter holiday vacation.

In the performance of the patch testing and X-raying programs, the schools and the county Board of Health assigned nurses to work with me. Without exception, each was superbly supportive. Ada Mang, Irene Westerh, Helen Beck, Sarah Bayes and Dora Wilson, all white, were of tremendous help over the years. They, with many other nurses, supported the annual Nurses' Institute gathering.

I wished my boss would become more supportive and change as many of my audiences had. There is an old saying that when an immovable object meets an irresistible force, something explosive is bound to happen.

It was in the making. I would not allow myself to feel demeaned and inferior. My boss would not relinquish his allegiance to white supremacy. The object and the force continued to meet. Something was happening to me. The brakes I had applied time and time again were losing their grip. I was tired of pumping my system to maintain control. I was headed for a collision.

Marcere Family Album

Percy, 27

Norma, 21

India Marcy

Rev. Henry Marcy

Sister (4 yrs.) and brother (1 yr.)

Al's first communion and Norma Jean's confirmation.

313

At St. Francis Academy.

Above: Norma Jean's first communion.

Right: High school graduation.

314

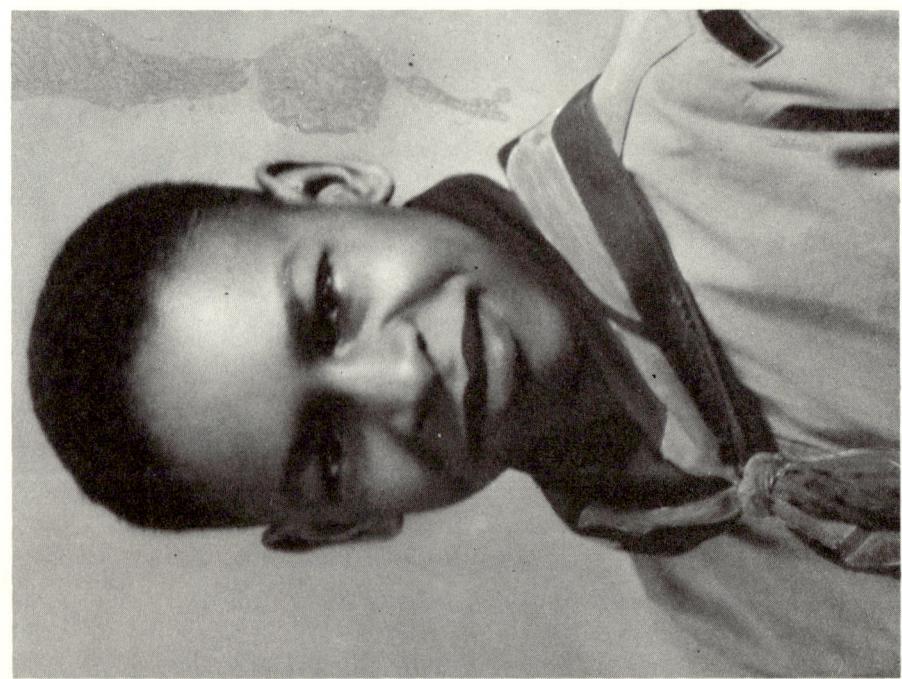

Al, Barbara and son Brent.

The Jane Hunter Civic Club Gypsy Ball, 1948. Seated: Rita Woods, Marjorie Frazier, Mary Meyers, Willa Webb, Dorothy Parker, Rosetta Bell. Standing: Elizabeth Carmichael, Norma Marcere, Elnora Stevens, Flora Spence Thomas, Dora Brown, Daisy Turner, Caldonia Harris.

Presentation of 5 year Volunteer Pin Award— Urban League annual meeting. Judge Clay Hunter, Austin Andrews, Mrs. Percy Marcere.

Norma and Percy on their 25th Anniversary.

317

Two views of our childhood home, 1424 - 5th St. S.W.

Home for 25 years at 817 Prospect Ave. S.W.

A souvenir from Zaire, Africa, 1970.

319

...orma Jean Marcere Snow ...her wedding gown.

The same gown worn by her daughter, Theresa Ann Snow Hood.

320

Top: Theresa Ann Snow Hood, a 3rd generation college graduate, receiving master's degree from Texas

Middle: Holy Rosary Choir Pahala, Hawaii.

Bottom: St. Paul's North Canton, Ohio Renewal group joins Norma on one of her Hawaiian trips.
Back Row: Jean Ners, Fr John Murray, Leroy and Jeanne Nist, Stella Spangler Carol and Bob Stanley, D Marcere; Ed Dick, Fr Thomas Heimann, Maxine Mears, Helen Bianchi.
Front row: Herm Spangler Robert and Maryann Fanno Donna and Arden Gill, Annette Thur, Pat Hansen.

XX

Confusion, Conflict, Confession, Compliance

Before the multifarious pressures of my job became a contributing factor (pushing me near the edge), many events transpired. Percy and I hosted our daughter's beautiful wedding while treading on thin ice in our marriage. Our son was faced with educational and career decisions.

Prior to those events, Percy was angered and literally devastated by his daughter's sojourn at boarding school. "She's not a fatherless or motherless orphan. She's not a delinquent daughter. She should be here at home. If there's enough room in this house for her brother and a foster child, why isn't she here?" he remarked more than once.

At St. Francis DeSales Academy, Norma Jean was experiencing a variety of adjustments to her new environment. She missed her daddy with whom there was a closeness she and I had never cultivated.

The curriculum at St. Francis encompassed the highest standards of middle class, Negro Catholic culture. Norma Jean continued her private voice and piano lessons. She was an "A" student. With a great many extracurricular activities, an exciting year was anticipated. The cadets from St. Emma's Military Academy shared their dances and other social events with the St. Francis girls. St. Francis graduates would return home to become the envied debutantes of their social set.

What our daughter did not tell us in her letters, a required weekly writing assignment, was her displeasure with the attention given to the girls with light skin and flowing long hair. Before the electric hot comb, before permanents and before the curl-free method of freeing the tight texture of Negro hair, the differences in the length and texture of tresses and a fair, mullato or octoroon complexion often became badges of acceptance and popularity.

How does one compete against Mother Nature's outward endowments? How does one call attention to one's academic strengths when intelligence is second in importance to an arbitrarily prescribed type of beauty? How does one rebel in a well-controlled Catholic environment?

Our teen-age daughter viewed several of the teacher-nuns as racist. There is no specific age when one is able to pinpoint, to define, to explain or to classify racist behavior. Once its sting has invaded the psyche of its victim, the victim is forever sensitized to like mannerisms in the next assailant and the next and the next.

Norma Jean reflected that by becoming a nun, some of the sisters were doing penance to atone for an aversion to Negroes. That which they could not handle in the outside world they tried to conceal by their sacrificial lives. The vivid recollection of Sister Carlotta's intent to keep her from participating in the Forty Hours Devotion at St. Joseph's justified her resentment of some of the nuns at St. Francis.

She came home from school one spring day, after her first communion, to announce, "Mother, Sister said today that our class was to march in the procession, but she didn't mean me."

"You must be mistaken, dear. Of course you will march. I marched at my church in the second grade, and so will you."

"No, Mother, Sister didn't mean me."

Immediately, without a word to my daughter, I walked the

fifteen-plus blocks to St. Joseph's and asked to speak to a priest, any one of the four. Sitting in the rectory office, I repeated my daughter's comments and added what was becoming a routine refrain: "I am not sending my child to a Catholic school to develop an inferiority complex. In everything that is required or expected of other children, I expect her to be included."

We talked awhile, calmly and politely, even though I was fighting mad. "I don't think," Father Nicolay explained, "that Sister intended to exclude your daughter. Just go ahead and reassure Norma Jean that she is to march. I shall see that she does."

The next day a very happy little girl rushed into the house after school shouting, "She did mean me, Mother. She did mean me. I am going to march in Forty Hours. The whole class is marching. Everybody!"

I did not know then that my daughter knew I had gone to school and talked to someone who had changed Sister Carlotta's mind.

Her daddy and I sat on the aisle seats during that processional pageantry so Norma Jean could see our smiles of pride and support.

At St. Francis, Norma Jean could not run home after school to tell us of her exclusion and her hurts, so she displayed her frustrations and her anger in her own way. She was never sassy or impolite. The things she did were first seen as innocent, unintentional coincidences, until they occurred with greater frequency.

She would emit a falsetto note in the middle of a solo or choral performance. She blamed it upon a sore throat. Her tonsils were acting up. A letter from school advised me to have her tonsils removed during summer vacation. Our family doctor found nothing wrong with her tonsils.

Near the finale of the junior class play, our daughter engaged in a fit of uncontrolled laughter which infected the entire cast and ruined the performance. The letter from school suggested that she not be enrolled as a senior the following September. "She is a disruptive influence."

Norma Jean returned to Mount Marie. When upon graduation she announced she was not going to college, her daddy and I were dismayed. We insisted she commute to Kent State for one year with the promise that we would not object to any later decision she made about her future. This she did and then started looking for a job. She contacted Monsignor Kotheimer, of whom she was very fond, for a reference letter to the Ohio Bell Telephone Company. She was hired. She was the first Negro girl to graduate from Mount Marie and the first Negro hired at Ohio Bell.

At the end of a year, our daughter began dating. Several months later she became engaged to the son of a Baptist minister from Alliance, Ohio. The young man, James Snow, agreed to convert to Catholicism when he understood she was looking for a Catholic husband.

Their wedding rivaled that of her grandmother, Ida Evans Snipes, and the grandfather she had never seen, Norman Sherwoood Snipes. Theirs was the first formal Negro Catholic wedding at St. Joseph's, just as the Snipes wedding had been the first formal church wedding of a Negro couple in the city of Canton.

I had sewn her wedding gown, a most beautiful creation of ice blue satin and antique lace. Her gown was my finest creation. It was truly a labor of love. After the wedding, I put Shuggie's sewing machine away. I would not sew anymore. Our little girl was grown up.

Shuggie made a strange comment after the wedding. "It was beautiful. I pray it will last. In a crowd like that, there are as many ill wishers as well wishers. It shows in people's eyes. I guess my girls did the right thing. They slipped off quietly to exchange their vows. They're all happily married." Percy was most unhappy about his daughter's marriage. He believed that Jim was impressed by our standard of living and saw himself marrying into money. "I just don't trust him," Percy said to me over and over again. "He doesn't mean our daughter any good. He's an opportunist. You'll see. You were so anxious to put on a big wedding, you couldn't see that you were throwing our daughter to a vulture," Percy accused more than once.

Al's Scout activity at St. Joseph's earned him city-wide recognition. He was the first Negro Eagle Scout in the area. Our family was nearing a record for firsts.

Preferring to go to a public rather than Catholic high school, Al did well at Lincoln. His teachers liked him. His favorite subjects were English and chemistry. He took part in track. As graduation drew near, he listened to his white classmates talk about getting jobs at various industrial plants.

"Al," one of his friends confided one day, "I've been hired in the chemistry lab at Timken's. Why don't you apply there? You're a better chemistry student than me. Why don't you?"

When Al applied, he was told there were no openings. Percy took Al to his foreman at Republic Steel. "This is my son, graduate of Lincoln High. He needs a job. No, I don't want him on the labor gang. My son's smart and good. Yes, I know. A summer laboring job is one thing. Now he's looking for something better and permanent."

Al was not hired at Republic Steel, either. Percy and I debated long about what to do. Should Al consider the Army, Navy, or Marines? If he joined any branch of the service, he might specify his interest in chemistry; but without any training or work experience he could be assigned to unskilled, unscientific tasks. We recalled my brother Eugene's experience in the Navy.

There was a school in Cleveland devoted to training medical

lab technologists. If we could send him there, the chemistry and laboratory training would prepare him for work in a hospital.

Carnegie Institute of Cleveland accepted Al's application. Our friends, Mr. and Mrs. Ellis, Mrs. Davis and Mrs. Mary Meyers, formerly of Massillon, made him welcome in their homes, providing room and board as he wished. On those weekends at home Al and I, son and mother, became very close. No matter how late the hour when he arrived home, he would awaken me with "Mom, Mom, are you awake?" and then proceed to discuss the week's events. We philosophized about people, morality, cultures and aired our viewpoints dealing with human issues. He had both feet on the ground. He was his father's son.

When Al had completed his year at Carnegie and had a certificate attesting to his qualifications as a laboratory technician, he was again unable to find work. The two local hospitals required at least a two-year college background.

Even with both feet on the ground, we feared that Al's unemployment would activate an uncertainty about his acceptance, his rights, his place in the total society. The fear was there. His unemployment could be reason enough to hang around street corners joining up with those who would put ideas in his head.

Percy knew the mindset of the street loafer. He knew the conversations, the words of envy and the taunts that Al could hear from youth his own age—the same taunts that upset my brother, Eugene.

"Buddy, you's no bettah dan de res' of us with all yo education. You'se speak like a white man. You'se gone to Catholic school. Whitey has 'lowed you to move in his nabo'hood, but what's it really got you? Wha's yoah good job? Git with it, niggah. We'se learn how to get some kicks out ah life."

Al told me his friends had coaxed, "Get your old man to

let you have his car this weekend, and we'll show you what life is all about. . . ."

In the wee hours of a Sunday morning Al wakened me from a prayerful sleep to tell me about the marijuana that was available to the decent young people in town. Then he suddenly announced: "Mom, I must get away from here. I would like to go to Xavier University in New Orleans. I understand the new pharmacist in town, Fred Johnson, graduated from there."

Alluren wanted to attend a college made possible by the visionary zeal of Mother Katharine Drexel, foundress of the Sister of the Blessed Sacrament and many schools and institutions. Norma Jean had attended her St. Francis De Sales Academy in Virginia. Many times I had renewed my spirit at the retreat house on the Drexel family estate in Philadelphia. Our son's interest in Xavier was heartening.

Al's choice of a Negro Catholic college in the Deep South meant we had to go to the bank for a loan. Not a single bank in Canton would have approved a loan to us after our furniture had been repossessed in 1934. It took us many years to establish a credit rating.

From my childhood habit of saving twenty-five cents a week for a twelve dollar and fifty cent Christmas Club, I began saving fifty cents a week and then a dollar. Some of this went into a savings account. Then I began to borrow fifty dollars from a Beneficial Loan Company, payable in full in six months. I paid it back in three months. I requested a loan of one hundred dollars and two hundred dollars and repaid it ahead of time. My part time attendance at Kent State University was used as a reason for borrowing money. I claimed a need for tuition, books and transportation to build up my credit.

When we walked into the bank to request a loan for our

son's expenses at college, we had a record of regular savings and exceptionally prompt loan payments. It was graciously and immediately approved. Al would go to Xavier, first class.

Al's year at Xavier broadened his insights into human behavior. A Catholic Afro-American culture was an eye-opener. He controlled his reactions to the off-campus apartheid with a triumphant sense of humor. Every time Al got on a bus, he pocketed one of the "colored" signs, took it back to his dormitory and hung it on the wall. He gathered close to one hundred "colored" signs during the year.

The multi-ethnic, multi-hued student body intrigued him. He was impressed with the Sunday afternoon invitations to the creole and native New Orleans family homes. "Mom," he wrote in one of his letters, 'I never realized how much fun one can have sitting in a living room discussing the history of a people, or gathered in a kitchen popping corn or making pecan fudge. The entire family makes us welcome in their homes. P. S. When it gets dark no one would think of turning the lights down low just to neck, as they do in Canton."

After one year at Xavier, Al was employed as a medical laboratory technologist at Mercy Hospital. When he enlisted in the Air Force, he was assigned to a medical division called Aviation Physiology. He became an instructor in "The Hazards of High Altitude Flying."

With both of the children gone, Percy and I behaved as strangers. We had little to say to each other. He blamed me for his loneliness. I became engrossed in my work, putting in many more hours than necessary, thus avoiding intimacy at home. There were days when we never saw or spoke to each other.

I kept my resolve never to use insulting, hurtful words in an argument. I was obsessively restrained to avoid an encounter at all costs. I also had another restraint. I never admitted to pain or physical discomfort. I had, since my sixteenth year, suffered excruciating menstrual cramps every twenty-one days and always on the weekend. I learned early not to expect any sympathy from anyone. There was always an abundance of tasks to perform. Fridays were generally test days at school. To miss a Friday test could lower one's grades.

Before my marriage, if Mom had bills to be paid on a Saturday morning, I could not say that I was in too much pain to walk to town to take care of business. I needed the two dollars I earned at Mrs. Oser's every Saturday as my week's lunch money and school allowance, so I stood at the ironing board, ironing nearly a dozen men's shirts, often crying with pain. The morning came to an end after I got down on my hands and knees to scrub and wax the kitchen and bathroom floors. If I had to cater a Saturday wedding breakfast, prepare a four-course Sunday dinner, I did what I had to do, perfectly, and endured without complaint this tri-weekly purgatory. I never confided to my Mom nor to my husband my discomfort. Neither indifference nor pity could have changed the inevitable.

On this Friday, however, doubled over in extreme pain, I walked into Dr. Helen's downtown office, just a block from work. I was in tears. "I can't take it any longer. I can't! I can't! These cramps are driving me out of my mind!" I cried.

She gave me some medication not to be taken until I was safe at home and scheduled me for a complete physical on Monday. On the way home, I began to anticipate the relief the medication would provide. How nice to lie in bed and pamper myself. No babies crying, no teen-agers in and out of the house. Just quiet, painless peace.

I was lying on the living room couch in a half-dazed, numbed stupor. The medication was working. The soothing sensation I was feeling frightened me. I wanted to be out of pain, but not out of control. When my husband came home from work, he seated himself in his comfortable chair and began reading the newspaper. He seemed not to notice that my lying down was unusual.

"Have you heard from Norma Jean this week?" he ventured.

"No."

"I wonder why she doesn't write."

"I don't know."

"Do you think if you . . . ."

"You" was the trigger word. I exploded! I sat upright, reached for the lamp on the end table and threw it at Percy screaming, "I can't make her write. I didn't force her to get married. Quit blaming me for everything. I can't take any more of this. Get out of my life or better still, I'll get out of yours!"

I thought I saw blood on Percy's face as he righted the lamp and walked out of the room. If I had not taken that medication, I would have left the house, gone to the bus station and taken a bus to Cleveland or Columbus or Philadelphia for a few days. Instead, I went to bed and stayed there.

On Monday morning, ignoring my doctor's appointment, I reported to work. During my lunch hour I went to see Father Heimann, pastor of St. Mary's Immaculate Conception Church. We had become very good friends. Knowing of my house-to-house visits as a caseworker and health educator, he had for a number of year pressed me into doing some pastoral home calls for him. He seemed particularly concerned about his Negro parishioners. He would ask me to drop by a home or two to say he had missed seeing them at Mass.

On this particular morning he began, "Norma, I have not seen Mrs. Williams in church for several weeks. When you are in her neighborhood, drop in to see how she is. Find out how Mr. Williams and the children are doing. See if there is anything they need. Do you think I would be welcome if I made a home call? Will you ask?" Father entreated this morning.

"Your wish is my command," I answered rather flippantly, and then blurted out my own concern.

"If I get a divorce, Father, can I continue to be a Catholic? Can I go to Mass and receive Holy Communion?"

"You are thinking of getting a divorce?"

"Yes."

"Why?"

"I just do not want to be married any more."

"Is there something seriously wrong with your marriage? Is Percy abusive?"

"Oh, no. Nothing like that. When I married it was . . . expedient. I wanted to go out into the world as an honorable woman. A single girl living away from home was looked upon with suspicion. We were married by a justice of the peace. I was never in love. I never intended to have children and never expected to stay married this long. The children are all grown now. I tried to be a good mother. I gave it my best. Our daughter is married, and our son is in the Air Force. I want my freedom. Percy and I have nothing in common."

"Are you wanting me to condone your reasoning? Am I to okay your plans to go your own way?" Father asked.

"I am not up to any mischief. I do not have a boyfriend. I shall not be looking for another husband."

"Be that as it may, a marriage does not cease just because one of the parties decides to call it quits. Your marriage is 'till death do you part.' It is just as valid as if you had all the formalities, all the trimmings of a royal ceremony."

"Father, we have been physically parted for nearly a year. We don't need each other any more," I insisted.

"You need, Norma, to be aware of how your decision will affect hundreds of people in this town who see you as a very fine Catholic woman. Many people know you. Many more people have been inspired by you. You have responsibilities and obligations. This is no time to think only of yourself."

"I am tired of responsibilities and obligations," I blurted out, on the verge of tears. "That is the story of my life, doing the right thing at the right time for the sake of others. I want to please myself, pamper myself for the first time in my life. I want my freedom!"

"And I want you today to tell your husband to come here to see me," Father interrupted authoritatively.

"He will not come. He is not a Catholic. He has no obligations to the church's teachings."

"Ask him. Tell him I want to speak to him and you be here, too."

"When I told Percy that Father Heimann wanted to see him (my first words to him in days), I was unprepared for his response.

"When does he want to see us? It's both of us, isn't it?"

I remember little of the detailed exchange of words while seated in Father's study. Father initiated the conversation relating how I was considering a divorce. From there he began lecturing Percy about his obligation to make me happy. I tried to interrupt. He was being unfair to scold Percy. It was not Percy, it was me . . . well, maybe it was both of us.

The embarrassing and somewhat frightening appointment ended. I suspected that within my husband's calm exterior there was a giant of a man capable of an explosive outburst. I actually feared going home. Then I heard Percy say, "You've given us much to think about, Father. Thank you for your counsel. I needed this."

We headed for home. Percy was gentle and attentive. I was confused. I felt trapped. Father had said something about loving one another. I had been taught not to hate, but not how to love. Had I denied the existence of conjugal love for fear of being hurt if or when a love I espoused would vanish as my mother's had? Were my frustrations on the job causing me to transfer unrelieved tensions to my mate and to our marriage? How long does it take to undo a marriage? How long does it take to incubate a nervous breakdown? What are the ingredients for creating an emotional illness? How many incidents of insult, denial, ridicule and ego deprivation does it take to engender helplessness, futility, shame, frustration, defeat? Are panic, fear and despair advanced states of all of the above? How high does the human thermometer of helplessness rise before anger, retaliation and revenge are considered to even the score? Are there biological components of hormonal activity, chemical imbalances or vitamin deficiencies that cause emotional-behavioral ups and downs?

A nervous breakdown! What is it? Is it all or part of one or more of the above? In the family, on the job, on the streets, in the churches, in travel and recreation, are there combinations of incidents that tip the scales of human endurance to a dangerous imbalance? Whence comes the cry, "Danger!" "Halt!"

After weeks of inner turmoil, I recall making an appointment to see Dr. Edmund Beshara. I was not sure why. I remember agreeing to go to Mercy Hospital for a rest. I did not tell Percy. I remember following the nurse down the sixth floor corridor. The nurse stopped to unlock a door to the psychiatric unit. I remember that I let out a scream and yelled, "No! No! No! I am not crazy!"

There was no "time" for awhile. Then I remember that wires were being attached to my body and shocks went all through me. I remember that I trembled so hard my bones felt like a bunch of marbles sprawled on the bed.

I was no longer a person. Something had been taken away from me. There was no cohesiveness to my spirit, my strength or my thinking. I recall eating some tasteless meals on a sun porch lounge. The women surrounding me reminded me of faceless zombies from another world. I tried to ignore them.

I recall feeling ashamed and angry when visitors came to see me. I was glad that my daughter lived in California and could not visit me. I recall going home some thirty pounds lighter and feeling like a limp rag. I recall being told to take it easy for three months.

Once at home I began having itching seizures. Every nerve in my anatomy seemed to rush to the surface of my body and engage in battle. I felt as though a thousand mosquitoes were stinging me. I rubbed, I scratched, I cried. I submerged myself in bathtubs full of water—hot, cold and lukewarm.

When the attacks subsided, I remember crying buckets of tears daily and not knowing why. I reached out to Percy and clung to him as a drowning person clings to a life raft. I asked him to hold me in his arms. "Just hold me. I don't want anything else. Just hold me." I felt so empty, so abandoned, so alone.

As he held me in his strong arms, close to his muscular body, I would continue to cry and cry and cry. I remember wondering why I had never said to my husband, "I love you." Did I need to put into perspective my convictions about love, sex and marriage? I had never wanted to be married, but I was.

I was thinking how lucky I was to have a husband who held and comforted me as he did. He made no demands of me. He allowed me to unfold at my own pace. I began to appreciate how loyal, how honorable, how patient and understanding he had been during the twenty-one years of our marriage. His love for me was real. It was true and everlasting.

It was hard for me to admit that I had held a part of me away from my husband. Had I ever considered him my equal? Many times co-workers and associates would ask, "What does your husband do?" "Is your husband a doctor?" "What is your husband's alma mater?" Why did I allow such questions to embarrass me?

Percy had never been inside a high school except to attend

his children's graduations. A college classroom was second nature to me. Popular opinion seemed to agree that it was all right for the banker's son to marry the scrub woman's daughter, but the scrub woman's daughter who had gone to college was expected to marry a doctor or lawyer.

Father Heimann had said to me, "Make a list of all the positive things about your husband and your marriage . . . and count your blessings."

Heading the list was that Percy was never an embarrassment. He was intelligent. He was well spoken. He loved and revered me. He loved his children. He never seduced other women. He worked every day. He allowed me space to do what I wanted to do. He never harnessed my freedom.

During my illness, I was given a book by Kahlil Gibran entitled *The Prophet*. Leafing through the book one day, the words "And What of Marriage" caught my attention. I read the poem over and over again.

"You were born together, and together you shall be forever more.
You shall be together when the white wings of death scatter your days.
Ay, you shall be together even in the silent memory of God.
But let there be spaces in your togetherness,
And let the winds of the heavens dance between you.

Love one another, but make not a bond of love:
Let it rather be a moving sea between the shores of your souls.
Fill each other's cup but drink not from one cup.
Give one another of your bread but eat not from the same loaf.
Sing and dance together and be joyous, but let each one of you be alone,

Even as the strings of a lute are alone though they quiver with the same music.

Give your hearts, but not into each other's keeping.
For only the hand of life can contain your hearts.
And stand together yet not too near together.
for the pillars of the temple stand apart,
And the oak tree and the cypress grow not in each other's shadow."

Gibran had described our marriage—a cypress and an oak not diminished but enriched by the other. I had a good marriage. I should not be afraid to love. With my illness behind me, I could now move forward toward a joyous love relationship.

Soon I was begging to be allowed to go back to work. My doctor was telling me that I could not go back to the Tuberculosis and Health Association. His words were, "Look for another job. You must! Your job was the chief cause of your illness. You thought you could change the conditions under which you worked. You could not, and you cannot ever. Those conditions will never change. How about teaching?"

"Could I go back to college?" I questioned.

"Of course. Why not?"

"I have had a nervous breakdown. I feel like damaged goods. I am afraid."

Dr. Beshara was most reassuring. "Please do not think that way. Your illness got rid of the cobwebs and excess baggage in your psyche. Go back to school, get your bachelor's and your master's degrees. Some day you may want to consider a doctorate. You can do it. You are a remarkable woman. Now be on your way. I shall want to see you in three years."

In the fall of 1955 I received a letter from Kent State informing me I had accumulated more than enough credits for a bachelor's degree. Those one and two classes a year had multiplied more rapidly than I had imagined. I was advised to meet with the registrar relative to some subjects that might be necessary, depending upon my plans for an elementary, a secondary or a dual teaching certification.

My visit with the registrar delighted me. I needed just five required subjects for my bachlor of arts degree. They were art, education, sociology, philosophy and speech.

Following my illness I requested and was granted a three-months' leave of absence from the TB office. I returned to Kent State the summer of 1956. I did not resign from my TB job until I had received my bachelor of arts degree in August and had enrolled in graduate school. The announcement of my resignation in September and my appointment as a graduate assistant at Kent State University made all of the local newspapers. The *Repository* carried an editorial lauding the quality of service that I had rendered to the community. An interesting future was just ahead.

When Dr. Dwight Arnold appointed me as one of his graduate assistants in the Psychology Department at Kent State University, I was forty-six years old. Nearing sixty, this vivacious white-haired gentleman exuded love and caring. He was just what my psyche needed.

Dr. Arnold became my inspiration. He was to me what Sister Mildred, Mr. Gilmore, Miss Swan, Mary Stanton and Delmar Serafy had been at crucial periods in my life. His confidence assured me that I could do the impossible, and I did.

For twelve months I commuted fifty miles a day from home to the university. I taught and counseled fifteen hours a week as Dr. Arnold's assistant. I carried a full load of graduate studies. I administered much of the Portage County elementary schools' achievement tests. On Saturdays I tested individual students from several counties. Parents and their children came for counseling relative to a multitude of school and home adjustment problems.

Many of the college students being counseled had suffered nervous breakdowns. I found it helpful for me to say and for the students to hear me say, "I have been there. I understand. Now pick up the pieces and forge ahead. You can do it."

In those twelve months I researched and wrote my master's thesis. It was entitled "The Social Interaction of Eighth Grade Students of Differing Socioeconomic Backgrounds."

I read no newspapers, watched no television, attended no movies or social events. I slept as little as four or five hours a night in two to three hour intervals. I was never happier or healthier. When I received my master of arts degree in Guidance and Counseling in August, 1957, the only person I saw was my husband. No other family members were present. Our embrace in the presence of hundreds of graduates and their families left no doubt of our gratitude to God and our rejoicing. We had overcome. We had done the impossible.

Weeks before graduation I began looking for a teaching job. Initially, I was eager to reopen my application with the Canton City Schools. Canton was considering Blacks for preschool or lower elementary assignments. Recalling how I had been denied a teaching job in 1929, I wanted no limitations now, based upon my race. It was the administration's timorous belief that a Negro would be more acceptable to very young children. A "mammy," "baby-sitting" role was the system's way of introducing Blacks to the teaching staff. My upper elementary and junior high school training was beyond their consideration. A counselor position was perhaps ten years away, I was told.

With an emotional intensity of anger and loathing that I was not afraid to admit, I embraced a Biblical command. I wiped the dust of the Canton school system from my feet. I would apply elsewhere in Ohio. I would never step my foot inside a Canton school to teach for one day or one year. I placed Massillon and Akron at the top of the long list of Ohio cities where I would apply. I was willing to commute to any city outside of Canton.

Mr. L. J. Smith, Superintendent of the Massillon City Schools, greeted me graciously as I walked into his office. He was a heavyset, distinguished individual with a friendly, charismatic personality.

"What can we do for each other today?" he asked as I seated myself in his office.

"I am applying for a teaching job in one of your schools," I replied.

"I read about your assistantship at Kent State. Congratulations!"

"Thank you."

"So you would like to work in the Massillon system?"

"I think so."

"I would not be hiring a stranger. You have been in and out of our schools for a good many years. You have spoken to our PTA groups, and you are known to many of our teachers. Do you have a grade or subject preference?"

"Yes, upper elementary or junior high."

"The only job that is open this close to the beginning of school is a gymnasium teacher at Jones Junior High School. How does that sound?"

My thoughts went back to my high school gym classes and my physical education classes at Kent State. I actually laughed out loud.

"You must be kidding. What would I look like in a gym suit, weighing nearly one hundred and sixty pounds. That's not exactly what I had in mind."

"There would be an English class or two to teach. You would enjoy that, I know. You have worked well with the journalism and English teachers with the School Press project.

What do you say?"

"Half of the job sounds fine. Let me sleep on it. I shall let you know."

I returned to the dormitory at Kent—my last two weeks' residence there—and shared with my Italian roommate, Rose, my interview. She remarked that she thought the superintendent was just being polite. "The application I submitted a month ago was turned down. A friend to a member of the School Board said it was because I am Catholic," Rose volunteered.

I did not return to see Mr. Smith. I went to Akron to reactivate my application there. Back in the dormitory a few days later, Rose waved a Massillon newspaper in front of me. "Look, you have been hired as a teacher at E. A. Jones Junior High. Here it is. A list of this year's teaching staff and their assignments. Do you suppose the Board has any idea that you are Catholic?"

"Of course not," I replied. "All Blacks are Baptist."

It was Shuggie's neighbor and friend, Mrs. Stewart, who told me many years later, "I remember when your mother came over to my house to show me the newspaper clipping about your teaching job. She was so proud of you. Your nervous breakdown had really upset her. Waving the newspaper in her hand, she said over and over again, 'She made it, she made it! My daughter made it! I knew she would!' "

XXI

Teaching

It was not only my dream of many years come true when I became a teacher, but the actualization of my mother's and grandmother's dreams of fifty and eighty years earlier. Virginia began teaching in the Akron school system in 1955, so I was not the first teacher in our family. It had been a long twenty-eight-year wait from the fall of 1929 to the fall of 1957 to hold a teaching contract in my hand. I was ecstatic and my husband, who had made many sacrifices and endured countless inconveniences, beamed with pride. He had played no small part in two women's college degrees—his sister's and his wife's.

Percy and I drove all over the E. A. Jones district to better understand the environment of the children I would teach. Massillon, a city of thirty-thousand citizens, was a sprawling area of single-residence, two-story homes with pleasing front lawns, rear yards and garden areas. The Jones School district was closest to the Republic Steel Plant, the railroad yards and other manufacturing companies. The area caught the smoke and the thundering sounds from the furnaces pouring out molten steel in readiness for machined products. Several small businesses—barber shops, taverns and a convenience grocery store—were inconspicuously nestled close to their owner-occupied residences next door. The neat outdoor environment suggested energetic families with pride in the appearance of their house and lawns.

The four Negro churches in the Walnut Avenue area—two Baptist and two Methodist—were not as imposing as the high spired Catholic church close to the Third Street railroad crossing. Their wood-framed structures were somewhat beyond the storefront category. Like miniature outposts, they seemed to transmit a feeling of religious surveillance over their neighboring inhabitants.

With our tour and the information I had obtained from Mr. Scourfield, I was forming a positive picture of my prospective students. E. A. Jones Junior High School, a sprawling multi-level, addition-enlarged building, had an enrollment of four-hundred students. One-hundred children were Negro. A large percentage of the Caucasian children were second-generation European ethnics or migrants from disadvantaged areas of the southeastern parts of the country.

I was the third Black teacher in the Massillon school system and the first at Jones. Mrs. Leader Brooks from Toledo and Alma Jones from New York preceded me. My assignment was that of physical education teacher for the seventh, eighth and ninth-grade girls, and the English teacher for three ninth-grade classes. I would have approximately fifty girls to a gym class and between thirty and thirty-five students in English. The English classes were of homogeneous groupings: A-B, C, and D-F achievers.

At the teachers' meeting just before the opening of school, I was startled by what I perceived as an atmosphere of pessimistic indifference. There was little of the exuberance of dedicated professionals. Mr. Scourfield, a mild-mannered gentleman with the appearance of an aristocrat, introduced me as the new English and gymnasium teacher with a master's degree in guidance and counseling.

"Mrs. Marcere is not a stranger to our school system. She has worked with the advisors and editors of our school publications while in the employ of the Stark County Tuberculosis and Health Association. Several of our students here at Jones have earned awards and gone with her on the Easter Monday tour to the Cleveland Health Museum," he elaborated.

A polite, silent, cautious acceptance emanated from the gathering. Mrs. Juanita Morgan, the eighth-grade English teacher and school librarian, smiled a warm welcome. We had met before and had worked well together. As for the majority of the staff, my senses caught the body language of suspicion, inspection, comparison, examination, reservation and all of those adjectives that shout, "So what! We have gotten along without Negro teachers all these years. What's the big deal?"

These teachers were not the Dean Verders or the Jesse Masons who would turn their backs and walk away from me. Neither would they be so uncouth as to refuse to work beside me, refuse to share the same teachers' lounge or use the same toilet as could occur in the Deep South. They were nevertheless telegraphing a perplexed uneasiness that told me not to look to them for anything. I was on my own. I wondered why they were distancing themselves from me.

"Do you know Jenny Lee Jones?" I was asked by one teacher before the day was over.

"No. I don't think I do," I replied.

"Oh, surely you have heard about Jenny Lee. She is a legend in this town. She has cooked for some of Massillon's finest families. A very nice person!"

"Maybe if I lived here I would know her," I explained. "Perhaps you can introduce me to her sometime."

Was this teacher trying to tell me something? I wondered. I would have appreciated a welcoming comment such as, "If I can be of any help since you are new here, let me know."

I never heard it.

What I did hear was the message to watch my step. I was there to teach, not to compete for acceptance or popularity; so I shrugged off my first impression messages. I taught three English and two gymnasium classes daily. I had a study hall, a free period and my lunch hour. There was no need to have daily contact with the staff at all if I avoided the teachers' lounge and the cafeteria.

After fifteen years of work with adults the ages of my students' parents and grandparents, I entered the classroom with definite teaching objectives. I hoped to encourage my pupils to study, to think and to discover. I would help them enjoy literature, become fluent in speech and cultured in manners and behavior. They should tower above their parents and relatives to take their rightful place in a nation that would some day accord them the dignity of full citizenship.

It took only a day or two to assess the monumental task ahead of me. My students shocked me by their unfamiliarity with discipline and purpose. They engaged in a calculated ritual for delaying the teaching process in every class they entered. They had no paper, their pencils needed sharpening, they had to go to the lavatory, they had left their books in another classroom, they were popping gum, they jostled with their friends as if they were on the playground.

Ground rules by me were established immediately. No gum-chewing, no pencil-sharpening after the class bell, no leaving the classroom for any reason whatsoever—never! When one outspoken young man protested with, "If I have to go, I have to go; and you know what will happen if you don't let me go."

I countered, "Yes, I do know what may happen, sir, and if there is a pool of liquid under your desk when the class period is over, you and the custodian can mop it up. You have five minutes to move from one class to another and to go to the lavatory. If your intestinal tract must be emptied every half hour or so, bring a statement from your parents and your doctor," I explained.

It took three days to convince my pupils I was there to teach and that they were to enter the classroom ready to learn.

The level of their basic skills in reading, writing and arithmetic was two to three grades below level. They seemed not to have advanced in anything since the fourth grade, except disruptive classroom behavior and a passion for fun with their peers. Their chief aim was merely to avoid failure by earning a "D." They were pupils with no thoughtful purpose in mind. They were not academically motivated.

The resigned, fatalistic, indifferent attitude of the teachers expressed at a staff meeting (not to mention the teachers' lounge) was hard to justify. They concluded that Jones School was no longer educable since the enrollment of Blacks had increased to thirty percent. The same percentage of ethnics from St. Joseph's School, described as not smart enough to go to a Catholic high school, would not demand quality attention. Just plain "poor" was the label attached to the other students. With two thirds of the student body unendowed mentally and many poor, teacher attitudes included low expectancy, pupil pity, racial, religious and cultural prejudice and "why sweat it."

My gymnasium classes were an unruly, disrespectful gathering of girls who came to class dressed in a variety of assorted colored shorts and blouses. With portable radios from home, they planned to spend the gymnasium class period dancing as they had the year before. I had been in enough Black churches and had heard enough sermons against dancing to know that most of their parents would not have approved. The children manipulated their environment to practice deception and disobedience.

Was the school gymnasium the place for pupils to practice

their own dance movements without instruction and direction? The dance as an art form had a place in a physical education curriculum. Through dance, discipline, gracefulness and physical fitness could become adjuncts to history, geography and multi-ethnic cultures. I enlisted the services of a dance instructor from another school for my ninth-grade classes.

Mr. Clyde Scourfield, my principal, listened to my request that all students be required to wear regulation gym outfits. I also requested new equipment. He reminded me that the students' parents could not afford and would refuse to purchase outfits. "They cannot afford uniforms. They have no money," he remarked.

"I can get the outfits," I told him. "I shall ask the Nannie Burroughs Club of Massillon to purchase one hundred outfits. I want blue shorts and white blouses numbered from zero to ninety-nine. The uniforms shall be the property of the school unless the pupils wish to purchase them at cost. The three to five inch numbers on the shorts and blouses will discourage borrowing and stealing," I explained.

Mrs. William (Lessie) Myricks was the second president of the Nannie Burroughs Club, which was affiliated with the State and National Associations of Colored Women's Clubs. Mrs. Myricks and her members gave unlimited support to Jones School. I shared with her my concerns about the wide gap between the home and the school. They were worlds apart, and each looked upon the other as uncaring opponents.

It took the greater part of a semester to get the gym classes organized as a well-controlled calisthenics and game activity period.

Convinced that a student's performance in a well-organized gym class set the tone for attention and performance in their academic classes as well, I enjoyed teaching physical education. Eventually it became my initial opportuniy for personal and group counseling.

Teaching English, a required subject, was a challenge. I had to develop a different teaching technique for each of my ninth grade classes. The "A-B" students were a delight to teach. Everything that had been taught in the methods courses at the university worked. With the students' well-grounded basic skills and a self-propelled motivation, learning was an adventure. They received enough positive strokes of "fine," "that is very good" and "excellent" to encourage further achievement. Of the thirty "A-B" English students, five were black.

The "C" students made no more demands of their teachers than they did of themselves. Their achievement scores were slightly below grade level. Their "average" performance was due as much or more to indifference, laziness, lack of motivation, immaturity and a lack of self-discipline as from diminished intellectual capabilities. They did just enough to avoid failing. With a little effort, they could have been "B" students. They were content to be "not as smart as the best" nor "as dumb as the worst." In this group of twenty-two, there were ten black students.

The thirteen black "D" and "F" students in a class of twenty required every innovative approach to teaching I could devise. They had fourth-and fifth-grade achievement scores. They hated school and would drop out or be kicked out between the ninth and tenth grades. They did all the things that spotlighted their disruptive tendencies and provoked ego-destroying rebuke. Their work was careless and untidy, they were absent from class frequently, and too noisy when present. They failed miserably when taking a test. No positive reinforcement ever came from a teacher who could say: "That is fine!" "Very good." "Show the class how you worked that problem." "I am so proud of you."

The "D-F" students heard instead, "Sit down and shut up!" "I'll have no more of that!" "You know that is not the right answer!" "Where is your work?" "Why haven't you done what you were told?" "You are assigned detention!" "Report to the Principal's office!"

With their self-image constantly assaulted, they would become so ego-maimed they stood to succumb to one of two choices: they could commit a criminal act to reclaim their lost self-esteem, and earn them retaliatory recognition, or they could "learn" non-school things that would designate them as intelligent, smart, cool, hip, etc. Their second choice would be to withdraw from the mainstream by pursuing an approach-avoidance existence. They would approach a situation until it became threatening and self-denigrating, then retreat to a safety zone of avoidance to be free of competition, comparison and failure. They would do nothing.

The ninth-grade English curriculum included twenty-four spelling and vocabulary words weekly. Literature required the reading of two classics, the *Odyssey* and *Great Expectations*. When I mentioned in a staff meeting that non-readers could not master such an assignment, I was told to get a supply of third-and fourth-grade reading-level books from the storeroom. "Try them!"

I wanted my "D-F" students to know about the Cyclops, the sirens, the sea voyages and the island dangers so vividly portrayed in the Odyssey. I wanted them to know about Pip and his youthful adventures. My pupils could not read, but they could hear, they could talk and they could see. If I could get them to listen to me while I read to them, maybe they would share their reactions in a class discussion.

In my most dramatic manner, remembering how Mom had read to me, I brought to life for twenty minutes daily the episodes from the pages the students could not read. Then followed a twenty-minute discussion. The last twenty minutes of the class period were spent with a dictionary and the twenty-four spelling words. Phonics was taught as we enunciated the vowel and consonant sounds. For many, it was an introduction to speech and basic reading skills.

The spelling and vocabulary unit became a drama class. Each weekend at home, I took the twenty-four spelling words and composed no less than three ten-minute, one-act plays of three or four characters each. On Monday, after I had read each play aloud, the pupils were assigned or chose a part in the play.

The students learned the meaning of new words by their usage. They also learned proper sentence structure and standard English. The cast gathered at lunch time and after school to rehearse their lines. They could supply any props or costumes they chose. On Friday they performed on the gymnasium stage. Their enthusiasm was extraordinary. School attendance and behavior improved immediately.

When I heard "D-F" students debating some detail about the Cyclops with students from the "A-B" group, I knew their knowledge was comparable. I began to wonder why teachers ceased to teach the non-reader. Why not make use of a child's ability to listen, to think and to memorize? When several of my students came to me expressing a desire to "read like you," I initiated oral reading sessions for the students. Reading, I was convinced, required auditory as well as visual alertness.

Study halls were time-wasters for most students. Few ever studied. The bright boys and girls were excused to engage in activities such as the yearbook, school newspaper, choir or band. The non-involved talked, asked to be excused to go to the lavatory, wrote letters to their sweethearts, drew pictures, defaced the desks or went to sleep. The mischief conceived in study halls often resulted in trips to the principal's office and expulsion from school.

I was given permission by my principal to supervise an activity room for students who created a disturbance in class. For one period a day in a little-used classroom, they became engrossed in a variety of hobbies and activities that encouraged their creative interests.

One lad, who trained carrier pigeons for distance flight contests, had a cage in a corner of the room. He brought the pigeons back and forth daily and explained how he trained them. Another two lads played chess. Both won awards in local chess tournaments. A girl was learning how to knit and crochet. Another with anything but an attractive figure spent her time drawing fashion designs. Several boys spent their study hours drawing cars and queer creatures from other planets.

Each had to give a three-minute oral report about his or her hobby. Once a week they put aside their work to watch a guidance film dealing with interpersonal relationships. They were on their best behavior in their other classes and maintained passing grades to remain in my activity room. Some teachers hinted I was rewarding the "bad" kids, but they also had to admit these young people could no longer be described as bad.

This activity and the improved performance of the gym classes undoubtedly led to my assignment as a guidance counselor after three years at Jones. When I first mentioned to Mr. L. J. Smith, the superintendent, that I was a qualified counselor, he commented, "Forget it. If I were to assign you to that position, the big boys downtown would serve my head on a platter." I wondered who the big boys were and what powers they wielded.

Mr. Scourfield, my first principal, gave me a great deal of latitude. It was gratifying to walk into his office to share ideas with the children's best interests at heart. A soft-spoken, genteel sort of person, he gave me the impression of not wanting to concede that his school could not be as good as the best. I asked, and he approved.

One teacher said to me, "I would not work as hard as you

do for all the tea in China. These kids do not deserve that much energy."

As a Black who had waited twenty-six years to be hired as a teacher, I felt in a squeeze. I was not to rock the boat. Was I also expected to do as little as necessary while striving to become "acceptable" to the members of the teaching staff? While many in the community applauded and envied my position in the school, they had no understanding of the the tall-stepping I made daily to be a good teacher. Trying to give my best to each and every child was like walking on hot lava in the fault area of a not-so-dormant volcano.

Some children resented a teacher who meant business and demanded performance. Some teachers took my enthusiasm and varying methods of teaching and counseling as trying to show off. I was aware I was courting disaster. A single misstep could jeopardize my job.

Upon Mr. Scourfield's retirement, Mr. Hollingsworth replaced him. I was faced with a principal whose concluding evaluation of my performance was to deny me tenure. He came into my classes periodically, evaluated my teaching techniques, scrutinized my lesson plans and apparently rated me satisfactory. He made one criticism: "Your vocabulary is much too large. I think you should water it down some."

"But I am a ninth-grade English teacher, and . . . yes sir, I shall watch myself," I replied.

I was shocked when a letter from the Board of Education announced that my request for tenure was being denied because "You are an 'ineffective' teacher. You may teach for one more year, however."

Immediately I went into high gear to disprove such an evaluation. I knew I was a good, effective teacher. I was not only going to fight for tenure, but for the preservation of my professional reputation and integrity. For as I had told L. L., "When it comes to performance, I am the damnedest bestest!"

Neither mediocrity nor incompetence could be attributed to my work. I had not been tardy nor absent a day in four years. I had attended all staff meetings and continued taking graduate courses at Akron University. I had no discipline problems in any of my classes. Of my students' parents, ninety-seven percent of them kept their conference appointments with me.

I contacted Attorney Sam Krugliak, a well-known Jewish lawyer, to represent me in my suit. He was determined to go all out in my behalf. My reputation as a first-rate professional while at the TB Association was an acknowledged fact. He gathered data on me painstakingly. We were ready for a fight.

Surprisingly, I was spared what I feared most—a lot of publicity with a court suit—when my attorney noted that the letter sent to me had been mailed a day late. Such dismissal notices should have been delivered by registered special delivery mail prior to the last day of May. My letter was postmarked June first. I had won and would remain at Jones for a total of eight years.

As a full-time guidance counselor, I was in charge of the ability and achievement testing and conducted regularly scheduled group guidance classes. I set up my own format. I had to relinquish my ninth-grade English classes but agreed to teach one seventh-grade Ohio history class.

Compared to the city-wide Junior High Achievement Test scores, Jones was at the bottom. Realizing that if my pupils did not catch up—catch up with inspiration, enthusiasm and the knowledge they could learn more and must learn more—I initiated an evening tutorial program.

My guidance classes were the starting point. I explained test scores, what they revealed about an individual's ability or determination to learn. My challenging comment to every class was this: "If you are already making "C" grades, chances are that you could be a "B" student with more study. You must pave a road for what you want out of life. As a junior high student, you must decide where you are going."

Referring to achievement levels, I explained that every year in school should equate a higher level of learning, like climbing stairs. "If you are in the seventh grade and achieving at the fourth grade level, whose fault is it? Have you been studying at least one hour daily? Do you read the newspaper? Do you read at least one book a month? How often do you write a paragraph, a story, a poem? Do you keep a diary? When was the last time you wrote a letter to your grandparents or cousins? These are the exercises," I would stress, "which put to use the basic skills of reading, writing and comprehension that your teachers have taught and continue to teach you. You must climb the achievement stairs. No teacher can do that for you."

I invited the students (seventh, eighth, ninth grades) to look at their grades and test scores and decide to be tutored one evening a week from 5:00 to 7:00 p.m. They made the decision to attend. The volunteer teachers were the "A" and "B" students from the three area high schools and Malone College. The one-on-one pupil-teacher ratio attracted sixty Jones boys and girls and as many volunteer teachers. A most interesting development was that the "B" students and a number of the "A" students also enrolled for tutoring.

"I have never studied with a smart person before and she helps me a lot," Mona spoke of her tutor from Central Catholic.

Mary, a "D-F" student after attending the tutorial sessions, requested that I assign her to the "A-B" groupings when registering her for the tenth-grade in the fall. "I may never be an 'A' student," she began, "but I can't learn anything from kids as dumb as me. If I am put in a class with smart kids, I can learn something from them and I will know how far

I have to go to be like them."

Her request was honored. Mary graduated from Washington High with a "C" average. That "C" made in the company of "A-B" students was more valuable than an "A" made in the company of "D-F" students.

Guidance classes and counseling sessions gave me the opportunity to address the needs of young teen-agers that necessarily went unattended by the classroom teacher. A teacher could not in a fifty- or sixty-minute subject matter class touch upon social courtesies, good manners, proper speech, dress and poise, cleanliness and body odors, family and peer relationships, respect for authority, citizenship, ethics and morality, not to mention thrift, bank accounts, careers and college preparation.

The nine once-a-week, regularly scheduled guidance units permitted the students and me to seriously share the incidents that could harm or benefit their young lives. Saturday and evening tours became a way of introducing the students to a larger culture outside their own. We toured industries, hospitals, City Hall, Council Chambers, the jail, museums, colleges and universities.

I recall that my principal and one of the faculty questioned why "D" students should go on the tour that included Kent State University, Malone College and Mount Union College.

"Why are you taking Hilda and Eddie? They will never make it to college. What good will a tour like this do them?"

Hilda's class report upon her return went something like this: "Mrs. Marcere, I couldn't believe my ears. Here were a hundred men and women eating in the Malone College cafeteria, and it was so quiet. They were eating and talking and moving around and there was no noise."

Noise and confusion were a normal part of our school halls and cafeteria that the teachers accepted as a cultural characteristic. I thought the noise level at Jones was disgraceful. It was an abandonment of administrative control and teacher monitoring to allow students to be so boisterously noisy.

I recalled two former Jones students, who with a half dozen girls, ruined my long anticipated dormitory experience that late summer of 1957 when I was completing my master's degree at Kent. They were boisterous, inconsiderate rowdies. Their antics, the volume of their voices and their language in the halls and corridors annoyed and angered me and many others who wanted to study or to relax.

There were at Jones teachers more concerned about expressing pity for their Black students than in teaching them. Many who had been in the classroom for twenty years sought to impress me with their theories and conclusions based upon experiences.

"I don't try to teach these kids," one teacher remarked. "I have been here for years. I love them, they love me. We have a lot of fun. If they don't do well in school, so what? There will be no jobs for them if they are too smart, so why help to make them unhappy, reaching for something they can never have?"

Another remarked, "I feel so sorry for them. The happiest hours of their day are here at school. The homes they live in—how hungry they are—you have no idea! I bring food every day for them." And she did.

The first fifteen minutes of her class were spent in eating apples, oranges and assorted foods instead of teaching an important basic skill subject. One day in the lounge this teacher dramatically related how her pupils devoured the food she placed before them.

I was paying little attention to her until she mentioned the name of a boy, the son of one of the Nannie Burroughs Club women. My mind's eye quickly shifted from that of a dilapidated home with children underfed, undernourished and underclothed to this well-dressed club woman, officer and leader. But there must be a mistake, a coincidence of names, I thought.

I decided to visit this home. If things were so deplorable, a welfare agency or a local church should be asked to inspect the environment so that the children's schooling was not hampered. No parent should send a child to school so hungry that the teacher must devote precious moments of her teaching time to feeding her class.

When I drove up to the address that Josie Rollstin, the school secretary, had given me, I knew there was some mistake. I was standing at the entrance of a brand new ranch style home in the twenty-five-thousand dollar range, according to 1960 real estate values.

An attractive young woman in her early thirties answered the door and assured me she was the mother of the two boys at Jones School. "Come in and tell me how they are doing."

To the left of the entrance was a dining area. On the table was a centerpiece of fresh fruit. I turned from there to the beautifully furnished living room to the right. I was being ushered to a comfortable chair.

"How are my boys doing in school?" she repeated her question.

"Not as well as they might," I answered hesitatingly. "They could do much better, I believe. They have a tendency to play in class and not get down to business."

I told her I had not come to talk about her sons or school, but to find out if her husband could service my car. (There was a sign on the lawn that read "Car Repairs Done Here.")

If these boys devour food in their classroom, they are exceptionally good actors, I was thinking. When they came in from school, they sheepishly acknowledged my presence and went right to their music practice.

As I left, I congratulated them and remarked that young

men who played instruments so well should apply some of that discipline to their school subjects.

"Who knows, some day you may decide to go to college to study to become a band master. You will need to have math, science and perhaps a foreign language before you can pass the entrance exams. Be careful not to jeopardize your future by playing games in junior high." I winked at the boys.

This family was better off financially than most of the teachers at the school where their children were being taught. Both husband and wife were gainfully employed. They also had a small auto repair business. Their grandmother was an active member of a civic club. Yet every teacher believed that these children were deprived, hungry and neglected.

It has often amazed and angered me that whites know so little about Blacks. The two worlds have been so far apart. The lower-middle to middle-class white teachers working in the school districts, of predominately Black residents, seldom have close associations with their pupils' world. They do not worship at the same church, do not shop at the same shopping centers, do not frequent the same beauty parlors, barber shops or restaurants. They have never been in a Black gathering and have never entertained or been entertained by a Black. Would they have sought to know more about the East Indian, Chinese, Mexican, Philippino or other ethnic minority if their teaching assignment had placed them in such a culture?

Black students play games with teachers whom they know will never meet their parents. They tell their parents all kinds of tales and half-truths interspersed with some real school happenings. They do this because they hear their parents make remarks about the prejudices, the hurts and the unfair tactics experienced in the larger white world.

I continued post-graduate studies to learn more about human psychology, child psychology and Black psychology. I went to workshops at Ohio State University, attended counselors' conventions, visited churches and observed gatherings of all kinds.

During those eight years at E. A. Jones, I traveled extensively throughout the states and also went to Canada, Bermuda and Europe (England, France, Italy). In many cities I made it my business to visit several schools, especially those public and Catholic schools serving Blacks.

I came to one general conclusion. The policies of the administrator determined the quality of the school and its emphasis upon academic excellence. If the administrator failed to maintain discipline because, among other things, he feared the wrath and the displeasure of Black parents; if he and the faculty felt high academic standards were unattainable, then the children ran the school and became underachievers.

Upon entering a predominately Black school in one large city, I ran into a state of bedlam. There were as many pupils roaming the halls as there were students in the classroom. A disturbance was in full bloom because a pupil from an art class had come down the hall spilling red tempera paint on the floor. A couple of adults ushered him into the Principal's office. He was told to sit there until his mother came to take him home. A curious group of teen-agers who should have been in class laughed and called out messages to the victim. No one could attend to me. I left.

Just a block away, I entered a Catholic school with Black students from the same general environment. There was order and decorum. I was greeted by a student hall monitor who took me to the Principal who was teaching a class. I was introduced to the students. They stood as one and welcomed me with a "We are pleased to meet you, Mrs. Marcere." They opened their books to read and study while the Principal and I conversed.

What made the difference between those two schools? Could I make a difference like that just being a guidance counselor in a school? I wanted to because the children I was teaching and counseling would be tomorrow's adults. These children could marry into and become members of my family, I wanted only the smartest and the best to call my own.

In addition to the guidance classes, I worked with small units of three and four students in group counseling. If the goal of counseling was to change the behavior and the attitude of one child, it was best to have a group change for some peer support. It was ill-advised to counsel a child and then turn him loose to become an oddball or misfit among his peers because of changed behaviors.

Gerry had a bad habit of playing the dozens, using "mother" in derogatory innuendoes to other children. A small group laughed and egged him on. It would have been counterproductive to have cleaned up Gerry's dirty mouth without his friends knowing the source and the inappropriateness of such language in a school setting. I included Gerry's gallery of supporters in the group counseling. They were to be responsible for refusing to acclaim Gerry. They were to help him refrain from obnoxious speech.

The presence of unwed teen-agers in the classroom was infrequent in the 1960s. Girls were not allowed to remain in school during their pregnancy. They were tutored at home. those who returned to school sought a counselor to help them make many adjustments. Often they resented the care and the responsibilities they had to assume. They did not know how to cope with the boys and young men in the high school and about town who openly remarked, "You've already been had. I think you're a nobody, but I'm not particular. I can give you what you want."

"Belle," an eighth grade mother of a six-month-old baby, come to my office in angry tears. "I can't make them stop. Every time I climb the stairs to the second floor, there's this bunch of boys. They grab my legs, lift up my dress and say,

'Let me see what it looks like. . . . I want some.' And just because I have a baby."

My group guidance classes that week stressed the qualities of a gentleman. I emphasized the respect that is due womanhood, one's mother, one's sister and the girl down the street. My strongest words were, "No nation, no race, no group of people can be strong if they lack self-esteem and respect for one another."

One young mother felt she had been made to feel cheap because she was born out of wedlock. She was always referred to as "Mary's kid." Another unwed mother at thirteen came to me for counseling every day at school for more than a year. She came to my home for a period of three years before she could cope with life. From her experiences and others like hers, I submitted an article to a guidance journal, "The Counselor Listens to the Illegitimate Teen-ager." Much is said about the unmarried girl who brings an unnamed baby into the world, but little consideration is given to the feelings of this "accidental, out-of-wedlock" child.

Johnny gave me some new insights about a single-parent home and promiscuous adults. He had been referred to me by his special education teacher because for some unexplained reason there were days when he would scream and become agitated when she called upon him in class. "He is a total non-reader, too," she remarked. "There are times when he is good-natured and very cooperative. See what can be done for him."

Johnny was invited to my office in the fall of that school year. He would not talk. He ignored every comment, every overture I made. Nevertheless, I scheduled him for half-hour weekly sessions and so advised his teacher. For that school year, Johnny was unresponsive. He was a well-dressed, neat-appearing child. I would compliment his nice clothing, his haircut, his pretty black eyes and then turn to my desk. At the end of the school year, I said good-bye, wished him a happy vacation and told him I would miss him.

When school opened in September, I notified his teacher that I would like to continue seeing Johnny. Upon his second visit he surprised me with, "Would you like to hear me read?"

"Of course!" I said, shocked beyond belief. He began reading from a book that was not a school text. I complimented him lavishly and then asked if he would read one of my books the following week. He agreed, his face full of smiles and his eyes twinkling.

The next week he read everything I placed in front of him. He could read as well as any seventh-, eighth- or ninth-grader in our school. I was teaching a seventh-grade Ohio history class, so I asked my principal if I could have Johnny in my class. "It is against the rules to take a child out of a special class and put him in the regular class unit," the principal said.

"This child is not a non-reader. He is not mentally retarded. Please let me have him for one period a day for a semester so I can observe his behavior in a regular classroom," I begged.

He consented. Johnny did "B" work in the class. He read aloud, he recited, he took the tests. He had a role in the Ohio history play at the end of the term.

What was wrong with Johnny? Why was he in a special class? Why did he explode into frightening tantrums from time to time? I began to inquire about his home life and family. Having been a social worker helped me to become "Hawkshaw the Detective."

Johnny's mother had never married, but she had had as many as six temporary "fathers" for her children. One of these men Johnny liked very much. One he despised. He would have liked to have been known as John Jones but his legal name was John Jackson, the name of his hated parent.

He actually exploded to near violence when his teacher in

calling the roll said, "John Jackson." After his rage he would go into periods of rebellious, autistic-like silence. Teachers and the psychologist, unable to communicate and attain a satisfactory test score, diagnosed him as a slow learner.

With this family information, I advised his teachers to address him only by his first name. After the successful experience in my Ohio history class, I submitted an article to the State Counselor's Journal called, "The Boy Who Could Not Read." It got me into big trouble. A representative from the state department made a trip to my school to inform me that once a child had been placed in a special class, he or she could never be returned to a standard, normal, regular classroom.

Teaching, the art of imparting knowledge, had its successes, helps and hindrances. Success in the classroom was enhanced and endangered by factors of birth, economic security or insecurity, the school environment, teacher attitude and expectancy, and religious and ethnic indoctrination.

I enjoyed my combined role as a teacher and counselor. In the classroom I was a rigid disciplinarian, demanding hard work and effort resulting in excellence. Every minute of a class period was precious. Counseling takes time to undo or rearrange the mixed up emotions and directions of the counselee. The counselor needs an abundance of empathy, understanding, acceptance and patience to direct his charges toward that goal of self-awareness and self-respect. Racial-ethnic pride is very essential to a positive life adjustment.

Massillon was good to me and for me. I learned much about the interrelationships of pupil, parent, teacher and community. I was disturbed that children who spent so much time going to school, quit or graduated from high school functionaly illiterate. My disturbance spawned the idea of a parent-community program to encourage academic excellence in the classroom.

During my summers I had been a counselor for the Upward Bound Program at Walsh College and a counselor-director of Stoydale-Brunnerdale Summer Camp. Throughout the year I was a career counselor for the Human Engineering Institute of the Republic Steel Corporation.

These experiences highlighted some general needs that could enhance a child's school performance. Parents, churches, social agencies and civic groups needed to become involved in producing scholars.

I began to dream of a four-hour Saturday morning school that would serve children from grades three through eight. The twenty-five-week school would be scheduled during the months of September, October, November, February, March, April and May.

The teaching unit curriculum would emphasize oral reading, speech and elocution, mathematics, ethnic cultures (history and sociology) and self-awareness. Writing would be incorporated in all units. Students and parents would agree to a daily two-hour study session.

Parents, senior citizens, high school and college students, community leaders, teachers and role models would volunteer their services. I would call the school PAX ("peace" in Latin), Program Academic Excellence.

At the junior high level I would emphasize the need to STRIVE. It would be a two-year, six-week summer program to Study, Think, Read, Investigate, Volunteer, and Excel.

I told myself that some day when I would no longer be concerned about an annual income to keep me above the poverty level, I would leave the teaching profession. A profession that condoned mediocrity, blamed parents, closed their eyes to environmental hazards and was not researching the best methods by which children from diverse cultural backgrounds could be taught was becoming frustrating. I would like to open my own school.

Such were my thoughts when the Akron school system sought me to become a counselor at Garfield Senior High. I was thrilled. To counsel in a comprehensive high school with a strong middle class White and Black student body would open new vistas of challenge and fulfillment. I decided with that acceptance to complete my studies at Akron University that would lead to certification as a school psychologist.

XXII

Venturing Away From Home

When early childhood excursions are pleasurable, exciting and educational; when there are frequent discussions in the family about the homelands of differing ethnic groups; when teachers make history and geography come alive with historical episodes and climatic attractions, there can be an insatiable desire to go places and see things.

The urge to travel, to get away from the day-to-day routine, was always a part of me. When everything about marriage, a home and family periodically built up to a feeling of confinement, I felt driven to travel for fulfillment. I could always put my hand on a five-dollar bill. I was never broke. I had learned how to save and hide money as a child. Just the feeling of having put a few quarters aside was comforting and "taking off" on the spur of the moment was possible.

"Taking off" meant leaving Canton on a Greyhound bus to Cleveland whenever I was annoyed. Annoyed? Yes, in many ways. Early one morning I asked Mrs. Tabbs to watch the children for me until Percy returned home from work. The note I left Percy went something like this: "I have no idea where I am going and I am not sure if I am coming back. I am sick of everything—you, the kids, this house, this town. Everything! If there was a pool hall for women, that is where

I would go."

Alighting from the bus in Cleveland, I spent the day window shopping, riding the elevator up to the top of the Terminal Tower, going to a movie or two and then boarding the last bus back to Canton. I never feared walking the deserted streets from the Square to home at one or two o'clock in the morning. Everyone at home would be sound asleep. If Percy heard me come in, he never let me know. Neither did he ever question where I had been.

Our first trip away from home and the children after eight years of marriage was to be our honeymoon. We planned to spend nearly a week at the Cleveland Exposition.

We would stay at the Majestic Hotel on East Fifty-Fifth and Central Avenue. We had driven by the hotel on infrequent trips to Cleveland and were impressed by its tall castle-like appearance.

In less than twelve hours we were so homesick we could talk of nothing but the children. Everything about our trip was annoying and disappointing. The lakefront Exposition, which at first resembled a combination of Meyers Lake, Coney Island, Springfield Lake, Ringling Brothers Circus and all the street carnivals we had ever seen, shed its exciting enchantment.

Our hotel room did not live up to our expectations of a romantic boudoir. After dark the night sounds surrounded the hotel mercilessly. There were quarrelsome and argumentative outbursts coated with music from static, ear-bursting radios.

I said to my husband, "This is so low-class, let's get out of here."

The early dawn streets were empty when we hailed a cab, the pumpkin carriage that had lost its way to fairyland. We headed home.

Traveling, running away, taking off for a day or two was

therapeutic for me. Besides a physical and psychological rejuvenation, it provided a new dimension in personal growth. Sometimes the underbrush about me became so entangled and so smothering that I could not see the forest (or the skyline) for the trees. I had to step outside and view my world from a distance.

Watching people on the street, listening to bits of conversations gave me a glimpse of others' lives. Meeting, talking to and observing people from a great many social, economic, religious and ethnic backgrounds helped me to recognize the differences and a common denominator in all of mankind.

My professional growth was enhanced more from my personal visits to more than two-hundred public and private schools in a score of towns, cities, states and three continents than from conferences, workshops and institutes. I gained insights that caused me to return home invigorated for the tasks ahead.

Because of my extensive travels, it came as a shock to learn how few of my fellow teachers had traveled. Even those who taught geography, civics and history had not been to the nation's Capitol or to New York City.

Their being free, white, twenty-one and gainfully employed had not made them travel-curious. I wondered if they had any idea of the racial roadblocks I encountered in my travels.

It took a lot of courage, whatever the purpose or destination, to travel in the '50s and '60s. It caused a lot of remembering and trying to forget.

We were driving to Meridian, Mississippi, to visit Percy's family when Emmett Till, the twelve year old lad from Chicago, was murdered. Entering and leaving the state, we were tensed with fear. Percy's personality changed so that he disgusted and angered me.

"Do you all suppose, good man, that we could have a little gas today?" he pleaded subserviently to the filling station attendant.

A moment later the attendant shouted at me as I headed for the rest room, "Hey, stop! We doan have a place for yo' people here!"

I expressed my anger by shouting, "Don't put another drop of gas in that tank!"

Percy was annoyed with me. He feared that with my attitude I would be returned North in a pine box, and he would be lynched.

Twenty miles down the road, Percy stopped the car for me to enter a stretch of woods to relieve myself. The fear of being bitten by a snake or arrested for trespassing panicked me.

With the birth of our first grandson, we decided to drive to California for his christening. We secured a special Green Book from the AAA. It designated establishments where Negroes could eat and sleep, traveling across these United States. My sister, Ruth, and Margaret Davis from Cleveland joined our son, Al, Percy and me on the three-week trip. We would go the southern route, spending a day or two in Mississippi and return by the northern route.

There were exhilarating moments when our hearts were free, moments when we exclaimed in awe and wonder the majesty of God's magnificent universe. Carlsbad Caverns, the Petrified Forests, the Painted Desert, Yellowstone National Park, Yosemite National Park and the Redwood Forest filled us with awe. We marveled at Mount Rushmore, Lake Tahoe, Salt Lake City, the Corn Palace, the Mormon Temple and Boys Town. The mountains, plains, forests, desert and bodies of water were perfect backdrops for the pictures we snapped.

There were frightening moments when some of the recommended lodges and motels appeared menacing or questionable. We continued on without sleep or rest. We ate the fruits, crackers and cheese Percy's relatives had packed for us, rather than venture inside stores or restaurants.

Holding our first grandson, James B. Snow II, in our arms was a blessing. Joy and peace surged through every fiber of my body when I, as his godmother, and his parents promised he would be reared in the faith to fear, to love and to serve God. Before his first birthday, our daughter and son-in-law moved to Bermuda. Grandaughters Theresa Ann and Jeannie Snow were born on British soil.

On each of my visits to Bermuda, I spent a great deal of time in the high school in Hamilton, BWI, where three-hundred Negro children were enrolled. I had seen no school in the United States with a student body showing such scholarship and racial pride.

It was there that I suspected the American Negro child was an underachiever because he did not know his racial roots. He had not been taught about the achievements of his African ancestors. He saw himself only as an ex-slave. I was equally as uninformed about my people and began to research the hidden achievements of Afro-Americans.

I discovered that membership in the NAACP was helpful. Groups of thinking, concerned Negroes could assess the racial incidents happening to themselves and others, locally and nationally. It helped to know we were not paranoid and that we had legal redress as American citizens.

There was another group I identified with in the 1960s. The Panel of American Women. It was composed of Jewish, Catholic, Negro and White Anglo-Saxon Protestant (WASP) women. As panelists, we spoke to groups about our personal experiences with racism and our concerns about our children.

We became a loving, understanding support group. No matter how weary after a day on the job and home chores, we were eager to address the most hostile audience. We believed our message and example could rid bigotry from our community.

Many times after our presentation at a human rights seminar

or interracial gathering, a defensive guilt-ridden individual would try to refute the Jewish or Negro panelist.

"You Negroes are in too big a hurry. You want too much all at once. I think the inequality is your fault. Your people lack initiative. They are lazy, irresponsible and not very smart. You Jews are shrewd and too smart. You wind up owning everything you get yours hands on."

Often, quite often, the emotionally charged remarks we could not voice in an audience of fifty or one hundred we expressed freely in our small gatherings of twelve to twenty women.

"I sat beside you on the panel with tears in my eyes," Barb Saltsman and Nancy Boylan said to me at one of our PAW business meetings. "We could feel your anger and your fear and yet you spoke calmly and smiled. Were we imagining something?"

"The American Negro lives in constant anger and fear. It is not imaginary. The human being that I am—wife, mother, teacher, counselor and psychologist— requires that I be sensitive to my emotions, my feelings and the incidents that initiate them," I explained.

"Because there are no KKK marches in the streets, no 'colored' signs on the drinking fountain on the Square and our children attend integrated schools, it is thought that we have nothing to fear.

"My husband goes to work. His foreman or a fellow worker can do or say something racist that could cause a confrontation. A confrontation is the forerunner of a disciplinary action. There could be the loss of a job or tension leading to increased blood pressure. He could become a statistic. I experience fear every day my husband goes to work.

"I as a Black and a mother not only have to cope with my encounters, but I must live and relive the incidents that happen to my children.

"My children can be called names and taunted on the way to and from school. They can be abused by a classmate and ignored, even belittled, by a teacher. I can look in their faces at the end of a school day and see their pain and their bewilderment," I tried to explain.

I recall sending Norma Jean and Alluren to the opening of the Dueber theater, which was just six blocks from our apartment. Looking out the bedroom window awaiting their return, I saw my children crossing Shroyer Avenue lugging two large flower baskets filled with withered flowers that had adorned the theater lobby and stage.

"The usher and another man gave us these flowers. Then they told us never to come back again," my children explained in unison.

What does a mother say and do? Show her anger? Yank the basket of flowers from the children? Frighten them by a shocking remark? Curse the manager?

No psychologist has yet written a "How To" book for Negro mothers who repeatedly face racial dilemmas. What did I do? I commented, "These flowers were very pretty once upon a time, but most of them are dead now. If you want to, we can make a small bouquet of the ones that are still pretty and throw the rest away. It is up to you.

"Now listen to me. We shall go back to that theater, but I will be with you. Just forget what they said." My tone was firm, not angry. "You are a free person and one-hundred percent American. You must always remember that."

I faced the manager the next day. In a decidedly firm tone, I told him that if ever my children came to the Dueber Theater again, he was not to harass them. "You had better treat them with the utmost courtesy and respect. And furthermore, please dispose of your own trash. Dead flowers have a most unpleasant stench! Good day!"

We lived just two blocks from the Sixth Street, Shroyer

Avenue swimming pool when our five- and eight-year-olds expressed a desire to go swimming. It had never dawned upon me, having lived in that vicinity for nearly thirty years, that they would be told to travel a mile and a half across town to the Jackson pool. "That pool is for colored people," they were told.

I became a one woman picket. I walked all around the fenced in pool saying to the adults watching their children, "My little girl and boy are not allowed to swim here. The people in charge won't let them in. Would you take your children out of the pool if my little children went into this water?"

Most said nothing, just walked away. I phoned the Park Commissioner and Mayor C. C. Curtis. I spoke with Ruth Robinson of the NAACP and to Dr. M. B. Williams.

It is strange how most of our rights come about only after protest, pressure and court rulings. Our rights have never been there free for the taking.

When I was assured my children could enter the pool, I feared for their safety. Would they come out of the pool alive?

Violence and rage accompany fear. James Baldwin, the author, wrote: "To be a Negro and to be relatively conscious is to be in a state of rage all the time."

When a home-owner failed to keep an appointment to allow me to see a house that was for sale, I penned these feelings in April 1970.

"You left me standing on your porch that Wednesday afternoon as thoroughly stripped of my dignity as if you had lynched me and left me hanging naked upon the town square. Your denial of my right to negotiate for a new home was literally to beat me and chase me back to the Urban Concentration Camp marked 'For Blacks Only.' "

The day-to-day tasks of just living, providing food, shelter and personal needs demand the utmost of every human being.

One does not need violent acts based upon another's racist assumptions to add to one's struggle to survive.

When we moved into our first home in North Canton, one of the neighbors voiced her fears to a friend of mine. "I never thought it would happen here," she complained. "I moved here to get away from their kind. Why would they want to move to an all-white town? I see they have school-aged children who come to their house. You can never tell what they will do. I don't feel safe any more."

Mrs. Sally Corrigan's comment to her was, "You should be so fortunate as to have that family as one of your neighbors."

"You must be crazy. Are you kidding?"

"No. I am not kidding. Those children who make you feel so unsafe have family relatives of the quality neither my nor your children can boast of yet."

Sally proceeded, "Can you count eight teachers, a college professor, two nurses, two school principals, a doctor, a businessman, an insurance agent, an electrical engineer and an interior decorator in your family?" she asked. My neighbor kept silent.

It took me nearly forty years to realize that the white reactions to my brown skin (described as colored, Negro, Afro-American and Black) had left an indelible negative imprint upon my psyche.

My trip to Rome, Italy, in 1962 for the May 6 canonization of St. Martin de Porres awakened me to color consciousness in a positive way. For nearly three weeks I traveled in the company of some of the finest people I have ever met. We ranged in ages from twenty to seventy-seven years. We were truly an interracial group with a variety of interests, a wealth of background experiences and a wide range of vocational pursuits. There were little idiosyncrasies and mannerisms that were pleasing, humorous and sometimes vexing, and yet the spiritual fervor of the group was heartening.

We crammed more sightseeing tours into our short visit than we can ever recount in a hundred hours of conversation. We traveled the underground in London, caught the trolleys in Paris and rode behind the hectic taxi drivers in Rome to visit some unscheduled places of interest. We felt the midnight spray from the fountain in Trafalgar Square in London and from dozens more during our leisurely sunset walk through the Tivoli Gardens near Rome. The churches, basilicas, cathedrals and monasteries revealed new wonders of art and architecture that aroused sentiments of deep religious and historic significance. The ancient castles, fortresses, squares, arches and ruins presented an awesome contrast to the modern construction in evidence everywhere.

The canonization ceremony in St. Peter's was the highlight of our trip. I was overwhelmed by the pageantry, the beauty and the solemnity of this once-in-a-lifetime experience. The resplendent painting of Martin de Porres being carried in procession, His Holiness, Pope John XXIII, officiating at the high altar, and the spontaneous burst of song from forty thousand worshipers who joined with the superb voices of the Sistine Choir, will never be forgotten.

I kept saying to myself, "All this in honor of a saint, a saint of Negro extraction. It can't be, it can't be." I looked at the dark skins about me, particularly the African clergy in their ebony dignity, and I was glad to identify with them. I was proud, very proud, of my dark-skinned heritage.

There was another personal reaction to this ceremony elevating St. Martin. It was my first experience of empathy with a saint and the knowledge that a saint could empathize with me. Little incidents in St. Martin's life were constantly crowding out other thoughts and prayers during that four-hour ceremony. I began to sense all the human emotions he must have sensed. I was aware of his feelings of rejection and of want. I felt his need for acceptance, his need to serve. I understood the sacrifices he endured and the patience he practiced to win the love of his fellow man. I came face to face with a saint who experienced all the real and imagined trials of the minority. I sensed the deep spiritual impact that turned the negative features of birth, environment and race into positive forces for God and man. He would be my close, close friend.

My last experience shows how a "conditioned" American minority reacted to an unstructured, unprejudiced situation. I am ashamed and much surprised that the land of my birth and residence afforded me so many negative experiences that, thousands of miles from home, my "learning" showed. The stimulus-response reaction to America's "separate" and "different" provisions was so taken for granted that when the stimulus-response resulted in acceptance rather than rejection, I, like the "conditioned" rat in the laboratory, became confused and made the wrong response.

I needed a shampoo and hairdo. I inquired of the desk clerk at the hotel where I could go to get my hair done. He sent me across the street to a much larger hotel and apologized that he had no accommodations. When I entered the beautiful, mirror-paneled salon, I addressed the manager with this question, "Can you tell me where I can go to get my hair done?"

"Right here," he answered (in very good English). "When do you wish an appointment? Now? Later today, perhaps? How about 6:30 this evening?"

"Yes," I said, "that will be fine."

"Do you desire a chiropodist, someone to trim your feet?"

"No, no, thank you. I'll be back."

I was as surprised and as confused as I could be. I had expected to be referred elsewhere, to a shop operated for Negroes across town, in someone's home perhaps. "Maybe he thinks my hair is of European texture," I said to myself. He was too natural, too willing to be of service, kind of naive, really. In the States, white barbers brought before the U.S. Civil Rights Commission claimed they could not cut Negro hair. If they could not cut it in Xenia, Ohio, how could they shampoo, dress and style it in Rome, Italy? I had all kinds of doubts about keeping the appointment and later phoned to cancel it. I was thoroughly confused.

That afternoon I excused myself from a shopping party on some pretense of wanting to sightsee on my own. In reality I hoped to meet another Negro, a resident of Rome, who might direct me to a beauty shop. I saw none; but when I passed an attractive beauty salon on the main thoroughfare with a sign in the large display window reading "English spoken here," I entered.

"Could you please tell me where I could get my hair done? A shampoo, press, curl and coiffure?" I asked.

"Yes, yes. When? Now? We are not busy; we shall take you now. Can you stay?"

The proprietor called a beautiful, dark haired operator and began giving her directions in Italian. An apprentice, a lad of eleven or twelve, handed me a magazine, then arranged an assortment of combs and jars and other equipment. Before I knew it, I was comfortably seated in the booth. I was being treated like a queen. I wasn't black or brown or white. I was a woman in a beauty parlor. I was a person. I was a human somebody.

This was what I felt all over Europe, this freedom from having a "place." It began on the jet plane out of New York. It continued on the streets, in the hotels, in the dining room, theater, parks, sidewalk cafes. We had run into no limits. There were no barriers, no signs, no covenants, no compromises, no lifted eyebrows, no "I'm sorry" comments. It was a strange, unfamiliar feeling—this being treated the same as any other person.

To my utter delight, I left the beauty salon even more

glamorous than I desired. I had a coiffure from one of the finest shops in Rome, Italy, and that was something that could not have happened in the town of my birth.

Often accounts of my travels were shared with my students to help them envision a world beyond their neighborhoods. One lad sneered, "All you teachers are rich. We could travel, too, if we had your money."

I told him, "Cigarette money pays for my travels."

"But you don't even smoke!"

"That's it," I replied. "If I smoked, I would go through at least two packs a day, because I never do anything half heartedly. You figure how much money I save daily and how far I can travel after one, two or five years by not smoking."

The entire class immediately engaged in a multiplication exercise that included a lifetime of smoking.

Many times when I meet a former student I am asked about my latest travels. All have remarked that the session about seeing the world on cigarette money was a greater deterrent against smoking than any lecture about endangering one's health.

XXIII

The Touch Of Our Hands

It was the middle of December 1966, when Percy greeted me as I came home from Jones School. He announced, "My doctor wants me to enter the hospital, immediately. There was blood in my urine today and well, something's wrong inside me."

I placed my three-foot miniature, live Christmas pine tree that I had just bought to decorate my unique study hall on the kitchen table. I tried to comprehend what my husband had just said.

"When did this happen? You said today? You are ill? Have you been in pain?"

"Well, no, I haven't been in any pain, but I saw this blood and went to see the plant doctor right away. He told me to see my family doctor and excused me to leave the plant early. Well, now you know. I'm to check in at Mercy Hospital this evening. I was waiting for you to come home. I haven't packed yet."

"You have never packed a suitcase in your life," I remarked. "Together we can do this up big. We can stop at the Shopper's Fair on West Tuscarawas and get a pair of pajamas, a robe and house slippers . . . your Christmas presents a couple of weeks early."

I was rattling on trying not to show my concern or arouse any fear in Percy. He had not been sick a day since the influenza he suffered while working on WPA in 1935.

"I wish I knew what's up," Percy spoke questioningly.

"You know for sure you are not having a nervous breakdown or a D and C scraping or treatment for a third-degree burn on your leg as I have had. Remember how you envied my leisure, my relaxation those times I was in the hospital, leaving you to manage the house and everything alone? Now it seems you are going to get even by taking a hospital vacation at the busiest time of the year, just before Christmas. Come, we had better get started. Oh, you can take this tree for your room. I can get another for the kids at the school or they can do without."

Percy was to undergo routine tests in the morning. He did not want me to return home that night. He begged me to stay. We learned that if he had a private room, I could stay as long as I wanted. The nurses even offered to put a folding cot in the room for me. Percy remarked, "That's not necessary. She can lay beside me in this bed."

"I'm sorry. That is not allowed in the hospital," one nurse exclaimed.

Every nurse on the floor came in the next morning to meet the new Don Juan. They asked Percy if he thought hospitals provided honeymoon suites for their patients. There was much laughter and teasing. It was comforting to know that the nurses were so friendly and so reassuring because Percy was mortally frightened.

The following morning Percy underwent surgery, the removal of kidney stones. The operation was a success, but three or four days later Percy took a turn for the worse. A staph infection had developed. His doctor suggested I obtain around-the-clock private-duty nursing care. "The regular duty nurses," I was informed, "cannot give him the attention he needs."

I appreciated the fact that the suggestion was made with the assumption we could afford the added expense. Percy became very ill. All his bodily functions began to diminish. Dr. Schumacker, his surgeon, called me aside and said, "Your husband has less than thirty-six hours to live. If any of his family wishes to see him alive, they had better come at once." He began questioning me about Percy's age, family history and living habits.

"His parents lived to celebrate their fiftieth wedding anniversary. Percy smokes cigars. He likes highly seasoned foods, seldom eats pork and seldom imbibes. He has never had a headache and does not snore," I told his doctor. With a "humph," he walked away.

I went immediately to the Mercy Hospital chapel and prayed this prayer. "Dear God, you heard what the doctor said. I shall call Percy's family in Mississippi. But why? He was as healthy as he could be a week ago. Why, God, why? I do not want to wail and cry. I want to say 'Thy will be done,' but it will be so hard. You promised man three score years and ten, and Percy is only sixty-three. Just help me to say, 'Thy will be done.' "

A hurried phone call was made to Percy's brother, Jonas, in Mississippi. I returned to Percy's room. His private duty nurse and the whole floor had been anxiously searching for me. "Dr. Schumacker has been looking for you. He wants your permission to transfer your husband to the Cleveland Clinic. There he can be placed on the kidney dialysis machine."

Dr. Schumacker was paged. He explained his recommendations to me. "I shall phone the Clinic and tell them to expect your arrival before five. You phone an ambulance while the nurse prepares your husband for the trip. Hand these records to the clinic physician."

In the briefest space of time we were ready for the Cleveland trip, but no ambulance arrived. Why should it take the ambulance so long? They were less than a mile away. I phoned to inquire about the delay. "The ambulance should be there," I was told.

I went over to the nurses' station and spoke to one of the sweetest nuns I had ever met. "Sister Anita, two men from this ambulance service were supposed to have been here by now. Please keep an eye out for them and tell them to hurry."

"There were two men here with a stretcher just seconds ago." she remarked, "but they left. I just saw them take the elevator. They've not had time to leave the parking lot yet, I am sure."

We both rushed to the window. The ambulance was pulling away. "They are leaving. Why, I wonder?" she queried. I knew the answer.

"I'll call them right back," Sister said.

"Never mind, Sister. I know of another ambulance service I can phone."

When I phoned Wackerly's, a former Union Avenue neighbor of my grandmother, I identified myself and stated the urgency. I was immediately assured, "Look for us in ten minutes and have no worry. You'll arrive in Cleveland as expected."

Seated beside my husband's unconscious body was the ambulance attendant and I. The driver was hitting the road full speed. We may have engaged in a whispered, intermittent conversation, but I do not remember. I recall very little, not even praying. I held one of Percy's hands in mine hoping to impart some strength, some hope, and the assurance I cared.

Not only that I cared, but that I loved him very much. I recalled the time nearly two years after my nervous breakdown when I first told Percy, I loved him.

"I went to see *Fiddler On The Roof*, tonight," I began, "and the lead characters, Golde and Tevya, reminded me of us. It was the most exciting play I have seen in a long time."

"Are you going to brief me on a play I didn't want to see?"

"I'd like to, but I'll just get to the point."

"Thank you."

"After twenty-five years of marriage Golde tells her husband Tevya that she loves him. The song she sang was so moving. 'Do I love you? . . . Yes, I love you.' I sat there crying like a baby."

"And that made the play exciting?"

"Not exactly, but I was reminded that we have been married nearly twenty-three years and I have never spoken the words, 'I love you' to the kindest, truest husband in the world."

Percy took me in his arms and waltzed me around the room. "You've loved me all along. You might have tried to fool yourself, about no such thing as love, but you never fooled me. However, I sentence you to whisper or shout at least twice each day, 'I love you. I love my husband.' "

Holding his hands on that ambulance ride, I hoped Percy could hear my litany of love. Slowly, quietly, peacefully, memories of our twenty-fifth wedding anniversary flowed back and forth like a soft melody in that tiny ambulance space. We were kneeling at the altar at St. Joseph's and having our marriage blessed. There were vows . . . "I promise . . . until death do us part."

After the early morning Mass, the young assistant priest joined us at home for breakfast. That evening some fifty guests gathered at our home to celebrate the occasion. Father Heimann was there to congratulate us.

Holding our hands in his, Father whispered, "Do you suppose anyone here, except the three of us, knows this evening was an improbability a few years ago? You seem happy that you took a mean old priest's advice and reconsidered. Congratulations!"

A few weeks after our anniversary celebration, Percy decided to go one step further. He announced his intent to join the Catholic Church. That same day he received notice of his acceptance as a candidate for the Masonic Lodge.

"All my life I've wanted to be a Mason, and Catholics can't be Masons. Do you think God will remember that I chose Him over pomp and ceremony and a very elite group of men?"

He had been seen with me so often during the Sunday masses that he was not required to undergo the lengthy catechism instructions. Mrs. Ellis came from Cleveland to be his godmother. She wept as she told me her husband had become so anti-Catholic he was forbidding some of her church activities.

Our holding of hands every Sunday as we approached the Communion rail to receive the body and blood of Jesus Christ was a real spiritual communion of oneness and love. I held his hand comfortingly and confidently during that ambulance ride. There was a strange peace that dispelled fear.

A corps of attendants met us at the Cleveland Clinic emergency entrance. The Wackerly driver and attendant left for dinner and said they would return in two hours allowing time for Percy to be in his hospital room. They would then drive me back to Canton. The emergency room was a beehive of activity as the doctors and nurses prepared Percy for the dialysis machine. I had no concept of a machine taking over a body function. I sat there intrigued as veins were exposed and tubes were inserted in his arms.

"You are a nurse, yes?" a doctor inquired.

"No, not at all," I answered.

"You are so calm, so . . . so . . ." He stopped.

"I think I am just curious. I have a big nose."

I phoned Mrs. Ellis and asked her to come to the hospital and spend the night with my husband. Would she also employ a private duty nurse for me? I had to leave immediately with the ambulance driver, but I would drive back by eight o'clock the next morning.

Mrs. Ellis greeted me at the clinic entrance upon my dawn arrival. "Mr. Marcere is very sick. We did not think he would make it through the night. You go to him now. I am waiting for the priest who is to give the last sacrament (Anointing of the Sick). He will be here any minute."

I hurried to Percy's bed. The oxygen machine had been removed, but tubes seemed to envelop every area of his still unconscious body. I could not touch his hands for fear of disturbing the tubes that were there. I could only look upon his still, almost death-like frame.

Soon two priests, Mrs. Ellis, a private duty nurse and I stood around the bed. The priests began to pray. One was anointing my husband with the holy oils. Both were chanting in Latin. I was incapable of comprehending the seriousness, the beauty or the deep spirituality of the moment. Then holding a crucifix in his hand, the anointing priest stood close to Percy and blessed him.

In that awesome moment with the ritual completed, we just stood there waiting. Our hearts beat as one. What would happen next? Not a word was spoken. Percy opened his eyes and smiled. The nurse suggested we leave the room. "Don't go far. Just step outside for a moment."

The next morning as strength flowed through his body, which was responding to the dialysis machine, Percy regained consciousness. "Where am I?" he asked.

Before we could explain, he said, "Jesus was here and smiled at me."

A month later Percy was returned by ambulance to Mercy Hospital to undergo a second surgery. On the fourteenth of February, three months after his pre-Christmas admission to the hospital, Percy returned home. Dr. Schumacker said to him, "You are my miracle man. That is the only way I can explain your existence today. A miracle. I want to see you every month for awhile. Take good care of each other."

As Percy regained his health, I wanted to branch out to new and exciting adventures. I dreamed of a new home in suburbia and I envisioned a trip to Africa, the land of some of our unknown forebears.

The Civil Rights movement and my trip to Washington, D.C., where I had heard and seen Martin Luther King talk about his dream, energized some unfulfilled desires. At the canonization of St. Martin de Porres in Rome in 1962, I experienced for the first time the freedom from having a "place." The two Martins made me very proud of my dark skin. I was ready to scale the highest fence.

Most of my travels had been alone. Now that God had lengthened Percy's days, I wanted to share every non-working day in venturous activities together. I felt a responsibility to move forward as first-class citizens. We could be role models for others.

As I drove back and forth from Canton to Akron, I passed many suburban communities close to my job. The homes were prettier, more modern, and set in landscaped settings of beauty and quiet.

"Percy, suppose we go house-hunting," I suggested one day.

"What for?"

"What for? Oh, for the heck of it."

"Are you thinking about moving to Akron, now that you're working over there?"

"I haven't thought anything in detail yet."

"How about me and my job at Republic Steel?"

"We could split the difference—halfway between—North Canton, for instance."

"You know no Negroes have ever lived in North Canton."

"I know. That is one of several villages in Stark County where it was rumored that a Negro had better not be seen in their town after sundown."

"And you want to look for a house there?"

"There's a first time for everything."

"Can we afford it?"

"Think so. Shall we find out?"

"It's up to you. If that's what you want. I'll be right beside you."

The four-year struggle to buy a home caused me to write an article, "Genteel Violence," printed in *Good Housekeeping* in April 1970. The charming one-story brick ranch we purchased was located on a half acre of land with a stream that flowed past the rear lawn. It was everything a home should be. It was perfect. The unique layout of the living room, family room, kitchen, breakfast nook, three bedrooms, two baths and utility area with its spacious windows spelled freedom.

The expansive lawn, the evergreen shrubbery, the rose garden, the crooked elm trees, the tiny vegetable and herb garden and the ducks and birds attracted to our patio caused us to meditate and to rejoice. We thanked God daily for the beauty of His creation and His bountiful blessings to us.

Our move to North Canton as the first Negro family in the town was a pleasant experience. Mr. and Mrs. Thomas Corrigan and Mr. and Mrs. Dutch (O. J.) DeMarco headed the list of loyal Catholic friends from the Christian Family Movement who hosted the more than three hundred persons who attended our open house gathering.

In 1970 the National Association of Colored Women's Clubs planned a trip to the Belgian Congo, Zaire, Kinshasa, as the guests of President Mobuto. I urged my husband to go with us.

"With all of you women?"

"There is bound to be at least three or four men."

"Maybe I should go. I'd be fulfilling my father's desire to walk on African soil."

Percy was the only man among the group of fifteen women

tourists. At a gathering of women burgomasters in Kinshasa, Percy forsook me to be the center of attention of those attractive women magistrates. They hovered over him as though he were a king. I had never known him to be so happy.

On the flight back to New York, before we knew that we would have the urge to kneel and kiss the American soil knowing it was home, Percy shared these thoughts with me.

"When I get to heaven, I'll tell my dad how wonderful this trip has been. What a feeling to know that we have origins as marvelous and wonderful as any Caucasian foreigner who landed on Ellis Island." Then he changed the subject.

"You know I've always been a little jealous, a little envious of the time you've spent with your club women. I should've pitied you. I should've been around to give you moral support. I don't like your hoity-toity, head-in-the-air, better-than-others women. They're vicious, envious, status-seeking vultures. From now on when you go to their meetings, I'm going to be beside you." He was.

When I became a member of the Youngstown Diocesan School Board, the Stark County Board of Mental Retardation, the Catholic Charities Board and other boards, Percy was there. Seated inconspicuously in the lobby, in an adjoining room or in the car, Percy was close by telegraphing the proud message that he was looking after me.

We developed an indescribable kind of closeness. At least twice a year Percy accompanied me to a state, regional or national convention. He met several other men who also accompanied their wives. They quipped about many things and engaged in the age-old debates about husbands and wives. Who ruled the roost . . . ? Who was the strongest . . . ? Who wore the pants . . . ? They reminded one another jokingly not to let their eyes linger too long on the women whose husbands were not there. "The little woman's bound to notice."

The men, even Percy, enjoyed the endearing attention of the other women even when they cattishly remarked, "You must be so proud of your wonderful wife."

XXIV

Counseling

During those years as a junior high counselor, I became firmly convinced that children experienced in early adolescence a quest for a spiritual meaning to life. In group counseling and on a one-to-one basis, I glimpsed the psyche of the twelve- to fourteen-year-old searching for the meaning of goodness. Questions were asked about right and wrong, religion, morality, justice, honesty, responsibility, fair play and the purpose for living.

In counselor training our professors had cautioned us, "Never speak of your own experiences to your counselees. Let your clients come to a decision through their own reasoning."

In gathering information for a research study, I randomly polled my students. I inquired about their church involvement; their knowledge of job probabilities and careers; the frequency of their interaction with neighbors and peers; how many people they knew who were or had been in jail; the number of deaths in their family due to accidents, violence or natural causes; and where they went and what they did on vacations.

Children from depressed, congested, amoral environments whose parents are functionally illiterate, underemployed and welfare-oriented and children acquainted with death, incarceration and violence have no storehouse of standards to help them make appropriate, upward-mobility decisions.

What career choices does a fourteen-year-old consider who hears exciting stories about the pimp, the gambler and numbers players? What moral stance does a twelve-year-old adopt who remarks boastfully, "I have two uncles and two older brothers in the state penitentiary."

What sexual restraints will a thirteen-year-old girl practice who asks of her counselor, "Do your two children have the same father?" "Don't you have boyfriends or other men you sleep with besides your husband? Why not?" "Are you supposed to let your mother's boyfriend feel you?" "If it's all right for our mom and dad to do it, why can't we?" "Why do boys talk about girls they do it with?" "Is it true you have to do it to prove that you're not queer?" "If you wait too late, like age eighteen, will you die of a strange disease?" The questions asked and the statements made revealed much about the adolescent's environment, the absence of a moral code and confusing parental messages.

My first book, *'Round the Dining Room Table*, took shape as I answered my young students' questions. They were not readers. They had not read *Heidi, Little Women, Rebecca of Sunny Brook Farm, Elsie Dinsmore, The Yearling, Anne of Green Gables* or the biographical sketches of Marian Anderson, Sojourner Truth or Paul Lawrence Dunbar.

They had been in no middle-class Negro homes and had read no books about Negro family life. My book would introduce them to my family. They could read about a mother who was an inspiring teacher. She had her trials and tribulations. She went through the heartbreak and struggle of holding together a broken home when her husband abandoned her and their six children; but she never lost hope.

My students could read how a mother said, "Welfare, no!" and took in washing to support the family. They could interact with children who were obedient, had chores to do at home and made good grades in school. They could read about the happy moments with an eighty-three-year-old Civil War veteran grandfather, an unmarried "fairy godmother" aunt and a history-telling seventy-three-year-old grandmother. They could identify with the hurts of skin-color isolation and name-calling and learn to declare, "I am somebody! No one can make of me a nobody!"

In my group guidance classes I encouraged delayed sexual activity and shared this with my pupils: "When I was nearly twelve, my mother said to me, 'As you grow older your body will change, and you will have strange body feelings. This is Mother Nature's way of preparing you for marriage some day. These feelings are called the mating call or the sex urge. Sex has been around a long, long time. Don't go crazy over it. Sex has ruined as many lives as it has brought happiness to.'

My mother continued, 'If you decide to try sex by laying with your boyfriend for ten minutes of pleasure, he and you will be responsible for the baby you invite into this world. Not me! Do not come to me for anything! You may not live at home. I will not feed you. I will not baby-sit for you. Your responsibilities are yours! Mine are mine!' "

In my guidance units I introduced my classes to exemplary role models. I took them on Saturday tours and invited them to my home. I urged them to think, to study, to read and to reach beyond their isolated ghetto world that held little promise for them. I shared these words of advice: "1. Learn to say no to your peers when they coax you to do something wrong. 2. Never let any condition in life permit you to hate yourself or others. And 3. Never regard yourself as a lesser person than you want to be."

By the time I began to serve the senior high student of sixteen-, seventeen- and eighteen-years-of-age, I realized that a valuable opportunity to intervene in a child's life may have eluded the counselor. Those youth to whom we had not ministered in junior high were beyond our grasp. Those we had let slip through our fingers, those whose questions we had not answered, those whose thoughts we had not listened to, those who had not been referred to the clergy for spiritual guidance or to a youth organization for supervised activities, those whom we had not helped to believe in themselves were headed toward self-destruction.

They dropped out or were kicked out of school. They had their babies, ran afoul of the law, were incarcerated or became homicidal statistics. They became the unlearned, underemployed candidates for welfare.

In 1966 I was assigned a counseling position at Garfield Senior High School in Akron. Our nation was still feeling the aftershock caused by Dr. Martin Luther King's march on Washington and the assassination of President John F. Kennedy. The two-thousand member student body and the nearly one-hundred-member faculty tried not to be uncomfortable with its nearly ten percent Black student enrollment.

The principal, Mr. Harlan Horton, and his assistant, Robert Simmons, administered well the predominate second-generation, European ethnic student body. I became the first Black counselor in the Akron, Ohio, school system. The other three counselors in the attractively designed, glass-enclosed office complex were most accepting. Mr. Leroy Dietz, the senior counselor, was a bachelor. Mr. Joseph Quinn was the father of twelve children. Miss Arlene Spahr was a bachelorette; I was the career housewife, mother of two. We worked as a well-coordinated team. Our communication was on the highest level of professionalism and deep respect.

We shared weekly our students' acute concerns and discussed recommendations. We were involved in curriculum content, faculty effectiveness, the interpretation of test scores, scholarship selectees, honor roll candidates, failures that could lead to dropouts, workshops, career nights and parent conferences. I leaned in the direction of the troubled student and the underachiever.

The faculty was uncomfortable with the new upsurge of militancy in the school. There was an atmosphere of fear and a subdued kind of anger. Black students were assertive. The white students became touchy and rejecting. The new visibility of the Negro students was disconcerting. They wore expansive Afro hairstyles. Loose, flowing multicolored dashikas replaced the formal blouse and the tailored shirt and tie. They made demands for observable integration and greater involvement in school activities.

"We want to sing Black songs in the chorus." "We want greater representation on the student council." "We want to invite our escorts to the junior-senior prom. There are not enough Black boys in this school to go around." "We want Black cheerleaders and Black baton twirlers." "We want you white girls to leave our Black boys alone."

We counselors had a busy year ahead of us. We were able to help the administration, the faculty and parents to see these demands as paralleling the new freedoms in the land. Some of the situations were near-explosive, some were funny and some just revealing.

* * * * * * * * *

SCARED

"My son is skeered of dogs, snakes, thunderstorms and niggers!" one mother said to me. I shall call her tow-headed, blue-eyed, ninth grade son Sam. I have not remembered his name. He had a temporary physical handicap caused by a summer playground accident. His mother requested that her son's classes be relocated for his convenience.

As the handicap persisted, the mother became unreasonably demanding about the location of Sam's classes. She was told he was being transferred to another school, better equipped for maximum mobility.

Sam's mother phoned me. With an ear-piercing shout she began, "You are my son's counselor? Yes? Well I want to tell you I will not permit my son's transfer to that school for the handicapped. His lameness is temporary, not permanent. Anyhow, there are too many niggers in that school."

She continued. "I must tell you, I am not prejudiced; but Sam is a very timid boy. He's not very big and he's easily frightened. He's skeered of dogs, snakes, thunderstorms and niggers. He won't be able to learn a thing in that school. Those niggers would skeer him to death."

"I am sorry," I replied. "This is an administrative procedure. Let me transfer your call to . . ."

"No! I want to talk to you. Can I come to your office right away?"

"Tomorrow would be better."

"Okay. I'll see you then. At this time?"

"Yes, that will be fine."

I alerted Arlene Spahr of the phone conversation and suggested she might face this irate woman as my substitute. "I really do not want to embarrass her by revealing I am the person to whom she spoke," I explained.

The next day Arlene did a casual, matter-of-fact job introducing this parent to me. Sam's mother never flicked an eyelash, never blushed and never hinted that we had conversed the day before. Sam was transferred without incident.

* * * * * * * * * *

DON'T TOUCH ME!

"Just bump into me and I'll knock the hell out of you," a Black girl screamed to a classmate. A student had dropped her contact lens in the lavatory wash bowl, and it was caught in the drain. In panic she dashed through the swinging door to call the custodian. She bumped into a Black girl. All that day the school was on an alert to avert a racial school disturbance.

The collision victim insisted she had been pushed aside on purpose. "She did. I know she did it on purpose. She never even said ''scuse me.' I'll tell anyone. I've said it all my life. 'Just bump into me and I'll knock the hell out of you!' "

"If I had not been so upset, I would have taken time to say 'I'm sorry,' " the girl explained to those in the guidance office. "I didn't mean to hurt you. I was upset. All I could think of was losing my contact lens and the dollars it would take to replace it."

Students trooped into the guidance office to express their concerns and even to take sides. "We don't want a racial incident here at Garfield," one commented.

"I don't care. If anyone bumps into me, they're in trouble."

"Why?"

"'Cause most cats are always sending us the 'stay away' message. Stay away from us in the cafeteria. Stay away from us on the gym floor."

"Yeah. In my English class they's always giving us Blacks the silent treatment. When one of us offers a topic for discussion, they keeps their mouth shut and says nothing. I feel like a damn fool when they discuss the silly stuff they gits all excited about."

"Well this school is a good school. It's a lot better than most. We must keep it this way."

"Maybe. But when they pass me in the halls, they bettah

not step on my toes or push me. As Flip Wilson say, 'Don't touch me. Don't ever touch me!' And I mean it!"

* * * * * * * * *

CAREERS OR WHAT?

I overheard a fellow classmate ask, "Eric, what's the counselor talking to your group about today?"
"Don't know—don't really care."
"I bet it's careers."
"Could be. Yeah. She goin' to try to make somethin' out of us to please whitey."
"Or keep her job."
"Yeah."
"Black folks with a job like hers is called Uncle Toms or Aunt Jemimas."
"Some folks just jealous of someone with a good job. Just jealous! That's why we trying to git an education, so we can git a decent job some day, too."
"That's a lot of bull; they's nothin' good out there for us."
"French, tell us 'bout the job you did las' night. Some career! Ha, Ha!"
"Shut your mouf!"
"Are you goin' to tell your counselor?"
"Tell her what?"
"That you trying to be a pimp."
"It's a damn sight bettah than the numbers or what you could do."
"Sez you!"
"Whitey's gotcha comin' an goin'. They ain't nothin' good out there for us."
"You have to be smart, man."
"Yeah, you have to be able to read. Which you can't. Come

to think of it, fool, how did you make it to the tenth grade? You can't read, like nothin'."

"No one asked for your two-cents worth."

"No, but when I gits ready to learn, I got some brains! You . . . You . . ."

I opened wide my office door and stood in the midst of three slighty embarrassed boys.

"Eric," I began, "I have a note here from your English teacher. She thinks you have real talent. You are doing very well on your oral reports, but you are not doing your written work. Why not?"

"I'm thinkin' about it."

"Well, think about it tonight and bring your work to me first thing in the morning. I want to look it over before you hand it in. Understand?"

"Yeah. I mean, yes ma'am."

"Here are some slips that will admit all of you to class. Now be on your way."

"Yes ma'am."

"Mrs. Marcere," Eric paused, "can you hear what we say when your office door is closed and that little transom is open?"

"If I were listening I suppose I could. You might try to lower your voices a little so as not to disturb others who are waiting for a counselor."

"Yes ma'am."

* * * * * * * * *

THE GARFIELD RIOT

The student disturbance happened because nobody was listening. School tradition was more important than communication, compromise, understanding and change.

Black students wanted three elected Blacks on the ten-member homecoming court. The administration, student council and athletic committee insisted upon the same traditional procedure for school elections, knowing that the votes of five-hundred-seventy-five White seniors would negate the choices of seventy-five Black seniors. The announcement that the football team would "select" three Blacks was an inflammatory insult.

Outside the school cafeteria, groups of students argued noisily while two-hundred of the less vocally inclined gathered for a sit-down strike in the auditorium.

"What do you all want?" a student was heard to shout. "Six black girls on the court? That's half the court. You are only twelve percent of this school. You are still a minority and don't forget it!"

A Black met the challenge with a louder retort. "We've never asked for more than three girls, but we want them elected—not hand-picked. Since you are so concerned about numbers and percentages, remember this: the team is more than fifty percent Black. And another thing! We are tired, very tired of you white girls shaking your fannies in front of our Black athletes!"

The principal, Mr. Moore, distributed a memo that the counselors and any teacher not on duty should monitor the halls and disperse any gathering of more than two people. I did not relish acting as a policeman, but I took my turn patrolling the corridors.

As I proceeded down one hall, I heard a barely audible chant of "W-h-i-t-e-y, W-h-i-t-e-y, W-h-i-t-e-y!"

I pretended not to have heard and walked over to a small group whose expression told me they had heard. I put my arms around one of the girls and whispered, "Go to class, please."

"I have a right to protest," she said and pulled away from

me.

"I have been protesting all my life," I confessed. "There are many different ways of protesting. Believe me, I know."

Minutes later as I was looking out my office window facing the southern entrance to the cafeteria, the city police arrived. They began loading the patrol wagon with students who were singing "We Shall Overcome." The young lady I had recently embraced was arrested with twenty other students.

I began to weep. Uncontrolled tears poured like a fountain from my eyes. I stood there paralyzed with anger. I hated the school system, the students, and myself.

The visionless, insensitive, traditional educators disgusted me. The leaderless youth, black and white, were pitiful. And me? I didn't know. I just asked the question, "What was my role? What should have been my position in a situation like this?"

Normalcy returns rapidly. No attempt was made to evaluate the positive or negative rioting experience. It was soon business as usual. Our four-hundred student case load awaited our services. The good students applied for scholarships, became involved in extracurricular activities and sought advice. The underachievers bypassed our office unless told by a teacher to "talk to your counselor."

Many times I overheard the raw language of a teen-ager being expelled from school. The vulgar, vicious epithets were worse than anything I had heard when I worked in the slums as a social worker. In the school environment it reflected contempt for authority and a low self-concept.

Was it possible for middle-class professionals from reasonably secure environments to understand the intensity and diversity of feelings experienced by young people from culturally different lifestyles?

The student body social class structure at Garfield Senior High was roughly as follows: eighty percent white middle-class, ten percent white poor, five percent black middle-class and five percent black poor.

The poor white child could anticipate being in the same shoes some day as the middle-class or upper-class white. His role models were eighty percent of the student body and ninety eight percent of the faculty.

A black child could not realistically identify with either. When would his parents, or even he, own his own business, play golf at the Firestone Country Club, have a vacation home on the lake, go to Europe or be elected to Congress?

The middle-class Blacks knew they lived well. They no longer lived in the heart of the slums. They were buying a nice house in a neat neighborhood. They were active church members. Their parents belonged to the NAACP and some sororities and fraternities. They traveled by car for summer vacations. A college education was in their plans.

The five percent Black poor did not see the five percent Black middle class as role models. They called them "Uncle Toms," "Aunt Jemimas," "Whitey," and "Oreo Cookies." They openly chided the achieving Blacks for their good grades and their proper speech.

When the Blacks (for the most part girls) made demands at Garfield to be cheerleaders, baton-twirlers, majorettes and student council representatives, they were fighting two battles. The first was equality with the white middle-class student who, like them, had private music and dance lessons and lived well. The second was to be extricated from the quicksand pull of the slum Black.

The impoverished Black had a way of telegraphing to his same-hued brothers a self-destructing message: "You're no better than the rest of us. . . . You're nobodies. Whites don't want you around them. You aren't going anywhere. Don't turn up your nose at us. We're survivors. We're just doing our thing. That's what you must do. Get some pleasure from your body.

Tell the whole cock-eyed, uncaring world to get the hell out of your way!"

The middle-class Black was between two opposing forces, one white, one black.

My transfer in 1971 to Central Hower, an inner city, predominately Black high school, separated me from some of the finest professionals with whom I have ever worked. Only pieces of what was effective counseling at Jones for eight years and Garfield for five years could be adapted to Central.

The student body generally evidenced a serious lack of purpose and self-esteem. Testing, scheduling and interviewing became routine procedures with no assurance that a difference was being made.

With or without this service the functionally illiterate would remain illiterate. They were already entrenched in their fifth- and sixth-grade tombs of ignorance. They had been marking time since their elementary school years. They were no longer inquisitive or enthusiastic.

With teachers expecting little, the underachieving "D" pupil entered classroom after classroom experiencing boredom and ego-destruction. Some pupils stayed in school to graduate and qualify for the armed services or a job in industry. Others, impatient for recognition, engaged in destructive activities leading to their expulsion from school.

Counselors are perhaps the highest trained professionals in the schools. They have a breadth of sociological, psychological and job information expertise in addition to classroom teaching skills. Yet too many fail to extricate themselves from the paperwork detail on their desks and do little to intervene on behalf of those pupils most seriously handicapped by the circumstances of their birth.

I looked at this unwholesome, uninspiring school environment and sensed our inadequacy to prevent the unhappiness, the underachievement, the dropouts and the kickouts of so many youths to whom learning had never been a mind-stretching experience. Could I do more? Should I point a finger at the teachers, the parents, the neighborhoods and churches for their obeisance to failure?

Jews and Catholics as minorities knew themselves. Negroes did not. In the Catholic school catechism classes, I had seen children inspired by the teachings that God created them to bring honor and glory to His name. I had observed the little Jewish boy on Housel Avenue and later Martha Philips on Fifth Street who went to the synagogue school. They had special feast days similar to the Catholic holy days. They never hung their heads in shame.

Except for the dramatic stories my mother read to us and the pride my grandfather expressed when he told of his parents' escape to freedom before the Civil War, where could I have learned about my heritage? No organization or church was teaching Negroes about their culture. We knew nothing of the ancient, historical significance of being of African stock. We just "growed" or were dumped on American soil.

For a brief early childhood period, the Black child is unaware there are human differences based upon skin color. When the shock of name-calling and rejection occurs, its impact is negative, nasty, degrading. The damage is so great the child never fully recovers unless someone takes him aside to assure him he is one of God's greatest miracles. He must be told he is somebody good and wonderful.

Many a day as I watched my students at school, I wanted to scream. I felt enraged that Negro boys and girls hated themselves so much and evidenced it by striking back at those who resembled them. The public schools had never done for the Black child what was being done for the Jewish and ethnic Catholic child in their church schools.

Black impoverished underachievers need a School of Self-Esteem. The school could remind each child that he is a human being created in the likeness of God and destined for greatness. Students could learn to appreciate the diversity of ethnic cultures with their multi-hued skin tones. The school could unveil the greatness of dark-skinned peoples and their contributions to the world. The curriculum could stress intellectual curiosity and encourage involvement in life-enhancing services.

A SELF-AWARENESS CLASS

After my first semester at Central Hower, I had a plan. I asked my principal, Mr. Lauer, to give me the names of twenty-five of the worst students in the school.

"I want those students who, as soon as they reach their sixteenth birthday, you plan to call to your office and recommend they quit school. My plan is to conduct a self-awareness class, one period daily for one semester. I would like to see if it is possible to penetrate this armor of purposelessness."

It was then I was told that the year before several eleventh- and twelfth-grade students had requested a credit course in Black History. They also asked for a Black teacher who would understand "when we tell it like it is."

I doubt if the petitioning students would have agreed to my leadership if there had been a younger, "more black" and "more obviously militant" teacher on the faculty. I was the only Black on the staff.

A great deal of effort was spent encouraging primarily those who were headed for immediate trouble to sign up for the class. I enlisted the assistance of six students—the best and the not-so-good.

With the approval of the superintendent of the Akron schools, Conrad Ott, I began a unit called Self-Awareness. Into a previously abandoned room on the third-floor, out of sight and sound from the regular classes, twenty-five Black students sauntered in cautiously.

"All I can tell you," I began, "is that this class will be different from any you have ever attended. It will be divided into four units called 'Who Are You?,' 'Where Are You?,' 'How Did You Get Here?,' and 'Where Are You Going?' Its chief aim is to help you know yourself better. The units will introduce you to psychology, sociology, Afro-American history and goal-setting."

For the first three days all were encouraged to express why they agreed to attend this class and what they expected to gain from it. They were specifically charged to express what bothered them about their school, their lives and being black. It became clear that ninety percent were more interested in the here-and-now than in Black history.

They attempted to tell it like it was to them. There were words, half-truths and misinformation, interspersed with feelings of bewilderment, fear and helplessness.

This is what these youths said to me and the entire class those opening days:

"I wish . . . I had never been told that the people I live with are not my real parents. I feel scared all the time. I'm afraid every day that somebody will tell me something I'd rather not hear."

"What worries me is all this talk about sterilization and abortions. We're on welfare. I'm afraid to go to a doctor for fear one of them will do something to me and I won't be able to have children when I'm full-grown. So I study hard, get a good job, marry and settle down only to find that my wife was sterilized when she was in her teens. What a hell of a society we live in. Who can you trust and who gives a damn?"

"Believe it or not, I'm afraid of people. Just walking through these halls ten times a day when we change classes makes me nervous. One teacher called me a stubborn slowpoke and

I wanted to slap her. She reminds me of my mom who yells at me all the time. Some day I won't be afraid of people and I'll show them all."

"When I started to school in the first grade, my whole world stopped until I returned home. I daydreamed or something until school was out and then I lived again. I couldn't take it. It was too different, too strange. It's not that much better now, but I'm older and I know I have to be here."

So much for their fears and their apprehensions. The confused logic of these youth is phrased in the following denunciatory statements:

"All big-shot blacks are Uncle Toms."

"Sammy Davis showed us he was an Uncle Tom when he jumped on Nixon's band wagon and sold us down the river."

"Yes, you too! How many asses did you have to kiss to get where you are?"

"Booker T. Washington did us more harm than good. He was a real cookie, an Oreo."

"President Nixon hates Blacks. To him we don't exist. He pretends we are not even around. The pigs who wear police uniforms haven't forgot that Blacks are around. They kill us every chance they get—from ten-year-olds to eighty-year-olds."

"Christianity is a white man's religion that preaches milk and honey and a lot of junk. Milk and honey have never been on a soul food diet, so we miss out here and now—and hereafter as well."

"All black ministers are in a religious racket that brings them money and women. They are also our 'Uncle Tom' spokesmen. They are all fakes."

"School is hell. It's one big joke and a waste of time. We're not taught anything important. A lot of facts about white cats and their history and a lot of crap about the white man's English. Who needs it?"

I had sensed these fears and similar bewilderments from teenagers for more than a dozen years. This was my first opportunity to have a full semester to listen daily to their feelings.

At the close of the third class gathering I laid down ground rules for the continuing group sessions in language expressing the same frankness most had shown me.

It was explained to them that the class would be an experience in trying to understand "why we think and feel as we do as a people." We would attempt to study ourselves, our history and our environment in order to gain a sense of hope, of power and purpose. They were told that they could express their personal feelings at any time, but all other statements, accusations and opinions must be documented or proved. They must be backed up by experts in the fields of history, sociology, psychology, religion and other disciplines. Each student was to read at least one historical book about Blacks, Negroes and African-Americans. They were to take notes daily.

I proclaimed my pride in myself, my family and my lineage. Perhaps the muted voices of middle-class Blacks relative to personal experiences and values is to be regretted. I set the record straight about myself.

"No, I've never kissed anybody's posterior. Neither have I compromised my honesty, my morals nor my values. You call me an Uncle Tom and an Oreo, but older, wiser citizens of my community have described me as a forthright Black. I am a woman who gets things done.

"America is my home. The blood of my ancestors who fought and died in the Civil War, who died freeing fellow slaves through the Underground Railroad, gives me a claim to America that no racist white nor militant black can ever deny me. I've been to Africa to walk on the soil where some of my forefathers may have walked. I've been to Europe to visit the countries where some of my other forefathers lived.

I hate no race of men, no individual man. A divine creator, whom I call God, is Father of us all. What right have I to shake my fist in the face of God and say that I hate His creation and that He should not have allowed this person or that race to exist?"

I was in business. We were off and running. The first unit was an introspective psychological focus on the self. The class was asked to ponder the question, "Who am I?" These young people looked inward and some for the first time in their young lives examined their "I am" and their "I feel" emotions. I stood at the back of the room frequently, speaking to them as a voice from their conscience.

The class was told to start from a base of personal, unalterable acceptances. They had to accept their race, their sex, their skin color, their height, the quality and texture of their hair, their parentage. From here we enumerated factors that could be changed: attitude, obesity, acne, study habits, manners, life goals and the determination to excel in something.

Each individual looked for some trait he liked about himself. All were asked to look in the mirror daily and say, "I like me because there's nobody in the world exactly like me. I'm unique."

It was surprising how easily they verbalized their dislike of themselves.

"I want to like myself," one teenager commented, "but I need other people to like me, too."

Another commented, "Yeah! Maybe I can accept the fact that I'm only five-feet-four and can never be a football player, but why do people laugh at me and make jokes about my size?"

"He's right," another volunteered. "Little people get picked on a lot. One of my teachers in grade school always blamed me if sonething went wrong around my desk. Even the kids lied on me because I was too small to fight back."

The second unit, "Where Am I?," was sociological. It highlighted culture and social-class status. The students came face-to-face with the labels and characteristics of lower, middle, and upper-classes.The differences in lifestyles, values and attitudes were touched upon. The possibility of mobility from lower-class to middle-class through the attainment of a good education, the level of employable skills and social standards of behavior was reviewed.

These youth examined the disadvantages of one-parent families and the welfare subculture. They discussed the impact of pimps and the urban hustler upon fatherless males. They reviewed the unmet emotional needs of the fatherless girl. They spoke freely of criminality, drugs, family neglect and brutality.

They reviewed the essentials for developing a positive self-image. The family and the school took a beating for deflating the self-image of Blacks.

Most of these teenagers had a limited concept of the world beyond their neighborhood. Their environment included the corner tavern, the crowded housing allotment, the store-front churches, the numbers runner, the area pimp, the neighborhood madam, the drug pusher, and some small business people. Their excitement involved the extremes of tragedy and good times. Homicide, illnesses, prison and welfare shared the spotlight with fine cars, money, clothes, music and parties.

The new movie images, male effeminacy and the conspicuous comsumption of goods crowded out the goal of a strong, parent-dominated family life.

In fact, their socialization—their culture—had little indoctrination in the mother-father role regarding children and family responsibilities. Dr. Frances Cress Welsing gave a vivid description of the negative socializing influences on Black youth in the September 1974 *Ebony* article "The Conspiracy to Make Blacks Inferior."

I seemed to have held these youths in the palm of my hand. Their minds were electrified with enthusiasm. I think at some points they were willing to attribute "soul" to me. I lost some when I attempted to refer to transitional changes that could bridge the gap between their world and the larger environment. Only the successful pupil, the honor roll student and student council members had experiences to make this concept meaningful. Athletes would possibly fit this category, but there were no athletes in this unit of study.

The third unit was a review of the Black man's role in American history. "How Did I Get Here?" Their book reports reviewed the culture of Africa, the disorientation of a people through slavery and the beginnings of a new racial awareness with the Civil Rights movement of the '60s.

Racism was discussed as a part of the fabric of American life. We identified institutional, psychological, scientific and educational racism. My students were asked to consider combatting racism as "every man's," rather than a "one-man, one-leader" omnipotent role. They were asked should a group depend solely upon a Dr. Martin Luther King, a Malcolm X, a Booker T. Washington or a new "Moses." What could young people do to draw attention to their dedication toward a quality life?

The class tried to put into perspective the various social and community agencies with their particular thrusts for improving racial conditions. The NAACP, the Urban League, the Muslims, the traditional Christian churches, labor unions and politics took on new meanings.

This was not an easy unit to summarize. These young people found it difficult to identify with an ideal. The national figures of a Kennedy or a Martin Luther King satisfied some. For still others their pastor, family doctor or corner druggist reflected their goals. They seemed hard-pressed to focus on a model or to believe that anyone had their interest at heart. Neither could they see themselves as the kind of leader they felt they needed in their lives. Their questioning was "How?" "How?"

In this unit there was a career-oriented session, "Where Am I Going?" We took a look at jobs, careers and incomes as a means of self-support and service to mankind. The "work" concept in an urban environment of the "hustler" and "welfare life style" was not fully understood nor fully accepted. School achievement and good grades had less meaning than rapping with their peers and being considered "hip."

At the close of this unit some students expressed a better understanding of themselves. Some were able to discern half-truths and faulty logic. Some were less afraid because they realized that fear could be conquered. Some were aware that the most mature act of a human being was to "Know Thyself."

Some general conclusions expressed by individuals in this unit were:

"I must know myself. I am important to me."

"I must like myself and others will respect this in me, even if they do not want to like me."

"I must combine saying 'I'm black and beautiful' with acting black and beautiful."

"It may be wise to seek the advice of elders. We might benefit from their experiences if not their conclusions."

"Do I have the right to demand of anyone—parents, teachers, leaders—a greater sacrifice of time, money or talent than I would be willing to give if I were in their shoes?"

"I have a right to enter the mainstream of American society and contribute my fair share to its development, so I will begin with my school. I will not be a complaining critic nor a cheering bystander but will help make policy at the student council level and pay attention to high academic achievement."

"I must prepare myself for employment in a world that demands real skills, yet is racist and discriminatory."

"I must vote and encourage others to vote."

"I must contribute to the strength and moral fiber of my race by being the kind of young adult and future parent whom other youth and my children can model and respect."

Of the thirty-five students who completed the class unit, thirty-two thanked me personally for this experience in self-awareness. Even if fifteen weeks were not sufficient to remove all their fears, destroy all the half-truths and replace all the faulty logic with reasonable rationalization, my young people seemed relieved and more self-confident. It appeared that their pent-up frustrations had been directed toward constructive goals.

I did not achieve one hundred percent holding power. Two students were asked to leave because they would not research their views and were disruptive in their negativism. One student dropped the class, stating that he was a well adjusted individual and did not need to be there. Three young men remained, but nonverbally tuned me out as a "square." They had involvements that interfered with an honest attempt at introspection. Nevertheless, three of the six came to me later for personal counseling.

In all, these young people brought me closer to the poor, environmentally disadvantaged youth than I had ever been before. Their outward behaviors masked a powder keg of fear, insecurity, mistrust and lack of direction. Unless parents, teachers, counselors, psychologists and sociologists recognize this plight and help youth to verbalize and understand their purpose in life, they will heed the voices of their peers and pseudo-leaders who will fan their fears into hatreds and acts of violence.

Is this not what happens when a teenager knifes a fellow student or shoots a teacher in the school corridor? Is it not likely that the neighborhood homicide of an aged pensioner or the taxi driver is the result of the absence of hope and purpose and the presence of a consuming misdirected hate within a youth who needs help? (1)

At the end of the term, my Self-Awareness Class arranged a bus tour to New York City. We saw the Black Broadway play, "Don't Bother Me, I Can't Cope." With the addition of two honor students, my granddaughters, six white students and several parents, the bus was filled to capacity. At the close of the theater performance, all forty of us were in tears. Embracing one another we exclaimed, "This is the best thing that has ever happened to us."

There was not one incident of misbehavior. We stayed at the Piccadilly Hotel. The students chided me for "picking a dilly," but the management praised my group for their ladylike and gentlemanly conduct.

It happened that Duke Ellington died while we were in New York. We toured Harlem and stopped at the funeral home to pay our respects. "He was one of our finest role models," I reminded them. "You can become somebody, too!"

I have often wondered where my Self-Awareness pupils are and what they are doing. Whatever their successes and failures, they made choices with their eyes open. They had a clearer view of "Who they were," "Where they were," and "How they got there." They could, with the proper motivation and devotion to learning, determine where they were going.

The concept of Self-Awareness excited me. I was ready to move into the area of psychology. I wondered what a school psychologist could do to make a difference in the quality of life for the Negro child.

(1) In the Akron, Ohio, city there were thirty-one homicides in 1972, twenty-eight in 1973. For the first eight months of

1974, there were thirty-four. Of this number, twenty-two were committed by blacks. A total of eight would fit the racial percentage.

XXV

The Shocking Truth!

An acquaintance who glanced through the first draft of my manuscript remarked, "I think you need some sex and scandal in your book. Readers want to be shocked by a sordid affair. They look for skeletons to fall out of the closet. It makes them feel righteous to say, 'So-and-so fell from grace. She wasn't all that goody-goody. She sinned.' Ordinary people read books for fantasy, thrills and a confirmation of human weaknesses. You have omitted what they most want to read about."

There was an awkward silence. I had no immediate comment. Fearing, I presume, that he might have offended me, he asked, "Why are you writing your autobiography? What message do you want to get across, and to whom?"

"Oh, originally," I sort of mumbled, "I thought my grandchildren might like to know a little of their heritage. Perhaps students of today and tomorrow will be interested in knowing what it was like growing up in the early 1900s."

"Were there no scoundrels, no black sheep, no acts of violence in your family to laugh or cry about?"

"No, there were none. Why should I want to memorialize the misdeeds of a family, truth or fiction, who have been the prodigal sons and daughters of society?"

"Why not?" he challenged.

"The bookshelves are crowded with the true stories of statesmen, movie stars, athletes, industrial magnates, religious leaders, lords and ladies of the evening, clergymen and bluebloods who have descended to the pits of hell. They have wallowed in the mud and slime of drugs, alcohol, murder, multiple sex relationships and whatever else you can name," I answered.

"Now, you get my point?" my friend remarked. "Those biographies make the Best-Seller list. Writing is a competitive market. Your life story may not even get published."

"Many such books and the notoriety about the greats who have fallen teach our young people two things. There is very little goodness in people, and it is natural to do everything unlawful and indecent until one decides to change. Then they confess and settle down to be role models. A teen-ager remarked in one of my guidance units, 'Oh I can sow my wild oats for a few more years. Some day I'll get religion and go to church and be dull and good.' "

"I sense the teacher in you has a message to your reader," he conceded.

"The only message may be this. Millions of young people with their unique genetic endowments and variable hues have lived exciting, rewarding lives. In the midst of the struggle to overcome obstacles and turn challenges into victories, they never sacrificed decency, honor and their commitment to others," I explained.

"Were you never tempted to follow the crowd, drink, have extra-marital sex, steal or plot to get even for a wrongdoing?" he inquired.

"My answer is no," I replied. "Temptation to me implies a choice of doing right or wrong. When I withstood the urge to slip my hand inside a college professor's purse and 'borrow' money to allay the pangs of three foodless days, I became impervious to all temptation. Temptation is not limited to youth. It pops up at any time in one's life. Would you like to know about one or two 'awful truths' in my life?"

"You're the author, continue," he said.

"I realized quite early in life there were enough fences between me and the good life, just being a Negro. I did not need to erect additional stumbling blocks.

"There have been situations where a wrongdoing could easily have taken place. I never wanted to do what others were doing. When at age twenty I, quite by accident, found myself sitting in the living room of a bootleg brothel in Cleveland, I made a choice.

"Nothing in this world, least of all the fear of peer ridicule, could have caused me to accompany the eight to ten couples on the second and third floors having sex. The bug to be popular with the crowd never bit me. I never lusted after a man, or fantasized what it would be like to be in the arms of a rich man, poor man, beggar man, thief, doctor, lawyer, Indian chief or whomever.

"My closest experience with fantasy occurred when I was nearly sixteen. The old saying 'sweet sixteen and never been kissed' encouraged most young ladies in high school to giggle and cast their eyes in the direction of a suitable recipient or donor, in time for the junior-senior prom.

"One night I dreamed of a very handsome young man, the color of gold. He stood before me and smiled. I must admit I scanned hundreds of audiences hoping to see this man of my dreams. No one ever came close to such sparkling grandeur. Finally I regarded that image as my Guardian Angel. My husband's flattering remark, 'You're so damn dumb it's pathetic,' seemed to confirm that an extraordinary angel had a special assignment to keep an eye on me."

My listener interrupted, "You're really serious about this angel business, aren't you?"

"Yes, very much," I replied, "and the following explains why.

"I was to attend a conference of social workers in Detroit. A few days before, I received a phone call from one of the young women I had met at a workshop. Would I be interested in sharing a suite of rooms with her and two to four others? 'We can be closer together, have room service and get acquainted with some of Detroit's finest.'

"Percy was as excited about the trip as I was. He urged me to take my first airplane flight rather than drive our car or ride the train or bus. He insisted I purchase a new outfit. I had long since abandoned the three-outfit maximum as an adequate wardrobe. I still sewed most of my suits and dresses. Percy complimented me upon my creations, but added, 'I hope the day will come when we can walk into Stern and Mann's or Parisian's and purchase a really first-class outfit.'

"Checking into the hotel, first-class outfit and all, I was delighted with the suite. Since the conference would begin with breakfast the next morning, an evening of fun had been planned. An inviting buffet was spread out in one room. People came and went all evening.

"I kept hearing, 'Norma, you will really be excited about this professor I want you to meet. He is sure to be late, but he is such a neat person and loaded with the bucks.'

"Shortly after this long-awaited guest arrived, the party enlivened considerably. Then I noticed that couples began to pair off. It dawned upon poor, dumb me like a flash out of nowhere that I was to share my bed with this stranger.

"Taking my purse and throwing my coat about me, I concocted some excuse about picking up a message at the desk. I slipped out of the room. I sat in the ladies toilet off the lobby rest room. I stood in the telephone booth as though I was talking on the phone. I found a chair at the end of the first floor corridor and sat there in the darkness. I was frightened, angry, sleepy and tired.

"About 4 a.m. I thought I saw this 'honored' guest and several other people alight from the elevator and pass through the deserted lobby. I waited awhile and returned to my room to lie fully clothed on my bed for a two-hour nap.

"I was eating breakfast when my friends sauntered into the coffee shop asking, 'Where have you been?'

" 'Wouldn't you like to know?'

" 'But you ditched Dr. So-and-so, and was he uptight!'

" 'Maybe I had a bigger fish to snare in my net,' I crowed and then wondered why I had made such a remark, suggesting that I did the things they did.

" 'Uh oh, sounds like we have a pro in our midst,' I heard.

"The convention convened. I attended every session and stayed out of my roommates' way. They eyed me with questioning glances.

"My respect level for a good many professionals crumbled that night and day. I felt that educated, intelligent people had a responsibility to be morally upright. I could understand the poor, illiterate, disease-ridden individuals, surrounded by crime and injustice seeking forbidden pleasures. They might feel the need to add a bit of spice to their lives, but not these people."

"Am I boring you?" I asked.

"No, no, continue," he replied. "Continue."

"Widening my circle of associates meant contact with a diversity of people. Percy often expressed fear that I would find myself in a 'touchy' situation.

" 'You can't mix oil with water. It's bad enough that you're a Catholic surrounded by Baptists and a northern-born outnumbered by southern-born. Don't stretch your luck by mixing people with a lot of different views together.' "

"I paid little attention and cultivated, in small groups and with individuals, lasting friendships. My beautician Elizabeth

Carmichael and I developed a sister-like relationship. She was an accomplished elocutionist. This exciting, vivacious woman was in many ways my opposite. Our husbands worked at Republic Steel. Our daughters were about the same age. Elizabeth supervised a group of fifteen to twenty teen-age girls known as the Junior Jane Hunter Civic Club. Our friendship almost ceased when I disagreed with her talks to the girls about sex. She was for protection. I was for abstinence."

"I've heard of her," my friend, now comfortably seated, remarked.

I continued, "We shared the same views about the good life. We were committed to an adequate income (freedom from want), an attractively furnished home, college education for our children and some status in the community gained through community services.

"Carmichael had a flair for entertainment, whether it was parties in her home or as chairman of the annual Pink Ball for the Jane Hunter Civic Club. Her ability to execute spectacular high class affairs helped to gain her and her husband membership in the elite BBB Club. Percy and I never made it. We were on the guest list to their affairs, but we were never invited to become members.

"Elizabeth was sharp, attractive and outgoing. She always made a grand entrance fifteen to thirty minutes tardy at whatever affair. This only accentuated her suave, debonair appearance. Her strut, her poise, her showmanship electrified her audience. It mattered not whether she was modeling in a style show, walking down the aisle in church or entering the Mayor's office in City Hall. She was queenly.

"When I wanted someone to go with me to a restaurant to test our ability to be served as first-class citizens, Carmichael was the only person I knew who had the courage to sit it out as long as necessary. She could portray the image of undaunted determination and ladylike composure.

"She was barely awake one morning at 7 a.m. (my hair appointments were early so I could be at work by 8:30) when I asked, 'How much money do you spend at the Stark Dry Goods Company in a week or month?'

"I followed this with a second question, 'Have you ever eaten a meal in their dining room downstairs, next to the Bargain Basement?'

"No," she replied.

" 'Neither have I, and I work downtown. Hundreds of people from the downtown offices eat their lunch there, but Stark's refuses to serve the Negroes who are employed downtown. What happens to those shoppers who might decide on the spur of the moment to enjoy a light meal there? I can go to a ten-cent store hot dog stand and that is it. How would you like to join me at Stark's some day soon, to see if we can be served?'

" 'I'm game if you are.'

"Elizabeth and I spent one and a half hours (11:30 to 1:00) sitting at three different locations in the most humiliating and insulting test of endurance imaginable.

"When we entered the dining room, the hostess made no attempt to seat us so we sat in an area where six tables were already filled. Before long, signs reading 'This Section Closed' were all around us and customers were being directed to another dining area.

"We moved to this section and were completely ignored as the white patrons were being served. We made polite attempts to attract a waitress's attention. 'Miss,' I called out several times.

"As one group after another finished their lunch, a 'Reserved' sign was placed on the table. Our third move produced the same treatment.

"We two, neatly dressed Negro women, were total nonentities. We did not exist. Institutional racism controlled the moral, religious, civil behavior of each employee in that store. The store was owned by a Jew. Less than ten years earlier, the Jew had experienced from 1930 to 1945 a period of near extermination in Germany. Yet an American Jew would concede to the Caucasian American's racist mandates.

"The poor white waitresses and store clerks, fearful of losing their low-paying jobs, put aside any religious or moral conscience they might have had. They wielded with a vengeance their racial superiority over their dark-skinned victims. Had Hitler been their Fuhrer, they would just as zealously have done his bidding in the massacre of an identifiable minority.

"Mrs. Carmichael, Dr. M. B. Williams, Mrs. Ruth Robinson, president of the NAACP, and I called upon Mr. Erlanger, owner of the Stark Dry Goods Company. We announced that we had enough evidence and witnesses to file a civil suit against his store. We urged him to immediately serve Negroes. He was easily convinced.

"I never ate in the dining room at Stark's, but other Negroes did. I could not relive the memories of that dehumanizing one-and-a-half hours. I would attempt and I did, alone, to test the discriminatory practices in other cafeterias and restaurants.

"Carmichael earned my highest respect in that department store dining room. Sometime later I think I earned from her a new kind of esteem. Sitting in her shop, between a shampoo, the dryer and hairstyling, I told her of a forthcoming trip. I would be attending the National Convention of the Urban League in Buffalo, New York. My brother Carl lived in Buffalo.

"Elizabeth commented, 'You are always traveling somewhere. Would you invite me to come along? It's a slow season and I can get away. Am I invited?'

"I was delighted to have her join me. Carl met us at the

bus terminal, drove us to his exotic little apartment and thrilled me with exciting details about his new job. He was the first Negro manager of the all-white East Aurora Country Club.

"He showed us where the food and liquor was, gave me the key to the apartment and promised to see me before I boarded the bus home. We retired in anticipation of a busy day.

"The second night, Elizabeth and I returned to the apartment, listened to some records, bathed and retired.

"As we were eating breakfast the next morning, Elizabeth said, 'Tell me, Norma, what are your plans for this evening?'

' 'Nothing in particular. The last session is not likely to be over before 10:00 or 10:30. It looks like another hectic day. Why?'

" 'Don't you ever go to the bars or nightclubs or join the delegates' parties?' she asked.

" 'Nope.'

" 'You mean to tell me that you attend all of these sessions and go back to your hotel room and sleep?'

" 'Yep.'

" 'Don't you have a boyfriend who meets you at these conferences and wines and dines you?'

" 'Nope.'

" 'I don't want to believe you. All these years I have told myself, 'Norma goes to all those conferences and conventions to let her hair down. She goes there to meet some highly educated muck-a-de-muck big shot and whoops it up—high fashion.' "

"I could not believe what I was hearing.

" 'Everybody knows your reputation is without blemish in Canton. I credited you with being careful and discreet. If I hear you straight, you are for real. You're not putting me on? What would you do if I took a room at the hotel and left you alone the next two nights?' I was asked.

" 'What do you think I would do in my brother's apartment?

Degrade it? Are you asking me if I would commit adultery in my brother's house, my brother's bedroom?'
" 'Have you ever committed adultery?' she asked.
" 'Are you my priest, wanting to hear my confession?'
" 'You don't have to answer. It is really none of my business.'
" 'I am glad to say no to your question. I gave my virginity to my husband. I am a married woman. There will never, ever be another man in my life.'
" 'I don't want to believe you, but I do. Forgive me for the many times I have imagined you engaged in an illicit romance when you left town. Does your religion have anything to do with your willpower?'
" 'I am sure it does. I believe in God. I believe in the Ten Commandments. I think of my body as the temple of my Lord and Savior. It is not a slop jar for sin and lust and fornication. Some day I must stand in judgment before my God and account for everything I have done with and to this body.'
" 'My mother is a Catholic. Did you know that?' Elizabeth asked.
" 'Yes I did. She is a wonderful woman.'
"We remained the best of friends and had the highest respect for each other."
My acquaintance said, "And that's it? That's the extent of your temptation to do what the world believes comes naturally? You didn't steal, fornicate, nor succumb to anger or dispair?"
"That's it," I replied. "I don't have to look back and regret that I stole or lied or hated or played my body cheap. I don't flaunt a holier-than-thou attitude, either. I'm just terribly grateful to my Guardian Angel for whispering loudly to me, 'I wouldn't do that, Norma, if I were you. It's wrong.'
"I got in the habit of saying, 'Thank you, God,' and walked away from temptation. That's the shocking truth."

XXVI

Stormy Weather

There are those days when the rain falls from gray skies all day long. As if to drown out the joyousness of the holiday season that Saturday between Christmas and New Year, the torrent from the heavens was relentless. The winter temperature just one and two degrees above freezing was on the threatening edge of an ice storm. Many inches of wet, clinging snow began to form chunks of frozen slush.

Streams of sluggish water flowed lazily on the oiled township road and lingered in low lying spots beside curbless lawns. Now and then a motorist on a mission that could no longer be delayed hit a deep puddle, releasing water in an angry spray of swish, ker-plop wetness.

Watching from my window I commented, "Percy, those chuckholes are getting larger and larger. We had better call the sheriff's office before someone is hurt or damages his car."

"No need to phone today. Every road crew and every street department will be on an alert for a freeze or more snow."

"It could put a dent in the BBB formalities tonight if this keeps up."

"It seems to me that a few years ago one of the winter formals had to be cancelled because of bad weather.

"I hate to see you go out in this weather right now. Why

not wait until after lunch? It should not take long to pick up your tuxedo and my corsage," I said.

"It's better to go now and get it over with. I need to go to the barber shop, and Saturdays are their busiest even in bad weather. I'll try to be back here by lunch time. Do you have everything you need for the breakfast?" he asked.

"Think so."

"How many guests are you . . . we expecting?"

"Between twenty and twenty-five. One or two of our friends have house guests. There could be more. They will all be here, you can be sure—weather permitting, of course—curious to see our new home.

"Remember when we were nobodies? Nobody important enough to host guests or to be invited to share an evening with the 'Four Hundred' elite?" I recalled.

"Nobodies, somebodies, a lot of nonsense no matter how you look at it. We are the same as we have always been, you and me, doing the best we could, treating others respectfully and struggling to enjoy some of the good things of life.

"We've done some unusual things. We started out with nothing, raised two wonderful children, shared our home with ten foster children, two of your nephews and half the kids you've been teaching. We have five grandchildren, we've bought two homes, traveled to Africa, and . . . ."

"And more than anything else, I think our marriage has proved something. We have proved that couples can grow together. It is good when college graduates can marry college graduates, but it is even more commendable when a couple starts from different beginnings and moves together as we have—North, South, Catholic, Baptist, professional, laborer. Ha, you never expected me to utter such words, did you?" I confessed.

"Knowing you all these years, nothing surprises me."

"One of the nurses at the hospital called my attention to

our marriage and scolded me a bit. I think she fell in love with you or at least thought I did not really appreciate what I had."

"Oh, she did, did she? That was a few years ago. I'll want to hear all about it. So, a secret admirer I never knew about put you wise to me, huh? Hold it until I come back. I won't be gone long. Got to go."

Percy gave me a big hug and started for the door. He called to say, "I'm taking the Buick instead of my old Chevy. It's heavier and safer in this kind of weather. See you."

The Better Business Buddies (BBB) Club was comprised of a small group of professionals, an agency executive or two and a number of energetic entrepreneurs. Each member invited six to eight couples to join them at their annual formal Christmas Ball. Their holiday tables were artistically arranged and laden with exotic hors d'oeuvres and expensive liquors. The guest lists were carefully scrutinized to guard against undesirables with questionable morals and boisterous social conduct. Nathan and Marian Doyle were first to invite us as their guests. It became a standing invitation until Mr. Doyle's passing. Then Booker and Bernice Haygood added us to their guest list.

The anticipation of the evening ahead was as thrilling as the occasion itself. A Negro assemblage is the most beautiful on earth, with its range of skin colors from midnight black through all shades of brown and tan to yellow-white. The ladies' gowns, dazzling and fashionable, would transform the ballroom into a paradise of majestic beauty. Part of the excitement was to see if this year's gowns, many personally designed, could out-distance the previous year's elegance.

The Black men in their tuxedos could make me want to shout or weep. They exhibited such grandeur, such dignity. It would be so nice if the hour of two o'clock never arrived to signal the ball was over.

So much pride, self-esteem and purpose was always in evidence at the BBB affairs. Everywhere one recognized an individual who had somehow pushed aside the roadblocks to accomplishment and had dispelled the predictions of incapability. Their achievements were monumental. The scrub woman's son had become a doctor. The steelworker's daughter had become a college professor. No one present had succumbed to failure.

I wondered if the highest type of white gatherings were quite as heterogeneous as ours. Did postal clerks, dog wardens, sheriff's aides, telephone operators, city councilwomen, beauticians and typists fraternize together with the town's finest doctors, lawyers, dentists and business executives?

The economic range of the BBB guests in the '50s and '60s ranged from the forty-to fifty-thousand-dollar incomes of the physicans to the fifteen-to eighteen-thousand-dollar salaries of the teachers, social workers and steelworkers. The single-digit salaries of typists, store clerks and elevator operators fluctuated between six-thousand and nine-thousand dollars.

The common badge of being eligible to be present at the BBB gathering was respectability. All were role models, exemplifying stable marriages, steady jobs, a business or professional skill, home ownership, good morals, promising children (evidence of good parenting) and participation in community endeavors. One indiscreet incident could remove a guest's name from the invitation list.

It was a thrilling experience to be on the same dance floor with Dr. and Mrs. P. M. Ross, Judge Clay and Mary Hunter, County Prosecutor Ira and Genevieve Turpin, Dr. and Mrs. S. W. Gregory, Dr. and Mrs. William Wilson, Mr. and Mrs. Douglas Matthews, the Dr. and Mrs. Thompson from Alliance and Dr. and Mrs. Robert Richardson. It was even a greater thrill to see the camaraderie as the BBB members and their guests stopped at table after table to greet their professional peers.

Good dancers at the BBB affairs never had an opportunity to sit out a dance. Even a clumsy dancer like myself would be invited to a half dozen or so dances. Percy danced two dances with me, the opening grand march and the last dance. I cherished that last dance when the lights were low and the music soft and slow. It was our precious moment. I had never seen Percy escort another woman to the dance floor.

I must have reminisced for an hour or so while arranging the food for the predawn breakfast. The fruit cup was prepared, the egg and milk batter was mixed for scrambled eggs and the biscuit ingredients placed in a bowl. It would take just twenty minutes after our guests arrived around 3 a.m. for me to heat the oven, put the sausage and bacon in, shape the biscuits and connect the coffee pot. All was in readiness. I could lie down and nap for awhile.

Preparing to doze off, I recalled the first affair I had planned for Percy in 1932 or 1933. His birthday was approaching. I wanted to give him a party. We had no young married couple friendships. Percy had a host of pool hall friends, so why not a stag party? I urged Eva, Percy's cousin, to enlist the aid of Dolphus Brinson and Crip to select ten to twelve of Percy's friends and invite them to the house. The menu would be fried chicken, potato salad, rolls, beer, coffee and cake. The party was to be from 9:00 to 12:00. Each card table had a brand new deck of cards awaiting expert hands. Dolphus was to keep Percy occupied at the pool hall and then accompany him home around 9:15.

The guests arrived early and quieted themselves in the dimly lit living room. Percy and Dolphus came into the house through the dining room side entrance. When he turned the lights on, a dozen of his "around the pool table" buddies shouted, "Happy Birthday, Pup-Pup!" Pup-Pup was one of Percy's nicknames.

He was surprised, shocked and angered. He let out a,

"What the . . . ?"

"It's your birthday, man, Happy Birthday!" several voices shouted.

"Excuse me a minute," Percy interrupted, looking at all of the intruders in his home. He placed one hand on the stairway door leading to the second-floor. "Excuse me, please."

The door closed behind him as he made his way upstairs. I supposed that he had gone to the bedroom to change his clothing. After a period of time when he had not come back downstairs, I decided to find out why the delay.

"You are not dressed? Your friends are waiting for you. What in the world are you doing?" I blurted, trying to hide my annoyance.

"I'm getting ready for bed."

"You can't, Percy. This is your party."

"No, no, this is your party. You invited them. These are not people who belong in my home."

"But they are your friends, the people you have to be with and play cards with every day."

"The men downstairs are my pool hall, Cherry Avenue, barber shop buddies. What I do and who my friends are downtown or up the street is one thing. What goes on and who comes to my house is another. I don't want them here!"

"What shall I tell them?"

"Tell them anything you like, but just get them out of here."

I returned downstairs and called Dolphus aside in the kitchen. "Dolphus, Percy is upset with me. He has gone to bed. He won't join the party."

"Don't worry. I think I understand Pup-Pup. We'll be out of here in a jiffy. I'll know what to say to the boys. You go back upstairs and let me handle everything."

Percy continued to enjoy evenings with his pool hall buddies, but they never came to our house. I lay there awhile, recalling other near-forgotten incidents. I did not fall asleep.

When the clock chimed 2 p.m., I realized my husband should have been home more than an hour ago. What was his delay? Maybe he had a longer wait at the barbershop than he anticipated. By 3 p.m., I was concerned. Where could he be? The weather had not worsened, but it was still an ugly day. I phoned the barber shop. No, "Pup-Pup" had not been there.

I phoned the shop where he was to pick up his tuxedo. "His suit is still here."

"Thank you."

I brought his dog "Spot" in from the garage to keep me company.

It was four o'clock. I phoned Dr. Gregory's office. Maybe Percy had taken ill. There was no answer. I was about to get out the old Chevy and drive eight miles to town, but where would I go to look for him? I began pacing back and forth from the kitchen, to the family room, to the living room where the large north and west floor to ceiling picture windows allowed me to see the length of Pleasant View Avenue to Schneider Road. My, it was nasty out! Could he have had an accident? I phoned Aultman and Mercy Hospitals. His name was not on the emergency lists.

Dark descends around 4:30 p.m. in Ohio in late December and early January. As the darkening shadows merged with the gray skies, I heard Percy pull up in the slush-filled, graveled driveway. I rushed to the door.

"Percy, where have you been?" I was looking at my husband who had aged ten years since leaving the house six hours earlier. A purple gray hue discolored his deep brown countenance. He said not a word but handed me a plastic bag containing his formal and a florist box with my corsage. He entered the family room, motioned his pet Dalmation to the floor and slumped into his favorite chair. He began to sob.

"Percy, what is wrong? Tell me. Are you ill? Where have

you been?"

"I've been in jail!"

"Jail?"

"Yes, downtown in the city jail."

"Not for tasting grapes in the supermarket," I quipped lightheartedly. Whenever we went grocery shopping and passed the fruit section with those beautiful transparent white grapes from California, Percy would pluck three or four before filling a sack of his favorite fruit.

"No . . . I . . . my car splashed water on a couple of women on West Tuscarawas across from the Mellett Mall. It wasn't anything that could've been avoided. The streets were full of water. I hit a chuckhole. The traffic cop came after me and signaled me to the curb. He asked me why I hadn't tried to avoid splashing the pedestrians."

"I couldn't help it. How was I to know that chuckholes were there? I didn't fill the chuckholes with water," I replied.

"Don't talk back to me, nigger!" he shouted. "You and your big Buick don't impress me."

"I can't repeat all that he said. He put on his siren and lights and ordered me to follow him to the police station. I've been in jail since 11:30 this morning."

"Why didn't you phone me?"

"How could I? I tried. I asked to phone you. No one paid any attention to me. No one told me why I was there, what I was being charged with. This cop pushed me into a cell, locked the door and forgot all about me. I would still be there if Judge Clay Hunter had not come to the jail for some reason and spied me. He looked at me and remarked, 'Percy, what the hell are you doing here?' "

"I just cried, 'I don't know. I don't know!' "

"Within minutes he had me out of there and here I am. He told me to phone him Monday morning if I wanted to file charges for unlawful detention. I'm to bring him . . . I don't know what I'm to do . . . or can do."

Percy was sobbing with the sounds of anger and humiliation that only come from deep within the soul of a wounded grown man. He frightened me as he continued his story.

"You don't know how I felt behind those bars. I was fenced in like an animal. It was a nasty, filthy place and so cold. I'm chilled to the bone. I can't go to the dance tonight. I don't have a haircut for one thing. Do you mind going alone?"

"Yes, I do mind going alone. You don't really need a haircut anyway. All you need is a shave. So dry your tears, take a good hot bath and get into bed. By midnight you will feel a lot better. We just won't let a two-bit cop spoil the rest of this evening for us."

I kept up a constant stream of chatter as I drew his bath, but I was thinking that an angel must have sent Judge Hunter to the city jail on such a wintry Saturday afternoon. I dreaded to think what could have happened to Percy if he had been detained that whole weekend without his medication.

After his bath, I lay down beside my husband and cradled him in my arms as he had held me so often following my nervous breakdown. I sang to him my favorite song. His was still "My Blue Heaven," by Whitting and Donaldson. Mine was "For the Good Times," by Kris Kristofferson, with a phrase change here and there.

I sang:
>Lay your head
>Upon my pillow,
>Hold your warm
>And tender body
>Close to mine.
>Hear the whisper
>Of the raindrops,
>Blowing soft
>Against the window

And make believe
You love me,
One more time—
For the good times.

Soon after midnight we drove to the BBB formal. No one could tell from our outward appearance and demeanor the inner turmoil we felt. I insisted that Percy dance every other slow dance with me so we could be in a close consoling embrace. His heartbeat felt like a fast-racing motor boat. I knew his blood pressure was dangerously high.

I was worried. Just a few years earlier Dr. Thompson from Alliance dropped dead on that same dance floor while dancing. "Dear God," I prayed, "do not let that happen to Percy."

The breakfast that followed in our home was a joyous, festive affair. We were repeatedly complimented for our beautiful home. We made no mention of the police and jail episode. The Booker Haygoods, our BBB hosts, were the last to leave. Having seen the pond and stream at the rear of our land, they suggested we get together for a fishing party "as soon as the weather permits."

There was never any word from the police department, city hall or Judge Clay E. Hunter. No summons, no charges, nothing. Daily as he scanned the mail, Percy would question, "I wonder why they don't mail me something and get this ridiculous thing over with. I can't stand it."

One evening he cried, "It makes no difference how good a life a Black man lives, he is still a slave to a White man's bigotry. A Negro can avoid a life of crime, he can be a good husband, a good father, a good provider, but some red-necked cracker, a white policeman, some Ku Klux Klanner or John Bircher at heart who hates the color of my skin can insult me, arrest me, beat me up, deny me and if I were in Mississippi, lynch me for no legitimate reason whatsoever!

"I left the South in fear of the lyncher's rope, but I have

been lynched right here in Canton, Ohio, in a different way. Look at me. Look at you. Are we respected any more than the pimp, the whore, the thief, the murderer or the dope peddler from skid row? No, we're just niggers!"

"Hush, Percy, hush! Don't talk like that. You must not think like that," I begged.

"I've got to talk about it or I'll burst from the pain inside." He was crying and trembling.

"When we lived on Prospect and Ninth Street Southwest," he continued, "it's hard to recall how many times as I walked home around midnight or after that a policeman in a cruiser would pull up to me and say 'Hey, Bud, what you all doing in a white neighborhood this time of night?'

" 'I live just a few blocks up the street, 817 Prospect,' I would say. 'You could drive me home, but I need the exercise.'

"I was polite, I smiled; but I wanted to bash his bigoted face in. You see, me—you—we as Negroes should not have lived west of Shroyer Avenue. The police trailed me until I got on the porch and walked into my house.

"Sometimes I purposely stayed out late to see who would stop me next. You'll never know what I would have said or done if you had met me at the door complaining and quarrelsome about my coming home so late at night. But you never bothered me, and I never said 'Thanks! Thanks for not adding to my anger and frustration.' "

"So, militant you had other reasons for staying out late. You had me thinking all these years that you could not stand my company or that you were a true night owl person." I tried to sound as though a mystery had been solved.

"When we had just one car, I was always faced with the decision, should I have the car so I could drive home without interference or should I leave the car with you in case of an emergency?" He paused to calm his voice.

"The other day I was in my own car, but it was not a beat-up

Ford. And I was in the wrong neighborhood. Today, in 1971, Negroes are not to be driving Buicks in a suburban shopping district on a rainy day unless they have the power of Houdini or a Moses. We must be able to part the flood waters so not a drop splashes even to the curb. We can never win with our Black skin. We are so visible. We can never know how the white man reasons or how much he hates us."

Many an evening as I came in from Central Hower High School, I would observe my husband sitting in his favorite chair, affectionately petting his Dalmation while copious tears rolled down his cheeks.

I feared for his health. He had done so well in the five years since his illness. His purple-gray pallor frightened me. He continued working. His physician was examining him every three months. His prognosis had been very good. In February, one month after the jail incident, Percy's doctor advised him to come in for monthly checkups for awhile.

Calling me aside, Doctor asked, "Is there anything in particular bothering your husband? His heart, his kidneys, his blood pressure all show disturbing changes. Make sure he takes his medication, watch his diet and keep him out of mischief."

How does one soothe a broken heart of humiliation, insult, disrespect, contempt and ridicule? How does one bolster another's self-esteem and transmit a feeling of strength to one who feels so powerless?

Percy's moods began to affect me. One day I said to him, "If you retire this spring, I shall take a year's sabbatical or a leave of absence so we can travel leisurely, enjoy our home and do a lot of fun things together."

The next day I shared with him, "Akron University, after an eight-year silence, has just told me that I have been accepted as a school psychologist intern. I am to contact Mr. Cardinal of the Kent City Schools for an interview. I think

I shall turn the internship down or ask for a year's delay. I am not too keen about traveling twenty-five miles back and forth each day. You will be here alone from 7 a.m. or earlier until 6 p.m. That is not fair to you.

"Anyhow, I am not sure that I am that keen about being a pioneer again. To become the first Black school psychologist might be a challenge I can do without. I am darn close to retirement anyhow. I am almost sixty-two years old."

Percy stopped me. "I've never known you to be so full of excuses. Why are you hesitating? You've wanted to become a psychologist for years. Were you not going to file a suit against the college for not assigning you to an internship? Now it's in your grasp and you hesitate. I don't like that. It's not like you. And don't talk to me about my retirement.

"I wouldn't know what to do away from Republic Steel and away from my buddies on the pool gang. I may take three or four weeks off and enjoy the ducks on the pond out back. I may go fishing with Haygood, but that's no reason for you to delay accepting this opportunity. You accept!"

Changing his tone to one of real joy he remarked, "Can you imagine? My wife is going to be a psychologist! . . . A real honest-to-goodness psychologist! Wait till I tell the boys downtown about this!" We embraced and both of us were glad.

One week later, May 13, Percy was dead. We were retiring. Percy was telling me how he had arranged the television in the bedroom. Did I want to turn it on and see how beautiful the color was?

"No. I would like to read awhile. Will I disturb you?"

"No, of course not. Your reading in bed all these years is just par for the course."

"What was the rest of the day like?" I asked.

"Nothing special. The dog and I watched the ducks swimming up and down the stream. There's some new ducklings and there will be more."

"How do you know that?"

"I found a nest of duck eggs under the evergreen shrubbery by the kitchen window."

"Really! Tomorrow I may take a peek. You look a bit tired. Are you taking your medicine?"

"Yes, for all the good it's doing. Well, good night."

"Good night."

We kissed. I propped my pillow, adjusted the bed lamp and began to read.

Within the hour Percy began breathing strangely. He was leaving me, I knew. I phoned our daughter, a half-mile away, to come immediately. There was an ambulance, a trip to the hospital, a priest, anointing, telephone calls and arrangements.

Three days later eight priests concelebrated the funeral Mass. Among those paying tribute were members of the Third Order of St. Francis, Christian Family members, Cursillo members, members of the Masonic Lodge, co-workers from Republic Steel and hundreds from all walks of life. A police escort solemnly saluted the funeral cortege. I was alone. I did not wail or cry. There were and still are tears of thanksgiving for God's gift to us of five additional years filled with a new kind of love approaching heaven on earth.

Percy's death followed that of my mother, Shuggie, by nearly a year and a half. I might not have made the move to North Canton if she had been alive. When she and Ruth lived alone, there were few days when I did not stop for a visit. We had a close relationship.

A Sunday routine was to take Mom to her Mass at St. Peters, go to my favorite Mass at St. Josephs, pick up Mom to take her back home and then go to St. Marys to teach a CCD class of junior high students.

Both Aunt Clella and Shuggie were widowed after a four year mid-life and late life marriage. Aunt Clella returned to Canton and worked as a cook at Aultman Hospital. Shuggie kept house and cared for Rae, a mentally retarded child, whose mother would not place her in an institution. Ruth, despite Aunt Clella's influence, could not adapt to the part-time kitchen jobs at the hospital. She became Mom's helper about the house and yard.

Each summer Shuggie enthusiastically cared for Eugene's and Carl's children, Robert, Carol and Raymond. Ethel, Virginia, and I contributed financially to Shuggie's support.

Mom slept peacefully away on January 4th after telling Ruth to take the radio upstairs to her bedroom and leave her alone to rest awhile. Three hours later when Ruth thought she ought to urge Shuggie to have some lunch, she discovered that Mom had died. It was as she had predicted she would, and similar to Aunt Clella's death two years earlier.

"You will never have to worry about doctor bills, hospital care or a rest home for me," Mom reiterated more than once. "When my time comes to leave this world, I'll just lie down on my living room couch and that will be it."

Ruth lived alone in the family home. I even considered sharing my home with her, but she upset me emotionally. She insisted that Percy was not dead. She would call me on the phone to report that she had seen him on the square when she was in town shopping.

That summer I supervised a children's camp at Brunnerdale Seminary for more than one-hundred inner city boys and girls. The children, the staff and the activities helped to allay my grief. I also sensed Percy's presence. He walked by my side and whispered to me. Whenever I was about to make a decision or arbitrate some differences between staff personnel, I would hear Percy's warning. "Remember, you can be so damn dumb at times. Please take it easy."

Toward the end of summer as I prepared to commute to Kent to begin my internship, it became more difficult for me to enter our dream home. The flood of memories overpowered me and drained me of all vitality. "Spot," Percy's Dalmatian, would jump upon his favorite chair and whine, as much as to say, "Where is he? Why doesn't he come and walk with me in the woods?"

I missed Percy's whistling, his eager greeting when I entered the house. I found it difficult going to Mass on Sunday. We always held hands, and that was before the Catholic Church shook hands with their fellow worshippers or uplifted them in prayer. This Sunday ritual between us became a gesture of pure love. It began as a reprimand, a gentle slap to keep me from picking my fingers. When I was a bundle of nerves I used to dig at the cuticles of my fingers until they bled. Percy would grab my hand and hold it firmly in his. That message of love and concern calmed me. It also caused me to thank my God, my Guardian Angel and the saints that I was so blessed to have such a caring mate.

The first month of internship at Kent initiated many changes. I engaged a single room with the DeFranges, a white family in Kent. I put our dream home up for sale. My new tasks, new surroundings and new co-workers were exciting. I had no time to grieve. Remembering Percy's words of encouragement and his pride in my pursuing a new career, gave me strength beyond belief, until the weather began to turn cold.

As the chilling December days of rain and snow heralded the approach of Christmas, I became very depressed. My first Christmas alone. What would I do? There would be no midnight Mass to which we had always invited some fifteen to twenty Catholic and non-Catholic friends. Percy would not be there to co-host the after-midnight breakfast that had become a twenty-five-year tradition in our home. I was sure to refuse to attend the BBB holiday affair as a widow.

With a two-week winter school vacation ahead, what should I do? Where should I go? I did not want to intrude upon a family unit. My sister, Virginia, lived in Chicago and Ethel lived in Columbus. I enjoyed frequent visits with them, but Christmas was their family togetherness. It should not include me.

Our son, Alluren, and his wife, Barbara, and their son, Brent, lived in East Hartford, Connecticut. What would I do there? Percy and I had spent our last Christmas together with Al and Barbara the year before. We had gone shopping and Percy tried his best to get me to purchase a beautiful, quite-expensive fur coat. I said no.

Percy remarked to Al, "What is it about your mother that makes her so afraid to spend money on clothes? Oh, she always looks neat, don't misunderstand me, but I want her to look elegant. Is your wife like that?"

"Have you looked in Barbara's clothes closets?" Al asked. "Note I used the plural when I said closets. She was a model before we married; but I'm like you, Dad, I want the best for my wife, too."

"Say that loud enough for your mother to hear," Percy urged.

Al was so much like his father. I would visit him at another time and season when memories were not so fresh.

Norma Jean's marriage had terminated in a divorce. Her father's fears were real. She and the four children were living in North Canton. She was having a difficult time making new adjustments. She was enrolled in college, had a job and a household to manage.

Norma Jean was devastated by her father's death. They were so close. Her whole world had fallen apart.

At a time when we should have been drawn closer together, a deep chasm seemed to be separating us. She came to my home less than a month after Percy's passing and found me sobbing. She had never seen me so disturbed. Looking at me she screamed, "Stop crying! I can't stand it! I need you. I am so alone. No one understands what I am going through.

No one, not even you."

She rushed from the house. Her grief distressed me. I remembered my mother's Gethsemane when my father deserted her. I could not witness my daughter's agony or even think about her one-parent family adjustments. I knew she was going through the torments of hell.

"Not now, dear God," I prayed. "It is too soon after Percy's passing. I don't have him to lean on. I can't be drawn into her sorrow. I have to back away. Please, please forgive me."

In Kent my brain was in a whirr. It zigzagged, from bank notes to projective techniques, from attorney fees to intelligence tests, from car repairs to operant behavior, from dry cleaning and laundry to parent conferences, from a physical examination to group dynamics, and from eating and sleeping to loneliness. A fragmented melody crept into my consciousness. It filled me with the undeniable emptiness of widowhood.

I kept hearing . . . "Stormy weather . . . Since he's gone away . . . Don't know why . . . Stormy weather . . . There's no sun up in the sky . . . My man and I ain't together . . . It's rainin' . . . rainin' . . . When he went away . . . Stormy weather . . . Now he's gone to stay . . . gone to stay . . . I'm weary all the time . . . All I do is pray . . . The Lord above will let me . . . let me . . . Walk in the sun once more." Walk in the sun once more!

That was it. That was what I needed. Sun. To see and feel the sun in December. I had to get away! Take off! Travel! Escape to a land of sunshine.

Mrs. Willa Mae Webb was a former neighbor of mine. She was also a fellow club woman and friend. She was the kind of warm, caring individual who did a multitude of kindnesses to bring a smile to one's heart. A greeting card, a flower arrangement, a linen handkerchief, a basket of fruit, a telephone call that followed a birthday, a holiday, an anniversary or a hospital visit was Mrs. Webb's way of saying, "I'm thinking of you."

She often invited me to community gatherings and introduced me to Blacks I would never have met in my multi-ethnic Catholic world. I reciprocated by inviting her to my world. Often, when we were the only Blacks in a large gathering, I wondered if we had ever been referred to as the "Gold Dust Twins."

"Willa," I phoned one day in early December, "how would you like to go to Hawaii with me and a group of teachers over Christmas? We could get a suntan on Waikiki Beach."

She accepted the invitation. When during our stay in Honolulu we had a choice of island-hopping or shopping, I flew to the "Big Island," Hawaii. I wanted to visit our family friend and confidante, Father Thomas Heimann. He was pastoring the small one-hundred member Holy Rosary parish in Pahala.

Father arranged for me to spend the night with the Bowmans. Mr. Bowman was one of the sugar plantation managers. I was introduced to a number of the villagers who were some of the most gracious people I had ever met. The next morning we toured as much of the island as time would permit before I boarded the plane for Honolulu.

The palm trees, the black sand beaches, the jagged, lava-rocked ebony soil from which sprouted odd shaped trees and the strangest foliage with magnificent flowers caused me to exclaim, "I love this place. I love it! I love it!"

There were no snakes slithering in the thick underbrush of the rainforests or the mountain slopes. Within an area of twenty miles one could traverse volcanic basins, lush rolling valleys or the stark desert plains. Gentle breezes stirred the ocean waves, tickled the tall sugar cane stalks and lovingly caressed each inhabitant.

When Mrs. Webb and I boarded the plane home, I knew I would return again and again. There might be many years of unfinished work ahead of me in Canton, Ohio, the town of my birth, but I had just adopted a second home, Hawaii.

When the cold Ohio rains of winter fall from the heavens and snow clouds threaten to cover the ground with whiteness, I fly away. I go where the weather is warm, where some of the friendliest people on earth greet me with sincere alohas and colorful leis. In Hawaii the sun shines during the rain, and rainbows—often double-rainbows—glorify the sky with multicolored wonderment. God loves colors.

At night the stars appear in the midnight-hued heavens with such brilliance. The feeling abounds that if I stretched my hands up far enough, I could touch the hand of God. Then, with my hand in His, I would understand the promise that some day the stormy weather would pass. There would be no more denials, no more racial and ethnic disparities and no fences between.

The End

Author's Notes

Racial designations

The racial designations applied to the descendents of the African slaves brought to America in the 1600s have varied.

Colored

The term colored was widely used by Americans until the mid-thirties. Even the terms mulatto and octaroon were commonly used to designate degrees of Caucasian-African mixture and skin color differences. Many "colored" displayed a consciousness of their Caucasian roots and enjoyed some privileges among whites.

Negro

Negro, meaning black in Latin, enjoyed prominent usage from the mid-thirties until the Civil Rights movement of the '60s. Efforts to displace Negro with Brown American were unsuccessful.

Afro-American

The designation, Afro-American, combines a people's African origins with their American birthright. Afro-American is the most academic classification of nearly 30 million of America's dark-hued citizens.

Black

In the 1960s, with the impetus of the Civil Rights movement, a race of people put aside their emphasis upon their variable Caucasian mixtures. They chose to express pride in their dominant African roots. Black became their identity. In this book black is used as an adjective (black), referring to skin color, and as a proper noun (Black), designating a race of people.

People of Color

As this book goes to press there is a growing tendency for many Blacks to refer to themselves as "people of color." This term appears to seek identity and unity with people of dark skin from a diversity of nations and cultures.

Index

AAA, 368
  Green Book, 368
Abbott, Robert, 256
Africa, 66, 218, 225, 387, 406
  Belgian Congo, 387
  Kinshasa, 387, 388
  burgomasters, 388
  Zaire, 387
African, Methodist Episcopal (AME) Church, Canton, Ohio, 51
  Zion Conference, 83
African, 141
Afro-Americans, 58, 141
  hair styles, 393
  History, 404
Aida, 148
Akron, Ohio, 230
  crime, 412-13
  School system, 339, 341, 364, 392
  First Black Counselor, 392
Akron University, Akron, Ohio, 352, 436
Alliance, Ohio, 324, 434
Alexander, Anne, 201
American minority reactions, 375-76
Anderson, Marian, 229, 390
Andrews, A. A., 256
Anne of Green Gables, 390
apartheid, 328
Archer, Esther, 273
Archer, John, 256
Armstrong School of Social Service, Philadelphia, Pa., 71, 112, 127
Arnold, Dr. Dwight, 337
Assumption of the Blessed Virgin Mary, 246
Atlantic Tea Store, Canton, Ohio, 83
Aultman Hospital, Canton, Ohio, 143
"Aunt Jemimas", 396, 400

BBB Club, 420, 425, 427-28, 429, 434, 440
B & O Railroad tracks, 12, 144, 164
Baptist Churches, 308, 419
Barnes, Owen, 195

Barrett, Father, 250
Barrick, 120, 123
Barthel, Catherine, 245
Bayes, Sarah, 310
Beane, Frank, 256
Beavers, Louise, 71
Beck, Helen, 310
Bellevue, Ohio, 51, 219
Bender's Restaurant, 296
Beneficial Loan Company, 327
Bennett College, N. Carolina, 241, 281
Bermuda, 358, 369
  Hamilton High School, 369
  curriculum, 369
Bernhardt, Sarah, 289
Beshara, Dr. Edmund, 333, 335
Bethune, Mary McLeod, 229
Bircher, John, 434
Black community, Stark Co., Ohio, 70
  employment, 70
  Churches, 309
  impoverished underachievers, 402
  heritage awareness, 402, 415
  negative socializing influences, 408-11
  self-image, 408
Black Hand Gang, 10
Black History, 403-4
Blessed Martin DePorres Catholic Service Store, 230, 236
Blessed Sacrament, 234
Bluford, Mrs. Ida, 217-20
Bowmans, 443
Boy Scout Troop 16, St. Joseph, Canton, Ohio, 301
  Oath & Promise, 302
  Scout Law, 302
  Eagle Scout award, 325
Boylan, Nancy, 370
Boys Town, 368
Brinson, Dolphus, 429-30
Brooks, Mrs. Leader, 342
Brookside Country Club, Stark Co., Ohio, 153-55, 172, 289
Broomhandle, Mrs., 217, 241, 306
Brown, Mrs., 57, 60, 61
Brumbaugh Lumber Co., Canton, Ohio 144, 275
Brunnerdale Seminary, 363, 439

Stoydale-Brunnerdale Summer Camp, 363
Buffalo, New York, 422
East Aurora Country Club, 288, 423
Burwell, Eva, 168, 174-76, 429
Louise, 194
"Buster", 82, 83

Calhoun, James, 256
California, 368
Calvary, 305
Canada, 358
Canton, Ohio, 14, 59, 60, 66, 70, 150, 158, 386, 435
Administration Building, 62
'City of Diversified Industry', 14
City Auditorium, 54
City Jail, 103
industries, 273
Family Service and Children's Bureau, 168
Foster Care Agency, 168, 174
patromen, 432-33
Public Schools, 194, 338
Public Square, 120
School Board, 59, 60, 61, 199
School Superintendent, 62
Urban League, 71, 112, 114, 129, 166, 183, 193-94, 200, 208, 272, 409
drama club, 207
Canton College Center, 32
Canton Repository, 268, 337
Cape Verde Islands, 307
Cardinal, Mr., 436
Carlsbad Caverns, 368
Carmichael, Elizabeth, 419-20, 422
Carnegie Institute of Cleveland, 326
Catholic Church, 221, 228, 233, 240-41, 307, 309, 419
Afro-American culture, 328
Anointing of the Sick, 385
Board of Education, 388
Catholic Diocese, 232
Catholic Grade Schools, 242
Catholic High School, 345
Christian Family Members, 438
Cursillo, 438
Council of Catholic Women, 309
Interracial Council, 309
Mass, 305
Order of St. Francis, 438
traditions, 277, 292
Central Catholic High School, Canton, Ohio, 242, 324, 353
Central Hower High School, Akron, Ohio, 401, 403, 436
Self-Awareness Class, 403, 412
bus trip to New York, 412
Chicago, Illinois, 367
Chicago Defender, The, 256
Chinese, 141
Christian Family Movement, 387
Christianity, 276, 304, 405
Christ's journey to Calvary, 225
Christmas Seals, 275
chairman, 306
Cincinnati, Ohio, 238
Civil Rights Movement, 386, 409
Civil War, 140, 271, 286
Veteran, 391
Clark, Miss Sadie, 272
Cleveland, Ohio, 42, 46, 57, 79, 148, 246, 366, 382, 418
East Side, 79
Exposition, 366
Health Museum, 310, 343
Clinic, 381, 384
Cleveland Call & Post, The, 256
Climalene Co., Canton, Ohio, 144
Cole, Dr. Simon, 16
Collison, Margaret, 306
Columbia University, 16
Communicable Disease Control, 275
Congress Lake, Stark County, Ohio, 17, 45, 46
Cook, Sadie, 120
Corn Palace, 368
Corrigan, Sally, 373, 387
Thomas, 387
Cotton Club, New York, 236
Council for Interracial Justice, 247
Council of Catholic Women, 232
Courtland Hotel, Canton, Ohio, 154
Crawford, John W., 183, 193-94, 197, 200-3
Crisis, The, 256
Curtis, Mayor C.C., Canton, Ohio, 103, 372

Day, Dorothy, 230, 236, 239
Hospice, 236, 238
soup kitchens, 237
farms, 237
Daily Worker, The, 230, 236

INDEX 449

Davis, Margaret, 230-31, 235, 242, 326, 368
  Sammy, Jr., 405
DeFranges family, 440
DeMarco, Mr. and Mrs. Dutch (O.J.), 387
Democratic Party, 207
Depression, 99, 137, 254
Deshler Wallick Hotel, Columbus, Ohio, 243
Detroit, Michigan, 172, 246, 418
DeWeese, Dr. O., 107, 131
Dietz, Leroy, 392
divorce, 331-32
Douglas, Melvyn, 267
"Don't Bother Me, I Can't Cope", 412
Doyle Confectionary, Canton, Ohio, 195
Doyle, Nathan, 256, 427
  Marian, 427
Drexel, Mother Katharine, 327
DuBois, W.E.B., 193, 256, 289
Dueber Hampden Watch Works, 216
Dueber Theater, Canton, Ohio, 371
Dueber School, Canton, Ohio, 12, 215, 286
Dunbar, Paul Lawrence, 390

Earle Theater, Philadelphia, Ohio, 130
East Hartford, Connecticut, 441
Easter Sunday, 226
Eastern Star, 218
Ebony Magazine, 282, 409
  "The Conspiracy to Make Blacks Inferior", 1974, 409
Elder Finney's Pentecostal Cong., Canton, Ohio, 221
Elks Lodge, 218
Ellington, Duke, 412
Ellis Island, 58, 388
Ellis, Iola, 230-36, 242, 326, 384-85
Elsaesser, Louis, 103, 167
Elsie Dinsmore, 390
England, 358
Employment Services Office, 271
Episcopal Church, 51
Eppy, Ben, 38
Erlanger, Mr., 422
Eskimo, 141
Evans, Clella (aunt), 9, 10, 11, 13, 45, 54, 72, 109, 118, 172, 241, 292, 307, 438-49
  Clella Dorsey (Grandma), 9, 13, 17, 49, 51, 55, 80, 86, 111, 117-18, 136, 140, 146-48, 161, 170-71, 178, 241, 297
  Clem, Aunt, 40
  Eugene (Uncle), 23, 154
  Ida
    see Snipes
  James Robert (Grandpa), 13, 51, 55, 67, 86, 111, 136, 154, 161, 170-71, 241, 271, 286, 391

Faust, 148
Federal Works Program, 193
Ferguson, Clotild, 71, 112, 113
"*Fiddler On The Roof*", 382-83
Firestone Country Club, 400
Fisher, Ruth, 182
  Aunt Lib, 182
Ford Motor Plant, Canton, Ohio, 290
Forty Hours Devotion, 322-23
France, 358
Francis, Mae, 245
  Rita (Mother Angelica), 245
Frazier, Charles, 256
Frease, Mrs. Harry, 9

Garbo, Greta, 267
Gardner, Eva, 307
  Mae, Perry, 307-08
Garfield Senior High School, Akron, Ohio, 364, 392, 399
  riot, 397
  Black students, 398, 400
  football team, 398
  cheerleaders, 400
Garvey, Mack Moziah, 218
Gibran, Kahlil, 335, 336
Gibson, Rev. S.E., 256
Gillespie radio repair, Canton, Ohio, 15
Gilmore, Mr., 39, 337
Good Friday, 224
Good Housekeeping, 387
  "Genteel Violence", April 1970, 387
Goodwill Union Industries, Canton, Ohio, 134
Great Britain, 268
Gregory, Dr. and Mrs. S.W., 428
Greyhound bus, 365
Group Guidance Classes, 391

Guardian, 256

Habig, Monsignor, 306-07, 309
Hannah Theater, Cleveland, Ohio, 149
Harbert, Larry, 301
Hardy, Ed, 291
Harlem, 412
Harlem Hostel, 236, 239
Harris, Baldwin, 256
Harter Bank, George D., 201
Hassel, Father, 220
Haygood, Brenice, 427, 434
  Booker, 427, 434, 437
Hawaii, 443-44
  Holy Rasary Parish, Pahala, 443
Hawkins, Wilson, 62
Heimann, Father Thomas, 239-40, 242, 294, 297, 330-32, 335, 383, 443
Helen, Dr., 329
Hollingsworth, Mr., 351
Holy Saturday, 226
Horton, Mr. Harlan, 392
Howard University, 241, 272
Hughes, Robert, 256
Hunter, Judge Clay E., 101, 104, 112, 113, 119, 256, 428, 432-34
  Jane E., 295
  Mary, 428
  Z.A., 256
Hunter's Restaurant, Z.A., 195
Hutchison's Restaurant, Canton, Ohio, 113, 115, 195

Indian, 141
Insbruck, Austria, 240
Interracial Council, 246
Italy, 358

Jackson Pool, Canton, Ohio, 372
Jacobs, Rev. Donald, 256
Jane Hunter Civic Club, 309, 420
  Pink Ball, 420
Japanese, 268
Jehovah's Witnesses, 232
Jerusalem Baptist Church, Canton, Ohio, 221-22
Jewish community, 422
"Jim Crow" Laws, 18, 70
John Carroll University, 240
Johnson, Ben, 288
Johnson, Fred, 327
Jones, Mr. and Mrs., 24, 25, 26, 29, 30, 32, 40, 45, 57
  Alma, 342
  Alvin, 32
  Jenny Lee, 343
  Suzie, 27, 28, 29, 31
Jones Junior High School, Massillon, Ohio, 339-42, 346, 352, 355, 358, 401
Joyce, Albert, 256
Junior High Achievement Test, 352
Junior Jane Hunter Club, 302
Juvenile Court, 270

Katharine Drexel's Monastery, 233
Kennedy, President John F., 392, 409
  assassination, 392
Kent, Ohio, 57, 66
  City Schools, 436
Kent State University, 16, 17, 23, 61, 65, 105, 118, 128, 200, 207, 324, 327, 336-37, 339-40
  Bachelor of Arts degree, 337
  internship, 439
  Normal School Extension Unit, Canton City School, 169
  Administration Building, 16
  Normal College, Kent, 17, 19, 21, 30, 32, 35, 37, 38, 44, 60, 64, 83, 103, 131, 274
  Psychology Dept., 337
King, Dr. Martin Luther, 177-78, 386, 409
  March on Washington, D.C., 392
Kintz, Peter, 220
Klu Klux Klan, 58, 218, 370, 434
Knights of Columbus, 246
Kobacher's Department Store, 267
Kotheimer, Monsignor, 216, 220, 222, 324
Krugliak, Sam (Atty.), 352

Lake Tahoe, 368
Latin rite Catholic church, 58
Lattimer, Mrs., 119
Lauer, Mr., 403
League of Women Voters, 207
Leahy's Grocery Store, Canton, Ohio, 164
Leatherman, Jeanette, 125, 126
LeFarge, Father, 247
Lefkowitz, Mr., 165
Leftwitch, Elder, 83
Leichenstein, Miss, 39

INDEX 451

Lend Lease Act, 268
Leonard, Mrs. John, 16, 59
Liberty Avenue School, Canton, Ohio, 60, 262
Lincoln, Abraham, 110
Lincoln High School, Canton, Ohio, 325
"Little Chicago", 10
Little Flower and Jesus, 244
Little Women, 390
Loew's Theater, 268
Lohengrin, 148
London, England, 182, 374
Lowe's State Theater, 267

Macy's Department Store, New York, 291
Majestic Hotel, Cleveland, Ohio, 366
Mang, Ada, 310
Marcere, Alberdeen (Johnson), 16, 17, 84, 85, 116
  Alluren Percy, 177-78, 181-83, 206-07, 275, 278, 301, 326-28, 371
  Barbara, 441
  Brent, 369, 441
  Jonas, 381
  Norma Jean, 146, 152, 162, 165, 167, 169-71, 181, 183, 205-07, 222, 224, 242, 275, 278, 302, 321, 322, 323, 330, 334, 371
  Percy Alluren, 11, 12, 15, 16, 17, 75, 81, 82-85, 111, 113-16, 118, 120-23, 132, 136, 140, 144-46, 150, 155, 158, 161-62, 163-64, 166-70, 173-76, 194-98, 201, 227, 231, 241, 279, 281-83, 291, 302, 321, 325, 326, 328, 329-34, 341, 366-68, 379-88, 418, 425, 427, 430-31, 434-35, 438
  Heritage, 116, 140, 142
  foster child Ella Mae, 205, 206
  foster child Johnny, 206
  foster child Marcella Oliver, 207, 242
Marcere, parents
  father, Rev. Henry Marcy, 116, 312
  mother, India Marcy, 312
Mason-Dixon Line, 308
Mason, Jesse H., 62, 64, 65, 69, 104, 343
Masonic Lodge, 384, 438

Massillon, Ohio, 200
  Board of Education, 351
  City Schools, 339
  English curriculum, 348
  tenure, 351
Master of Arts Degree, 338
  master's thesis, 338
Matthews Funeral Home, Canton, Ohio, 195
Mr. and Mrs. Douglas, 428
Mayfair Tea Room, 126
McBrady Goods, 25
McFadden, Bishop, 232, 246, 303
McKenzie & Jones, Canton, Ohio, 139
McGeehon, Miss, 12
McKinley High School, Canton, Ohio, 37, 38, 39, 64, 170, 257
McKinley Hotel, Canton, Ohio, 101
McKinley Park, Canton, Ohio, 12
McKinley Theater, Canton, Ohio, 119
McPherson, Aimee Semple, 54
Mellett Mall, Canton, Ohio, 432
Menelick Culture Club Scholarship, 16, 110, 241
Mercy Hospital, Canton, Ohio, 143, 243-44, 328, 333, 379, 381, 385
  School of Nursing, 300
Meridian, Mississippi, 168, 196, 367
Methodist Church, 308
Metropolitan Life Insurance, 143
  Nurse, 176
Metropolitan Opera House, New York, 149, 291
Meyers, Mary, 326
Mills Brothers, 82
Minor, Catherine, 306
Missionary societies, 309
Mississippi, Meridian, 16, 194, 434
Mobuto, President, 387
Model T Ford, 82
Molly Stark Tuberlosis Hospital, 259
Moore, Mr., 398
Morgan, Mrs., 343
Mormon Temple, 368
Motley, Dan, 288
Mount Calvary Baptist Church, Canton, Ohio, 221
Mount Marie H.S.
  see Central Catholic H.S.
Mount Rushmore, 368

Mount Vernon, Ohio, 282
Muslims, 409
Myricks, Mrs. William (Lessie), 346

Nannie Burroughs Club, Massillon, Ohio, 346
National Assoc. of Colored Women's Club, 387
National Urban League, 194
  Convention, Buffalo, 422
Negro History Club, 156
N.A.A.C.P., Canton Chapter, 22, 69, 70, 72, 76, 240, 247, 250, 369, 372, 400, 409, 422
  National, 194
NRA minimum wage scale, 209
Negroes, 15
  Catholics, 246
  Catholic Culture, 321
  Citizens Council, 309
nervous breakdown, 333-35, 338
  shock treatment, 333
New Orleans, Louisiana, 328
New York, New York, 182, 247, 376, 412
  Broadway, 412
Nicolay, Father, 323
Nixon, Richard, Pres., 405
North Canton, Ohio, 373, 386
Norwalk, Ohio, 22

O'Dea's Estate, 246
Ohio Bell Telephone Company, Canton, Ohio, 324
Ohio Schools, 60
Ohio State University, 357
Oliver, Marcella
  see Marcere foster child
Omaha, Nebraska, 293
"Oreo Cookies", 400, 406
Oser Mrs., 329
Ott, Conrad, 403
Ottomwa, Iowa, 247

Paddy's Restaurant, New York, 291
Page, Howard, 256
  Mrs. Howard (Georgianna Umbles), 242
  children, 242
Page's Bakery, Canton, Ohio, 195
Painted Desert, 368
PTAs, 309
Panel of American Women, 369

Paris, France, 374
Parisian Clothing Store, Canton, Ohio, 165, 418
Pathfinder Roller Skating Rink, 256
Pearl Harbor, 268, 270
Pearson, Henry, 256
Pemberton, Rev. and Mrs., 12
Pennsylvania Railroad tracks, 10
Perry, Andrew, 307
Peoples Baptist Church, Canton, Ohio, 221
Petrified Forests, 368
Philadelphia, Pa., 125, 130, 131, 132, 149, 161, 182, 226
  Amusement Park, 130
  Father Divine's dining room, 130
  Germantown, 125
  Mayfair Tea Room, 126
  YWCA, 125
Philadelphia Urban League, 71, 112, 127
Philippino, 141
Philips, Martha, 402
Phyllis Wheatly Assoc., Canton, Ohio, 155, 156
Piccadilly Hotel, New York, 412
Pittsburgh, Pa., 246
Polynesian, 141
Pope John XXIII, His Holiness, 374
Portage County Elementary Schools, Ohio, 337
Portuguese, 307-08
Poor Clair Nuns, 245
Powe Brothers, 256
  Shellie, 282-83
  Gary, 282
  Lindsey, 282
  Myra, 282
  Carl, 282
Powells Grocery, 195
Powell, Bill, 242
  Marcella Oliver, 242
  Moses, 256
Premmer, Mr. and Mrs. John, 10, 11, 125
  restaurant, Canton, Ohio, 13, 195
Program Academic Excellence, 363
Prophet, The, 335
Protestant church, 58
prostitution, 265
Public Health, 275
  nurse, 254

INDEX 453

Quinn, Joseph, 392
Quaker, 51

racism, 229, 236, 243, 249, 255, 293-310, 322, 355, 370-73, 394-403
  caucasian American racism, 422
Raleigh, North Carolina, 14, 18, 69
Ravenna, Ohio, 57
Rebecca of Sunny Brook Farm, 390
Redwood Forest, 368
Reeves, Arthur (family), 17, 19, 31
Reeves, Mrs., 45, 46, 47
Republic Steel, Canton, Ohio, 201, 266, 271, 308, 325, 420, 437
  Human Engineering Institute, 363
  Massillon Plant, 341
Richardson, Dr. and Mrs. Robert, 428
Richman Bros. Men's Clothing Store, Canton, Ohio, 16, 17, 75, 111, 115, 131, 149
Ritchie, Mr. Oscar, 200
Ritterspaugh, Miss Lena, 12
Roberts Grocery, Canton, Ohio, 36
Robinson, Ruth, 372, 422
Rollstin, Josie, 356
Roman Catholic Church, 59
Roman Legionnaires, 225
Rome, Italy, 373, 374, 376
  Tivoli Gardens, 374
Roosevelt, Eleanor, 229
F.D.R.. 263
Rosary, the Divine Office, 232, 247
Rosary and Altar Societies, 309
Ross, Dr. and Mrs. P.M., 428
Rotarians, 229
'Round the Dining Room Table, 390

St. Agnes, Cleveland, Ohio, 231
St. Emma's Military Academy, 321
St. Francis DeSales Academy, Virginia, 303, 321-23
  Blessed Sacrament Mother House, 327
St. Johns A.M.E. Zion Church, Canton, Ohio, 19, 21, 53, 76, 119, 221
St. Johns Catholic Church, Canton, Ohio, 224, 248
  minstrel show, 240, 248
St. Joseph Catholic Church, Canton, Ohio, 53, 216, 226, 323, 324, 383, 438
  school, 215, 220, 222, 322, 345
St. Martin de Porres, 373, 386
  canonization, 373-74
St. Mary's Catholic Church and School, Canton, Ohio, 13, 51, 52, 64, 205, 215, 220, 225, 330, 438
St. Mary's Seminary, Cleveland, Ohio, 240
St. Patrick's Cathedral, New York, 291
St. Patrick's Catholic Church, Kent, Ohio, 44, 51, 56, 57
St. Paul's AME Church, Canton, Ohio, 53, 119, 221
  Sunday School, 53
St. Paul's Catholic Church, Canton, Ohio, 308
  rectory, 308
St. Peter's Basilica, Rome, Italy, 374
St. Peter's Catholic Church, Canton, Ohio, 239-41, 304, 306, 438
  rectory, 242, 294
Salt Lake City, Utah, 368
Saltzman, Barb, 370
Salvation Army, Canton, Ohio, 134, 138
Sancta Clara Monastery, Canton, Ohio, 245
  Day of Recollection, 246
Saturday Evening Post, 23
Schario, Hortense, 220
Schools, Public, 310
  Parochial, 310
Schneider Lumber Co., Canton, Ohio, 144, 167, 269
Schumacker, Dr., 381, 385
Scott, George, 195
Scourfield, Clyde, 342, 346, 350-51
Seiser's, 286
Self-Awareness Class
  see Central Hower
Sharon, Pennsylvania, 45, 172, 241
Shearer, Norma, 146
Shoppers Fair, Canton, Ohio, 379
Shroyer Field, 286
"Shuggie",
  see Ida Evans Snipes
Simmons, Robert, 392
Simon of Cyrene, 225
Simpson, Father Allen, 247
Sister Anita, 382
Sister Bernadine, 234
Sister Carlotta, 322-23

Sister Gertrude, 234
Sister Hortense, 234
Sister Juliana, 246
Sister Mildred, 39, 51, 58, 225-26, 234, 337
Sixth Street swimming pool, Canton, Ohio, 372
Slaughter, L. L., 256
Slovac, 295
Smallwood, Bud, 256
Smith, Al, 76
Smith, L.J., 339, 350
Snipes, Ida Evans (Shuggie) (Mother), 9, 12, 14, 17, 18, 25, 30, 36, 40, 46, 49, 51, 52, 57, 58, 61, 68, 69, 73, 76-78, 83, 85, 99, 103-6, 109-14, 120, 123, 134-36, 150-52, 159-61, 163, 171-75, 182, 199, 206, 218, 281, 283, 284-87, 290, 324, 329, 340, 391, 438
"Snipes Bar & Grill", Canton, Ohio, 69
Snipes, Norman Sherwood (Father), 14, 36, 106, 107, 114, 123, 154, 163, 164, 181-82, 218, 283
  Carl, 36, 84, 104, 107, 119, 154-55, 172, 236, 241, 275, 281-82, 285, 288, 290-91, 301, 422, 439
    Betty, 236, 291
    Raymond, 236, 291, 439
  Ethel, 27, 28, 36, 83, 84, 85, 103, 104, 106, 107, 109, 110, 114, 120, 154-56, 172, 241, 281, 439-40
  Eugene, 36, 84, 104, 107, 114, 152-55, 172, 270, 281-83, 285, 290, 301, 325, 326
    Mary (wife), 283, 290
    Robert Eugene, 153, 283, 439
    Carole, 283, 439
  Ruth, 36, 84, 107, 123, 158, 172, 281, 285, 292, 368, 439
  Virginia, 36, 68, 84, 158, 171, 172, 241, 281, 283, 285, 341, 439-40
Snow, James B. II, 324, 369
  Jeannie, 369
  Theresa Ann, 369
Social Workers Institute, Columbus, Ohio, 243, 309
South Market School, Canton, Ohio, 60
Spahr, Miss Arlene, 391-92

Spencer, Vera, 82, 83
Stabat Mater, 224
Stanton, Mary Quinn, 207-08, 224, 225, 230, 242-44, 337
Stark County
  Board of Mental Retardation, 388
  County Ohio commissioners, 103, 167, 210
  County Tuberculosis and Health Assoc., 274, 293, 295, 310, 336, 343, 352
    office, 296-98
    Board of Directors, 306-07
Stark Dry Goods Company, Canton, Ohio, 421-22
State and Nat. Assoc. of Colored Women's Club, 295, 346
Statue of Liberty, 291
Stebbins Typewriter Rental, 269
Stephanic, Father, 309
Stern & Mann's, Canton, Ohio, 149, 418
Stewart, Mrs., 340
Stow, Harriet Beecher, 249
Strand Theater, Canton, Ohio, 119
STRIVE, 363
Supreme Court, 193
Supreme Liberty & Life Ins., 282
Swan, Miss, 39, 40, 41, 42, 43, 44, 337

Tabbs, Mrs., 119, 161, 365
  Lucille, 119, 120
  Dan, 119, 120
Talmadge, Norma, 146
Taylor, L.L., 293-300, 303-07, 309
T.V. Repair School, 290
Temple University, 31, 71, 105, 112, 114, 126, 129, 179, 207
Thanksgiving, 84, 277-78, 283
The Ten Commandments, 55, 424
Theresa Hotel, New York, 237, 291
Thompson, Dr. and Mrs., 428, 434
Till, Emmett, 367
Timken Roller Bearing Company, Canton, Ohio, 100, 128, 216, 325
Titus, George, 256
  James, 256, 269
Tomalet, Mrs., 128
Treiber, Monsignor, 215
Trotter, William Monroe, 256
Truth, Sojourner, 229, 390
tuberculosis (TB), 206, 275, 294, 300

patch testing, 310
x-raying, 310
Turner, Everhart, 282
  Everhart II, 282
  Robert, 282
  Kenneth, 282
  Diana, 282
"Two-Faced Woman", 267

Umbles, Floyd, 256
United Fund agencies, 309
United States Air Force, 328
  Aviation Physiology, 328
United States Navy, 286
"Uncle Toms", 396, 400, 405-06
Uncle Tom's Cabin, 249
Underground Railroad, 51, 406
University of Michigan, 274, 276
U.S. Civil Rights Commission, 376

Verder, Dean, 20, 21, 22, 23, 35, 65, 343

Wackerly Funeral Home ambulance service, 382, 384
Walker, Dr. J.B., 81, 113, 121, 198, 306
  Mrs. Etna, 155
  O.W., 256
Walsh, Bishop, 247
Walsh College, 363
  Upward Bound Program, 363
Wapakoneta, Ohio, 293
Warren, William, 256
Washington, Booker T., 193, 405, 409
Washington D.C., 182, 386
Washington Hotel, Canton, Ohio, 164
Webb, Willa Mae, 442-43, 444
Webster, George, 256
Weir family, 100, 101
Welfare, 278
Welsing, Dr. Frances Cress, 408
Western, Irene, 310
Westinghouse General Electric, 271-73
Westlawn Cemetery, Canton, Ohio, 241
"Whitey", 400
Wilberforce College, 81
Williams, Dr. Mantle Burt, 143, 144-45, 176, 182, 206, 372, 422
Wilson, Dora, 310
  Dr. and Mrs. William, 428
  Flip, 396
Wise, Rhoda, 243-45
Woolworth's, Canton, Ohio, 43, 166, 296
WPA, 182-83, 194, 199-203, 207-10, 211-12, 221, 261-62, 264, 270

X, Malcolm, 409
Xavier University, New Orleans, 327
YMCA, 81, 118, 286
YWCA, 23, 81, 118
Yearling, The, 390
Yellowstone National Park, 368
Yosemite National Park, 368
Youngstown, Ohio, Diocese, 247
  School Board, 388

Zollinger's, 139

Songs:

My Blue Heaven, 16, 85, 150, 227, 433
Let Me Call You Sweetheart, 6
Ain't Misbehavin, 16
When The Red Red Robin Comes Bob Bob Bobbin Along, 84
Among My Souvenirs, 84
On Seeing Two Brown Boys In A Catholic Church, 234
Dark town Strutters Ball, 248
My Gal Is A High Born Lady, 248
My Wild Irish Rose, 248
Bill Bailey Won't You Please Come Home, 248
We Shall Overcome, 399
For The Good Times, 433